# WISDOM'S APPRENTICE

# WISDOM'S APPRENTICE

*Thomistic Essays in Honor of*

## LAWRENCE DEWAN, O.P.

*Edited by Peter A. Kwasniewski*

Os Justi Press
Lincoln, NE

New edition copyright © 2023
Os Justi Press
All rights reserved

(Originally published by the Catholic University of America Press in 2007. This edition features a new addendum.)

No part of this book may be reproduced, stored in a retrieval system, or transmitted in any form, or by any means, electronic, mechanical, photocopying, or otherwise, without the prior written permission of the publisher, except by a reviewer, who may quote brief passages in a review.

Os Justi Press
P.O. Box 21814
Lincoln, NE 68542
www.osjustipress.com

Send inquiries to
info@osjustipress.com

ISBN 978-1-960711-45-8 (paperback)
ISBN 978-1-960711-46-5 (hardcover)

# Contents

Editor's Introduction     vii
Biography of Lawrence Dewan, O.P.     xiii
Publications of Lawrence Dewan, O.P.     xv

### PART I. *Metaphysics*

Is Truth *Not* a Transcendental for Aquinas?     3
Jan A. Aertsen

Thomas Aquinas and "What Actually Exists"     13
Stephen L. Brock

Really Distinguishing Essence from *Esse*     40
David B. Twetten

The Real Distinction between Supposit
and Nature     85
J. L. A. West

### PART II. *Natural Theology*

From Shadows and Images to the Truth     109
Ralph McInerny

Re-thinking the Infinite     122
Leslie Armour

Is Thomas's Doctrine of Divine Ideas
Thomistic?     153
Gregory T. Doolan

## PART III. *Philosophy of Nature*

The Impossibility of Action at a Distance     173
*Christopher A. Decaen*

Physics and Philosophy     201
*Jude P. Dougherty*

Two Masters, Two Perspectives: Maritain
and Gilson on the Philosophy of Nature     214
*Ralph Nelson*

## PART IV. *Ethics and Spirituality*

Moral Taxonomy and Moral Absolutes     237
*Kevin L. Flannery, S.J.*

Interior Peace: *Inchoatio vitae aeternae*     260
*Heather McAdam Erb*

Works Cited     283
Contributors     299
Index of Names     303

# Editor's Introduction

It is with commingled pleasure and reverence that I introduce this volume of essays offered to Lawrence Dewan, O.P., for the occasion of his seventy-fifth birthday on March 22, 2007. For all of the contributors to this volume, Father Dewan has been a redoubtable interlocutor, a vitally important teacher, or an esteemed colleague—in some cases, all three. To those who have had the good fortune to know him and work with him, he has been a model of that loving pursuit of wisdom in which Socrates, and the whole Western tradition inspired by his incisive questions, locates the highest natural aspiration of man. Beyond this, Father Dewan is a faithful son of Saint Dominic who has placed his immense intellectual gifts at the service of the Church, carrying forward her mission of illuminating natural reality with supernatural light. His more than one hundred publications on a wide variety of subjects have made a decisive contribution to the development of Thomistic thought in recent decades. In addition to his own research and writing, which one would think of as more than enough work to fill his days, Dewan has shown a signal dedication over the years to instructing students even at the humblest beginnings of undergraduate philosophy, and has spared no effort to assist those who approach him for help (the number of e-mail consultations or requests for critiques of papers in progress is probably incalculable). To young and old, Thomist and non-Thomist, Catholic and non-Catholic, he has made himself available as thinker and critic, as pastor and friend. For all this, we are deeply grateful, and it seemed only *dignum et iustum* to seize an opportunity to pay tribute with a collection of essays focusing on some of the many topics that have exercised his genius.

The title of this volume, *Wisdom's Apprentice,* is largely intended as a reference to the wisdom literature of the Old Testament, in which we so often read about the wise man who instructs others in the way of truth and right, the way pleasing to God. The Church in her liturgy applies such texts to her teachers of sacred doctrine. "The mouth of the just shall meditate wisdom" (Ps. 36:30); "The mouth of the just shall bring forth wisdom" (Prov. 10:31); "I have taught you the way of wisdom" (Prov. 4:11). One of my favorite verses—"In the ancient is wisdom, and in length of days prudence" (Job 12:12)[1]—is particularly well-suited for the honoree of this volume, and in a double sense. In an age when every attempt had been made to relegate classical metaphysics (and not infrequently classical ethics) to the dustbin of historical curiosities or to reinterpret them into irrelevance, Dewan, among others, continues patiently to expound truths metaphysical and moral, illuminating and defending them with the aid of his great spiritual mentor, Saint Thomas Aquinas. But it is not Aquinas alone who features in Dewan's writings; he shows an abiding interest in the Presocratics, Plato, Aristotle, Boethius, Dionysius, Augustine, Capreolus, Cajetan, and a range of other "ancients," to whom we must always be prepared to look for guidance and inspiration. Indeed it was Father Dewan who, in his presidential address to the American Catholic Philosophical Association, referred to himself as a mere "apprentice." Referring to his choice to speak about truth as happiness "according to Thomas Aquinas," he stated (with characteristic humility):

> I almost always give papers presenting what I take to be the doctrine of St. Thomas. Usually they get placed in the "history of philosophy" category. Generally my aim is philosophical, and, with Thomas, I insist that ". . . the study of philosophy is not in order to know what it is people have thought, but what is the truth about reality." However, agreeing as I do with my teacher Étienne Gilson that "great philosophers are very scarce," and that the soundest approach in philosophical education is to live a sort of apprenticeship with a great philosopher, I have lived an apprenticeship with Thomas Aquinas. That at this relatively late date in my life I am still presenting his views, as well as I can, simply means that I am still an apprentice.[2]

Today, after some decades of motley and meandering pluralism in Catholic philosophical circles, we are witnessing a renaissance not only of Thomistic studies but of classical philosophical inquiry in general, with the philosophy of being at the forefront. Dewan has demonstrated in a sustained and convincing way just how "relevant" and even, one might say, ahead of us are so many remarkable thinkers of former centuries—or millennia. In this way he has underlined the truth we find eloquently expressed in the Book of Job:

---

1. As translated in the Douay-Rheims version, rendering the Vulgate's *in antiquis est sapientia et in multo tempore prudentia*.
2. "Truth and Happiness," in *The Importance of Truth: Proceedings of the American Catholic Philosophical Association*, vol. 67 (Washington, DC: The American Catholic Philosophical Association, 1993), 1–21; here, 1.

Editor's Introduction ix

"In the ancients there is wisdom"—*sophia,* the highest virtue of the speculative intellect, preoccupied with ultimate questions, poised to contemplate God, the first and best of causes—"and in length of days, prudence," that sublime and indispensable virtue of the practical intellect, which directs and harmonizes human actions with a view to man's final end, happiness.³

But inquiries of such magnitude and difficulty are neither mastered overnight nor quick and easy to pass on. Hence this book's title is meant also to emphasize the personal commitment of a philosopher and scholar who, ever since his studies in Toronto and Paris in the 1950s, has been "at the books" for over fifty years. His is a knowledge that has matured and ripened, and we have benefited from that process. Though occasionally *sapientia* and *prudentia* will be found *in iuvenibus* (as when Friar Thomas d'Aquino between the ages of twenty-seven and thirty-one composed the *De ente et essentia,* and soon showed himself capable of juggling many occupations at once), it is rare; *in antiquis* is its customary home.

The Festschrift is divided up into four parts, representing four areas of steady interest to Father Dewan and to people who work within the Thomistic tradition, the *philosophia perennis:* I. Metaphysics, II. Natural Theology, III. Philosophy of Nature, and IV. Ethics and Spirituality.

Part I contains four essays bound together by their common endeavor to clarify the precise meanings and relationships of basic aspects of metaphysical analysis: essence, nature, *suppositum* or existent, and *esse* or the act of being. Jan Aertsen respectfully continues a debate with Dewan concerning truth as a transcendental, Stephen Brock and David Twetten tackle, from different perspectives, St. Thomas's doctrine of *esse* (on which, be it recalled, Dewan defended his doctoral dissertation in 1967, choosing Capreolus as his route of entry), and Jason West explores a real distinction different from the one that attracts so much attention.

Part II climbs further up the mountain of inquiry, into the domain of natural theology. Ralph McInerny and Leslie Armour pose questions about the basis, limits, and naturalness of man's knowledge of the divine, Armour as a non-Thomist wondering his way through the paradoxes of traditional theological discourse and McInerny reflecting on why John Paul II urged

---

3. Admittedly, the verse, translated more literally from the Hebrew, is more an adage about experienced people: "Wisdom is found in the old, and discretion comes with great age" (as the New Jerusalem Bible renders it). Our more "patristic" reading is based on the Vulgate's choice of the words *sapientia* and *prudentia.*

us, especially now in the exhausted afterblaze of modernity, to resume the ancient quest for God that takes the path of rigorous philosophical reasoning rooted in a wakeful encounter with the world around us. Gregory Doolan peers into the internal constitution, so to speak, of the divine mind itself, showing that Aquinas's doctrine of divine ideas is not a pious holdover from Augustine but a deliberately wrought element, and a central one at that, in his distinctive metaphysical vision.

Two authors in Part III, Jude Dougherty and Ralph Nelson, take up a time-honored *topos* in Thomistic thought, namely the relationship, not always peaceful and free of polemics, between contemporary natural science and an Aristotelian-Thomistic philosophy of nature. Our newspapers and journals are filled with discussions about the reach and range of "science," the competence of its practitioners to pronounce upon big questions of meaning and morality, and the responses made, for better or for worse, by representatives of various religious traditions. There is a palpable need, more urgent than ever, for the renewal of a properly *philosophical* study of nature, marked by an energetic engagement with modern thinkers yet drawing upon a vast inheritance of profound analysis from Aristotle down through Aquinas and his disciples. Christopher Decaen's essay on action at a distance (along with his other work in recent years) brings before us a surprising wealth of resources available in an older tradition that was almost obliterated in the heyday of positivism. As Dougherty reminds us, the partisans of positivism have not gone away, in spite of the beating they have received from a wide array of thinkers across the disciplines.

After things divine and things natural, Part IV turns to things specifically human. Borrowing a phrase from Dewan ("moral taxonomy"), Flannery shows that there is abundant reason to see Aristotle and Thomas as unanimous in their affirmation of the intrinsic goodness and badness of certain kinds of free action, in pursuit of which human beings will flourish in virtue, perish in vice, or flounder in between. Heather McAdam Erb writes of man's most fundamental quest, which is not for any mere knowledge nor for any mere morality, but finally for a "peace that passes all understanding" (Phil. 4:7)—the peace of eternal life, which the soul at peace with God can already begin to taste in this mortal life.

Publication of this Festschrift would not have been possible without generous donations from Jim Holman, a member of the Board of Trustees of the International Theological Institute for Studies on Marriage and the Family in Austria, and from the Aquinas Center for Theological Renewal at Ave Maria University in Florida, whose directors, Matthew Levering and Michael Dauphinais, are longstanding admirers of Fr. Dewan. I thank Jim, Matthew, and Michael for their gracious help on behalf of a most worthy project. I also warmly thank Carol Kennedy for her expert copyediting. Finally, I am indeed grateful to the entire staff of the Catholic University of America Press, especially David McGonagle, director, and Gregory LaNave, former acquisitions editor.

Lastly, I am indebted to my wife, Clarissa, for her support and patience during the planning and execution of this project. She was also one of Dewan's students at the Catholic University of America and shared with me the joy, a number of years later, of hosting him at our home in Austria when he came to teach as a guest professor in the spring semester of 2005. As the Byzantine-rite students of the Institute would happily sing for Father Dewan: *Mnohaja lita! (Ad multos annos!)*

# Biography of Lawrence Dewan, O.P.

Lawrence Dewan was born March 22, 1932, at North Bay in Ontario. He undertook his undergraduate and graduate studies at St. Michael's College, University of Toronto (where his teachers included Marshall McLuhan), save 1953–1954, when he studied in Paris (frequenting the weekly *salon* of Gabriel Marcel). Other well-known teachers included Étienne Gilson, Armand Maurer, and Jacques Maritain. (According to Father Dewan, his single *private* meeting with Maritain was a complete failure: when the young student excitedly announced his desire to "get at the *real* thought of St. Thomas," Maritain only muttered: "Archaeology, pure archaeology." In point of fact, among his many services to Catholic scholarship has been his effort to recover, elucidate, develop, and, at times, critique Maritain's rich legacy.) Dewan's doctoral dissertation in philosophy, "Doctrine of Being of John Capreolus: A Contribution to the History of the Notion of *ESSE*" (University of Toronto, 1967), completed under the advisorship of Joseph Owens, C.Ss.R., seemed to announce, in advance, a lifetime's fascination with one of the most distinctive and challenging areas of the thought of St. Thomas and the Thomistic tradition.

Dewan taught philosophy from 1959 to 1965 at the University of Ottawa (at that time a Catholic university) and from 1967 to 1971 at St. Mary's University, Halifax, Nova Scotia. This latter position he resigned upon entering the Order of Preachers in 1972. Between 1971 and 1976 he did his theological studies, finishing with degrees both civil (M.A.) and canonical (Licentiate). He was ordained priest in 1976. From 1974 to the present he has been teaching at the Collège dominicain de philosophie et de théologie/Dominican College of Philosophy and Theology, now called the Collège Universitaire Dominicain/Dominican University College, in Ottawa, Ontario (as associate professor, 1976–90; as professor, 1990–present). He served as vice president of the same college for six years (1984–90). Among many appointments as visiting professor of philosophy special mention should be made of his spring semesters at the Pontifical Institute of Mediaeval Studies and the Centre for Medieval Studies, School of Graduate Studies, University of Toronto (1983–89) and at the Catholic University of America, Washington, D.C. (1990–97 except for one year). He accepted an invitation to spend the spring of 2005 in Austria, where he was visiting professor of philosophy at the International Theological Institute. From 1991 to the present he has also been recognized as adjunct professor of philosophy and member of the School of Graduate Studies and Research at the University of Ottawa. As a much-loved professor, Father Dewan has influenced the lives of countless students, many of whom have gone on to become professors of Thomistic philosophy and theology in their own right.

In over one hundred articles published from 1971 onward, he has engaged in lively discussions of Thomistic metaphysics, natural philosophy, and ethics, with a particular penchant for detailed critiques often bearing the title "St. Thomas, So-and-so, and Such-and-such." Many of these articles are now being readied for republication as thematic collections edited by their author, which will make them conveniently available to a new generation of students and teachers. Dewan's great service to the community of Catholic thinkers does not end with publications and teaching, but extends to involvement with professional organizations: he was president of the American Catholic Philosophical Association 1992–1993, and president of the Canadian Maritain Association 1988–1995.

In recognition of many years of loving labor dedicated to the pursuit of wisdom and its communication to men and women, Father Dewan received from the Dominican Order on May 1, 1998, its highest theological award, the honorary degree Master of Sacred Theology *(Sacrae Theologiae Magister)*. From December 1999 he has been a member of the prestigious Pontifical Academy of St. Thomas Aquinas, in which membership is gained only on the basis of an invitation from the Vatican.

# Publications of Lawrence Dewan, O.P.

## 1971–Present

### 1971
†"Leslie Dewart and Spiritual Hedonism." *Laval théologique et philosophique* 27 (1971): 25–39. [Entitled in the Fordham University Press volume: "Is Thomas Aquinas a Spiritual Hedonist?"]

### 1973
"Leslie Dewart, St. Thomas, and Knowledge." *Downside Review* 91 (1973): 51–64.

### 1974
"Number and Order of St. Thomas's Five Ways." *Downside Review* 92 (1974): 1–18.
†"St. Thomas and the Ontology of Prayer." *Divus Thomas* 77 (1974): 392–402.

### 1977
"St. Thomas, Capreolus, and Entitative Composition." *Divus Thomas* 80 (1977): 355–75.

### 1978
"Being *per se*, Being *per accidens*, and St. Thomas' Metaphysics." *Science et Esprit* 30 (1978): 169–84.
"St. Thomas and the Causality of God's Goodness." *Laval théologique et philosophique* 34 (1978): 291–304.

### 1979
"St. Thomas and the Possibles." *The New Scholasticism* 53 (1979): 76–85.
"St. Thomas, Ideas, and Immediate Knowledge." *Dialogue* 18 (1979): 392–404.
Review of A. Guindon, *La pédagogie de la crainte dans l'histoire du salut selon Thomas d'Aquin*. *The Thomist* 43 (1979): 670–72.

### 1980
"St. Albert, the Sensibles, and Spiritual Being." In *Albertus Magnus and the Sciences*, ed. James A. Weisheipl, 291–320. Toronto: Pontifical Institute of Mediaeval Studies, 1980.
"St. Thomas and the Divine Names." *Science et Esprit* 32 (1980): 19–33.
"The Distinctiveness of St. Thomas' Third Way." *Dialogue* 19 (1980): 201–18.

\*"St. Thomas, Metaphysics, and Formal Causality." *Laval théologique et philosophique* 36 (1980): 285–316.
†"The Real Distinction between Intellect and Will." *Angelicum* 57 (1980): 557–93.
\*"St. Thomas and the Ground of Metaphysics." In *Philosophical Knowledge: Proceedings of the American Catholic Philosophical Association*, vol. 54, 144–54. Washington, DC: American Catholic Philosophical Association, 1980. [Title changed to "St. Thomas and the Seed of Metaphysics" in the book *Form and Being*. See below under 2006.]

### 1981
†"St. Thomas, Jacques Maritain, and the Philosophy of Religion." *University of Ottawa Quarterly* 51 (1981): 644–53.
†"OBIECTUM: Notes on the Invention of a Word." *Archives d'histoire doctrinale et littéraire du Moyen Âge* 48 (1981): 37–96.
Review of G. Kopaczynski, *Linguistic Ramifications of the Essence-Existence Debate*. *Laval théologique et philosophique* 37 (1981): 107–8.

### 1982
"St. Thomas, Joseph Owens, and Existence." *The New Scholasticism* 56 (1982): 399–441.
"St. Thomas Aquinas against Metaphysical Materialism." In *Studi Tomistici* 14: *Atti del'VIII Congresso Tomistico Internazionale*. Vol. 5, *Problemi Metafisici*, 412–34. Vatican City: Libreria Editrice Vaticana, 1982.
Review of Francis J. Kovach and Robert W. Shahan, eds., *Albert the Great: Commemorative Essays*. *Canadian Philosophical Reviews* 2 (1982): 282–85.

### 1983
"Charles De Koninck." Article *ad loc.* in *The Oxford Companion to Canadian Literature*, ed. William Toye. Toronto/New York: Oxford University Press, 1983.

### 1984
†"Punzo on Ethics." *The New Scholasticism* 58 (1984): 464–70. [Entitled in the Fordham University Press volume: "Is Liberty the Criterion on Morals?"]
"St. Albert, Creation, and the Philosophers." *Laval théologique et philosophique* 40 (1984): 295–307.
"St. Thomas, Joseph Owens, and the Real Distinction between Being and Essence." *The Modern Schoolman* 61 (1984): 145–56.
"St. Thomas and the Integration of Knowledge into Being." *International Philosophical Quarterly* 24 (1984): 383–93.

### 1985
\*"St. Thomas and the Principle of Causality." In *Jacques Maritain: philosophe dans la cité / A Philosopher in the World*, ed. Jean-Louis Allard, 53–71. Ottawa: University of Ottawa Press, 1985.

## 1986

†"Jacques Maritain and the Philosophy of Co-operation." In *L'Alterité: vivre ensemble différents*. Actes du Colloque Pluridisciplinaire Tenu à l'Occasion du 75ᵉ Anniversaire du Collège Dominicain de Philosophie et de Théologie (Ottawa, 4–6 octobre 1984), ed. Michel Gourgues and Gilles-D. Mailhiot, 109–17. Montréal: Éditions Bellarmin / Paris: Éditions du Cerf, 1986.
"La Mort dans la perspective de la sagesse divine, selon saint Thomas." In *Urgence de la philosophie*, ed. Thomas De Koninck and Lucien Morin, 571–79. Quebec: Les Presses de l'Université Laval, 1986. (English trans. published in *Angelicum* 65 [1988]; see below.)
†"St. Thomas, Our Natural Lights, and the Moral Order." *Maritain Studies/Études maritainiennes* 2 (1986): 59–92. (Reprinted in *Angelicum* 67 [1990]: 285–307.)

## 1987

"Something Rather than Nothing, and St. Thomas' Third Way." *Science et Esprit* 39 (1987): 71–80.
Review of Joseph Owens, *Elementary Christian Metaphysics* and *An Interpretation of Existence* (reprints). *Dialogue* 26 (1987): 572–74.

## 1988

"St. Thomas, St. Bonaventure, and the Need to Prove the Existence of God." In *Philosophie et culture*. Actes du XVIIᵉ Congrès mondial de philosophie, ed. Venant Cauchy, 3:841–44. Montréal: Éditions du Beffroi/Éditions Montmorency, 1988.
"Laurence Foss and the Existence of Substances." *Laval théologique et philosophique* 44 (1988): 77–84.
†"Death in the Setting of Divine Wisdom." *Angelicum* 65 (1988): 117–29. [Originally published in French in 1986.]
†"Communion with the Tradition: For the Believer Who Is a Philosopher." *Science et Esprit* 40 (1988): 315–25.

## 1989

"Saint Thomas, Alvin Plantinga, and the Divine Simplicity." *The Modern Schoolman* 66 (1989): 141–51.
*"Saint Thomas, Metaphysical Procedure, and the Formal Cause." *The New Scholasticism* 63 (1989): 173–82.
†"Concerning the Person and the Common Good." *Maritain Studies/Études maritainiennes* 5 (1989): 7–21.
"Some Observations on Professor Armour's Paper (on God)." *De Philosophia* [Ottawa] 8 (1989): 115–24.
*"Saint Thomas, Form, and Incorruptibility." In *Être et Savoir*, ed. Jean-Louis Allard, 77–90. Series: Philosophica 37. Ottawa: Les Presses de l'Université d'Ottawa, 1989.

## 1990

"St. Thomas, Our Natural Lights, and the Moral Order." *Angelicum* 67 (1990): 285–307. (Originally published in *Maritain Studies/Études maritainiennes* 2 [1986]: 59–92.)

"Big Bang, If There Was One, Was No Big Deal" [letter to the editor, title given by the editor], *New York Times*, May 27, 1990.

### 1991
"S. Thomas et le bien: métaphysique et moral." *Maritain Studies/Études maritainiennes* 7 (1991): 27–48.

"Aristotelian Features of the Order of Presentation in St. Thomas Aquinas' *Summa theologiae, Prima pars*, qq. 3–11." In *Philosophy and the God of Abraham: Essays in Memory of James A. Weisheipl, OP*, ed. R. James Long, 41–53. Papers in Mediaeval Studies 12. Toronto: Pontifical Institute of Mediaeval Studies, 1991.

"The Interpretation of St. Thomas's Third Way." In *Littera, sensus, sententia. Studi in onore del Prof. Clemente J. Vansteenkiste, O.P.*, ed. Abelardo Lobato, O.P., 189–200. Milan: Massimo, 1991.

"St. Thomas, James Ross, and Exemplarism: A Reply." *American Catholic Philosophical Quarterly* 65 (1991): 221–34.

"St. Thomas, Aristotle, and Creation." *Dionysius* 15 (1991): 81–90.

Foreword for the republication of John N. Deck, *Nature, Contemplation, and the One: A Study in the Philosophy of Plotinus*, 9–10. Burdett, NY: Larson Publications, 1991.

### 1992
"St. Thomas, God's Goodness, and God's Morality." *The Modern Schoolman* 70 (1992): 45–51.

"A Book on the Philosophical Theology of St. Thomas Aquinas." Review-article on Leo J. Elders, *The Philosophical Theology of St. Thomas Aquinas*. *Science et Esprit* 44 (1992): 205–20.

### 1993
†"Antimodern, Ultramodern, Postmodern: A Plea for the Perennial." *Maritain Studies/Études maritainiennes* 9 (1993): 7–28.

*"What is Metaphysics?" *Maritain Studies/Études maritainiennes* 9 (1993): 145–60.

†"Philosophy and Spirituality: Cultivating a Virtue." *Homiletic and Pastoral Review* 94, no. 2 (November 1993): 25–30.

†"Truth and Happiness." Presidential Address to the American Catholic Philosophical Association. In *The Importance of Truth: Proceedings of the American Catholic Philosophical Association*, vol. 67, 1–21. Washington, DC: American Catholic Philosophical Association, 1993.

### 1994
"Thomas Aquinas, Creation, and Two Historians." *Laval théologique et philosophique* 50 (1994): 363–87.

"Man: The Perennial Metaphysician." *Maritain Studies/Études maritainiennes* 10 (1994): 11–33.

## 1995

"History of Philosophy, Personal or Impersonal?: Reflections on Étienne Gilson." *Maritain Studies/Études maritainiennes* 11 (1995): 7–31.
"St. Thomas and Pre-Conceptual Intellection." *Maritain Studies/Études maritainiennes* 11 (1995): 220–33.
†"St. Thomas, James Keenan, and the Will." *Science et Esprit* 47 (1995): 153–76.
"St. Thomas's Fourth Way and Creation." *The Thomist* 59 (1995): 371–78.
"St. Thomas's Successive Discussions of the Nature of Truth." In *Sanctus Thomas de Aquino: Doctor Hodiernae Humanitatis. Miscellanea offerta . . . al Prof. Abelardo Lobato, O.P.*, ed. Daniel Ols, O.P., 153–68. Vatican City: Libreria Editrice Vaticana, 1995.
†"St. Thomas and the First Cause of Moral Evil." In *Moral and Political Philosophies in the Middle Ages: Proceedings of the Ninth International Congress of Medieval Philosophy*, ed. B. Carlos Basan et al., 3:1223–30. Ottawa: Legas, 1995.
Review of James A. Weisheipl, *Frère Thomas d'Aquin: sa vie, sa Pensée, ses oeuvres*. *Science et Esprit* 47 (1995): 122–23.

## 1996

"St. Albert, St. Thomas, and Knowledge." *American Catholic Philosophical Quarterly* 70 (1996): 121–35.
†"Natural Law and the First Act of Freedom: Maritain Revisited." *Maritain Studies/ Études maritainiennes* 12 (1996): 3–32.

## 1997

"Capreolus, Saint Thomas et l'Être." In *Jean Capreolus et son temps 1380–1444: Colloque de Rodez* [special number, #1 of *Mémoire dominicaine*], 77–86. Paris: Cerf, 1997.
"Jacques Maritain, St. Thomas, and the Birth of Metaphysics." *Maritain Studies/Études maritainiennes* 13 (1997): 3–18.
†"St. Thomas, Lying, and Venial Sin." *The Thomist* 61 (1997): 279–99.
*"St. Thomas, Physics, and the Principle of Metaphysics." *The Thomist* 61 (1997): 549–66.
Critical notice/Étude critique on Norman Kretzmann's *The Metaphysics of Theism: Aquinas's Natural Theology* Summa Contra Gentiles I. *EIDOS* [University of Waterloo] 14 (1997): 97–121.

## 1998

"Torrell on Aquinas." Review of Jean-Pierre Torrell, O.P., *Saint Thomas d'Aquin, Maître Spirituel*. *The Thomist* 62 (1998): 623–31.
"God and the Big Bang" [excerpt from a lecture]. *Thomas Aquinas College Newsletter*, Summer 1998, p. 8.

## 1999

"St. Thomas and Creation: Does God Create 'Reality'?" *Science et Esprit* 51 (1999): 5–25.

*"St. Thomas and the Distinction between Form and *Esse* in Caused Things." *Gregorianum* 80 (1999): 353–70.
†"St. Thomas and the Causes of Free Choice." *Acta Philosophica* 8 (1999): 87–96.
*"The Individual as a Mode of Being According to Thomas Aquinas." *The Thomist* 63 (1999): 403–24.
"Jacques Maritain and Toronto (A Visit to P.I.M.S.-S.M.C. Archives)." *Maritain Studies/Études maritainiennes* 15 (1999): 13–51.
"Étienne Gilson and the *Actus Essendi*." *Maritain Studies/Études maritainiennes* 15 (1999): 70–96.
†"St. Thomas and Moral Taxonomy." *Maritain Studies/Études maritainiennes* 15 (1999): 134–56.
"St. Thomas and the Existence of God: Owens vs. Gilson, and Beyond." In *God and Argument*, ed. William Sweet, 115–41. Ottawa: University of Ottawa Press, 1999.
Review of Vivian Boland, O.P., *Ideas in God according to Saint Thomas Aquinas: Sources and Synthesis*. *Review of Metaphysics* 53, no. 2 (1999): 429–30.

### 2000

"Some Philosophers on the University." *Maritain Studies/Études maritainiennes* 16 (2000): 35–58.
†"St. Thomas, John Finnis, and the Political Good." *The Thomist* 64 (2000): 337–74.
"Jacques Maritain's Legacy in Canada." *Catholic Insight* 8, no. 2 (March 2000): 32–34.
"Politics of the Heart: Elián in the Middle" [letter to the Editor, title given by the Editor]. *New York Times*, April 15, 2000.

### 2001

"Thomas Aquinas, Gerard Bradley, and the Death Penalty: Some Observations." *Gregorianum* 82 (2001): 149–65.
†"Wisdom as Foundational Ethical Theory in St. Thomas Aquinas." In *The Bases of Ethics*, ed. William Sweet, 39–78. Milwaukee: Marquette University Press, 2001.
"Some Remarks Occasioned by a Reading of Otto Hermann Pesch [concerning Thomas and theology of history]." *Science et Esprit* 53 (2001): 143–53.
"Étienne Gilson." In *Penseurs et Apôtres du XXme siècle*, ed. Jean Genest, 170–82. Montreal: Fides, 2001.
"St. Thomas and Infinite Causal Regress." In *Idealism, Metaphysics, and Community*, ed. William Sweet, 119–30. Aldershot, England: Ashgate, 2001.
Review of Mark Wynn, *God and Goodness: A Natural Theological Perspective*. *Review of Metaphysics* 54, no. 4 (2001): 954–55.

### 2002

"Étienne Gilson and the *Actus Essendi*." *International Journal of Philosophy* [Taipei] 1 (2002): 65–99. [A revised and expanded version of the 1999 publication of the same title.]
"A Note on Metaphysics and Truth." In Proceedings of the Pontifical Academy of St. Thomas Aquinas, published as *Doctor Communis* N.S. 2 (2002): 143–53.
†"Jean Porter on Natural Law: Thomistic Notes." *The Thomist* 66 (2002): 275–309.

"Which *Esse* Gives the Answer to the Question: 'Is It'? for St. Thomas." *Doctor Communis* N.S. 3 (2002): 80–97.
"Maritain, Einstein, and Special Relativity." *Maritain Studies/Études maritainiennes* 18 (2002): 29–44.
†"La sabiduría y la vida humana: lo natural y lo sobrenatural." In *Idea cristiana del hombre. III Simposio Internacional Fe cristiana y cultura contemporánea*, ed. J. Aranguren, J. Borobia, and M. Lluch, 303–38. Pamplona: Ediciones Universidad de Navarra, 2002.

### 2003
"Thomas Aquinas and Being as a Nature." *Acta Philosophica* 12 (2003): 123–35.
"On Milbank and Pickstock's *Truth in Aquinas*." *Nova et Vetera* [Eng. ed.] 1 (2003): 199–212.

### 2004
"Is Truth a Transcendental for St. Thomas Aquinas?" *Nova et Vetera* [Eng. ed.] 2 (2004): 1–20.
"Does Being Have a Nature? (Or: Metaphysics as a Science of the Real)." In *Approaches to Metaphysics*, ed. William Sweet, 23–60. Dordrecht: Kluwer, 2004.
"St. Thomas's 'Fifth Way' Revisited." *Universitas* [Taipei] 31.3 (March 2004): 47–67.
*"What Does It Mean to Study Being 'as Being'?" *International Journal of Philosophy* [Taipei] 3 (July 2004): 63–86.
"Cosa significa studiare l'ente '*inquanto ente*'?" In *Tommaso d'Aquino e l'oggetto della metafisica*, ed. Stephen L. Brock, 11–34. Studi di Filosofia, 29. Rome: Armando Editore, 2004. [Italian translation of the preceding item.]

### 2005
"Richard Swinburne, St. Thomas, and Many Gods." In *Essays in Medieval Theology and Philosophy in Memory of Walter H. Principe, C.S.B.: Fortresses and Launching Pads*, ed. James R. Ginther and Carl N. Still, 143–53. Aldershot, England: Ashgate, 2005.
"On Anthony Kenny's *Aquinas and Being*." *Nova et Vetera* [Eng. ed.] 3.2 (2005): 335–400.
"Maritain on Religion in a Democratic Society: *Man and the State* Revisited." *Maritain Studies/Études maritainiennes* 21 (2005): 32–60.

### 2006
"St. Thomas, Norman Kretzmann, and Divine Freedom in Creating." *Nova et Vetera* [Eng. ed.] 4.3 (2006): 495–514.
*Form and Being: Studies in Thomistic Metaphysics*. Washington, DC: The Catholic University of America Press, 2006. [Comprising thirteen of the articles mentioned in this bibliography, namely, those marked with an asterisk.]
†"Faith and Reason from St. Thomas Aquinas's Perspective." *Science et Esprit* 58 (2006): 113–23.

## Forthcoming

*Wisdom, Law, and Virtue: Essays in Thomistic Ethics.* New York: Fordham University Press, exp. 2007. [Comprising twenty-seven of the articles mentioned in this bibliography, namely, those above and below marked with a dagger symbol.]

†"St. Thomas, Metaphysics, and Human Dignity." A paper read at Fu Jen University, Taipei colloquium on Christian philosophy and human dignity, December 2002.

†"Suicide as a Belligerent Tactic: Thomistic Reflections."

"What Does Creation Look Like?" In *Omnia in Sapientia: Essays on Creation in Honour of the Rev. Dr Robert D. Crouse,* ed. W. Otten, W. Hannam, and M. Treschow. Studies in Intellectual History. Leiden: Brill, in press.

*"St. Thomas, Ralph McInerny, and Analogy." In *Laudemus viros gloriosos: Essays in Honor of Armand Augustine Maurer, C.S.B.,* ed. Rollen E. Houser. South Bend: University of Notre Dame Press, forthcoming. [In the collection *Form and Being,* the essay is entitled "St. Thomas and Analogy: The Logician and the Metaphysician."]

"Aristotle as a Source of St. Thomas's Doctrine of *esse.*" In *Aquinas's Sources: The Notre Dame Symposium,* ed. Timothy L. Smith. South Bend, IN: St. Augustine's Press.

*"Nature as a Metaphysical Object." In *Restoring Nature: Essays in Thomistic Philosophy and Theology,* ed. Michael M. Waddell. South Bend, IN: St. Augustine's Press.

*"The Importance of Substance," to be included in a set of papers on science and philosophy and religion, from the Notre Dame University Thomistic Summer Institute.

"Creation, Metaphysics, and Cosmology." Read to the Canadian Maritain Association meeting in Toronto, May 2002. Publication forthcoming in a volume edited by William Sweet.

"St. Thomas and the Renewal of Metaphysics." Read to the American Maritain Association, Washington, D.C., October 2005. Publication forthcoming.

PART I

# METAPHYSICS

Jan A. Aertsen

# Is Truth *Not* a Transcendental for Aquinas?

IN A RECENT ESSAY, Lawrence Dewan has asked whether truth is a transcendental for St. Thomas Aquinas. The answer seems to be self-evident, for Thomas states at several places in his work that "being," "one," "true," and "good" are transcendental terms. Nevertheless Dewan raises this question, since in his view an important change of doctrine concerning truth is to be found as we move from *De veritate* q. 1 to the *Summa theologiae* I, q. 16. The most fundamental revision concerns Thomas's presentation of the "truth of things." In the latter treatment, he eliminated any reference to a "truth" said of things relative to the *human* mind. He also eliminated any intrinsic form called "truth," *even one identical with entity*. A thing is called "true" in relation to the *divine* intellect.[1] The passage in *Summa theologiae* I, q. 16, a. 6—so crucial for Dewan's interpretation—reads: "And thus, though there are many essences or forms of things, nevertheless there is one truth of the divine intellect, according to which all things are denominated 'true.'"[2]

Dewan concludes his paper with the following observation:

When I presented this view of change of doctrine to my friend Jan Aertsen, he protested that the truth would no longer be a "transcendental." Is this so? I said to him, and I continue to believe, that it would be a "logical transcendental." After all, the transcendentals are so called as transcending the Aristotelian categories. The doc-

---

1. L. Dewan, "Is Truth a Transcendental for St. Thomas Aquinas?" *Nova et Vetera* [Eng. ed.] 2 (2004): 1–20. Cf. his earlier paper, "A Note on Metaphysics and Truth," *Doctor Communis* N.S. 2 (2002): 143–53 (*The Contemporary Debate on Truth*, Proceedings of the II Plenary Session of the Pontifical Academy of St. Thomas Aquinas).

2. *Summa theologiae* [hereafter *STh*] I, q. 16, a. 6: "Et sic, licet plures sunt essentiae vel formae rerum, tamen una est veritas divini intellectus, secundum quam omnes res denominantur verae."

trine of the categories is one that pertains to logic, but is used in metaphysics as well. It should not be surprising that some transcendental predicates have different sorts of verification than others. This seems, in Thomas's mind, to be the case with "good" and "true."[3]

In my contribution to this volume I would like to continue the discussion with my learned friend and debate his unusual answer to the question "Is Truth a Transcendental for St. Thomas Aquinas?" The notion to which Dewan appeals will be first examined. Is there something like a "logical" transcendental, and does the true belongs to this type of term? I will show that both questions can be answered affirmatively: the true can, in Thomas's mind, be regarded as a logical transcendental. Yet this does not exclude at all that the true *(verum)* also is a metaphysical transcendental for Thomas. In this respect I disagree with Dewan's interpretation; apparently truth has several modes in Aquinas's work. The most distinctive feature of his treatment of truth in *De veritate*—his account of the true as a transcendental property of being—has not been abandoned in the *Summa theologiae*. The transcendentality of *verum* forms a continuous moment in his metaphysics.

## The True as a Logical Transcendental

Dewan's essay claims that Aquinas ultimately understood the true as a "logical" transcendental, but what is meant by this expression? Is there anything like a medieval doctrine of logical transcendentals? The answer can be affirmative, if we take the term "doctrine" not in a strict sense, for the conception of logical transcendentals was not elaborated as systematically as its metaphysical counterpart.[4] In Aquinas's work we do not find an explicit account of such notions, but only some observations pointing to them.

The idea of logical transcendentals was strongly suggested by what Aquinas calls the "affinity" between logic and metaphysics, which becomes apparent in their "commonness":[5] both sciences deal with that which is common to all things, that is, with being in general. Aquinas elaborates on

---

3. Dewan, "Is Truth a Transcendental," 17.
4. Cf. G. Pini, "The Transcendentals of Logic: Thirteenth-Century Discussions on the Subject Matter of Aristotle's *Categories*," in *Die Logik des Transzendentalen. Festschrift für Jan A. Aertsen zum 65. Geburtstag*, ed. M. Pickavé (Berlin: de Gruyter, 2003), 140–59.
5. *In VII Metaph.*, lect. 3, 1308: "Haec scientia [sc. metaphysica] habet quandam affinitatem cum logica propter utriusque communitatem." Cf. *In Boethii De Trinitate* q. 6, a. 1: "Utraque scientia communis est et circa idem subiectum quodammodo."

Aristotle's remark in his *Metaphysics* (IV, c. 2, 1004b 1) that the task of the philosopher is similar to that of the dialectician or logician, insofar as "he is able to consider all things." Thomas explains the similarity by claiming that the two kinds of being that underlie the domains of logic and metaphysics, being of reason *(ens rationis)* and real being *(ens naturae)* respectively, are coextensive *(aequiparantur)*. The proper subject matter of logic is "being of reason," which covers those concepts that reason attaches *(adinvenit)* to the things it considers, such as the notions of "genus" and "species." Since every being that exists in nature falls under the (logical) consideration of reason, the subject matter of logic has the same extension as that of metaphysics.[6]

The metaphysical consideration of the *communia* is, of course, different from the logical one. Metaphysics deals with things themselves by considering what is common to them, such as "being" and its transcendental properties. Logic is concerned with the "intentions of reason" that can be formed of all things as understood. These intentions can be regarded as "logical" transcendentals, since they are applicable to every categorial being. Aquinas mentions as examples "proposition" and "predicament."[7]

Dewan holds that the true *(verum)* also belongs to the list of logical *communia*, and not without reason. The basic idea running through Thomas's discussion of truth like a scarlet thread is that the proper place of truth is the intellect. In his account of truth in both *De veritate* and the *Summa theologiae*, he cites a text from book VI of Aristotle's *Metaphysics* (c. 4, 1027b 25) to the effect that "truth and falsity do not exist, as good and evil, in things, but in the mind." This thesis forms a formidable obstacle to any metaphysical conception of the transcendentality of truth. Thomas accordingly employs Aristotle's saying as a counterargument to the view that truth resides solely in things.[8]

The context of Aristotle's statement is the discussion of one of the mean-

---

6. *In IV Metaph.*, lect. 4, 574. Cf. R. te Velde, "Metaphysics, Dialectics and the *Modus logicus* according to Thomas Aquinas," *Recherches de théologie ancienne et médiévale* 63 (1996): 15–35.

7. *In I Post. Anal.*, lect. 20: "Sciendum tamen est quod alia ratione dyaletica est de communibus et logica et philosophia prima. Philosophia enim prima est de communibus, quia eius consideratio est circa ipsas res communes, scilicet circa ens et partes et passiones entis. Et quia circa omnia que in rebus sunt habet negociari ratio, logica autem est de operibus rationis; logica etiam erit de hiis, quae communia sunt omnibus, id est de intentionibus rationis, que ad omnes res se habent; non autem ita quod logica sit de ipsis rebus communibus sicut de subiectis: considerat enim logica sicut subiecta syllogismum, enunciationem, praedicamentum aut aliquid huiusmodi."

8. *De veritate* q. 1, a. 2 *sed contra* and *resp.*; *STh* I, q. 16, a. 1 *sed contra*.

ings of "being" that he had distinguished in the fifth book of the *Metaphysics*, namely "being as what is true" *(ens ut verum)*. "Being" is designated as "true," because it expresses the composition and division of terms in a proposition. "Being as what is true" is being as a verbal copula, a sign of the composition of subject and predicate in a sentence. Since this composition occurs in the intellect, the origin of the "veridical" sense of being is in the intellect forming a proposition. In order to emphasize that "being as what is true" does not signify something extramental, Aristotle then says: "Falsity and truth are not in things—it is not as if the good were true, and the bad were in itself false—but in thought."[9]

Thomas's commentary on the *Metaphysics* makes clear that he takes the statement of the Philosopher as more than merely an argument from authority. He enters at length into the distinction between the true and the good and gives a philosophical justification for Aristotle's statement. This justification, which recurs in *De veritate* q. 1 and the *Summa theologiae* I, q. 16, is based on the insight that a spiritual substance relates to reality in two different ways. A human being directs himself at things by knowing and desiring them. The object of knowledge is truth, the object of desire is the good. Between the processes of knowing and desiring there is a fundamental distinction, which becomes evident in their termini. Cognition is a process of "assimilation" that is completed when the similitude of the thing known is in the knower. Truth indicates this completion or perfection of knowledge and is therefore in the mind. The appetite, by contrast, is not a process of assimilation but a movement toward things. It is an "inclination" toward a thing in itself, which is desirable because it is perfect. Good is therefore a perfection in things.[10] In his accounts of truth, Thomas follows

---

9. Aristotle, *Metaphysics* VI, c. 4, 1027b 17–25. Aristotle's text does not quite say what Thomas's quotation states, but Thomas's reading is taken from the medieval Latin translation of the Arabic text. Cf. J. F. Wippel, "Truth in Thomas Aquinas," *Review of Metaphysics* 43 (1989–90): 297n5.

10. *In VI Metaph.*, lect. 4, 1234: "Sciendum est autem, quod cum quaelibet cognitio perficiatur per hoc quod similitudo rei cognitae est in cognoscente; sicut perfectio rei cognitae consistit in hoc quod habet talem formam per quam est res talis, ita perfectio cognitionis consistit in hoc, quod habet similitudinem formae praedictae. Ex hoc autem, quod res cognita habet formam sibi debitam, dicitur esse bona; et ex hoc, quod aliquem defectum habet, dicitur esse mala. Et eodem modo ex hoc quod cognoscens habet similitudinem rei cognitae, dicitur habere veram cognitionem: ex hoc vero, quod deficit a tali similitudine, dicitur falsam cognitionem habere. Sicut ergo bonum et malum designant perfectiones, quae sunt in rebus: ita verum et falsum designant perfectiones cognitionum." And in 1240: "Apparet etiam ex his quae hic dicuntur, quod verum et falsum, quae sunt obiecta cognitionis, sunt in mente. Bonum vero et malum, quae sunt obiecta appetitus, sunt in rebus." Cf. *De veritate* q. 1, a. 2: "Motus autem

Is Truth *Not* a Transcendental? 7

the Aristotelian approach by recognizing that the proper place of truth is not in things but in the mind.

In *Metaphysics* VI, Aristotle draws a far-reaching conclusion from his discussion of "being as what is true." This kind of being falls outside the inquiry of metaphysics; it "must be passed over" by the science that deals with being in the proper sense, extramental being, because the cause of being-as-what-is-true is an operation of the intellect. Being in this sense belongs rather to logic or the science of the intellect.[11] The same conclusion can be phrased in another way. Since truth and falsity are in the mind, their consideration is the proper task of the logician.[12] Viewed from this perspective, one could say that truth belongs to the "logical" transcendentals. The conditions necessary for truth to be a transcendental property of being seem to be absent.

## The True as a Metaphysical Transcendental

The logical approach does not give a complete picture, however, of Thomas's conception of truth. He also acknowledges that there is truth in every being, as it already becomes clear from the order of questions in his treatment of truth in *Summa* I, question 16. After having replied affirmatively to the questions asking whether truth is only in the intellect (a. 1) and whether it is only in the composing and dividing intellect (a. 2), Thomas discusses in the third article the convertibility of "the true" with "being." What is surprising is that for this idea Thomas again appeals to Aristotle's *Metaphysics*. As a counterargument against objections suggesting that being and true cannot be convertible because truth is only in the intellect, he cites a statement in book II of the *Metaphysics* (ch. 1): "There is the same disposition of things in being and in truth."[13]

---

cognitivae virtutis terminatur ad animam (...) sed motus appetitivae terminatur ad res (...) et quia bonum (...) dicit ordinem entis ad appetitum, verum autem dicit ordinem ad intellectum, inde est quod Philosophus dicit in VI Metaphysicae quod bonum et malum sunt in rebus, verum autem et falsum sunt in mente." Cf. *STh* I, q. 16, a. 1.

11. Aristotle, *Metaphysics* VI, c. 4, 1027b 25–1028a 3. Cf. Thomas Aquinas, *In VI Metaph.*, lect. 4, 1242: "Et ideo (...) est praetermittendum (...) ens quod significat verum (...). Illius vero, scilicet entis veri, causa est (...) operatio intellectus componentis et dividentis. Et ideo pertinet ad scientiam de intellectu."

12. *In IV Metaph.*, lect. 17, 736: "Verum autem et falsum pertinent proprie ad considerationem logici; consequuntur enim ens in ratione de quo considerat logicus: nam verum et falsum sunt in mente."

13. *STh* I, q. 16, a. 3: "Sed contra est quod dicit Philosophus II *Metaph*. quod eadem est dispositio rerum in esse et veritate."

The context of Aristotle's statement is his argument that "philosophy is rightly called the science of truth," and, of all the philosophical disciplines, metaphysics preeminently considers truth. Since we cannot know the truth without the cause, Aristotle advances a general proposition concerning causality: the cause of an attribute or property that is common to both the cause and its effect is the maximal instance *(maximum)* of that attribute. Fire, for example, is the hottest of things because it is the cause of heat in all other things. The general proposition on the causality of the *maximum* is next applied to truth: What causes other things to be true is itself most true. Hence the principles of eternal things are most true, because these are always true and the cause of being of other things. From this reasoning Aristotle infers the corollary "that each thing is related to truth in the same way as it is to being"—or, as Thomas puts it, "that there is the same disposition of things in being and in truth."[14]

This argument must have had a strong appeal to Thomas, for he makes use of it at several places in his work. One example is his extension of the claim from *Metaphysics* II concerning the relation between being and the true to the transcendental "good" as well: "There is the same disposition of things in goodness and in being."[15] Another telling example is the beginning of the *Summa contra gentiles* (I,1), where he develops the thesis that truth is "the ultimate end of the whole universe." Aquinas sustains this thesis from two different perspectives: Christian revelation and metaphysical knowledge. In the latter case he clearly has in mind Aristotle's account in the second book of the *Metaphysics*.

The Philosopher determines first philosophy, too, as "the science of truth," not of any truth, but of that truth which is the origin of all truth, namely, the truth which belongs to the first principle of being of all things. Therefore, its truth is the principle of all truth, for there is the same disposition of things in truth as in being.[16]

The idea that there is the same "disposition" in being and in truth means that the order *(ordo)* in both is identical. That which is being in the highest degree is true in the highest degree. The reason is not that being and

14. Aristotle, *Metaphysics* II, c. 1, 993b 19–31.
15. *STh* I-II, q. 18, a. 4: "Eadem est dispositio rerum in bonitate, et in esse."
16. *Summa contra gentiles* I, c. 1: "Sed et Primam Philosophiam Philosophus determinat esse *scientiam veritatis;* non cuiuslibet, sed eius veritatis quae est origo omnis veritatis, scilicet quae pertinet ad primum principium essendi omnibus; unde et sua veritas est omnis veritatis principium; sic enim est dispositio rerum in veritate sicut in esse."

the true are conceptually identical but rather that "a thing is apt to be conformed *(adaequari)* to the intellect in the degree to which a thing has entity *(entitas)*. Consequently, the notion of truth follows upon that of being."[17] Truth now appears in its ontological dimension, as a transcendental property of being.

The two approaches taken by Thomas in his accounts of truth result in two basic conclusions. The first approach based on Aristotle's claim in the sixth book of the *Metaphysics*, that truth is not in things but in the mind, results in the conclusion that "being-as-true" falls outside metaphysics. The second approach follows Aristotle's statement in the second book that there is the same disposition in being and in truth and results in a metaphysical conception of truth as being. Thomas himself speaks of a "twofold" truth, that of the intellect and that of the thing.[18]

Thomas's procedure in dealing with the ontological conception of truth suggests that he does not see the two conceptions as incompatible. He does not appeal, as one might expect, to Augustine's definition of truth, "The true is that which is," but appeals to Aristotle. A deliberate strategy could underlie this choice. Precisely by appealing to the same philosopher, who claims that the place of truth is the intellect, Thomas suggests that the two conceptions of truth belong together.

Instructive is his explanation of the convertibility of "true" and "being" in the *Summa theologiae* I, q. 16, 3. Convertibility is one of the marks of transcendental terms. It expresses their real identity; because of their commonness, they include one another. Yet they are no synonyms, for transcendental terms differ conceptually *(secundum rationem)*. The other transcendentals add something to "being."[19] We first present Thomas's argument for the convertibility, and then draw it out, for his reasoning remains rather implicit.

17. *De veritate* q. 1, a. 1 ad 5: "Dispositio non accipitur ibi secundum quod est in genere qualitatis sed secundum quod importat quendam ordinem: cum enim illa quae sunt causa aliorum essendi sint maxime entia et illa quae sunt causa veritatis sint maxime vera, concludit Philosophus quod idem est ordo alicui rei in esse et veritate, ita scilicet quod ubi invenitur quod est maxime ens, est maxime verum. Unde nec hoc ideo est quia ens et verum ratione sunt idem sed quia secundum hoc quod aliquid habet de entitate secundum hoc est natum adaequari intellectui, et sic ratio veri sequitur rationem entis."
18. *Super Ioannem* c. 18, lect. 6, 2365. Cf. *STh* I, q. 16, a. 3 ad 1: "Verum est in rebus et in intellectu."
19. Cf. J. A. Aertsen, *Medieval Philosophy and the Transcendentals: The Case of Thomas Aquinas* (Leiden-New York: Brill, 1996), 30–38.

As "good" has the *ratio* of desirable, so "the true" has an order to knowledge. Now everything is knowable insofar as it has being *(esse)*. For this reason it is said in the third book of *De Anima* (431b 21) that "the soul is in a sense all things," through the senses and the intellect. And therefore, as good is convertible with being, so is the true. But as good adds to being the notion of desirable, so the true adds a relation to the intellect.[20]

Thomas clearly indicates the *ratio* of "the true" in a metaphysical sense: it expresses "an order to knowledge." Truth is conceived here as knowability. Thomas consistently speaks of ontological truth in terms of "aptitude": something is called "true" insofar as it is apt to be conformed to the intellect or "is apt to bring about a true idea of itself." Knowability is the possibility or condition for truth in the formal sense, which is a conformity between intellect and thing, and as such fully compatible with the "logical" mode of truth.

Characteristic of the medieval doctrine of the transcendentals is the conceptual derivation of the other transcendentals from the first notion, "being": they are seen as an inner explication of this first. In his argument, Thomas underlines the inner basis of the truth of things: "Everything is knowable insofar as it has being *(esse)*." The real identity of the "true" and "being" is mediated by the notion of "act." Everything is knowable, not insofar as it is in potency but insofar as it is in act.[21] Insofar as a thing is in act, it is called "being" *(ens)*, for the name "being" is taken from the act of being. Actuality is the ground of both the knowability and the entity of things. From this follows the convertibility of the true and being.

Earlier in the *Summa*, Thomas had argued that "being" is the first conception of the intellect, because something is knowable insofar as it is in act. Therefore, "being" is the proper object of the intellect and thus the *primum intelligibile*.[22] This fundamental knowability is expressed by the transcendental "true," since it adds a relation to the intellect.

20. *STh* I, q. 16, a. 3: "Sicut bonum habet rationem appetibilis, ita verum habet ordinem ad cognitionem. Unumquodque autem inquantum habet de esse, intantum est cognoscibile. Et propter hoc dicitur in III *de Anima* quod *anima est quodammodo omnia* secundum sensum et intellectum. Et ideo sicut bonum convertitur cum ente, ita et verum. Sed tamen sicut bonum addit rationem appetibilis super ens, ita et verum comparationem ad intellectum."
21. *STh* I, q. 87, a. 1: "Unumquodque cognoscibile est secundum quod est in actu, et non secundum quod est in potentia, ut dicitur in IX *Metaph.* (c. 9): sic enim aliquid est ens et verum, quod sub cognitione cadit, prout actu est."
22. *STh* I, q. 5, a. 2: "Illud ergo est prius secundum rationem, quod prius cadit in conceptione intellectus. Primo autem in conceptione intellectus cadit ens: quia secundum hoc unum-

## Is Truth *Not* a Transcendental? 11

*Verum* is a relational transcendental. Thomas indicates the term to which being is correlated by quoting Aristotle's statement "the soul is in a sense all things." It is illustrative for the continuity in Aquinas's conception of truth that the idea of the correlation between *anima* and being, which is central in his argument for the transcendental character of the true in *De veritate*, recurs in the *Summa*.

Thomas understands Aristotle's statement as a reference to the special position of human beings in the world. Man is all things *quodammodo*, namely, not by his being, but by his knowing; it is that in which the perfection of an intellectual substance consists. Knowing beings are distinguished from non-knowing beings in that the latter have only their own form, whereas knowing beings are by nature able to assimilate also the forms of other things. Their nature has "a greater amplitude and extension."[23] An intellectual substance has "more affinity" to the whole of things than does any other substance. Through its intellect it is able to comprehend the entire being *(totius entis comprehensiva)*.[24] The human mind, one could say, is marked by a transcendental openness.

Aquinas's argument for the convertibility of "true" and "being" draws a parallel to the convertibility between "good" and "being," which he had discussed earlier in the *Summa* (q. 5,1 and 5,3). Such a parallel is meaningful only if "the true" and "the good" are not heterogeneous, as Dewan suggests. In his reading, "true" and "good" have different sorts of verification; they are different kinds of transcendentals, because "true" is a logical predicate and "good" a metaphysical one.

Interestingly, in the *Summa theologiae* I, q. 16, a. 4, Thomas discusses the order of the notions "true" and "good." His thesis is that despite their real identity and convertibility, "the true" is conceptually prior to "the good." One of his arguments for this priority is based on their relationship to the

---

quodque cognoscibile est quod est actu (...). Unde ens est proprium objectum intellectus: et sic est primum intelligibile, sicut sonus est primum audibile."

23. *STh* I, q. 14, a. 1: "Cognoscentia a non cognoscentibus in hoc distinguuntur, quia non cognoscentia nihil habent nisi formam suam tantum; sed cognoscens natum est habere formam etiam rei alterius, nam species cogniti est in cognoscente. Unde manifestum est quod natura rei non cognoscentis est magis coarctata et limitata: natura autem rerum cognoscentium habet maiorem amplitudinem et extensionem. Propter quod dicit Philosophus (...) quod *anima est quodammodo omnia*."

24. *Summa contra gentiles* III, c. 112: "Naturae autem intellectuales maiorem habent affinitatem ad totum quam aliae naturae: nam unaquaeque intellectualis substantia est quodammodo omnia, inquantum totius entis comprehensiva est suo intellectu."

first transcendental. The true is closer to being than is the good, for the true is related to being absolutely and immediately, while the *ratio* of the good is consequent upon being, insofar as this is perfect and appetible.[25] In the preceding article on the convertibility of the true and being, Thomas had explained that the true expresses a relationship to knowledge and that everything is knowable insofar as it has being. The *ratio* of the good expresses appetibility. A thing is appetible insofar as it is perfect. Consequently, the good has the aspect of the "ultimate."[26] The *ratio* of the true, knowability, is therefore closer to being than is the *ratio* of the good. Neither Thomas's argument in art. 4 nor his explanation in art. 3 suggests a heterogeneity between the true and the good: both are metaphysical transcendentals.

25. *STh* I, q. 16, a. 4: "Licet verum et bonum supposito convertantur cum ente, tamen ratione differunt. Et secundum hoc verum, absolute loquendo, prius est quam bonum. Quod ex duobus apparet. Primo quidem ex hoc, quod verum propinquius se habet ad ens, quod est prius, quam bonum. Nam verum respicit ipsum esse simpliciter et immediate: ratio autem boni consequitur esse, secundum quod est aliquo modo perfectum; sic enim appetibile est."

26. *STh* I, q. 5, a. 1 ad 1: "Sed bonum dicit rationem perfecti, quod est appetibile: et per consequens dicit rationem ultimi."

Stephen L. Brock

# Thomas Aquinas and "What Actually Exists"

IT WOULD BE DIFFICULT to overstate the importance of Fr. Lawrence Dewan's contributions over the years to our understanding of St. Thomas's doctrine of being *(esse)*. Best known, I imagine, are Fr. Dewan's masterly treatments of the relation between the "act of being" *(actus essendi)* and essence. Among other things, he has made us appreciate how tight the bond is, and how subtle the distinction, between these two "targets of metaphysical attention" (to use a characteristic phrase of his).

Perhaps not as well known is some rather recent work of Fr. Dewan's on the relation between *esse* and truth.[1] In this area, one of his findings took me somewhat by surprise. It concerns Thomas's assertion that the *esse* which properly answers the question "is it?" or "does it exist?"—the question *an sit*—is the *esse* that signifies the truth of a proposition *(esse ut verum)*. The *esse* that signifies the act of being *(esse ut actus essendi)* is something else. What surprised me was how strictly Fr. Dewan takes the assertion.[2] I had thought that at least in some cases the affirmative answer to the question *an sit* could signify a thing's *actus essendi*. But Fr. Dewan insists that it always signifies the truth of a proposition.

---

1. Papers of his on this topic include: Lawrence Dewan, O.P., "St. Thomas's Successive Discussions of the Nature of Truth," in *Sanctus Thomas de Aquino: Doctor Hodiernae Humanitatis*, ed. Daniel Ols, O.P. (Vatican City: Libreria Editrice Vaticana, 1995), 153–68; "A Note on Metaphysics and Truth," *Doctor Communis* N.S. 2 (2002): 143–53 *(The Contemporary Debate on Truth*, Proceedings of the II Plenary Session of the Pontifical Academy of St. Thomas Aquinas); "Which *Esse* Gives the Answer to the Question: 'Is It?' for St. Thomas," *Doctor Communis* N.S. 3 (2002): 80–97; "Is Truth a Transcendental for St. Thomas Aquinas?" *Nova et Vetera* [Eng. ed.] 2 (2004): 1–19. There is also some pertinent material in his "Anthony Kenny's *Aquinas on Being*," *Nova et Vetera* [Eng. ed.] 3 (2005): 335–400.

2. Dewan, "Which *Esse*."

Experience has taught me that when one's reading of St. Thomas is at odds with Fr. Dewan's, it is best to revisit one's assumptions. So here. What I have found is that I had been influenced by a way of understanding the distinction between *esse ut actus essendi* and *esse ut verum* that, I now see, is not quite Thomas's way. It was originally proposed, I believe, by Peter Geach. My title alludes to one of Geach's papers on the matter.[3] Geach assimilates Thomas's distinction to a distinction that he takes from Gottlob Frege, between existence in the sense of *Wirklichkeit* (actuality) and existence in the sense of the existential quantifier. Following Christopher Martin, I shall call the latter *Es-gibt-Existenz* (literally, "there-is"-existence).[4] Since Geach's Fregean interpretation of Thomas enjoys some currency, I thought that my results might be worth putting forward.[5]

Geach is well aware that Thomas holds that the question *an sit* concerns only *esse ut verum*, not *esse ut actus essendi*.[6] On Geach's account, this would be because the question *an sit* has nothing to do with whether what is asked about is "presently actual." Existence in the sense of present actuality would be precisely *esse ut actus essendi*. Since it seemed to me that at least sometimes the question *an sit* could concern present actuality, I drew the conclusion that in those cases it must concern *esse ut actus essendi*.[7] Clearly my

---

3. Peter Geach, "What Actually Exists," in *God and the Soul* (South Bend: St. Augustine's Press, n.d.; repr. of the 1969 ed.), 65–74. Geach also discusses the distinction in "Aquinas," in G. E. M. Anscombe and Peter Geach, *Three Philosophers* (Ithaca: Cornell University Press, 1961), 65–125; and "Form and Existence," in *God and the Soul*, 42–64.

4. See Christopher Martin, "The Notion of Existence Used in Answering An Est?," in Martin, *Thomas Aquinas: God and Explanations* (Edinburgh: Edinburgh University Press, 1997), 50–79. (He introduces "*Esgibtexistenz*" on p. 66.) Martin follows and develops Geach's interpretation of Thomas, and I shall be drawing upon his study at certain points. For some of the development, he expresses a debt to Alejandro Llano, *Metafísica y lenguaje* (Pamplona: EUNSA, 1984). Llano also uses Geach in his reading of Thomas, in Alejandro Llano, "'Being as True' according to Aquinas," *Acta Philosophica* 4 (1995): 73–82; Alejandro Llano, "The Different Meanings of 'Being' According to Aristotle and Aquinas," *Acta Philosophica* 10 (2001): 29–44.

5. Another work showing the influence of the Fregean interpretation is Anthony Kenny, *Aquinas on Being* (Oxford: Oxford University Press, 2002). Up to a point, the influence can also be seen in Gyula Klima's generally very negative appraisal of Kenny's Fregean approach: Gyula Klima, "On Kenny on Aquinas on Being: A Critical Review of *Aquinas on Being* by Anthony Kenny," *International Philosophical Quarterly* 44 (2004): 567–80. For why I say "up to a point," see below, nn. 7 and 77.

6. Geach, "Aquinas," 88–89; "Form and Existence," 57.

7. Klima appears to have drawn the same conclusion. What he takes to characterize the "exists" that is a "first-level" concept and a *verbum substantivum* (i.e., the "exists" that signifies *actus essendi*) is its signifying that something is "one of the things that presently populate our actual universe," its telling us that "the thing in question *actually*, at the moment of our

conclusion was mistaken. But the mistake does not lie in thinking that the question *an sit* could concern present actuality. It lies in thinking that present actuality coincides with *esse ut actus essendi*. For even in the *esse ut verum* sense, "exists" concerns the present; that is, it is not "timeless." And in its most proper use, it too signifies actuality. This even seems to be why it gets the name of existence.

First I shall look at some ways in which the Fregean distinction is indeed comparable to Thomas's, together with some uncontentious differences between them. In the second section, I argue that unlike *Es-gibt-Existenz*, Thomas's *esse ut verum* is variable over time in a way that makes it similar to *actus essendi*. This is connected with a difference between *esse ut verum* and *Es-gibt-Existenz* that may at first seem rather insignificant, namely, that whereas *Es-gibt-Existenz* attaches to "concepts" (in the Fregean sense), *esse ut verum* attaches to propositions. Propositions are a sort of composite, and it is to a sort of composite that the *actus essendi* which is subject to time also attaches. This is the *actus essendi* which we first and properly understand, and from which, according to Thomas, our notion of *esse ut verum* derives. In the third section I make the case for the claims that *esse ut verum* chiefly signifies actuality and that this is what explains its derivation from *actus essendi*. I conclude with some remarks on the nature and importance of *esse ut verum* actuality, and a suggestion as to what is truly distinctive about *actus essendi*.

## Convergences between Frege's Distinction and Thomas's

Here is a brief sketch of the Fregean distinction, as presented by Geach.[8]

According to Frege, the question whether a certain item exists can have two quite different senses. In one sense, what is being asked is whether "there is *(es gibt)* any such thing as" that item. To ask this, Frege holds, is nothing other than to ask whether the meaning of the item's name has at

---

consideration, exists." (I am putting together remarks from Klima, "On Kenny," 571, 574, 579.) For more discussion of this sense of "exists," Klima sends us to Geach's "What Actually Exists," which he calls a classic paper (Klima, "On Kenny," 571n6).

8. Since it is Geach's interpretation of Frege that has directly influenced the reading of Thomas, the question of the accuracy with which it represents Frege's own thought is incidental to my purpose here.

least one instantiation. It is in this sense, for example, that we might ask whether a centaur exists. To say that it does is to say that the meaning of "centaur" is instantiated by at least one thing. This is *Es-gibt-Existenz*.

What is especially to be noted about *Es-gibt-Existenz* is the sort of item that it can be ascribed to (or denied of). If we say that a centaur exists, what we are ascribing existence to is not the individual thing or things instantiating the meaning of "centaur." That would make little sense. It would mean that what instantiates the meaning of "centaur" has at least one instantiation. What we are ascribing existence to is the meaning of "centaur" itself. Frege would call it the "concept" of centaur. A thing that instantiates a concept is what he calls an "object." *Es-gibt-Existenz*, then, is attached not to things or objects, but to concepts. Objects instantiate concepts, but the "instantiatedness" belongs to the concepts, not the objects.

A Fregean concept is not to be understood as a purely "subjective" or "mental" affair.[9] Of course it is something that the mind conceives or understands, but it may also be found "outside" the mind—in an object that instantiates it. It is rather like what Thomas would call an intelligible form or a simple *ratio*.[10] Instead of speaking of a "concept," we could speak of a "kind" or a "class," or even a "description."[11] When we ask whether a centaur exists, we have in mind the description of a certain kind or class, and we want to know whether the number of members of the kind or class so described is not nought.[12]

The other sense of existence is *Wirklichkeit*. In this sense, "exists" means "is presently actual." This sense, Geach tells us, "corresponds to the uses of the verb 'to exist' in which we say that an individual thing comes to exist, continues to exist, ceases to exist, or again to the uses of 'being' in which we say that thing is brought into being or kept in being by another thing."[13] Geach says that "a provisional explanation of actuality may be given thus: $x$ is actual if and only if $x$ either acts, or undergoes change, or both."[14]

*Wirklichkeit* is never a feature of concepts, but only of some individuals or "objects." Not all objects admit of *Wirklichkeit*, for Frege, because he

---

9. See Geach, "Form and Existence," 45–46.
10. On how a *ratio* is "in" a thing, see *In I Sent.*, d. 2, q. 1, a. 3.
11. See Geach, "Aquinas," 90.
12. See Gottlob Frege, *The Foundations of Arithmetic*, trans. J. L. Austin (Oxford: Basil Blackwell, 1950), 65.
13. Geach, "Aquinas," 90–91.
14. Geach, "What Actually Exists," 65.

considers pure numbers to be objects, and they do not have *Wirklichkeit*.[15] The objects that may (and may not) be subjects of *Wirklichkeit* are what we might want to call "real things": Socrates, the planet Mars, the desk I am sitting at, your nose, and the like.

So in the *Wirklichkeit* sense, when we ask whether something exists, we are not asking whether the meaning of its name is instantiated by anything. We are asking whether the thing named is presently actual or not. In the case of an animal or a plant, this would amount to asking whether or not it is now alive. Being alive is something very different from being instantiated.

Now we can begin to consider how Frege's distinction compares with Thomas's.

In many of the places in which Thomas invokes the distinction between *esse ut verum* and *esse ut actus essendi*, he refers us to a passage in Book 5 of Aristotle's *Metaphysics*. It will be useful to have part of his commentary on that passage before us. Aristotle is presenting the various ways in which things are said "to be." His first distinction is between being *per accidens* and being *per se*. After explaining being *per accidens*—coincidental being—he distinguishes three other ways in which things are said to be. According to Thomas, all of these fall under being *per se*. The first is being as divided into the ten categories; the second, being in the sense of the truth of a proposition; the third, being as divided into the potential and the actual. Our passage falls within the discussion of being in the sense of the truth of a proposition.

Then when he says *amplius autem* he posits another mode of being, according to which "to be" and "is" signify the composition of a proposition, which the intellect fashions by composing and dividing. Whence he says that "to be" signifies the truth of a thing; or better, as another translation has it, that "to be" signifies that some stated thing is true. Whence the truth of a proposition can be called the truth of a thing by its cause. This is because it is from the fact that a thing is or is not that a statement is true or false. For when we say that something is, we signify that a proposition is true; and when we say that a thing is not, we signify that [a proposition] is not true. And this holds both in affirming and in negating. In affirming, as when we say that Socrates is white, because this is true. In negating, as Socrates is not white, because this is true, namely that he is non-white. And likewise we say that the diameter is not incommensurable with the side of a square, because this is false, namely, that it is not non-commensurable.[16]

---

15. See Frege, *The Foundations of Arithmetic*, 20.
16. The last two sentences of this paragraph are rather confusing. Perhaps there is a prob-

But you should know that this second mode [of being *per se*] is related to the first [viz., being as divided into the categories] as effect to cause. For truth and falsity in a proposition, which the intellect signifies by this verb "is" insofar as it is the verbal copula, follows from the fact that something is in reality. But because the intellect considers as a sort of being something that in itself is a non-being, such as a negation and the like, "to be" is sometimes said of something in this second mode and not in the first. For blindness is said to be in the second mode, on account of the fact that the proposition is true which says that something is blind; yet it is not said to be true[17] in the first mode. For blindness does not have any being *(esse)* in things, but is rather the privation of a certain being. However, it is merely accidental to a thing that something be truly affirmed about it in the mind or in speech. For a thing is not ordered to knowledge, but rather the reverse. But the being that each thing has in its own nature is substantial. And so when it is said that Socrates is, if the "is" is taken in the first mode, it is a substantial predication. For "a being" is superior to each of the beings, as animal is to man. But if it is taken in the second mode, it is an accidental predication.[18]

---

lem with our text of the commentary, or even with the translation(s) that Thomas was working with. What Aristotle is getting at here (1017a33–b1) is clear enough: no matter whether the predicate is positive ("Socrates is musical") or negative ("Socrates is non-white"), "is" signifies truth; and "is not" signifies falsehood, even when the predicate is positive ("the diagonal is not commensurable"). There is certainly no reason to suspect that Thomas thinks otherwise.

17. I would be inclined to omit "true" *("vera")*. It ruins the parallel with the previous clause. Of course we must await the Leonine critical edition of the commentary.

18. "Deinde cum dicit amplius autem ponit alium modum entis, secundum quod esse et est, significant compositionem propositionis, quam facit intellectus componens et dividens. Unde dicit, quod esse significat veritatem rei. Vel sicut alia translatio melius habet quod esse significat quia aliquod dictum est verum. Unde veritas propositionis potest dici veritas rei per causam. Nam ex eo quod res est vel non est, oratio vera vel falsa est. Cum enim dicimus aliquid esse, significamus propositionem esse veram. Et cum dicimus non esse, significamus non esse veram. Et hoc sive in affirmando, sive in negando. In affirmando quidem, sicut dicimus quod Socrates est albus, quia hoc verum est. In negando vero, ut Socrates non est albus, quia hoc est verum, scilicet ipsum esse non album. Et similiter dicimus, quod non est diameter incommensurabilis lateri quadrati, quia hoc est falsum, scilicet non esse ipsum non commensurabilem.

"Sciendum est autem quod iste secundus modus comparatur ad primum, sicut effectus ad causam. Ex hoc enim quod aliquid in rerum natura est, sequitur veritas et falsitas in propositione, quam intellectus significat per hoc verbum est prout est verbalis copula. Sed, quia aliquid, quod est in se non ens, intellectus considerat ut quoddam ens, sicut negationem et huiusmodi, ideo quandoque dicitur esse de aliquo hoc secundo modo, et non primo. Dicitur enim, quod caecitas est secundo modo, ex eo quod vera est propositio, qua dicitur aliquid esse caecum; non tamen dicitur quod sit primo modo vera. Nam caecitas non habet aliquod esse in rebus, sed magis est privatio alicuius esse. Accidit autem unicuique rei quod aliquid de ipsa vere affirmetur intellectu vel voce. Nam res non refertur ad scientiam, sed e converso. Esse vero quod in sui natura unaquaeque res habet, est substantiale. Et ideo, cum dicitur, Socrates est, si ille est primo modo accipiatur, est de praedicato substantiali. Nam ens est superius ad unumquodque entium, sicut animal ad hominem. Si autem accipiatur secundo modo, est de praedicato accidentali." *In V Meta.*, lect. 9, §895–96 (Marietti).

In the rest of the paper I shall refer to this as the *Meta.* 5 text.

Plainly the distinction that Thomas draws here invites comparison with the Fregean one. For instance, like *Wirklichkeit,* what Thomas speaks of here as the "first" mode of being belongs squarely to the domain of "real things," the things that act or are acted upon.[19] Although he does not say it in so many words, this is the mode to which *esse ut actus essendi* belongs. I believe this is uncontroversial in the literature. It is how Fr. Dewan takes it.[20]

We should not be misled by the fact that Thomas ascribes this mode of being to things in all of the Aristotelian categories. This may seem to be in conflict with the Fregean restriction of *Wirklichkeit* to certain individuals or "objects," but really it is not. For one thing, Thomas holds that there are individuals or particulars in all of the categories.[21] More to the point, he does not mean that this sort of *esse* is something of which things in all of the categories are properly subjects. The proper subject of any *actus essendi* is an individual substance, a subsistent.[22] The substance's primary and unqualified *actus essendi* is that which it has through its substantial form. An accident is only an additional nature or form composed with the substance. By subjection to it, the substance takes on an additional, qualified *actus essendi.*[23] An accident "is" in just this sense: by it, the composite to which it belongs somehow is. "Whiteness is said to exist, not because it subsists in itself, but because by it, something has 'being white.'"[24] In fact, not even the substantial form is a proper subject of *esse.*[25] The proper subject is the composite of form and matter, the substance itself. So what the *Meta.* 5 text means is that there is *esse,* in the first mode, "according" to the natures of things in all the

---

19. Thus pure mathematicals, abstracting from motion and action, exist only "in the mind"; see *Summa theologiae* (hereafter *STh*) I, q. 5, a. 3, ad 4. Mathematicals do exist "in reality," but not in a pure state. They must be attached to things that are not mathematicals. See *STh* I, q. 30, a. 1, ad 4.

20. Dewan, "Which *Esse,*" 87. Texts invoking the distinction and clearly associating the first mode with *actus essendi* include *In I Sent.,* d. 33, q. 1, a. 1, ad 1; *In III Sent.,* d. 6, q. 2, a. 2; *De potentia* (hereafter *De pot.*), q. 7, a. 2, ad 1; *Quodl.* IX, q. 2, a. 2; *STh* I, q. 3, a. 4, ad 2. There is also *Quodl.* II, q. 2, a. 1, although Fr. Dewan raises doubts about its authenticity (Dewan, "Which *Esse,*" 97).

21. *STh* I, q. 29, a. 1.

22. The subsistent is also the proper subject of action and passion: *STh* I, q. 75, aa. 2 & 3.

23. See *STh* I, q. 5, a. 1, ad 1.

24. "Albedo dicitur esse, non qui ipsa in se subsistat, sed quia ea aliquid habet esse album"; *Quodl.* IX, q. 2, a. 2.

25. See *STh* I, q. 75, a. 2, ad 2. Even the human soul is only a partial subject of the *esse* that it gives.

categories.[26] But the proper subject of such *esse* is always an individual composite of form and subject or form and matter.[27]

There is also a clear similarity between Thomas's second mode of being, which of course is *esse ut verum*, and Frege's *Es-gibt-Existenz*. Neither of them attaches directly to real things. *Es-gibt-Existenz* attaches to concepts, and *esse ut verum* attaches to propositions.

This obviously is also something of a difference between them. Thomas holds that concepts or simple *rationes* are not true or false, except in an indirect way.[28] I shall want to argue that the difference is more telling than Geach leads us to think it is. But they at least have this in common, that neither a concept nor a proposition is a "thing." Indeed, prima facie, what attaches to propositions might seem to be even more removed from things than what attaches to concepts is. For concepts can be instantiated by things, whereas propositions are only in the mind. If *esse ut verum* can be predicated of things in an accidental way, this is not because propositions can be in things. It is because they are about things, and because their truth is somehow an effect or a function of things. A proposition is a composition of terms that is formed by the mind to signify that the items expressed by the terms are composed *in re*.[29] But the composition *in re* is not a proposition, for the simple reason that it is not a signification. Things do not instantiate propositions. They only verify (or falsify) them.[30]

In addition to the fact that what *esse ut verum* attaches to is a proposition, not a concept, there is also at least one other obvious difference between it and *Es-gibt-Existenz*. This has been pointed out by Christopher

---

26. We might wonder why the *Meta.* 5 text says that the *esse* that each thing has in its own nature is "substantial." Thomas does not always confine the term "substance" to what is in the category of substance. He sometimes calls the essence or nature of something in another category its "substance." See for example *STh* I-II, q. 10, a. 1.

27. Geach is quite clear about the fact that every *actus essendi* is through and according to some form; see "Form and Existence," 60.

28. See *In VI Meta.*, lect. 4, §1233; *In IX Meta.*, lect. 11, §1906–9; *In I Periherm.*, lect. 3, §35; *STh* I, q. 17, a. 3.

29. Thus, "hoc ipsum esse quod significat veritatem, et non esse quod significat falsitatem, uno modo dicitur, scilicet in compositione, scilicet quod est verum si componitur in re quod intellectus componit: falsum autem si non componitur in re quod intellectus componit, intelligens aut denuncians"; *In IX Meta.*, lect. 11, §1914. This is at the place where the Latin text of Aristotle speaks of *"esse ut verum."*

30. On the fact that for Thomas, truth in the proper sense is not "in things," see Dewan, "St. Thomas's Successive Discussions of the Nature of Truth"; "A Note on Metaphysics and Truth"; and "Is Truth a Transcendental?"

Martin.³¹ Thomas says that "Socrates exists" can be taken in the *esse ut verum* sense. For Frege, the word "Socrates" would signify an object, not a concept, and so the only sense in which Socrates could be said to exist or not would be that of *Wirklichkeit*. Martin does not give this discrepancy much importance, nor would I. The doctrines can at least be brought into proximity with each other. This will take some explaining.

Although of course a proper name does not signify a class or a kind, it does, for Thomas, signify a certain *ratio*.³² Moreover, unlike Frege, Thomas has no difficulty with the idea that a proper name can play a predicative role.³³ No doubt it would be odd to ask whether anything "instantiates" the *ratio* of Socrates, since that sounds as though many things might conceivably do so. But it surely makes sense to ask whether in truth there is any such thing (or any such person) as Socrates.

Of course if our question is whether *an* F exists, the name of F can signify only a class or kind. It makes no sense to ask whether *a* Socrates exists, or whether the class of Socrates is not empty. Geach seems to hold that the question *an sit* must always be about a class or kind.³⁴ However, he does not simply rule out questions such as "whether there is any such thing as Socrates." To cite his own example, he holds that the statement "There is no such thing as Cerberus" is significant, and that the "there is" does not at all refer to *Wirklichkeit*.³⁵ Only, instead of saying that what the statement means is that the concept of Cerberus is not instantiated, he says it means that the word "Cerberus" is not a genuine name. In Geach's view a genuine name always refers to something.

Here we seem to have a disagreement between Geach and Thomas on what counts as a name. I suppose it complements the disagreement between Frege and Thomas on whether proper names can be predicative. Our concern, however, is not with names, but with the meaning of "exists." I think it is clear that the *esse ut verum* which Thomas ascribes to individuals can

---

31. Martin, "The Notion," 67.
32. See *STh* I, q. 13, a. 9: a name imposed to signify a singular is incommunicable "et re et ratione." I suppose the *ratio* of an individual would be a kind of "definite description."
33. See *In VII Meta.*, lect. 2, §1273; Gottlob Frege, "On Concept and Object," in *Translations from the Philosophical Writings of Gottlob Frege*, trans. and ed. P. T. Geach and Max Black (Oxford: Basil Blackwell, 1980), 50.
34. It is true that for Thomas, the properly *scientific* question *an sit* is always about a kind, a universal. But not all truth is scientific.
35. Geach, "Form and Existence," 55ff.

be judged comparable to a sense of existence that Geach does recognize and that is at least similar to *Es-gibt-Existenz*. It is certainly very different from *Wirklichkeit*.

Still, I also think it would be important not to push the comparison too far. Even if Thomas were to grant that a genuine proper name must refer to something, I do not believe he would simply equate a name's having reference with an "existence," in *any* sense. It is here that we can begin to see the significance of the difference between saying that existence attaches to a concept and saying that it attaches to a proposition.

## The Instantiation of Concepts, the Truth of Propositions, and Tense

Suppose we grant that "the name 'Socrates' refers to something" is one sense of "Socrates exists." Let us also grant that, as Geach insists, a person's name never ceases to refer to the person. It does so even after the person has died. "The reference of a name admits of no time qualifications; names are tenseless."[36] I think this second supposition is quite right, and I find it hard to imagine that Thomas would not. But combining it with the first supposition gives this result: in some sense, dead Socrates continues to exist. (I hope it is obvious that the immortality of the human soul is irrelevant here. If not, then for "Socrates," read "Mei Xiang.")

This is exactly what Christopher Martin says about *esse ut verum* as applied to Socrates: "for St. Thomas, . . . a sentence such as 'Socrates exists', taken in the *esse ut verum* sense, makes perfectly good sense; *indeed, it is even true*, while the same sentence taken in the real *esse* sense has not been true since the hemlock took effect."[37] A little later he states the point in a general way: "some individual exists in the *esse ut verum* sense if we can affirm of it some predicate that implies its present or past real existence."[38] He also lays down a parallel thesis about the *esse ut verum* that would apply to a concept: "some concept is instantiated if we can affirm it of some present or past real existent."[39]

Now, taken by itself, this last assertion does surely make sense. The present instantiatedness of a concept does not depend upon the presence of any

36. Ibid., 59.
37. Martin, "The Notion," 67 (emphasis added).
38. Ibid., 72.  39. Ibid.

"What Actually Exists"   23

of its instances. They may just as well all be past. The concept of "dinosaur" is no more fictional than that of "panda." It applies to a reality, though one that is no longer actual. Instantiatedness, *Es-gibt-Existenz*, is as tenseless as reference.

But what this shows, I believe, is precisely that instantiatedness is after all not quite the same as *esse ut verum*. There is a remarkable passage in Thomas's commentary on Book 10 of the *Metaphysics* that leaves little doubt about this. He is discussing Avicenna's view that *ens* is only an accidental predicate. Avicenna, he says,

was deceived, on account of the equivocation of "being" *(ens)*. For the being that signifies the composition of a proposition is an accidental predicate, because the composition is brought about by the mind according to a determinate time. To be in this time or that is indeed an accidental predicate. But the being that is divided into the ten categories signifies the very natures of the ten genera, insofar as they are in act or in potency.[40]

Clearly the being that is an accidental predicate here is nothing other than *esse ut verum*, "the being that signifies the composition of a proposition." But here its accidental character is shown, not by the reason given in the *Meta*. 5 text—the fact that things are not ordered to knowledge—but by the fact that the composition is formed "according to a determinate time."

What does this mean? I see no reason not to think that Thomas is alluding to the teaching of the *Perihermeneias*, that the verb in a proposition always "co-signifies" a time.[41] That is, it is always tensed. Thomas explains that this is owing to the temporal condition of our mind.

Because our cognition falls under the order of time, either directly or indirectly—on account of which the soul, in composing and dividing, must adjoin a time, as it says in the third Book of *De Anima*—the result is that things fall under its cognition under the aspect of present, past or future.[42]

---

40. "Similiter etiam [Avicenna] deceptus est ex aequivocatione entis. Nam ens quod significat compositionem propositionis est praedicatum accidentale, quia compositio fit per intellectum secundum determinatum tempus. Esse autem in hoc tempore vel in illo, est accidentale praedicatum. Sed ens quod dividitur per decem praedicamenta, significat ipsas naturas decem generum secundum quod sunt actu vel potentia"; *In X Meta.*, lect. 3, §1982. Earlier in the *Metaphysics* commentary Thomas criticizes Avicenna on the same point, saying that although the *esse* of a thing is other than its essence, it is not something added on as an accident, but rather is "constituted through the principles of the essence": *In IV Meta.*, lect. 2, §558. By *"esse"* there he means *actus essendi* (see §553). The principles of the essence would be the matter and the form.
41. See *In I Periherm.*, lect. 5, §53–58.
42. "Quia igitur cognitio nostra cadit sub ordine temporis, vel per se vel per accidens—

Of course the tense of the verb may not signify the very time at which the mind is forming the proposition. That is, it may not signify the present. What a tense signifies is the time of "the things falling under the mind's cognition," that is, of the matter that the proposition is about, as such. It signifies the time of the matter's being so disposed as to make the proposition true. This is why, when the proposition is about a variable matter, its own truth is also variable.

> The being *(esse)* in which the composition of the intellect is constituted as an affirmation indicates a certain composition and union; while the non-being *(non esse)*, which negation signifies, removes composition and designates plurality and diversity. Hence, in matters that can be both composed and divided, one and the same statement may be sometimes true, sometimes false; as this statement, "Socrates is seated," is true while he is seated, and the same is false when he gets up.[43]

If "Socrates is seated" is true now, it is because seatedness belongs to Socrates now. Likewise, if "something is blind" is true now, it is because the *ratio* of blindness belongs to something now.

Here we should recall that, as Martin himself observes, according to the *Meta.* 5 text "something is blind" means the same as "blindness is."[44] Martin explains rightly that for Thomas, to shift from the abstract "blindness" to the concrete "blind" is not to change what is being talked about; the difference between them is only in the mode of signifying, not in the matter signified. So "blindness is" is merely elliptical.[45] The verb "is" signifies the truth of a proposition, the text says, "insofar as it is the verbal copula." Evidently it can play this role even when the statement's grammatical form does not show it.

I suppose that the possibility of converting "something is blind" into a

---

unde et anima in componendo et dividendo necesse habet adiungere tempus, ut dicitur in III *De Anima*—consequens est quod sub eius cognitione cadant res sub ratione praesentis, praeteriti et futuri"; *In I Periherm.*, lect. 14, §194. The reference seems to be to *De anima*, bk. 3, ch. 6, 430b1–4.

43. "Esse autem in quo consistit compositio intellectus ut affirmatio, compositionem quamdam et unionem indicat: non esse vero, quod significat negatio, tollit compositionem, et designat pluralitatem et diversitatem. Unde manifestum est, quod in his, quae contingit componi et dividi, una et eadem oratio sit quandoque vera, quandoque falsa; sicut haec oratio, Socrates sedet, est vera eo sedente, eadem autem falsa eo surgente"; *In IX Meta.*, lect. 11, §1900.

44. Martin, "The Notion," 68.

45. Later in the *Metaphysics* commentary Thomas dwells at some length on the possibility of transforming the question "whether so-and-so exists" into the question "whether something is so-and-so" (and correspondingly, "what so-and-so is" into "why something is so-and-so"); see *In VII Meta.*, lect. 17, §§1650–51 and §§1662–63. Cf. *In II Post. An.*, lect. 1, §414.

statement with only two terms—"blindness is," or "blindness exists"—lies in the fact that its subject is merely indefinite. In fact, a proposition with a more definite subject might not tell us that what the predicate signifies exists, or at least not unqualifiedly. "Something that I am thinking about is a chimera" does not imply that a chimera exists, except in a qualified sense: "in my mind."[46] This is because "something that I am thinking about" need not be, unqualifiedly, some *thing*—some *res* or reality.[47]

Of course in some contexts we might affirm a thing's existence unqualifiedly, even though we do not mean that it exists "in reality." An arithmetician might very well say simply that a prime between 10 and 20 exists. He means that some number between 10 and 20 is prime. He can speak in this way without reifying numbers, because in the context of mathematics, "exists" can be understood as "exists in the qualified manner in which pure numbers exist," namely, "in the mind." To use a Fregean notion, the arithmetician's "universe of discourse" is pure numbers. I do not think Thomas would have any problem with this notion. He would, however, judge that the universe of discourse of pure numbers is itself only a qualified one. Our unqualified universe of discourse, and the one from which all the others are somehow derived by an operation of the mind, is . . . the universe, the real one. What exists altogether unqualifiedly, in the *esse ut verum* sense, is whatever is true of something *in rerum natura*.[48]

It would be a mistake, I take it, to think that the "is" in the proposition "something is blind" signifies *another proposition* affirming the truth of this one. It is not as though even "something is blind" is merely elliptical, for "it is true that something is blind." That would create an infinite regress, since "something is blind" shows up again in the expanded proposition. But in order to "signify" the truth of a proposition—or let us say, in order to present a proposition as true—one does not need another proposition saying that it is true. In fact every proposition presents itself as true, even though it does not predicate truth of itself. Thomas's thought seems to be simply that when one has a proposition in which "is" is used as a copula, the function of "is" is just this: to serve as that by which the proposition presents itself as true.

---

46. See Gyula Klima, "The Semantic Principles Underlying Saint Thomas Aquinas's Metaphysics of Being," *Medieval Philosophy and Theology* 5 (1996): 87–141, at 125. Klima's study is very helpful for unraveling the intricacies of the relation between existence and predication in Thomas.
47. See *STh* I, q. 48, a. 2, ad 2; *De malo*, q. 1, a. 1, ad 19.
48. See *In II Post An.*, lect. 6, §461; *STh* I, q. 48, a. 2, ad 2; *In II Periherm.*, lect. 2, §212.

Presumably then, "Socrates is" and "a dinosaur is," taken in the *esse ut verum* sense, can likewise be converted into "something is Socrates" and "something is a dinosaur." But would Martin or Geach hold that "something is Socrates" and "something is a dinosaur" are indeed now true in the *esse ut verum* sense, and false only in the *actus essendi* sense? This would surely be strained. The blindness example is enough to show this. Since blindness is a privation, "something is blind" can bear only the *esse ut verum* sense. But suppose there were no present cases of blindness, only past ones. Some things were blind, but now nothing is. Given that the concept of blindness remains instantiated, *Es-gibt-Existenz* would give us a sense in which "blindness exists" remains true. But we can hardly say that for Thomas, there is a sense in which "something is blind" is still true, since now "nothing is blind" is also true, and "is" must bear the same meaning in both. The statements are in contradiction.

Geach does express approval of Thomas's identification of the "existence" that answers the question *an sit* with the truth of an affirmative proposition. "This is exactly right," Geach says, "for 'an F exists' is true if and only if 'F' is truly predicable of something or other."[49] Yet note that Geach does not quite say that "an F exists" is true if and only if "something is an F" is true. His formulation leaves room for the possibility, asserted explicitly by Martin, that the only true predication of F be in the past tense: "something was an F." If "an F exists" means "the concept of F is instantiated," then "an F exists" is true if and only if *either* "something is an F" *or* "something was an F" is true.[50] And so the truth of "an F exists" is not quite identical with the truth of "something is an F." The one statement is not simply elliptical for the other.

At first it looked as though *Es-gibt-Existenz* was closer to "things" than *esse ut verum* is, because things can instantiate concepts, whereas they cannot instantiate propositions. But now it is *esse ut verum* that seems closer to things. The truth of "something is blind" is never "in" things, but its fate is tied to the fate of things. It lasts only so long as the composition of blindness with something or other *in re* lasts. By contrast, the instantiatedness of the concept of blindness will remain forever, no matter what happens to things.

I do not mean that it would be impossible to make affirmations of *Es-gibt-Existenz* line up with affirmations of *esse ut verum*. We could simply confine our universe of discourse to what is present. Then a concept will be

---

49. Geach, "Form and Existence," 57. See also Geach, "What Actually Exists," 65.
50. Some might wish to add "something will be an F," but this is incidental.

instantiated only if some instance of it is present. But Thomas's *est* does not require any such maneuver. It has the restriction to the present built in. (Of course the "present" is not always restricted to the present *moment*.)[51]

The passage from *Metaphysics* 10 (hereafter *Meta*. 10) might almost make it seem that if any *esse* in Thomas is timeless, it is the *esse* that is "in things," the *esse* that pertains to the natures of the categories—*esse ut actus essendi*. In the *Summa theologiae*, in fact, he tells us that the proper measure of *esse* is not time but eternity.[52] However, he also qualifies this, saying that insofar as a given *esse* recedes from permanence and is subject to change or "transmutation," it is subject to time.[53] Clearly the *esse* that is according to the natures of the categories is subject to transmutation, because it is a term of generation and corruption. It begins as the result of a composition of form and matter or form and subject, and it ceases as a result of their decomposition. The *Meta*. 10 text in fact signals this transmutability, when it says that the being that is divided into the categories signifies the natures of the ten genera insofar as they are in act *or* in potency. Of course it is only insofar as they are in act that they have *actus essendi*.[54]

So there is a clear parallel between the statement "whiteness exists," taken as referring to *esse ut actus essendi*, and the statement "blindness exists," which can refer only to *esse ut verum*. Although the "exists" seems to attach to a simple item, what it signifies is understood to be a result of the item's composition with something, and one that lasts only as long as the composition itself does. In one case the result is real. In the other, it is "only in the mind."[55] *Esse ut verum* is a very "weak" mode of *esse*.[56] Nevertheless, the par-

---

51. See *In I Periherm.*, lect. 5, §63.
52. *STh* I, q. 10, a. 4, ad 3.
53. Still, the *esse* that is merely "subject" to transmutation is subject to time only by association, *per accidens*. What is properly and directly measured by time is the *esse* that "consists" in a transmutation (to use Thomas's expression in *STh* I, q. 10, a. 4, ad 3); i.e., a motion, a "being moved." This *esse*, however, is not a full-fledged *actus essendi*. A motion is only an "imperfect" act. Thomas even speaks of motion as a sort of mixture of real being and being of reason; see *In IV Meta.*, lect. 1, §539–43.
54. This is not at all to say that the being that is divided into the categories altogether abstracts from act and potency, or that it does not always refer to *actus essendi*. There is still a reference to *actus essendi* even when the nature is signified merely as being in potency. To be in potency is nothing other than to have an order toward being in act. The division into act and potency is *per prius et posterius*, and a nature is signified *simpliciter* as a being only when it is signified as in act. See *STh* I, q. 5, a. 1, ad 1.
55. *In V Meta.*, lect. 9, §889; *Quodl.* IX, q. 2, a. 2.
56. "Nam unum eorum [scil., modi essendi], quod est debilissimum, est tantum in ratione,

allel does help us to begin to see that the use of "exists" to signify the truth of a proposition is not a merely arbitrary appropriation of the term.

> The deformity [of sin] is said to be, not because it has *esse* in reality, but because the intellect composes a privation with a subject, as a sort of form. Whence just as from the composition of a form with a subject or with matter there results a certain substantial or accidental *esse*, so the intellect signifies the composition of a privation with a subject by a certain *esse*.[57]

## *Esse ut Verum* as an Actuality

The parallel does not stop here. To say that blindness exists is not only to signify a composition of blindness with something and to co-signify it as "present." Said most properly, it is also to signify the present composition as "actual." In its primary use, *esse ut verum* signifies actuality. That this is Thomas's view can be shown, I believe, very readily.

We do not even have to look very far from the *Meta.* 5 text. In the immediately following section of the same *lectio*, Thomas takes up Aristotle's third mode of being *per se*, being as divided into potency and act. I suspect that some readers may be thinking that it is really here, and not in the being of the categories, that we hone in on *actus essendi*. But Thomas says this:

> Then when he says *amplius esse* he posits the distinction of being according to act and potency, saying that being and to be signify something sayable or utterable in potency, or sayable in act. For in all the aforesaid terms that signify the ten categories, something is said in act, and something is said in potency. And from this it results that each category is divided according to potency and act. And just as in things that are outside the soul, something is said in act, and something in potency, so too in the acts of the soul, and in privations, which are merely things of reason.[58]

---

scilicet negatio et privatio, quam dicimus in ratione esse, quia ratio de eis negociatur quasi de quibusdam entibus, dum de eis affirmat vel negat aliquid." *In IV Meta.*, lect. 1, §540. See also *In VI Meta.*, lect. 4, §1243.

57. The passage in full runs thus: "Ens dicitur dupliciter. Uno modo quod significat essentiam rei extra animam existentis; et hoc modo non potest dici ens deformitas peccati, quae privatio quaedam est: privationes enim essentiam non habent in rerum natura. Alio modo secundum quod significat veritatem propositionis; et sic deformitas dicitur esse, non propter hoc quod in re esse habeat, sed quia intellectus componit privationem cum subjecto, sicut formam quamdam. Unde sicut ex compositione formae ad subjectum vel ad materiam, relinquitur quoddam esse substantiale vel accidentale; ita etiam intellectus compositionem privationis cum subjecto per quoddam esse significat. Sed hoc esse non est nisi esse rationis, cum in re potius sit non esse. Et secundum hoc quod in ratione esse habet, constat quod a Deo est." *In II Sent.*, d. 37, q. 1, a. 2, ad 3.

58. "Deinde cum dicit amplius esse ponit distinctionem entis per actum et potentiam; di-

"What Actually Exists" 29

This could hardly be clearer. Act and potency are not a wholly new order of being *per se*. Rather they are a division within the two modes previously explained—*both* of them. They apply not only to the natures of the categories, but also to the acts of the soul, and even to privations, which are only things of reason. Blindness exists only in the *esse ut verum* sense. Yet it is not nonsense to speak of the potential and actual existence of blindness. Its actual existence, of course, can hardly be an *actus essendi*. The lesson is rather that not every actual existence is an *actus essendi*. Sometimes it is only an actual truth.[59]

We find rather striking confirmation of the applicability of potency and act to privations in Book 9.[60] Aristotle argues that the actuality of a good is better than the potential for it, whereas the actuality of a bad is worse—more truly bad, we might say—than the potential for it. The reason is that what is in potency to one contrary is the same as what is in potency to the other, so that it is in a way both (or neither), whereas the actualities are mutually exclusive. For instance, what is potentially healthy (good) is also potentially ill (bad), but what is actually healthy is not actually ill. As Thomas points out here, "the bad" is characterized by being "deficient."[61] Badness is a privation, and it admits of both potentiality and actuality.[62]

But most explicit about *esse ut verum* as chiefly signifying actuality is the ensuing portion of Thomas's commentary on *Metaphysics* 9 (hereafter *Meta.* 9). He tells us that after comparing act and potency with respect to good and bad, Aristotle compares them "with respect to the understand-

---

cens, quod ens et esse significant aliquid dicibile vel effabile in potentia, vel dicibile in actu. In omnibus enim praedictis terminis, quae significant decem praedicamenta, aliquid dicitur in actu, et aliquid in potentia. Et ex hoc accidit, quod unumquodque praedicamentum per actum et potentiam dividitur. Et sicut in rebus, quae extra animam sunt, dicitur aliquid in actu et aliquid in potentia, ita in actibus animae et privationibus, quae sunt res rationis tantum." *In V Meta.*, lect. 9, §897.

59. Cf. Llano, "The Different Meanings," 39, where he contrasts "veritative existence" with "being as actuality."

60. Already in *Metaphysics* 5 we are presented with a long discussion of potency, but not of act. Thomas tells us that Aristotle does not discuss act at this point, because he could not sufficiently explain its meaning unless the nature of forms were first shown, which he will do in Books 8 and 9; *In V Meta.*, lect. 14, §954.

61. *In IX Meta.*, lect. 10, §1883.

62. Apart from the *Metaphysics* commentary Thomas does not seem to speak often of "the bad in act" or "the bad in potency," but it seems clear that he has no trouble with the notions. See *De ver.*, q. 22, a. 6 ad 3; *De malo*, q. 1, a. 3, obj. 7 & obj. 8; *De malo*, q. 1, a. 5, ad 20 (here he cites the *Meta.* 9 passage).

ing of the true" (*secundum intelligentiam veri*).⁶³ Thomas divides this comparison into two parts. The first concerns potency and act with respect to the very act of understanding. The general argument of this part, he tells us, is that "things that are understood must be in act." This is shown by the fact that "their truth is discovered when they are reduced from potency to act."⁶⁴

The second part, which is long and rather complex, concerns potency and act with respect to truth and falsity themselves. At several places in his commentary on this part, Thomas asserts the connection between truth and actuality quite explicitly. Within the limits of this paper I can do little more than to signal these places.

Aristotle's text begins with a difficult passage that invokes the various senses of being—or rather, the senses of both being and non-being. As Thomas reads it, the thought is that

while being and its opposite, non-being, are divided in two ways—in one way, according to the various categories, which are substance, quantity, quality, and so on; and in the other way, according to potency and act, whether of one or the other of the contraries, since it can happen to both of the contraries to be in act and in potency—that which is in act is most properly said to be true or false.⁶⁵

I take it that the "contraries" here are the beings and non-beings of the categories, for instance white and non-white. Potency and act belong to both of them. And in either case, whether we are dealing with a being or a non-being, that which is most properly called true or false is that which is in act.

At first it may seem odd that Thomas should speak of the being or the non-being of the categories as true or false. But we must remember that the beings of the categories are not solely beings in the real or *actus essendi* sense. Socrates is (I mean, was) a real being, in the category of substance, but we can also speak of him as a being in the *esse ut verum* sense. As becomes abundantly clear in the sequel, the discussion of this entire section concerns being and non-being in the *esse ut verum* sense.⁶⁶ Even in this sense, being

---

63. *In IX Meta.*, lect. 10, §1888.   64. Ibid., §1894.

65. "Dicit ergo primo, quod cum ens et non ens ei oppositum dividantur dupliciter: uno modo secundum diversa praedicamenta, quae sunt substantia, quantitas, qualitas et cetera; alio modo secundum potentiam et actum, vel unius, vel alterius contrariorum, quia utrumque contrariorum contingit actu esse et potentia: hoc quod est in actu, maxime proprie dicitur aut verum aut falsum"; ibid., lect. 11, §1895.

66. Thomas announced earlier that the last part of *Meta.* 9 concerns the being that signifies truth; see *In VI Meta.*, lect. 4, §1233.

and non-being can be divided in accordance with the categories. After all, the categories are not only modes of being, but also modes of predication; that is what "categories" *means*. "Those [genera] into which being is first divided are said to be categories *(praedicamenta)* because they are distinguished according to the diverse modes of predicating."[67] What Thomas is telling us is that of the being which is the true, and the non-being which is the false, that which is most properly such is that which is in act.

The next points concern the true and the false "about composite substances."[68] Aristotle says that "in things," the true and the false are nothing other than being composed and being divided. Thomas explains that when it is a matter of composite substances, the truth of the composition in thought is founded upon some composition in the things. This may be a composition of form and matter, or of what functions in the manner of form and matter *(per modum formae et materiae)*, or of accident and subject. This covers truths about privations, since the mind treats these as "a sort of form."[69] He also makes the observation we saw earlier, that if the components may be either composed or divided *in re*, then the composition of them in thought may be either true or false.[70] On the other hand, he says, if the components are always composed *in re*, then their composition in thought is always true, and if they are always divided, it is always false.

There follows an extended discussion of what truth is in simple substances. It is not the same as in composites, Thomas says, because *esse* is not the same—the *esse* of composites flows *(surgit)* from the components, but this is not so in simples—and because truth follows *esse*.[71] We can skip over the details of the account of truth in simple substances, because here it is not a question of the truth of a proposition. To the truth of a proposition there is always opposed the falsehood of the contradictory proposition; but what we learn here is that concerning simples, as such, the only alternatives are truly understanding what they are, or else not understanding them at all, even falsely. However, one of Thomas's remarks toward the end of this

---

67. The quotation is the second sentence of the following: "Unde oportet, quod ens contrahatur ad diversa genera secundum diversum modum praedicandi, qui consequitur diversum modum essendi; quia quoties ens dicitur, idest quot modis aliquid praedicatur, toties esse significatur, idest tot modis significatur aliquid esse. Et propter hoc ea in quae dividitur ens primo, dicuntur esse praedicamenta, quia distinguuntur secundum diversum modum praedicandi." *In V Meta.*, lect. 9, §890.
68. *In IX Meta.*, lect. 11, §1896–1900.
69. See above, n. 57.
70. See above, n. 43.
71. *In IX Meta.*, lect. 11, §1903.

is worth noting. He says that Aristotle eventually applies everything that he says about simple substances to his chief aim. The aim is "to show that the true is more in act than in potency *(verum magis est actu quam in potentia)*." This is shown by the fact that with regard to composites, the true is a matter of composition and division, which "designate act"; and that with regard to simple substances, there is no false, but only true, "on account of which they are not in potency but in act."[72]

The account closes with what Thomas calls a corollary. I think he means that it is an offshoot of the earlier remark about propositions that are sometimes true, sometimes false. It is that concerning immobile things, there is no error directly about the time, as there is concerning contingent things. For instance, if someone says that Socrates will sit at a time when in fact he will not, or that there will be an eclipse when in fact there will not, he errs about the time. But if someone regards something as immobile, then although his judgment about it may be false, the error will not be about the time. One who thinks that a triangle does not change will not think that it sometimes has angles equal to two right angles and sometimes does not. Nor will someone think that a given number is sometimes prime and sometimes not. Remarkably, Thomas sees even this point as aimed at showing that the true is chiefly the actual. "From these things it is clear that the true is concerned more *(magis)* with act. For immobiles, as such, are always in act."[73] We can speak of actuality, it seems, even in the domain of pure mathematics.

Throughout this discussion, Thomas has said that the true is "more" or "more properly" in act. Evidently it can also be in potency, but only in a diminished way. This too is in parallel with real existence. What is white, simply speaking, is not what is white in potency but what is white in act. The unqualified existence of whiteness is the *actus essendi* that corresponds to it, the act of being white.

We may wonder whether any reason can be given for this connection between *esse ut verum*, or the *esse* signified by the copula, and actuality. The *Metaphysics* commentary is not of much help. But the nearly contempora-

---

72. "Et omnes adaptat quod dixerat de substantiis simplicibus ad principale propositum: scilicet ad ostendendum quod verum magis est actu quam in potentia. Ostenderat quidem hoc circa composita, pro eo quod verum est circa compositionem et divisionem, quae actum designant: in substantiis vero simplicibus ex eo quod non est in eis falsum, sed tantum verum. Propter quod non sunt in potentia, sed in actu"; ibid., §1910. See also §1912.

73. "Ex quibus apparet, quod verum est magis circa actum. Immobilia enim, inquantum huiusmodi, semper sunt actu"; ibid., §1919.

neous *Perihermeneias* commentary is. There we learn that the reason lies in the very meaning of the word *"est."*

The Aristotelian passage concerns *"est"* as signifying a composition in which there is truth or falsity, the *"est"* that is the verbal copula. What Aristotle is arguing, Thomas says, is that such a composition cannot be understood without components. To say *"est"* by itself is not yet to say something true or false. In the course of this, Thomas notes that Aristotle says that *"est"* only "co-"signifies a composition. Thomas takes him to mean that this signification of *est* is merely secondary. He proceeds to show how it arises from the primary signification.

He says that this verb *est* co-signifies a composition because it does not chiefly signify this, but as a consequence. For it primarily signifies that which falls into the understanding in the mode of an absolute actuality. For *est*, said simply, signifies to be in act. And therefore it signifies in the mode of a verb. But because the actuality that this verb *est* chiefly signifies is commonly the actuality of every form or act, whether substantial or accidental, hence it is that when we want to signify that any form or act is actually in a subject, we signify it by this verb *est*, either unqualifiedly or in a qualified way: unqualifiedly, according to the present tense; in a qualified way, according to the other tenses. And so as a consequence, this verb *est* signifies a composition.[74]

What does Thomas mean by an "absolute" actuality? I would suggest that he is seeking to distinguish the actuality signified by *"est"* from the actualities signified by other verbs. (The topic under discussion, after all, is verbs.) Other verbs signify items understood in the manner of actions and passions. Actions and passions too are actualities, but they are "relative" ones, in the sense that they bear upon something—they have "objects." They are the actualities of active or passive powers, which likewise have objects. Existence does not have an object. That of which it is the actuality is not a thing's active or passive power, but rather its essence. The essence of a thing is what the thing is just in itself, absolutely.[75]

---

74. "Ideo autem dicit quod hoc verbum est consignificat compositionem, quia non eam principaliter significat, sed ex consequenti; significat enim primo illud quod cadit in intellectu per modum actualitatis absolute: nam est, simpliciter dictum, significat in actu esse; et ideo significat per modum verbi. Quia vero actualitas, quam principaliter significat hoc verbum est, est communiter actualitas omnis formae, vel actus substantialis vel accidentalis, inde est quod cum volumus significare quamcumque formam vel actum actualiter inesse alicui subiecto, significamus illud per hoc verbum est, vel simpliciter vel secundum quid: simpliciter quidem secundum praesens tempus; secundum quid autem secundum alia tempora. Et ideo ex consequenti hoc verbum est significat compositionem." *In I Periherm.*, lect. 5, §73.

75. "Actio enim est proprie actualitas virtutis; sicut esse est actualitas substantiae vel essen-

In the primary sense, "that which falls into the understanding in the mode of an absolute actuality" must surely be *esse* in the sense of *actus essendi*. This is what *est* primarily signifies. We were told in the *Meta.* 5 text that its copulative or veritative signification is an effect of this. It would be in keeping with this that the *Perihermeneias* text mentions only "positive" or "real" items—forms and acts—as things whose actual inherence in or composition with a subject is signified by *"est."* These are the items to which *actus essendi* pertains. Such items are indeed what provide our first predicates, our first intelligibles. Their privations and negations can only follow, since the intelligibility of these is a function of the intelligibility of what they remove. Still, once we apprehend privations and negations, we treat them too in the manner of forms that may actually inhere in or be composed with a subject, and we also signify the actual composition by *est*.[76] Eventually we even say simply that they "are" or "exist."

So the fact that the verb *"est"* chiefly signifies an actuality is the very reason why it comes to function as the copula; that is, to signify the truth of a proposition. What we learn from the commentary on *Meta.* 9 is that just as its eventual use to signify what only potentially has *actus essendi* is a less proper one, so too its use to signify what is only potentially true is less proper. As signifying truth, *"est"* is used most properly for what is actually true.

The *Perihermeneias* text also gives us the reason why *esse ut verum* is not tenseless. What it signifies is an item's actually inhering in a subject. In the present tense, it signifies the inherence as actual in an unqualified way; in the other tenses, in some qualified way. It is hard to imagine how it could signify the inherence as actual in a way that is neither qualified nor unqualified. To signify the inherence in a tenseless way would seem to require abstracting altogether from its actuality—which apparently is just what *Es-gibt-Existenz* is supposed to do. This may very well be an intelligible move. But I do not think Thomas would recognize it as yielding any natural sense

---

tiae"; *STh* I, q. 54, a. 1. Similarly: "sicut autem ipsum esse est actualitas quaedam essentiae, ita operari est actualitas operativae potentiae seu virtutis"; *De spir. creat.*, q. un., a. 11.

76. See above, n. 57. It should not be thought that the "actual inherence" of a privation in something is any more "real" than the privation itself. Thus: "quod autem privatio possit significari ut habitus, et ut aliquid habitum, ex hoc contingit, quod ens aequivoce dicitur. Et secundum unum modum et privatio et negatio dicitur ens, ut habitum est in principio quarti. Et sic sequitur quod etiam negatio et privatio possunt significari ut habitus"; *In V Meta.*, lect. 14, §964. More generally on the lack of "ontological commitment" in Thomas's inherence theory of predication, see Klima, "The Semantic Principles," 97–110.

of the verb *"est."*[77] At any rate what it yields is not the *esse* that answers the question *an sit.*

Geach says that Aquinas realized that in the sense in which it answers the question *an sit,* the "proposition 'an F exists' does not attribute actuality to an F, but F-ness to something or other; e.g., 'there is evil' does not mean 'evil has actual existence' but 'some things have defects' (Ia q.48 art.2 ad 2um)."[78] In fact the text cited does not mention "actual existence" at all. What it says evil does not have is *entitas.* This, I would suggest, means "the nature of a being *(ens).*" Although we can speak of evil as a being—and either as a being in act or as a being in potency—it is not in the sense in which "a being" signifies anything real, any nature. It is only in the sense in which it signifies the true.[79] But whatever *entitas* means, I think it is clear that even though "an F exists" does not attribute actuality to F-ness by itself, or make F-ness a proper subject of actuality, it does for Thomas attribute actuality to "F-ness in something or other." (That is, it does so when said most properly.) It means that something or other actually has F-ness. And "F-ness" may be either something positive, or something negative or privative.

Should we say that Thomas merely has a broader notion of "actuality" than Geach does, one that begins from "real" or "positive" acts, but then extends to other items? That seems true, but it is not the whole story. Thomas is saying that we all have the broader notion. The extension comes quite naturally to our minds. And it serves to explain the broader notion of "existence," the one that applies both to real natures and to their privations and negations, *esse ut verum.*

This is perhaps where the Fregean interpretation of Thomas does him the least justice. Thomas has a reason why the two senses of existence are signified by the same word. One sense derives from the other. The Fregean reading leaves the derivation quite obscure.[80] One might wonder whether

---

77. Here is where Klima definitely parts company with Geach. He holds that in medieval philosophy there is no concept of existence that corresponds to the Fregean existential quantifier. See Klima, "On Kenny," 572. Interestingly, he suggests here that what might come closest to the Fregean notion (though still not the same) are the medieval logicians' *signa particularia,* e.g., *quidam.* These of course are as tenseless as names.
78. Geach, "Form and Existence," 57.
79. On the true as not giving us any "nature of being," see *In VI Meta.,* lect. 4, §1243.
80. I find no mention of it in Geach. Martin does *say* that for Thomas, the notion of *esse ut verum* is derivative from that of real *esse.* But instead of explaining this along the lines of the *Perihermeneias* passage or even of *In II Sent.,* d. 37, q. 1, a. 2, ad 3 (above, n. 57), he takes it to mean that "a sentence affirming *esse ut verum* in some way depends for its truth on some sen-

the word is not totally equivocal. Thomas insists that its equivocity is not total. It is analogical.[81]

How far Thomas is from considering it totally equivocal can be seen in his treatment of God's knowledge of "enuntiables," that is, truths that can be expressed in propositions. "An enuntiable composition," he says, "signifies some *esse* of the matter; and so God, through his *esse*, which is his essence, is the likeness of all the objects that are signified by enuntiables."[82] He even says that insofar as the deformity of sin has *esse* in reason, "it plainly comes from God."[83] However "weak" this mode of *esse* may be, it is still strong enough, "perfect" enough, to be judged modeled upon the *esse* that is a pure, subsistent actuality.

## The Act of Being True and the Distinctiveness of *Actus essendi*

Lest there be any doubt about it, the actuality that *esse ut verum* signifies is not itself something subsistent. Although it is not "in things," it by no means dwells in some mysterious region divided both from the physical world and from the mind. It is in the mind. It is not anything other than a proposition's being true—that is, its "actually" being true. What it is divided from is the proposition's only potentially being true. When the proposition is actually true, it is most properly true. That, together with the total exclusion of "only potentially being true" from simple substances, is the gist of the discussion of truth in the *Meta.* 9 commentary.

---

tence affirming real existence"; Martin, "The Notion," 72–73. It is not clear to me that Thomas even holds this (see *De malo*, q. 2, a. 1, ad 9), and in any case it is not really to the point. It tells us only that the use or application of one notion presupposes that of the other. This does not at all mean, or even entail, that the one notion derives from the other. A sentence affirming color of something depends on a sentence affirming surface; does the notion of color derive from the notion of surface?

81. *In IV Meta.*, lect. 1, §535.

82. "Compositio enuntiabilis significat aliquod esse rei; et sic Deus per suum esse, quod est eius essentia, est similitudo omnium eorum quae per enuntiabilia significantur"; *STh* I, q. 14, a. 14, ad 2. It strikes me that Klima goes too far when he says, "Were there no humans to form the concept of blindness, there would be no blindness, even if there were animals that lacked sight, for the actuality of blindness consists in the actual lack of sight conceived by humans by applying the concept of negation to the concept of sight"; Klima, "The Semantic Principles," 125. It is not just that there does in fact happen to be a divine mind. The very coherence of the account of truth as primarily "in the mind" eventually requires one. See *STh* I, q. 16, a. 1, obj. 2 & reply. I do, however, note that here, Klima speaks of "actuality" where there is no question of *actus essendi* (see above, n. 7).

83. *In II Sent.*, d. 37, q. 1, a. 2, ad 3, quoted above, n. 57.

So put, the association of truth with actuality may even sound trivial. Can we not say the same about anything? What is most properly alive, or white, or blind, or even false, is what is actually so, not what is only potentially so. This however is exactly what Aristotle is driving at throughout his comparisons of potency and act in *Meta.* 9, chs. 8–10: wherever we find potency and act, it is act that has the upper hand. This is so in composite substances, and in actions, and in good and bad, and in intelligibles, and in propositions. Moreover, it is as applied to truth that the comparison of potency and act reaches its greatest universality, since truth extends both to all real beings and to all beings of reason. Potency and act do not extend any further. They are a division of *being*. They do not extend further even when they extend to the false. For just as the negations and privations of real beings (the "non-beings of the categories") are beings of reason, the negations and privations of beings of reason are beings of reason too. Even falsehood, which is nothing but the privation of truth, is a being of reason. "Socrates exists" IS false. Once, it was only potentially false; now it actually is, and most truly is. It is only because the false is a being of reason, only because there is truth about it, that potency and act apply to it.

The actuality of *esse ut verum* is "in the mind," in a proposition. It should not, however, be identified with the mind's very act of forming the proposition. Truth is not a "psychological" actuality.[84] This fits quite well with its being signified by *"est"* rather than some other verb. Like *actus essendi*, being true is neither an action nor a passion. It is a sort of "absolute" actuality, in the sense explained earlier.[85] For this reason, its character as an actuality is perhaps difficult to catch hold of. But then, and for the same reason, so is that of *actus essendi*. The actuality that most strikes us is that of motion.[86] Even if *actus essendi* belongs only, as Geach says, to things that can act or undergo change, to be is not itself to act or to undergo change.

In fact, Geach's criterion for *actus essendi* will not even suffice to distinguish it from the actuality of truth, since minds too are capable of acting and undergoing change. Should we say that only *actus essendi* is a *term* of change? But this is not correct either. If things begin to exist and cease to exist, propositions also begin and cease to be true. Geach would no doubt say that the change in a proposition's truth is only a very weak sort of change, a

---

84. Cf. Frege, *The Foundations of Arithmetic*, 20.
85. Above, after n. 74. Pertinent here is *STh* I, q. 82, a. 3, ad 1: "ratio causae accipitur secundum comparationem unius ad alterum . . . , sed verum dicitur magis absolute."
86. See *Meta.* 9, ch. 3, 1047a31–35.

"Cambridge" change, not a "real" one.[87] The real change is in what the proposition is about. This is quite Aristotelian.[88] But even a Cambridge change is not no change at all.

So if we want to find what is truly distinctive about *esse ut actus essendi* vis-à-vis *esse ut verum*, it is neither to the notion of actuality nor to that of change that we should appeal. Is it not rather to the very notion of the "real"? *Esse ut verum* is not *in rerum natura*.[89] It is in a proposition, and a proposition is not part of *rerum natura*. It is not, we might say, "foundational."

Even if truth is in some way an "absolute" actuality, what it is the actuality of is very far from being an absolute item. A proposition is not a self-contained affair. It is a signification, and what it signifies is not just its own truth. What only signifies its truth is the copula. The copula signifies truth insofar as it signifies the composition of subject and predicate. But subject and predicate also signify, and they are not their own *significata*, their own "matter." Their composition signifies the composition of the *significata*. And this is how the copula signifies the proposition's truth: as a function of how the matter stands. For it signifies the proposition's truth precisely as a certain *esse* of the matter. To be sure, this *esse* is only an accidental predicate. It is not even "in" the matter. It is in the mind's proposition, and ordering the matter to it is the mind's work. But it is strictly proportioned to the matter's disposition, "founded" thereon.

This is why truth, as a mode of "being," is so weak. What it is in does not stand on its own. The proposition's components do not make the proposition true by themselves. They make no pretense of doing so. They do not suffice to "give being" to the proposition in the way that the components of a thing's essence do suffice to give being to the thing. A proposition is not a substance, and a predicate is not an essence.

Both *esse ut verum* and *actus essendi* are actualities, but only *actus essendi* is the actuality of an essence, *actus essentiae*.[90] That this is the proper

---

87. On "Cambridge" changes see Geach, "What Actually Exists," 71–72.
88. See *Categories*, ch. 5, 4a22–4b18.
89. I note that Martin prefers to call *actus essendi* "real" existence rather than "actual" existence (Martin, "The Notion," 75n16). But his only reason for the preference is that "actual" is needed for the distinction with "potential." I do not find him applying either "actual" or "potential" to *esse ut verum*.
90. Texts on *esse* as *"actus essentiae"* or the equivalent: *De pot.*, q. 5, a. 4, ad 3; *In I Sent.*, d. 4, q. 1, a. 1, ad 2; d. 19, q. 5, a. 1, obj. 1; d. 33, q. 1, a. 1, ad 1; d. 37, q. 1, a. 2; *De ver.*, q. 10, a. 1,

note of *actus essendi* seems really rather explicit in most of the places where Thomas refers to the *Meta.* 5 distinction. In these places he nearly always mentions essence, or at least the things that have essence—the beings of the categories. Often, as in the *Meta.* 5 text itself, he does not even speak of *actus essendi*; and when he does, he associates it with essence.[91]

This is why *actus essendi* is always "extramental." It is always tied to an essence, and an essence is always extramental—always in the *res* whose essence it is.[92] It is what the thing is "in itself." Only the beings of the categories have essence, and they have it only insofar as they are *in re*. However perfectly the mind understands an essence, and even if it is the mind that produces the essence, what is in the mind is not the essence itself, but only its *ratio*.[93] But it is unnecessary to belabor this here. Any student of Fr. Dewan's knows it very well.

---

obj. 3; *De spir. creat.*, q. un., a. 11; *STh* I, q. 54, a. 1. See also *De pot.*, q. 9, a. 5, ad 19; *In IV Meta.*, lect. 2, §558.

91. See the texts cited above, n. 20. Places where he mentions only essence or the categories include *De ente et essentia*, ch. 1; *In I Sent.*, d. 19, q. 5, a. 1, ad 1; *In II Sent.*, d. 34, q. 1, a. 1; *In II Sent.*, d. 37, q. 1, a. 2, ad 3; *In X Meta.*, lect. 3, §1982; *STh* I, q. 48, a. 2, ad 2; *De malo*, q. 1, a. 1, ad 19.

92. See, e.g., *STh* I, q. 59, a. 2.

93. See *De pot.*, q. 3, a. 5, ad 2.

*David B. Twetten*

# Really Distinguishing Essence from *Esse*

GIVEN THE DEVELOPMENTS in contemporary analytic philosophy over the last thirty years, one no longer need apologize for theorizing about essence. Metaphysics in general, of course, is once again an acceptable philosophical project. Many analytic philosophers defend such counterintuitive positions as the Platonic reality not only of Universals but also of Propositions; a Counterpart Theory affirming the genuine existence of every possible world; and an Unrestricted Mereology affirming that this letter *e* taken together with the last breath of Shakespeare constitute as much a single entity as do you. After the resuscitation of such medieval theories as haecceity and middle knowledge, the call for a doctrine of Aristotelian essence to found a Kripkean essentialism should seem a modest claim.[1]

Of course, as philosophical developments bring the medievals into conversation with contemporaries, they also introduce such in-house disputes

---

I am very grateful to Stephen Baldner, Jeffrey Brower, Lawrence Dewan, Owen Goldin, Sebastián Kaufmann, Gyula Klima, Cyrille Michon, Stephen Pimentel, Thomas Prendergast, Brian Shanley, Thomas Sullivan, Richard Taylor, Roland Teske, Gregory Traylor, John Wippel, Yu Wong, and Michael Wreen for help and suggestions at various stages in the composition of this paper.

1. Baruch Brody, "Why Settle for Anything Less than Good Old-Fashioned Aristotelian Essentialism?" *Nous* 7 (1973): 351–64; Gyula Klima, "Contemporary 'Essentialism' vs. Aristotelian Essentialism," in *Mind, Metaphysics, and Value in the Thomistic and Analytic Traditions*, ed. J. Haldane (Notre Dame, IN: University of Notre Dame Press, 2002), 175–94. Klima is quick to observe that a metaphysical theory of essence will have to be accompanied by revised theories of predication and semantics. See Gyula Klima, "The Changing Role of *Entia Rationis* in Medieval Philosophy: A Comparative Study with a Reconstruction," *Synthese* 96 (1993): 25–59; "Ontological Alternatives vs. Alternative Semantics in Medieval Philosophy," *S-European Journal for Semiotic Studies* 3 (1991): 587–618. For a defense of Realism, see Michael Jubien, *Contemporary Metaphysics: An Introduction* (Cambridge, MA: Blackwell, 1997).

## Distinguishing Essence from *Esse*  41

as those over the reality of the common nature and the plurality of substantial forms. I wish to consider one such dispute, that over the 'real distinction' between essence and *esse*,[2] most famously ascribed to Thomas Aquinas.[3] No contemporary philosopher untouched by 'Thomism' entertains the

---

2. When speaking of Aquinas, I normally retain the Latin term *esse* rather than use a translation or paraphrase such as 'being,' 'existence,' 'act of existence,' or 'act of being,' each of which, though defensible, is destined to raise objections where there should be none. In this practice, I intend *esse* not in every sense, but in one of the four significations distinguished by Aquinas following Aristotle; see Thomas Aquinas, *Scriptum super libros Sententiarum* [*Sent.*], ed. P. Mandonnet and M. Moos (Paris: Lethielleux, 1929-1947), 1, d. 33.1.1 ad 1 (quoted below in n. 94); Aquinas, *In duodecim libros Metaphysicorum Aristotelis expositio* [*In Met.*], ed. M.-R. Cathala and R. Spiazzi (Turin/Rome: Marietti, 1950), 5.7, lect. 9. According to this signification, *esse*, as the verbal noun corresponding to *est* just as running *(currere)* corresponds to runs *(currit)*, signifies an act, "that by which it is said [of something] that it is" (Aquinas, *Questiones de quolibet* [*Quodl.*] 9.4.1c, ll. 117-121, in *Opera omnia: iussu impensaque, Leonis XIII*. P.M. edita [Rome: Commissio Leonina, 1882-], vol. 25; Aquinas, *Summa contra gentiles* [*SCG*], ed. C. Pera et al. (Turin/Rome: Marietti, 1961), 2.54, n. 3 [*Secundo autem*]), or "that it is in act" (*Sent.* 1, d. 8.1.1c; *Sent.* 2, d. 3.1.1c); "the act of an *existing x* insofar as it is a being" (*Sent.* 1 d. 19.2.2c); "that by which [*x*] subsists in the nature of things" (*De ente* 4, ll. 163-64) or "by which each thing formally is" (*De ente* 5, ll. 27-28); "that which first falls in the intellect through the mode of actuality absolutely speaking; since '*est*' said simply signifies actually to be, ... [signifies] the actuality of every form" (Aquinas, *Expositio libri Peryermenias* [*In Peryerm.*] 1.3, lect. 5, ll. 393-99, in *Opera omnia*, vol. 1.1*). *Esse*, then, pertains to the question 'whether *x* is' and is not an essential predicate of a thing; Aquinas, *Quaestio disputata de spiritualibus creaturis* [*QDSC*] 8 ad 3, ll. 340-49, in *Opera omnia*, vol. 24.2. As a result, "that which has *esse* is rendered an actually existing thing"; Aquinas, *Quaestiones disputatae de potentia Dei* [*QDDP*] 7.2 ad 9, in *Quaestiones disputatae*, ed. P. Bazzi et al. (Turin-Rome: Marietti, 1953), vol. 2. As some of these texts indicate, Aquinas at times uses '*existens*' or '*existentia*' as synonymous with this signification of *ens* or *esse*; see also, for example, Aquinas, *Quaestiones disputatae de veritate* [*QDDV*] 1.2 ad 3, in *Opera omnia*, vol. 22; *SCG* 2.84, n. 17 (*Secundo quia*); Aquinas, *In librum beati Dionysii De divinis nominibus expositio*, ed. C. Pera (Turin/Rome: Marietti, 1950), 2 (73-75), lect. 6, nn. 216-18; c. 4 (188), lect. 14, nn. 474-75; c. 5 (284), lect. 3, nn. 669-73; c. 6 (286-87), lect. 1, nn. 678-79; *In Peryerm.* 1.6 (17a26-29), lect. 9, ll. 63-70; *In Met.* 7.17 (1041a27-32), lect. 17, nn. 11, 13-14 (1658, 1660-61); *In De generatione et corruptione* 1.2, lect. 4, n. 4 (29), in Aquinas, *In Aristotelis libros De caelo et mundo, De generatione et corruptione, Meteorologicorum expositio*, ed. R. Spiazzi (Turin/Rome: Marietti, 1952). Nevertheless, since in many contemporary contexts, 'exists' and 'existence' have a debased sense, I shall use, where possible, 'is' and 'to be' to translate *est* and *esse*; or, I shall use 'actually to be' to specify this one among the four senses of 'to be.' For the purposes of this paper, it remains an open question whether "*esse* as the act of all acts, perfection of all perfections" (*QDDP* 7.2 ad 9) signifies more than "the act and perfection by which all *other* features—whether logically or really other—*are* or have *esse*."

3. I use the terminology 'real distinction' between 'essence and *esse*' ('Real Distinction') as familiar labels. Aquinas speaks literally only of a "real diversity" or "real composition" (*Sent.* 1, d. 13.1.3c; *QDDV* 27.1 ad 8), although he also says that *esse* "differs in reality" *(differt re)* from that of which it is the act (*Sent.* 1, d. 9.2.2c); that *esse* and 'that which is' "really differ" *(differunt realiter)* or are "really other" *(aliud realiter)*, as opposed to that which "differs in conception" *(differunt secundum intentiones)* or to that which is "really one and the same" *(unum et idem realiter)*; Thomas Aquinas, *Expositio libri Boetii De ebdomadibus* [*In De ebdom.*] 2, ll. 198-220, in *Op-*

plausibility of such a theory, yet I wonder whether it will not be required in a revived Aristotelian theory of essence. After all, there already are philosophers who defend 'is' or 'existence' as a predicate, perhaps even as a first-order property or actuality.[4] I write, then, assuming that it is possible—although it is no mean feat—to defend Aristotle's theory of form and matter.[5] In Aquinas's version of the Aristotelian theory, remember, form and matter together comprise 'essence.' Given form and matter, is it necessary to affirm *esse* or 'to be' as a further ontological principle of real substances—as another feature of our ontology besides essences and properties? Thomists are, in the main, the philosophers who will answer, yes. I maintain that they give this answer usually without hearing the major objection of the non-Thomist against them. I call this the Aristotelian's 'Question-Begging Objection.' Aquinas himself fails to see the force of this objection, hence fails to develop an argument immune to it, hence fails to prove, as I show, that 'to be' is really other than the matter-form composite which is. I propose an alternative argument that addresses the objection, an argument inspired by Aristotle's philosophy and modeled on some neglected argumentation of Aquinas. Something similar to my argument is needed to meet the Question-Begging Objection. Finally, I suggest that the difficulty of refuting

---

*era omnia*, vol. 50.2. Cf. Joseph Owens, "Aquinas's Distinction at *De Ente et Essentia* 4.119–123," *Mediaeval Studies* 48 (1986): 264–87, at 266–73; Cornelio Fabro, "Circa la divisione dell'essere in atto e potenza secondo San Tommaso," in *Esegesi tomistica* (Rome: Pontificia Università Lateranense, 1969), 109–36; "Neotomismo e neosuarezismo: una battaglia di Principi," ibid., 137–278, at 190–97. Some, of course, claim that Aquinas affirms only a conceptual distinction; see Francis Cunningham, *Essence and Existence in Thomism: A Mental vs. "the Real Distinction"?* (Lanham, MD: University Press of America, 1988). Aquinas does not hold that *esse* and essence are two subsisting *things* as if we should then ask with Giles of Rome, Can God cause one to be without the other? But 'something,' 'thing,' and 'real' for him are terms that transcend the categories, as does 'being'; cf. *Sent.* 1, d. 8.5.1–2; *Sent.* 2, d. 37.1.1c; *QDDV* 1.1c, ll. 129–50. I take 'real' in 'real distinction' to mean 'in the nature of things,' prior to an act of the mind (without necessarily being separable). Ultimately it would be preferable to speak of a 'real distinction between the individual substance (or supposit) and its *esse*'; cf. *SCG* 2.52–54; *Quodl.* 2.2.1c, ll. 73–76; 2.2.2c, ad 1–2, ll. 93–102, 145–49, 154–58. Yet, even when Aquinas makes such precisions he also speaks of a "composition of essence and *esse*"; cf. *Quodl.* 2.2.1, ll. 5–12, 73–76; 2.2.2c, ll. 99–100.

4. Cf. thinkers as disparate as Henry Leonard, "The Logic of Existence," *Philosophical Studies* 7, no. 4 (1956): 49–64; J. L. Mackie, "The Riddle of Existence," *Proceedings of the Aristotelian Society*, suppl. vol. 50 (1976): 247–67; Peter Geach, *God and the Soul* (South Bend: St. Augustine's Press, n.d. [repr. of the 1969 ed.]), 65–74; Gareth Evans, *The Varieties of Reference*, ed. J. McDowell (Oxford: Clarendon Press, 1982), 345–48; William L. Craig, "Is Presentness a Property?" *American Philosophical Quarterly* 34, no. 1 (1997): 27–40; Barry Miller, *The Fullness of Being: A New Paradigm for Existence* (Notre Dame, IN: University of Notre Dame Press, 2002).

5. For a contemporary defense, see James Ross, "The Fate of the Analysts: Aristotle's Revenge," *Proceedings of the American Catholic Philosophical Association* 64 (1990): 51–74.

Distinguishing Essence from *Esse*   43

this objection and of establishing the Real Distinction reveals that what is at stake are first principles—which can be defended only with probable arguments or with arguments showing that their rejection entails the absurd.

## The Question-Begging Objection

The form of this objection will not be foreign to readers of Aquinas since it is the same as that of the leading objection that Aquinas himself levels against Anselm's 'Ontological Argument.' For Anselm, That Than Which Nothing Greater Can Be Thought (TTW) is not TTW if it does not exist in reality; for if it does not exist in reality, then something greater than it can be thought, namely, the same thing existing *both* in the mind and in reality.

(1) Suppose that one thinks of TTW, as is possible.
(2) TTW, then, exists in the mind.
(3) But TTW existing *both* in the mind and in reality is greater than TTW existing only in the mind.
(4) Therefore, if TTW exists *only* in the mind, then TTW is not TTW (because a greater is thinkable).
(5) Consequently, TTW exists both in the mind and in reality.

In Aquinas's judgment, the real problem with this argument is that it begs the question.[6] Most contemporary critics attack Steps (1) through (3), whereas Aquinas concedes that it is possible to think of TTW, and that if TTW is thought, it exists in the mind.[7] For him, the problem lies in Step (4). The contradiction derived there, that TTW is not TTW, results only if one has already assumed:

(6) TTW exists in reality.

---

6. *SCG* 1.11, n. 2 *(Nec oportet)*: "[N]on enim inconveniens est quolibet dato vel in re vel in intellectu aliquid maius cogitari posse, nisi ei qui concedit esse aliquid quo maius cogitari non possit in rerum natura." See also *Sent.* 1, d. 3.2 ad 4; *ST* I.2.1 ad 2.

7. Aquinas's concession of Step (3) is only implicit. But in one place he apparently concedes what in any case one must concede who grants Steps (1) through (3): that if TTW is thought, it cannot consistently be *thought* not to exist, and so must be thought to exist. Still, it follows not that it exists in reality but only that while thought, it must be *thought* to exist in reality. See Thomas Aquinas, *Lectura romana in primum Sententiarum Petri Lombardi*, ed. Leonard E. Boyle, O.P., and John F. Boyle (Toronto: Pontifical Institute of Mediaeval Studies, 2006), d. 3.1 ad 2. On this reading, just as only if TTW is thought does it follow that either it must be thought to exist in reality or it is not truly TTW in thought; so only if TTW exists in reality does it follow that either it must exist in reality or else it is not truly TTW, but only TTW in thought.

As Aquinas puts it, that TTW is not TTW is no problem for one for whom there is no TTW in reality in the first place. That a centaur is not a centaur, we may say, or that a square-circle is not a square-circle is of no consequence outside logic. For Aquinas, then, the conclusion that either TTW exists in reality or it is not TTW depends on the question-begging assumption that there is in reality a TTW in the first place.

Aquinas introduces a number of arguments in defense of a real distinction between essence and *esse*. They each involve the general structure: given that things have essences, and given that there is also in reality the actual being or *esse* of those essences, it follows, for a series of reasons, that *esse* in things must be really other than their essence. Imagine the reaction of the Aristotelian, who can agree with Aquinas that form and matter are really distinct principles within extramental reality.[8] But Aristotle, as nearly everyone today agrees, never theorized about *to einai* as really distinct from matter and form. The Aristotelian can concede, as Thomas can concede in the case of Anselm's TTW, that the reasoning from premise to premise in the various arguments for a Real Distinction is valid. Nevertheless, the conclusion depends on one's already having granted, in addition to the familiar substance-level constituents of Aristotelian ontology—namely, matter and form—a third constituent of one's ontology: *esse*, the actuality of essence. For the Aristotelian, however, the *to einai* or 'to be' of material things is nothing apart from form and matter, is merely a word that we use to describe the actualized composite of the two. The 'to be' of material things is nothing but whatever comprises their essence, however 'essence' is explicated, whether as individual form alone, as form and matter, or as the actuality of form in matter. There is no *esse* in the Thomist sense as an ontological actuality beside matter and form, beside whatever actuality essence already has of itself. If there is no 'Thomist *esse*' in the first place, runs the objection, there is no need to affirm a real distinction between essence and *esse*. All of Aquinas's arguments beg the question by assuming that there *is* 'to be' as the actuality of an essence in potency to it, that there is Thomist *esse*.[9]

---

8. Aristotle in *Metaphysics* Z.17 famously identifies individual essence or *to ti ēn einai* with a substance's form. Aquinas ascribes to Aristotle, based on *Metaphysics* H.1–2, 6, the doctrine that essence includes both form and matter. Aquinas takes the conclusions of *Metaphysics* Z to be provisional insofar as the investigation is preliminary to that of Book H; see *In Met*. 8.1, lect. 1, n. 1 (1681); Lawrence Dewan, "St. Thomas, Metaphysics, and Formal Causality," *Laval Théologique et Philosophique* 36 (1980): 285–316, at 293–94.

9. The objection need not charge Aquinas with explicitly starting from the assumption of

Whether or not this Question-Begging Objection holds must depend on an examination of Aquinas's arguments, to which we shall turn in the next section. Here, however, we may address some initial Thomist reactions. The Thomist asks, How can one question that there is *esse* or 'to be' in the world? Is that fact not obvious? The Aristotelian agrees that it is evident that things 'are' but disagrees that their 'to be' requires more ontological resources than those of Aristotle. After all, was Aristotle blind to the fact that things are? And yet, he affirmed no more than form and matter in accounting for their 'to be.' If Aristotle did not affirm an ontological act of 'to be' to explain why things are, then it is not obvious that such an act is necessary. To this many Thomists have a ready response: the Aristotelian thinks of 'to be' as a state that can be *conceptualized* and therefore reduced to the static principles of form and matter. That things 'are' is not known in the concept of what they are, but is known only in a distinct act of the mind, the act of judgment. Hence, that things are is not reducible to the *conceptualizable* principles of form and matter.

Now, the most sophisticated statement of this Thomist reaction will acknowledge that one is not thereby allowed to affirm a real distinction between the essence of things and the act by which they are.[10] Still, whatever their 'to be' is, it would seem that it cannot be the object of a concept, and therefore that it cannot be reducible to essence, form, or matter, each of which can be conceptualized. The Aristotelian counters that if 'to be' here is a feature of reality that is not reducible to matter and form but is necessary so as to account for the actuality of material things, then this 'to be' is

---

the conclusion, namely, that there is a real distinction between *esse* and essence. Rather, the objection charges that Aquinas assumes without proof the side of the real distinction that is in contention, namely, *esse*. The objector accepts essence.

10. For this acknowledgment (not this reaction), see Joseph Owens, "Aquinas on Being and Thing," in *Thomistic Papers*, vol. 3, ed. L. Kennedy (Houston: Center for Thomistic Studies, 1987), 3–24, at 10–13; cf. also n. 36 below. For Owens, existence as known through judgment prior to the Real Distinction is not *esse* as actuality or perfection, which is conceptualizable, but is the composing or synthesizing of matter and form or substance and accident reflected in the (non-propositional) 'judgment' that '*x* is'—a judgment that is always temporally simultaneous with, though naturally prior to, conceptualization; Joseph Owens, "Aquinas on Knowing Existence," *Review of Metaphysics* 29 (1976): 670–90, at 678, 681–82; "Judgment and Truth in Aquinas," *Mediaeval Studies* 32 (1970): 138–58; repr. in *St. Thomas Aquinas on the Existence of God: Collected Papers of Joseph Owens, C.Ss.R.*, ed. J. Catan (Albany: State University of New York Press, 1980), 34–51, at 35, 43–44; *An Elementary Christian Metaphysics* (Milwaukee, WI: Bruce, 1963), 47–55, 73–75; *Cognition: An Epistemological Inquiry* (Houston: Center for Thomistic Studies, 1992), 168–70, 181, 192–96.

being affirmed as really distinct from essence either by a question-begging assumption or merely on the basis of our mental acts. One may as well label the latter basis the 'Judgment of *Esse* Argument' for the Real Distinction. The problem with such an argument is not only that it is not found in Aquinas, but also that its acceptance would ultimately make one wonder why Aquinas has criticized Anselm's Ontological Argument. In effect, the 'Judgment of *Esse* Argument' would be a variation of the 'Understanding of Essence Argument,' to which I shall turn first: as if from an understanding of an essence as matter and form and from the judgment that an essence is, one can know that 'to be' is not essence. Yet, if one can reason thus from one's mental acts, why cannot one infer from a property of TTW as thought, that it must be thought to be in reality, to the parallel property of TTW in reality: that it must be in reality? For one would be inferring from a property of 'to be' as thought to a property of 'to be' in reality: that it is other than essence.

All that I wish to suggest now is that the Question-Begging Objection is not easily dismissed. But suppose that the objection does turn out to hold: what are the consequences for Aquinas's thought? The Aristotelian will charge Aquinas with having introduced highly dubious innovations into the heart of Aristotle's philosophical theory.[11] 'To be' as actuality emerges in the history of ideas only in the Neoplatonic effort to describe the One beyond Being, beyond intelligibility, beyond Essence.[12] Neoplatonists came to concede that the First actually *exists*, even though it is beyond the Form of Being itself; that is, that there is 'to be' beyond essence. Aquinas participates in an old tradition of blending elements of Aristotle with Neoplatonism,[13] and his principal inspiration for the theory of a really distinct 'to be' appears to be Avicenna.[14] What is especially new in Aquinas is the adoption of the *esse*-essence dichotomy within the Christian project of faith seeking reason, inherited from Augustine. Aquinas uses 'to be' as act in his defense of such

---

11. For the charge developed in this paragraph, see especially Hans Meyer, in *Thomas von Aquin: Sein System und Seine Geistesgeschichtliche Stellung*, 2nd ed. (Paderborn: Schöningh, 1961), 103, 120–26, 131–33.

12. See especially the work of Richard C. Taylor, "Aquinas, the Plotiniana Arabica, and the Metaphysics of Being and Actuality," *Journal of the History of Ideas* 59 (1998): 217–39.

13. See especially Alain De Libera, "Albert le Grand et Thomas d'Aquin interprètes du *Liber de causis*," *Revue des Sciences Philosophiques et Théologiques* 74 (1990): 347–78.

14. Cf., for example, Anton Pegis, "St. Thomas and the Origin of Creation," in *Philosophy and the Modern Mind*, ed. F. X. Canfield (Detroit: Sacred Heart Seminary, 1961), 49–65.

theological doctrines as the creation of the world *ex nihilo* and the immortality of the human soul. But, our Aristotelian will argue, Aquinas misleadingly presents his most original claims as conclusions that are *philosophically* justifiable. In Aristotle's philosophy the major metaphysical player is the individual essence, *to ti ēn einai*. The 'to be' of a thing is expressed in its definition, and 'the what it was to be' or essence is a thing's individual form.[15] Once Plato's beard has been trimmed, the ontology sufficient to account for all extramental 'to be' comprises solely matter, form, and various accidents. *Esse* or *to einai* as an act of 'to be' really distinct from *to ti ēn einai* is unnecessary and therefore superfluous. I would hasten to add that if such *esse* is not philosophically justifiable, it should not be offered as helpful to theology, where it seems to be in no way required for belief. The real distinction between essence and 'to be' has long pitted Thomists against other theologians. If the Question-Begging Objection is correct, it seems opportune to jettison the distinction once and for all.

## An Existential Crisis: The Failure of Aquinas's Proofs

A major task in Aquinas scholarship is to catalog Thomas's arguments for philosophical theses according to a systematic order that he himself would recognize. We have made great strides in the last fifty years, but the recent book by John Wippel deserves special recognition in this regard. According to my count, there appear to be at least nine different *kinds* of the over forty individual arguments that Aquinas offers, or that Aquinas scholars have defensibly understood him to offer, on behalf of the real distinction between *esse* and essence. In arriving at this number I make no claim to be exhaustive, but I rely mainly on the previous lists of such leading scholars as Cornelio Fabro, Leo Sweeney, Joseph Owens, and John Wippel.[16] In what follows, I reclassify, rename, and reduce Aquinas's arguments to their

---

15. For a contrast of Aristotle and Aquinas, see Armand Maurer, "Form and Essence in the Philosophy of St. Thomas," in *Being and Knowing: Studies in Thomas Aquinas and Late Medieval Philosophy* (Toronto: Pontifical Institute of Mediaeval Studies, 1990), 3–18.

16. They themselves are indebted to, among others, Norbertus del Prado, *De veritate fundamentali philosophiae christianae* (Freiburg/CH: Ex Typis Consociationis Sancti Pauli, 1911), 23–70; M.-D. Roland-Gosselin, *Le "De ente et essentia" de s. Thomas d'Aquin*, Bibliothèque thomiste 8. Kain (Belgium: Le Saulchoir/Paris: Vrin, 1926; repr. 1948), 187–89; Joseph De Finance, *Être et agir dans la philosophie de Saint Thomas*, 2nd ed. (Rome: Gregorian University Press, 1960), 94–107.

essential steps, listing them in chronological order, so as to assess his preferred arguments in light of the Question-Begging Objection. I begin with the three stages in chapter 4 of the early, purely philosophical work, *De ente et essentia*. These three stages can and have been taken to correspond to three different and separable arguments, although in the *De ente* itself they constitute one whole in which each subsequent argument builds upon the one prior to it.[17]

### The 'Understanding of Essence Argument' and the First Stage of *De ente* 4

The *De ente* presents the fullest version of a form of argument that stands on its own in at least one other place, in Aquinas's early *Scriptum on Lombard's Sentences*.[18] According to many interpreters, Aquinas intends in this First Stage of *De ente* 4 to establish no more than a conceptual distinction between essence and *esse*. But if the argument is to be taken in defense of the Real Distinction, as would appear *prima facie* to be the case, and as the passage from the *Scriptum* suggests, it may be restated as follows.

(1) Whatever does not belong to the understanding of a thing's essence must be distinct from that essence.
   (1.1) For, no essence can be understood without its parts.
(2) Hence, [if such a feature belongs to a thing,] it must enter into composition with it [as really distinct from it, whether the feature is caused by the essence itself or] comes to it from without.[19]
(3) But one can understand what is a human or a phoenix (or an eclipse; *Sent.* 2, d. 3.1.1) without knowing whether it has 'to be' *(esse)* in reality.
(4) Therefore, the 'to be' of an essence [that exists] enters into composition with it as [really] distinct from it.

---

17. Three arguments are both distinguished and united, for example, in Cornelio Fabro, "Un itinéraire de saint Thomas: L'Établissement de la distinction réelle entre essence et existence," *Revue de Philosophie* 39 (1939): 285–310, repr. in *Esegesi tomistica*, 89–108, at 94, 99; *La nozione metafisica di partecipazione secondo s. Tommaso d'Aquino*, 2nd ed. (Turin: Società Editrice Internazionale, 1963), 218–19.

18. Thomas Aquinas, *De ente et essentia* [*De ente*] 4, ll. 94–103, in *Opera omnia*, vol. 43; *Sent.* 2, d. 1.1.1c; *Sent.* 2, d. 3.1.1c (for this passage as a 'God to Creatures Argument,' see below, n. 45). In three other early passages, though not again after 1260, Aquinas employs in a comparable way the principle that *esse* is not found in the understanding of a thing. See *Sent.* 1, d. 8.3.3 expos.; *Sent.* 1, d. 8.4.2c; *QDDV* 10.12c, ll. 174–78.

19. For this Step, see *De ente* 4, ll. 94–96, 127–30. The *De ente* makes no distinction between

There are a number of problems with this argument, some of which can be resolved. Here I am interested only in the Question-Begging Objection. The argument proceeds from the absence of our knowledge of 'to be' or *esse* in knowing essences to the presence of *esse* as really distinct from essence. But the argument presupposes that *esse* is something that must belong to the essence of a thing in order that it be. *Esse* as act of an essence is assumed to be part of our ontology. Consequently, the absence from an essence of its *esse* leaves that essence nonexistent. Thus, there is a tacit Step (5) between Steps (3) and (4) that may be spelled out thus:

(5) 'To be' *(esse)* is a feature that must *belong to* essences in order that they be.

The Aristotelian objector, however, denies Step (5). For the Aristotelian, it is not the case that things exist because of a 'to be' that, in the words of *De ente* 4, 'belongs to,' 'comes to from without,' 'enters into composition with,' or 'is received by' essence and that thereby actualizes that essence so as to be. 'To be' for material things is simply for form to actualize matter. For an essence to have its constituent parts is for it to be. The Aristotelian, then, can explain one's ignorance of 'to be' in knowing essence merely by appealing to individual matter. Knowing *what* a whooping crane is does not tell me whether one is, because individual material instances are not known in knowing essences. Whether there are whooping cranes is known only by perceiving individual instances of that species. One need not affirm a really distinct 'to be' to explain the difference between knowing a species and perceiving its instances. As a result, the Aristotelian's ontology is sparser here than the Thomist's, requiring only form, matter, and the relevant acts of knowing universals and particulars.

### The 'Hypothetical Essence That Is *Esse* Argument' and the Second Stage of *De ente* 4

Most interpreters agree that the First Stage of *De ente* 4 fails to establish a real distinction between essence and *esse*. John Wippel is well known for his vigorous defense of the Second Stage,[20] and he has recently isolated and

---

Steps (1) and (2); I have added material in brackets to bring out the argument, on the assumption, again, that a Real Distinction is intended.

20. John Wippel, *Metaphysical Themes in St. Thomas Aquinas* (Washington, DC: The Catholic University of America Press, 1984), 107–32; see also Scott MacDonald, "The Esse/Essen-

identified the argument of this Stage as a distinct form of argument for the Real Distinction.[21] On at least six other occasions, four in mature works, Aquinas offers what could be taken as an explicit instance of this form of argument. The version in the *De ente* begins by testing an hypothesis that will be affirmed with proof in the Third Stage.

(1) Suppose that there is something in which *esse* ('to be') is not other than essence, but whose essence is its own *esse*.[22]

(1.1) This would be '*esse* itself,'[23] that is, subsisting *esse*,[24] which is not received in another, but is '*esse* alone' *(esse tantum).*[25]

---

tia Argument in Aquinas's *De Ente et Essentia*," *Journal of the History of Philosophy* 22 (1984): 157–72.

21. John Wippel, *The Metaphysical Thought of Thomas Aquinas: From Finite Being to Uncreated Being* (Washington, DC: The Catholic University of America Press, 2000), 137, 143, 150–57. For the Second Stage as an independent argument, cf. Fabro, "Un itinéraire," 97–99; *La nozione metafisica*, 219, 221. Wippel groups under this category six instances of the 'God to Creatures Argument' as categorized by Leo Sweeney, "Existence/Essence in Thomas Aquinas's Early Writings," *Proceedings of the American Catholic Philosophical Association* 37 (1963): 97–131. Although four of these affirm God as actually existing, not as a mere hypothesis as in the *De ente*, the logic of their argument, based on the uniqueness of subsistent *esse*, does not require this affirmation, as Wippel observes (*Metaphysical Thought*, 136–37, 151–55, 585); for their reasoning, see below, nn. 41–44. Nevertheless, I include in the 'Hypothetical Essence That Is *Esse* Argument' only those seven passages that *actually* proceed without the explicit affirmation of God's actual existence. In fact, of the nearly twenty instances of the 'God to Creatures Argument' that can claim to be complete (besides *De ente* 4), most have a similar argumentative structure to that of arguments based on the mere hypothesis of God. And all but one argue from the fact that nothing but God can be its own *esse*, or *esse* itself. Even where this is not explicitly defended within the argument, in most cases it could be taken to have been previously established systematically within the work in question. In other words, if any instance of the 'God to Creatures Argument' that employs the actual existence of God should be grouped with the Second Stage of *De ente* 4, a good case could be made that nearly all of them should be so grouped. Yet, the 'God to Creatures' approach is well attested in Aquinas and is worth retaining as a distinct mode of arguing, a point that I develop below, in "Summary Observations."

22. Aquinas, *De ente* 4, ll. 103–26, specifically ll. 103–14; cf. *Sent.* 1, d. 8.5.2c; Thomas Aquinas, *In octo libros Physicorum Aristotelis expositio* [*In Phys.*], ed. P. M. Maggiolo (Turin/Rome: Marietti, 1950), 8.10, lect. 21, n. 13 (1153).

23. *In Phys.* 8.10, lect. 21, n. 13 (1153); *In De ebdom.* 2, ll. 216–58, specifically ll. 218–20. The latter passage forms an integral part of an argument that I present separately below, the 'Simplicity of *Esse* Argument.'

24. *De ente* 4, l. 115; *In Phys.* 8.10, lect. 21, n. 13 (1153); *SCG* 2.52, n. 5 *(Item. Si).*

25. *De ente* 4, ll. 114–17. It needs to be explained why *esse* could not be merely one conceptually distinct feature of a first essence even though not a really distinct feature; this feature could be unique to it, 'its own.' In other words, why must an existing essence in which there is no Real Distinction be identical to *esse itself*? It also needs to be explained whether identifying an essence with '*its own esse*' is a necessary and/or sufficient step prior to identifying an essence with '*esse* itself.' Cf. *Sent.* 2, d. 3.1.1c: "Alia autem natura invenitur de cujus ratione est ipsum suum esse, immo ipsum esse est sua natura."

(1.2) Such a thing cannot participate in anything else; for, *esse* is the ultimate act, which is participable by all but does not itself participate in anything else.[26]
(2) All other things are distinct from this hypothetical being.
    (2.1) For, something either is or is not its own *esse*, *esse* itself.[27]
        (2.1.1) But if there is something that is not its own *esse*, it must acquire its *esse* from another; hence, in itself it is possible with respect to *esse*.[28]
    (2.2) Also, there could be only one thing that is its own *esse*.
        (2.2.1) For, it could not remain '*esse* alone' and be pluralized in any conceivable way of pluralizing, such as by adding a *differentia*, or by being received in some subject, such as in matter.[29]
        (2.2.2) Also, it would be similar to a separate form, which would be unique.[30]
        (2.2.3) Also, subsistent *esse* must be infinite and therefore unique.[31]
    (2.3) Also, to be caused belongs to other things but cannot belong to subsistent *esse*. Otherwise, to be caused would belong to 'a being qua a being,' implying an infinite regress of caused causes.[32]

26. Thomas Aquinas, *Quaestiones disputatae de anima* [QDDA] 6 ad 2, ll. 268-77, in *Opera omnia*, vol. 24.1. Cf. also *In De ebdom.* 2, ll. 85-102, 249-51. This step, just as Step (3.1), below, n. 33, forms a 'Hypothetical Essence That Is *Esse* Argument through *Participation*,' an argument that in QDDA 6 ad 2 does not expressly use uniqueness. For this form of argument, cf. below, nn. 48-49, and below, the 'Participation Argument' and the 'Participation in *Ens* Argument.'

27. *Sent.* 1, d. 8.5.2c; *In De ebdom.* 2, ll. 219-20, 249-51; *In Phys.* 8.10, lect. 21, n. 13 (1153). The argument in these passages based on Step (2.1) can be called the 'Hypothetical Essence That Is *Esse* Argument through *Disjunction*,' which is completed by Step (2.1.1), (2.2.2), or (3.1).

28. *Sent.* 1, d. 8.5.2c. For what Aquinas regards as Avicennian reasoning from 'being caused' to the Real Distinction, see below, n. 73.

29. *De ente* 4, ll. 105-21; *In De ebdom.* 2, ll. 249-58. In these passages together with those in the following two notes is found the 'Hypothetical Essence That Is *Esse* Argument through *Uniqueness*,' comprising Steps (1) and/or (1.1), and (2.2), perhaps together with Steps (2.1) or (3.2). For this form of argument, cf. below, nn. 41-42.

30. Thomas Aquinas, *Super Librum de causis expositio* [*In LDC*], ed. H. D. Saffrey (Fribourg/Louvain: Société Philosophique, 1954), 4, pp. 29.27-30.30, at 29.27-30; *In Phys.* 8.10, lect. 21, n. 13 (1153); cf. *De ente* 4, ll. 110-13. For this step, cf. below, n. 43.

31. *In LDC* 4, p. 30.18-20. This step is completed by Step (3.2). For this form of argument, cf. below, n. 44.

32. *SCG* 2.52, n. 5 *(Item. Si)*. The argument of this passage, constituted by Steps (1.1) and (2.3), is singular in Aquinas's corpus, a 'Hypothetical Essence That Is *Esse* Argument through *Causality*,' relying on neither uniqueness nor Participation. For other arguments through causality, see below, the 'Effect to Cause Argument,' and n. 73.

(3) Therefore, in all other things there must be a [real] distinction between essence and *esse*.

(3.1) For, *esse*'s being participated by diverse natures allows for a plurality.[33]

(3.2) Also, *esse* that is received by essence is finite and therefore admits of a plurality.[34]

For years I, much as Wippel, taught that this Second Stage successfully moves beyond a mere conceptual distinction to establish a real distinction between essence and *esse*. But I was thinking as does a Thomist, not as does my Aristotelian objector. According to the Question-Begging Objection, why must we think that what lacks a Real Distinction must have Thomist *esse* in the first place? Another way of putting the objection is to ask, Why does Step (1), the supposition of something lacking the Real Distinction, imply Step (1.1), that such a thing must be 'pure' or subsistent *esse*? Are there not alternative ways of lacking a real distinction between *esse* and essence, for example, by being pure essence? In such a case, 'pure essence' would be instantiated, so that the proposition 'pure essence exists' would be justifiable, but one need not ask whether an ontological property 'to be' is identical to that essence—whether it is pure 'subsistent *to be* itself.'

Or, even were one to grant subsistent 'to be,' why affirm in Step (3) that all other things also have 'to be' in the sense required; namely, as an actuality over and above what they are? Why not say that such things are judged to be, but that to account for this judgment one need not affirm in reality any feature other than their essence?[35] Even if there were a subsistent 'to be,' then, that 'to be' would not compete with other things whose 'to be' is likewise taken to be indistinct from their essence; for such things 'have *to be*' only in the sense that their essence is *judged* to be instantiated. Thus, the Aristotelian can insist that 'to be' is simply for there to be form instantiated in matter—and that Thomist *esse* is nowhere in the picture. Joseph Ow-

---

33. *In LDC* 4, p. 30.2–8, 28–29; *In De ebdom*. 2, ll. 234–50; cf. *In Phys.* 8.10, lect. 21, n. 13 (1153). This step is implicit in QDDA 6 ad 2. Cf. above, n. 26.

34. *In LDC* 4, p. 30.18–30. This step is the completion of Step (2.2.3); cf. above, n. 31.

35. Cf. Daniel Utrecht, "*Esse* Means Existence," in *Saints and Scholars: Studies in Honor of Frederick D. Wilhelmsen*, ed. R. A. Herrera et al. (New York: Peter Lang, 1993), 87–94, at 87: "It is one thing to say *that* something exists. It is something else to say that it exists because it 'has' something called *esse* actuating it. . . . The Thomist needs to show how he knows there *is* such an act."

Distinguishing Essence from *Esse*   53

ens has leveled a similar objection against Wippel's reading of this Second Stage: "Nothing has been introduced to show that existing adds a positive content of its own over and above the quidditative content of the thing."[36] Without 'to be' in the picture as an ontological component, the objector is not compelled to draw the consequence that there can be only one instance of what lacks a composition of essence and *esse*. Instead, for the objector, all things lack this composition.

### The 'God to Creatures Argument' and the Third Stage of *De ente* 4

Joseph Owens defends the view, which he ascribes to Thomas, that it is possible to prove a real distinction between being *(esse)* and essence only after the proof for the existence of God—after the proof, that is, of 'being as a nature.' For Owens, the definitive 'God to Creatures Argument' is found in *De ente* 4 in the Third Stage, which after proving that *esse* as a nature exists, concludes to a Real Distinction.[37] In any case, it is widely agreed that the 'God to Creatures Argument' is well attested in Aquinas. Apart from the

---

36. Owens, "Aquinas's Distinction," 282. Of course, Owens's point is a different one: he rejects the Second Stage only because, for him, it operates with a *concept* of *esse*, not with *esse* grasped in judgment, and its reasoning ends as it begins with purely mental distinctions; see Joseph Owens, "Stages and Distinction in *De Ente*: A Rejoinder," *Thomist* 45 (1981): 99–123, at 108–10, 114–21. Only after the *esse* that is grasped in judgment is known to exist as a nature as in the Third Stage is it possible to establish the Real Distinction. Nonetheless, the reasoning of the Third Stage relies on that of the Second; ibid., 109; *Elementary Christian Metaphysics*, 101 (although it could also use the infinity of pure being, as in ibid., 103, 106–8). And Owens sees the first two stages as part of one continuous argument for the Real Distinction; ibid., 68–71, 77–82, 101–8; "Aquinas's Distinction," 276, 281, 286. In fact, according to Owens, each of the two Stages could be separated out and taken as concluding to the Real Distinction *after* it is known that God exists whose being is a nature; Joseph Owens, "Quiddity and Real Distinction in St Thomas Aquinas," *Mediaeval Studies* 27 (1965): 1–22, at 19.

37. Owens, *Elementary Christian Metaphysics*, 71–75, 101–8, 351; for the Third Stage as an independent argument, cf. also Fabro, "Un itinéraire," 104; *La nozione metafisica*, 220. Owens's reading of the Third Stage, as beginning only with a conceptual distinction between a thing and its being, faces the interpretative problem that the reasoning in *De ente* 4 appears to involve the reception of real *esse* from another. If, as is true, an argument *could* be mounted without such reasoning, that argument would still have to address the Question-Begging Objection, as must any 'God to Creatures Argument.' In other words, what entitles one to infer from the judgment that God exists to the fact that God's *esse* is a nature? Precisely at this point *esse* as an ontological act is introduced. Why is not God understood merely as pure form, which is judged to exist without introducing any further ontological components? The Third Stage at this point runs the risk of arguing from a mental operation to reality in a way that Owens himself has sharply criticized; see Joseph Bobik, "Some Disputable Points Apropos of St. Thomas and Metaphysics," *New Scholasticism* 37 (1963): 411–30, at 425.

*De ente*, there are at least nineteen instances of the argument, most of which are drawn from eight different mature works. I distinguish three general versions of this argument: some versions argue in a particular way through Uniqueness or Participation, whereas another version is Simplified. Paradigmatic of the 'God to Creatures' approach is the argument of *Summa theologiae* I.44.1c. Aquinas, having already systematically shown that God exists, that his *esse* is identical to his nature, and that there can be only one thing that is subsistent *esse*, now argues that therefore everything other than God is not identical to its *esse* but must participate in *esse* and must consequently be caused by the first unparticipated *esse*, the creator. In fact, most instances of the 'God to Creatures Argument' are introduced to distinguish creatures, especially immaterial or everlasting ones, from the divine: angels, the human soul, or celestial bodies. For the present purposes, I reduce the various versions of the 'God to Creatures Argument' to three steps, while I indicate within the first two steps the directions taken by the different versions.

(1) As is shown elsewhere, something exists that is its own 'to be' or *esse*, that is *esse* itself or *esse subsistens*.[38]

    (1.1) God alone is such a thing.[39]

        (1.1.1) For God as the sole first cause is the most perfect and actual thing, and to such a thing alone belongs to be actual in the most perfect way, to be *esse* itself.[40]

    (1.2) Further, there can be only one God, only one thing that is its own *esse* or *esse subsistens*.[41]

---

38. All instances of the 'God to Creatures Argument' have some version of this step, affirming one or more of these designations of God—whether through proof or not. 'Subsisting *esse*' by itself in Aquinas, *Quodl.* 12.4.1c, ll. 16–26 (1272), grounds a distinct version of the 'God to Creatures Argument'; see below, n. 49. On the classification of arguments using something whose essence is *esse*, see above, n. 21.

39. Apart from the aforementioned *Quodl.* 12.4.1c, all instances of the 'God to Creatures Argument' use some version of Step (1.1), which affirms divine otherness. Simplified versions of the argument, or those that argue through Participation, may not use Step (1.2), which affirms divine uniqueness; for these see below, nn. 45, 48–49.

40. *SCG* 2.52, n. 7 *(Item. Cum)*. I count this passage as a 'God to Creatures Argument Simplified' because it offers no defense of Step (2); cf. below, n. 45. Still, it implies that all things other than God acquire *esse* and as such are in potency; also, that anything that is first in potency, then in act is completed only by the perfect act of *esse*, which God alone is. To this extent the passage is similar to the 'God to Creatures Argument through Participation and Becoming' of *Quodl.* 12.4.1c, ll. 16–26; see below, n. 49.

41. Step (1.2) affirms not merely divine otherness but unicity, the target of the Second Stage

(1.2.1) For, since *esse* as such cannot be diversified, if it subsists, nothing can be added to it to diversify or pluralize it.[42]

(1.2.2) Also, it is one, as is a common nature considered in itself or taken to exist by itself.[43]

(1.2.3) Also, subsistent being must be infinite, possessing the fullness of being.[44]

(2) But other beings exist whose essence is not *esse* itself.[45]

(2.1) For there is a plurality of other beings,[46] whose *esse* is received and contracted to what receives it, and as a result is limited.[47]

---

of *De ente* 4, which serves as the model for the 'Hypothetical Essence That Is *Esse* Argument.' I refer to the general argument based on the step as the 'God to Creatures Argument through Uniqueness,' which is completed by Step (2), Step (2.1) or even (2.2), and some version of Step (3). In addition to the variations of this argument mentioned in the next four notes, I include Thomas Aquinas, *Compendium theologiae* [*CT*] 1.68, ll. 18–30, in *Opera omnia*, vol. 42; *De substantiis separatis* [*De sub. sep.*] 9, ll. 102–18, in *Opera omnia*, vol. 40; cf. *SCG* 2.15, n. 5 *(Item. Quod)*.

42. *SCG* 2.52, n. 2 *(Si enim)*. Step (1.2.1) together with Step (2.1) forms the 'God to Creatures Argument through Uniqueness Proper.' For a similar form of argument, see above, n. 29. For Roland-Gosselin (*Le "De ente,"* 188), Aquinas develops this argument in light of Avicenna's proof of the uniqueness of the necessary being.

43. *SCG* 2.52, n. 3 *(Amplius natura)*; also *Quodl.* 7.1.1 ad 1, ll. 143–59 (1256); *QDSC* 1c, ll. 357–408; *ST* I.44.1c; Thomas Aquinas, *Questiones disputate de malo* 16.3c, ll. 164–74, in *Opera omnia*, vol. 23; *De sub. sep.* 8, ll. 164–87; *Quodl.* 3.8c, ll. 37–48 (1270). This step forms the 'God to Creatures Argument through Uniqueness of a Common Nature.' For the reasoning, see above, n. 30.

44. This step together with some version of Step (2.1) forms the 'God to Creatures Argument through the Uniqueness *of Infinite Esse*,' used in *SCG* 2.52, n. 4 *(Adhuc. Impossibile)*; *QDSC* 1c, ll. 357–408. For this argumentation, cf. above, n. 31.

45. All instances of the 'God to Creatures Argument' use Step (2), but some argue simply through it and Step (1.1) alone: *Sent.* 1, d. 8.5.1c; *Quodl.* 7.3.2c (1256); *Quodl.* 9.4.1c, ll. 115–21 (1257); *SCG* 2.52, n. 7 *(Item. Cum)*; cf. *ST* I.47.1. This I call the 'God to Creatures Argument Simplified.' One 'God to Creatures Argument' is unique, defending Step (2) by means of the 'Understanding of Essence Argument': *Sent.* 2, d. 3.1.1c. Hence, I do not introduce it here as a special form of the 'God to Creatures Argument,' but instead I refer the reader to the 'Understanding of Essence Argument' and the First Stage of *De ente* 4 above. This passage, just as *Sent.* 2, d. 1.1.1c, uses reasoning of both the First and Third Stages of *De ente* 4—although the two passages use different parts of the Third Stage: the passage from Distinction 1 argues for the existence of subsistent *esse*, whereas that from Distinction 3 offers proof that all things other than God, including angels, have essence really distinct from *esse*.

46. This point is barely made explicit, but is used by all of the passages that reason through Step (1.2); see above, nn. 41–44. The conclusion of the Third Stage in *De ente* 4 reasons thus (especially on Owens's interpretation), relying on the conclusion of the Second Stage; see *De ente* 4, ll. 121–26; 143–45.

47. *Quodl.* 7.1.1 ad 1, ll. 143–59; *QDSC* 1c, ll. 357–408.

(2.2) Also, when some feature, in this case *esse*, belongs to something according to its own nature, it belongs to all others only by participation.[48]

(2.3) Also, things 'most' come to be in act by participating in the first, pure act: subsisting *esse*.[49]

(3) Therefore, in other beings *esse* and essence are really distinct.

(3.1) Consequently, in such things (a) *esse* as an act must be caused by another and is received by an essence that is in potency to it, so that (b) *quod est* is other than *quo est*.[50]

(3.2) Also, such things participate in being.[51]

Given these three steps, it is easy to see that the 'God to Creatures Argument' is vulnerable to the Question-Begging Objection at exactly the same points as was the 'Hypothetical Essence That Is *Esse* Argument'. Step (1) assumes Thomist 'to be' or *esse* in assuming that God is his own *esse* or *esse* itself. Leo Sweeney has put the objection strikingly: "Granted that the divine essence is *esse*, still for that statement to be meaningful one must have

---

48. This step, together with Step (1.1) forms the 'God to Creatures Argument through Participation,' whose purest form is found in SCG 2.52, n. 8 *(Ampliius. Ipsum)*; see also Thomas Aquinas, *Expositio libri Posteriorum* 2.7 (92b8–11), lect. 6, ll. 43–50, in *Opera omnia* 1.2*; cf. Sent. 2, d. 16.1.1 ad 3; Sent. 2, d. 37.1.2c; *In Phys* 8.10, lect. 21, n. 14 (1154); and especially *In De ebdom*. 2, ll. 234–50, recorded in Step (3.2) in the 'Simplicity of *Esse* Argument,' below, where participation in *esse* is ascribed to any determinate form, including Aristotle's separate substances, as a condition for its distinction from other things. In other places, the argument is formed with some version of Step (1.2), using uniqueness; hence I call it the 'God to Creatures Argument through Uniqueness and Participation': in fact, participation is defended in this version almost exclusively as an alternative to the uniqueness of subsistent *esse*. This argument is found in CT I.68, ll. 18–30; ST I.44.1c; *De malo* 16.3c, ll. 164–74; *De sub. sep.* 9, ll. 102–18; and Quodl. 3.8c, ll. 37–48; cf. SCG 2.15, n. 5 *(Item. Quod)*. The same argument is found in one 'Hypothetical Essence That Is *Esse* Argument': *In Phys* 8.10, lect. 21, n. 13 (1153). For arguments through Participation, see above, n. 26, and below, the 'Participation Argument' and the 'Participation in *Ens* Argument,' in addition to the following note.

49. Quodl. 12.4.1c, ll. 16–26. This step forms a 'God to Creatures Argument' that does not use divine otherness or uniqueness, but is completed, instead, only by Steps (1) and (3.2). The resulting argument, distinct from the one identified in the previous note, is a 'God to Creatures Argument through Participation and Becoming.' On this argument, see Lawrence Dewan, "St. Thomas and the Distinction between Form and *Esse* in Caused Things," *Gregorianum* 80 (1999): 353–70. For similar reasoning, cf. above, n. 40.

50. Step (3.1a) is found in Quodl. 7.3.2, ll. 24–35; and 9.4.1, ll. 115–21; Step (3.1b) is found in Sent. 1, d. 8.5.1c; whereas many passages witness both (a) and (b): Sent. 2, d. 3.1.1c; *De ente* 4, ll. 147–66 (Third Stage); *De sub. sep.* 8, ll. 164–87; Quodl. 3.8c, ll. 37–48.

51. Participation in the 'God to Creatures Argument' may be a consequence of rather than a means to establishing the Real Distinction, as for Step (2.2): QDSC 1c, ll. 357–408; cf. *In LDC* 4, pp. 29.27–30.18–30.

a prior recognition of what *esse* is and of what being is. Whence comes that recognition?"[52]

But even if one admits Thomist *esse* in Step (1), is it necessary to affirm Thomist *esse* in Step (3)? Grant, according to Step (2), that other beings exist whose essence is not *esse* itself. How does it follow that they are not mere essence, but that they also have a really distinct *esse*? In two versions of the 'God to Creatures Argument', Aquinas even adds a step between Steps (2) and (3):

(4) But everything that is has 'to be' *(esse)*.[53]

The Aristotelian rejects Step (4) in Aquinas's sense: there is no 'to be' or *esse* as a component to be had. That *esse* is a component of reality to be possessed must be proved and not merely assumed. A similar difficulty arises for the version of the 'God to Creatures Argument' that uses Participation: does it not presuppose that *esse* is a component of things that is really distinct from essence or substance? Only if so is it necessary to affirm a distinct participation in *esse* as opposed to a thing's participation in substance.

### The 'Genus Argument'

Aquinas alludes many times to a doctrine that he ascribes to Avicenna, that the essence of whatever is in a genus must be distinct from its *esse*. In at least seven passages, including from the *Summa theologiae* and three other mature works, Aquinas presents the reasoning behind this conclusion. In each of these seven passages, he must intend not a conceptual but a real distinction. Admittedly, in none of these seven is Aquinas systematically investigating the metaphysical composition of creatures: in all but one he is taking up the question whether God's essence falls into a genus. Nonetheless, in four instances, including in *De ente et essentia* 5, he *explicitly* uses the 'Genus Argument' to conclude to a Real Distinction in all things other than God.[54] The 'Genus Argument' can be captured in the following five steps.

---

52. Sweeney, "Existence/Essence in Aquinas's Early Writings," 130.
53. *De sub. sep.* 8, ll. 183–84: "Omne autem quod est esse habet"; *Quodl.* 12.4.1c, ll. 23–26: "Unde esse est completiuum omnis forme, quia . . . habet esse cum est actu; et sic nulla forma est nisi per esse." See also the quotation below, in n. 65; and *SCG* 1.22, n. 9: "Amplius. Omnis res est per hoc quod habet esse."
54. *Sent.* 1, d. 8.4.2c; *De ente* 5, ll. 5–14; *QDDV* 27.1 ad 8; *ST* I.3.5c. The other three passages are *CT* 1.14, ll. 12–19; *SCG* 1.25, n. 4 *(Item. Quidquid)*; *QDDP* 7.3c. Cf. the allusion in *Sent.* 2, d. 3.1.1 ad 1; Thomas Aquinas, *Super Boetium De trinitate* 6.3c, ll. 133–37, in *Opera omnia*, vol. 50.

(1) [Every essence, with one possible exception, has at least one genus that is predicated essentially of it (namely, its ultimate category), and there is no real distinction between an essence and its genus.]⁵⁵

(2) But whatever is identical to a class as such, whether to genus or species, belongs to every member of that class.⁵⁶

(3) Therefore, any essence that is really identical to its 'to be' or *esse* will be identical in *esse* to everything else in whatever class is predicated essentially of it.

(4) This has absurd consequences:

    (4.1) No genus or class will have within it a plurality of essences that actually are (*SCG* 1.25).

    (4.2) Also, either each individual thing that is will be identical to every other, or no two things that are will be of the same kind (cf. *De veritate* 27.1 ad 8).

        (4.2.1) For, the 'to be' or *esse* of each thing is proper to it and distinct from the *esse* of anything else.⁵⁷

(5) Therefore, the essence of everything in a genus or class must be really distinct from its *esse*.

Everyone acknowledges the problem with this argument, which lies in concluding from Steps (4.1) and (4.2.1) to Step (5). Grant, in other words, that there are many distinct individuals within each genus. The argument proves only that there must be some really distinct principle to distinguish two things that actually are and that belong to the same genus. Still, is 'to be' or *esse* as an ontological component necessary to make them distinct, or does not individuating matter alone suffice? Whatever is the source of individuality is also the source of pluralization within a class. And the Aristotelian can say that this is matter, not Thomist *esse*. To assume that it is *esse* is to beg the question, as Wippel has pointed out:

> But as it first appears in the argument, *esse* may signify nothing more than a particular actually existing member of a generic or specific class, that is, a particular concrete existent. One cannot yet assume what remains to be proved, i.e., that *esse* already signifies an act principle which is really distinct from the essence principle of each particular substance.⁵⁸

---

55. A step of this kind is presupposed in Aquinas's reasoning.
56. *De ente* 5, ll. 10–13; *SCG* 1.25; *ST* I.3.5c.
57. *QDDP* 7.3c; *De ente* 5, ll. 13–14.
58. Wippel, *Metaphysical Thought*, 161.

## The 'Simplicity of *Esse* Argument': The *Exposition of Boethius'* *De hebdomadibus* 2

Cornelio Fabro is well known for having identified a 'Participation Argument' (or mode of argument) for the Real Distinction, which Fabro considers the most important foundation for the distinction in Aquinas.[59] I see only two instances of the 'Participation Argument' that can claim completeness, that can claim to give grounds for participation in *esse* without presupposing the Real Distinction, and that appear to be actually intended by Aquinas to establish the Real Distinction. Most versions of the so-called 'Participation Argument' turn out to be versions of the 'God to Creatures Argument,' as I have pointed out.[60] Still, one other argument employs non-participation as a key part of its reasoning and uses Participation language, although it cannot be reduced to the 'Participation Argument.' I name the unique and important argument of the apparently early *Exposition of Boethius' De hebdomadibus* the 'Simplicity of *Esse* Argument.'

(1) 'To be' *(esse)* is simple.
    (1.1) For, 'to be' is not a subject either of 'to be' or of accidents.[61]
    (1.2) Also, 'to be' does not participate in anything else—whether logically, as in something more universal or in something concrete versus abstract, or ontologically, as in a substantial form or in an accident (ll. 68–113, 207–209).
(2) But if 'that which is' is composed of matter and form, it is obviously not simple.[62]

---

59. Fabro, *La nozione metafisica*, 217, 222, 243–44. According to Fabro, Participation is used in a fully systematic way in Aquinas's arguments for the Real Distinction only in the mature works, such as in the last argument of *SCG* 2.52 (ibid., 217, 221); yet, this use represents not a new argument, but merely a modification of earlier arguments (ibid., 243; but cf. below, nn. 67, 88). Only in later writings, however, does Fabro take up the apparent consequence that Aquinas's early *Exposition of Boethius' De hebdomadibus*, as opponents of the Real Distinction have charged, is itself marked by Avicenna's 'extrinsicist,' dynamic causal reasoning (ibid., 217, 222, 227). As Fabro later observes, the *Exposition* evidences the logical and formal character of Boethius's non-intensive notion of *esse*, and we see Aquinas there actually contradicting his own metaphysics, for example, in agreeing with Boethius that "*esse* is not yet"; Cornelio Fabro, "La problematica dell' 'esse' tomistico," *Aquinas* 2, no. 2 (1959): 194–225, repr. in *Tomismo e pensiero moderno* (Rome: Pontificia Università Lateranense, 1969), 103–33, at 104–8; *Participation et causalité selon s. Thomas d'Aquin* (Louvain: Publications Universitaires, 1961), 268–80.

60. For these versions, see above, n. 48.
61. Aquinas, *In De ebdom*. 2, ll. 48–63, 114–46, 204–12.
62. Ibid., ll. 206, 209, 212–13.

(3) Or, if 'that which is' is not composed of form and matter, either it is absolutely simple or it is in some other way composed (ll. 216–230).
  (3.1) But if 'that which is' is absolutely simple, so that its essence is identical to its 'to be,' there can only be one such (ll. 216–219, 249–258).
  (3.2) Or, if 'that which is' is without matter yet is not absolutely simple, it must have form that is other than, that enters into composition with, and that participates in 'to be' so as to be pluralized and to be distinguished from that which is absolutely simple (ll. 219–249).
(4) Therefore, in every case but one, simple 'to be' is really distinct from 'that which is.'

Aquinas explicitly draws attention to the fact that the early stages of this argument, as he discovers it in Boethius, conclude merely to a conceptual distinction between *esse* and essence, not to a real distinction (ll. 36–39, 198–220). For the early stages focus on properties of language, on the 'modes of signifying' of words and concepts. '*Esse*' ('to be') unlike 'that which is,' says Thomas, signifies in an abstract rather than in a concrete mode; '*esse*' signifies as 'that by which' rather than 'that which,' and as a formal part rather than as a subject whole.[63] Accordingly, we do not say that 'to run' *(currere)* runs or that 'to be' *(esse)* is, but 'what runs' *(id quod currit siue currens)* runs and 'that which is' *(ens siue id quod est)* is. Similarly, we do not say that a human is humanity or that 'that which is' is 'to be' or *esse* itself. It follows that 'to be' is conceptually distinct from 'that which is,' although not that it is really distinct, observes Thomas.

At the same time, Aquinas believes that his argument establishes a Real Distinction merely by introducing ontological components in place of 'that which is,' namely, form and matter. Given a form-matter composite, argues Aquinas, it is evident that its 'to be' insofar as it is simple is really distinct from the composite that is 'that which is.' But has Aquinas managed to evade the Question-Begging Objection? Granted, as the Aristotelian concedes, that all material things are form-matter composites, why do they have or why must there be in them, in addition, simple 'to be' as an ontological component? Why can simple 'to be' not be merely a term or predicate that we ascribe to them? Aquinas introduces no argument to show that

---

63. Ibid., ll. 39–45, 48–65, 87–102, 116–46.

Distinguishing Essence from *Esse* 61

simplicity must be a property not only of language or concepts, of the verb 'is' and 'to be,' but also of some feature of reality.

The 'Limitation of *Esse* Argument'

John Wippel first named this as a distinct form of argument in Aquinas's *corpus*.[64] It is found in germ in at least three passages in Aquinas, including in the *Summa contra gentiles*, although two of the passages do not propose to prove the Real Distinction, and the third cannot as such be ascribed to Aquinas insofar as it is an 'argument *sed contra*.' Despite the infrequency of the 'Limitation of *Esse* Argument,' its reasoning is entirely consistent with Aquinas's doctrine on *esse* and his Principle of the Limitation of Act by Potency. Given that, it is striking that Aquinas does not give preference to an argument that, if it succeeds, is the simplest and most cogent of all Aquinas's arguments for the Real Distinction. At the same time, this argument is perhaps more obviously susceptible than any other to the Question-Begging Objection. Hence, it is of special interest here. Was Aquinas aware of the vulnerability of this argument?

(1) All things [except one] must have 'to be' *(esse)* that is finite.[65]
    (1.1) [For, only one thing can be 'to be' itself.]
(2) But 'to be' that is not received in something subsists as absolute and infinite.[66]
    (2.1) For, as is true of any form, 'to be' is of itself common, so that it is limited only by being received in some subject.[67]

---

64. Wippel, *Metaphysical Themes*, 157–61; *Metaphysical Thought*, 170–76; yet the argument was previously identified by Battista Mondin, *St. Thomas Aquinas's Philosophy in the Commentary to the* Sentences (The Hague: Martinus Nijhoff, 1975), 52. See also Giles of Rome, *Theoremata de esse et essentia*, ed. E. Hocedez (Louvain: Museum Lessianum, 1930), 5, 24.21–25.18, and 20, 141.16–142.16. The argument was recognized by Renaissance Scholastics as central to Aquinas's exposition; see Cajetan, *In De ente et essentia D. Thomae Aquinatis commentaria*, ed. M.-H. Laurent (Turin: Marietti, 1934), 5, q. 12, n. 100.

65. "Omnis creatura habet esse finitum"; Aquinas, *Sent.* 1, d. 8.5.1 sc. See also above, n. 53. I modify Step (1) and add Step (1.1) to show that the reasoning as such does not depend on the actual existence of God. It is evident, in any case, that all bodies are finite.

66. *Sent.* 1, d. 8.5.1 sc; *SCG* 1.43, n. 8 *(Amplius. Ipsum)*. Cf. also n. 44 above.

67. See *Sent.* 1, d. 8.2.1c: "[E]sse enim recipitur in aliquo secundum modum ipsius, et ideo terminatur, sicut et quaelibet alia forma, quae de se communis est, et secundum quod recipitur in aliquo, terminatur ad illud; et hoc modo solum divinum esse non est terminatum, quia non est receptum in aliquo, quod sit diversum ab eo.... [I]llud enim in quo non est esse absolutum, sed terminatum per recipiens, non habet esse perfectum sed illud solum quod est

(3) Therefore, 'to be' must be received in something other than it so as to limit it.[68]

(4) Or, therefore, 'to be' must be limited by something other than it that is in some way its cause [formal].[69]

(5) [Consequently, 'to be' and the essence that receives and limits it are really distinct.]

This argument sharply reveals its dependence on a principle implicit in Step (1): that all things have Thomist 'to be' or *esse*.[70] If this is denied, as by our Aristotelian objector, then the argument fails. The Aristotelian can agree that things have finite being, can even accept in theory the Principle of the Limitation of Act by Potency. But why cannot the finitude of things be accounted for by the fact that form is received in matter in the case of material things? And if a plurality of immaterial forms is admitted, distinction within the plurality can be preserved by the finitude of the forms alone: each form has a different definition, as does each prime number, for Aristotle.

The 'Effect to Cause Argument'

One other explicit defense of the Real Distinction is well known since it falls within Aquinas's catalog of seven arguments for the Real Distinction in spiritual substances in *Summa contra gentiles* 2.52. Nonetheless, scholarly lists of Aquinas's arguments typically fail to classify it distinctly.[71] This is probably because, not unlike the 'Limitation of *Esse* Argument,' it is obviously vulnerable to objections, including the Question-Begging Objection.

---

suum esse: et per hoc dividitur esse aeternum ab esse rerum immobilium creatarum, quae habent esse participatum, sicut spirituales creaturae." Cf. also *ST* I.7.1c; I.7.2c. Notice that Fabro grounds his own résumé of the 'Participation (mode of) Argument' on the *finitude* of all created substance; see above, n. 59; Fabro, *La nozione metafisica*, 243–44; cf. also Cornelio Fabro, "Sviluppo, significato e valore della 'IV via,'" *Doctor Communis* 1–2 (1954): 71–109, repr. in *Esegesi tomistica*, 351–85, at 366–69. In fact, Fabro's exposition of *esse* as act in which all things participate as in a "separate perfection" seems to fit well with the passage from *Sent*. I, d. 8.2c quoted above (cf. Fabro, *Participation et causalité*, 195–202). Perhaps he does not invoke it because it uses 'dynamic' terms of 'reception' rather than merely terms of static Participation.

68. Aquinas, *Sent*. 1, d. 8.5.1 sc; cf. also *De sub. sep*. 8, ll. 255–73.

69. *SCG* 1.43, n. 8 *(Amplius. Ipsum)*.

70. See above, n. 53.

71. Thomas Dillon, "The Real Distinction between Being and Essence in the Thought of St. Thomas Aquinas" (Ph.D. diss., University of Notre Dame, 1977), 215, lists this as a fifth argument beyond the standard four summarized by Sweeney; cf. also Roland-Gosselin, *Le "De ente,"* 188: "proofs from the nature of created being"; Fabro, *La nozione metafisica*, 214–15, 220–21. The argument was central in medieval and Renaissance Thomism; cf., for example, Norman Wells, "Capreolus on Essence and Existence," *Modern Schoolman* 38 (1960): 1–24.

Distinguishing Essence from *Esse* 63

(1) Substance belongs to each thing through itself, not through another.[72]
(2) But 'to be' *(esse)* belongs to each created [or caused] thing through another.[73]
  (2.1) Otherwise, 'to be' [would belong to each such thing through itself, and] would be uncaused.
    (2.1.1) [For *x* is uncaused if it does not depend on another so as to be, just as for substance P to be a substance needs no cause.][74]
(3) Therefore, the 'to be' of each caused thing is really distinct from its substance.

The Aristotelian may admit, of course, that 'being caused' requires a really distinct cause. But the objector denies that 'being caused' implies that *esse* or 'to be' as an ontological component other than form and matter comes to belong to what is caused, as in Steps (2) and (2.1). Instead, why cannot a substance's being caused 'to be' merely mean that its matter is actualized by form, without introducing Thomist *esse* at all? Then the argument shows

---

72. Aquinas, *SCG* 2.52, n. 6 *(Amplius. Substantia)*.
73. For other places where such causal reasoning is reflected, see above, nn. 28, 40, and 49, as well as Step (2) in the 'Participation Argument' below, and Steps (1.1) and (4.2) in the 'Participation in *Ens* Argument'; for causal reasoning in general, cf. above, n. 32. Aquinas's 'Effect to Cause Argument' grows out of *his reading* of Avicennian arguments regarding the possible versus necessary being—according to which arguments a caused thing is only possible in itself and must receive *esse* from another in order to be; see *Sent.* 1, d. 8.5.2c; *Sent.* 2, d. 1.1.5 ad sc 2; *ST* I.3.7 ad 1, but especially *QDDV* 8.8c, ll. 121–26: "Omne autem quod aliquid non habet a se ipso sed ab altero, est ei praeter essentiam suam; et per hunc modum probat Avicenna quod esse cuiuslibet rei praeter primum ens est aliquid praeter essentiam ipsius quia omnia ab alio esse habent"; *In Met.* 4, lect. 2, n. 9 (556): "[Avicenna] dicebat, quia in qualibet re quae habet esse ab alio, aliud est esse rei, et substantia sive essentia eius." See especially Avicenna, *Liber de philosophia prima sive scientia divina*, ed. S. Van Riet (Louvain-Leiden: Peeters, 1977–1980), vol. 2, 8.3, pp. 395.12–396.28; cf. 8.4, pp. 400.7–402.47. Notice, though, that Avicenna's reasoning here, if it can be taken as a proof of the Real Distinction, proceeds from God to creatures. Fabro takes it as crucial that Aquinas departs from Avicennian causal and 'extrinsicist' lines of argumentation for the Real Distinction, such as mark Aquinas's early works, in favor of 'static and intrinsicist' lines through Participation; Fabro, *Participation et causalité*, 216; cf. Mario Pangallo, *L'essere come atto nel tomismo essenziale di Cornelio Fabro* (Rome: Libreria Editrice Vaticana, 1987), 34–37, 49–52. As Pangallo observes, however, Aquinas's shift is not as absolute as Fabro suggests; ibid., 36. Of course, the second half of Fabro's *Participation et causalité* develops in Aquinas's mature thought a causal line of reasoning *subsequent* to the Real Distinction that owes something to Avicenna but is completely rethought in terms of intensive *esse*; cf. Fabro, *Participation et causalité*, 341, 381–88, 431–41.
74. The brackets contain one way of completing the argument. For this step, cf. Aristotle, *Metaphysics* Z.17, 1041a15–24. For a cause as that from which the *esse* of another follows, see Thomas Aquinas, *De principiis naturae* 3, ll. 76–79, in *Opera omnia*, vol. 43.

that effects depend for their being on causes, not that they receive really distinct *esse* or being from their causes.

### The 'Participation Argument': *ST* I.75.5 ad 4

As mentioned above in "The 'Simplicity of *Esse* Argument,'" I see only two instances of an argument through Participation in Aquinas, which I present here and in the following section. The other purported instances either rely on the hypothetical or actual existence of God or assume outright Participation as an ontological reality—that is, they assume a participant and a really distinct *esse* participated by it.[75] One of the two instances, that from *Summa theologiae* I.75.5 ad 4, is nothing more than the core of the 'God to Creatures Argument through Participation,' extracted from its starting point assuming God's existence. This passage is the 'Participation Argument' in its pure form.[76]

(1) [No created form is subsistent 'to be.'][77]
(2) [Therefore,] any created form participates in 'to be' or *esse*.
(3) But everything that participates is compared to that in which it participates as potency to act, an act limited by the capacity of what receives it.
(4) Therefore, every created form is composed of *esse* as act and *essence* as receiving it.

I have already raised the difficulty with the 'Participation Argument' in discussing the 'God to Creatures Argument through Participation.' Step (2) seems to beg the question. It assumes that 'to be' or *esse* is a component of things that can be or must be participated in. But one can admit that created forms are beings and deny that they participate in *esse* as an ontological component distinct from form. Whatever Participation such things have, then, would be purely logical and would presuppose no Real Distinction—a possibility that Aquinas expressly allows in the *Exposition of Boethius' De hebdomadibus* 2.[78]

---

75. See above nn. 26, 48–49.
76. Compare the version of this argument in Giles of Rome, *Theoremata* 5, 25.19–26.5: were a creature its own unparticipated *esse*, it would be entirely simple.
77. I add Step (1) to show that the argument, although it uses 'created form,' need hinge only on there being something *other* than subsistent *esse*—whether or not such a thing is seen as caused.
78. Aquinas, *In De ebdom.* 2, ll. 36–39, 55–113, 198–206; cf. also Step (3) in the following section.

Distinguishing Essence from *Esse* 65

The 'Participation in *Ens* Argument':
*Quodlibet* 2.2.1

The second instance of an argument through Participation is worth considering separately because of its singular form: the argument found in a famous passage from the late Quodlibet, question 2 (1269). What makes this passage unique? It can claim to be a strong argument for the Real Distinction because it begins with participation as a fact about predication alone. I believe that Aquinas is aware that to assume ontological participation in *esse* is to assume a Real Distinction, and he does not intend passages where such an assumption is made, thought-provoking and suggestive as they are, as self-standing arguments. The same cannot be said, however, of the following five steps of *Quodlibet* 2.2.1.

(1) Everything [except one possible thing] is said to be 'a being' (*ens*) in a participative sense.[79]
  (1.1) For no *caused* thing is subsistent 'to be' (*esse*).[80]
(2) But whenever one thing is said of another in a participative sense, there be must something besides that which is participated; in this case, namely, besides 'to be' (ll. 46–52).
  (2.1) [This distinction will be conceptual if the participation is only logical; but if the participation is not logical, the distinction will be real and the participation ontological.][81]
(3) 'A being' (*ens*) can be said of 'substance' or 'accident' in a participative, yet essential, sense, as the more of the less universal; this is logical participation, implying no Real Distinction (ll. 52–54, 67–72).

---

79. *Quodl.* 2.2.1c, ll. 33–37. Aquinas contrasts "predicatur per participationem" or "predicatur participative" with "predicatur essencialiter"; for the distinction, see *In Met.* 7.4, lect. 3, n. 23 (1328). Aquinas elsewhere contrasts properties possessed "participative" with properties possessed "integraliter," "originaliter," "plenarie," and "secundum suam plenitudinem."

80. "[N]ulla enim *creatura* est suum esse, set est habens esse"; *Quodl.* 2.2.1c, ll. 37–38. I modify Steps (1) and (1.1) to make it clear, contrary to first appearances, that the argument need not presuppose either God's actual existence or the Real Distinction, unlike for Wippel, *Metaphysical Thought*, 169; cf. 105. Aquinas need maintain only the negative claim that nothing caused is subsistent 'to be,' and the argument does not need divine creation. As is clear from Step (4), *habens esse* need not be taken by itself to *signify* an *esse* really distinct from the *habens*, any more than 'animal' predicated in a participative sense of 'human' need *signify* a really distinct animality; cf. Aquinas, *In De ebdom.* 3, ll. 58–68. Aquinas has not yet ruled out logical participation, much as a species participates in its genus.

81. Step (2.1) is implied by Aquinas's use of Step (3).

(4) But 'a being' can be said of an efficiently caused thing only in a participative and *accidental* sense, not in an essential sense.[82]
    (4.1) For, 'a being' *(ens)* is not a genus or a difference.
    (4.2) Also, no efficiently caused essence 'is' by definition or explains its own 'to be.'
        (4.2.1) Hence the questions 'whether it is' and 'what it is' are different.
(5) But by applying Steps (2) and (2.1), accidental participation therefore implies that a thing's essence is [really] other than its 'to be' *(esse)*, which is 'accidental' or beside the essence, but which comes to belong to it. Such participation must be ontological (ll. 73–75).

The argument has intriguing features. It recognizes the difference between participation as found in language and as found in reality; only the latter requires a real distinction between participant and what is participated. Also, the argument seems to use causality in order to establish a real participation and a real distinction. Thus, from the fact that something is a creature (ll. 37–38) or is efficiently caused, the argument infers in Step (4) that it is called 'a being' *(ens)* in an accidental, participative sense, and therefore that it has 'to be' *(esse)* as a really distinct feature. Nevertheless, as in the case of the 'Effect to Cause Argument,' does the 'Participation in *Ens* Argument' not beg the question by assuming that to be caused is to receive 'to be' as an ontological component other than form and matter? What amounts to the same, can one assume that the only other kind of participation besides essential participation is ontological, as in Step (2.1)? It seems that Averroes himself, according to Aquinas's own account here, admits an *accidental* predication of 'to be' that introduces only conceptually distinct 'to be': that affirms only 'to be' 'in the sense of propositional truth,' as in 'Socrates is' (ll. 63–66). Even Aquinas admits that the proposition 'God is' signifies for us only 'to be' in the sense of truth, an accidental predicate.[83] In this life we cannot know God's nature, hence nor the *esse* that is identical to his nature. The term 'is' in 'God is,' then, seems to be an accidental predicate, conceptually distinct from 'God' without implying any Real Distinction in God. Why can one not hold that the same is true for other predications of 'is,' such as those in question in the argument?

---

82. *Quodl.* 2.2.1c, ll. 54–66. For the proposition that a caused being or 'creature' is called 'a being' as participating 'to be' or *esse*, see also *Sent.* 2, d. 16.1.1 ad 3.

83. See *ST* I.3.4 ad 2; *QDDP* 7.2 ad 1.

Distinguishing Essence from *Esse* 67

Summary Observations

All nine of Aquinas's arguments for the Real Distinction that we have reviewed seem vulnerable to the Question-Begging Objection. Aquinas seems never to have been aware of the objection. At the same time, his *Exposition of Boethius' De hebdomadibus* shows his awareness of the sharp difference between reasoning that establishes only a conceptual distinction and reasoning that establishes the Real Distinction. And there is some evidence that over the course of his career, Aquinas embraced less and less the 'logical reasoning' of the 'Genus' and 'Understanding of Essence' arguments in favor of 'metaphysical' reasoning, such as has been distinguished by Fabro.[84]

It appears to me that Aquinas did originally believe that his 'Understanding of Essence Argument' and the First Stage of *De ente* 4 established a Real Distinction. But he does not repeat this reasoning in the mature works, and this practice appears to be deliberate. He continues to use the 'Genus Argument' until 1265, but not as his preferred argument for the Real Distinction. The 'Simplicity of *Esse* Argument' of the early *Exposition of Boethius' De hebdomadibus*, much as the 'Participation in *Ens* Argument' of the late *Quodlibet* 2, begins 'logically' with properties of the words *esse* and *ens*, although it must be said that both make a transition to ontology: by introducing matter and form in the *Exposition of Boethius' De hebdomadibus* 2, and by introducing the contingency of a creature in the Second Quodlibet. The comparatively less logical, more ontological reasoning of the 'Hypothetical Essence That Is *Esse*' and 'God to Creatures' arguments appear to be preferred by Aquinas if mere numbers are considered. I see no good reason to think, however, that Aquinas in the mature works regards the 'God to Creatures Argument' as standing on its own, as does the 'Hypothetical Essence That Is *Esse* Argument.' I would argue, in other words, that on the most plausible reading of the *De ente* and the *Summa theologiae* alike, Aquinas thinks it is first necessary to prove the Real Distinction in material things prior to proving both God's existence and the identity of God's *esse* and essence; afterward these conclusions can be used to show that *all* things other than God, notably, all everlasting or immaterial things, must be caused by God by receiving *esse* as something really distinct from their essence. This is the singular role of the 'God to Creatures Argument' and the reason for its frequency.

A final point could be made concerning the 'God to Creatures' and 'Hy-

---

84. Fabro, *La nozione metafisica*, 215–22; see below, n. 88.

pothetical Essence That Is *Esse*' arguments. Much of the central reasoning in the different versions of these arguments does not depend on the actual or possible existence of God and could be extracted from this context to form an independent argument for the Real Distinction. Aquinas has already made this extraction in the case of the 'Effect to Cause' and 'Participation' arguments, and less clearly in the case of the 'Limitation of *Esse* Argument'.[85] In my view, however, the reasoning of these arguments is more obviously vulnerable to the Question-Begging Objection after the extraction is made.

## Help from Aristotle

If Aquinas's own arguments for the Real Distinction fail to meet an Aristotelian objection, in what sense do I speak of receiving "help from Aristotle?" The greatest names in Thomist scholarship have seen the need for help, I believe, but have found it in Scripture and/or in Plato. For Étienne Gilson and Cornelio Fabro alike, Aquinas fails to demonstrate the Real Distinction only in the sense that he never tried to demonstrate it in the first place. Gilson denies that anyone has ever proved the Real Distinction, and he cites what approximates the Question-Begging Objection as the reason that a proof should not even be attempted: "[A]ll the arguments one can use to establish the distinction between being and essence in Thomas Aquinas's doctrine presuppose the prior recognition of the notion of the 'act of being' *(esse)*."[86] For Gilson, Aquinas came to the Real Distinction in a theological rather than in a purely philosophical way, proceeding from God to creatures, reflecting on the words of Exodus 3:14: 'I am Who Am.'[87] Similarly, Fabro denies that the Real Distinction can be known through intuition, judgment, or deduction.[88]

---

85. Cf. above, nn. 48–49, 66, 72–75.

86. Étienne Gilson, *Elements of Christian Philosophy* (Garden City, NY: Doubleday, 1960), 130. See ibid., 128: "[N]o one has ever been able to demonstrate the conclusion that, in a caused substance, existence is a distinct element, other than essence, and its act." Cf. also Étienne Gilson, *The Christian Philosophy of St. Thomas Aquinas*, trans. L. Shook (Notre Dame, IN: University of Notre Dame Press, 1994), 82.

87. Gilson, *Elements of Christian Philosophy*, 130–35.

88. Fabro, *Participation et causalité*, 75, 79–81; "Notes pour la fondation métaphysique de l'être," *Revue Thomiste* 2 (1966): 214–37, repr. in *Tomismo e pensiero moderno*, 291–317, at 292, 312, 314; cf. Luis Romera, *Pensar el ser: Análisis del conocimiento del "Actus Essendi" según C. Fabro* (Bern: Peter Lang, 1994), 99–100. Notice the evolution in Fabro's thought and expression on this issue. In his 1939 article on the Real Distinction, he defends both what he calls the "logico-metaphysical argument" of the First Stage of *De ente* 4 and the two 'metaphysical arguments' of the Second and Third Stage; Fabro, "Un itinéraire," 94–97. In the 1950 revision of *La*

## Distinguishing Essence from *Esse* 69

It is reached only in a dialectical analysis[89] that starts from the intensive act of being, which is also identifiable with God.[90] The first source of this properly Thomistic analysis is thus Genesis and Exodus, but it subsequently proceeds

---

*nozione metafisica*, 217–22, 243–44, Fabro still distinguishes Aquinas's two logical arguments (*De ente* 4, First Stage, and the 'Genus Argument') from two early metaphysical arguments (*De ente* 4, Second and Third Stages), though the logical arguments must not be taken to stand on their own (ibid., 219); but Fabro favors Aquinas's third and subsequently developed *mode* of metaphysical argument, couched in Participation, such as is offered in the last argument of *SCG* 2.52. In 1954, Fabro highlights the centrality of three moments of the 'dialectic of participation' for Aquinas's metaphysics of the creature, within which *dialectic* the *argument* through participation becomes for Aquinas the *exclusive* way to *demonstrate* the Real Distinction; Fabro, "Sviluppo della 'IV via,'" 368–69. By contrast, *Participation et causalité* in 1960 does not speak of 'an argument' or 'demonstration' for the Real Distinction, except in reference to Aquinas's original Avicennian reasoning; see *Participation et causalité*, 216, 625. For three stages of development in Fabro's thought on the Real Distinction, beginning with *La nozione metafisica*, see Pangallo, *L'essere come atto*, 43–48, 67, 147–49. Only in the final stage, reacting to existentialism, does Fabro criticize and renounce the use of 'existence' as an unphilosophical term; ibid., 149. In this final stage, Fabro takes *existentia* to be a term of anti-Thomistic origin, foreign to the semantics of Thomistic metaphysics, whose appearance in Henry of Ghent and Giles of Rome is a landmark in the 'forgetfulness of being' lamented by Heidegger; Cornelio Fabro, "Platonismo, neoplatonismo, e tomismo," in *Tomismo e pensiero moderno*, 435–60, at 449; "Il nuovo problema dell'essere e la fondazione della metafisica," in *St. Thomas Aquinas, 1274–1974: Commemorative Studies*, ed. A. Maurer et al. (Toronto: Pontifical Institute of Mediaeval Studies, 1974), vol. 2, 423–57, at 454–55.

89. *Participation et causalité*, 73–75, 479, 625. Fabro speaks there of a "metaphysical reflexion," "resolutive dialectic," or "theoretic resolution," but elsewhere of a "dialectical" or "transcendental resolution"; Cornelio Fabro, "L'emergenza dello *esse* tomistico sull'atto aristotelico: Breve prologo," in *L'atto aristotelico e le sue ermeneutiche*, ed. M. Sánchez (Rome: Herder-Università Lateranense, 1990), 149–77, at 174, 176. For the stages of the resolution and its evolution in Aquinas, see also Fabro, "La problematica dell' 'esse,'" 107–10; *Participation et causalité*, 79–83; 195–244.

90. Sometimes Fabro suggests that he does not intend to reduce his approach to the Real Distinction to a simple 'God to Creatures Argument,' even when he accepts such an argument (*La nozione metafisica*, 192–205, 243–44; *Participation et causalité*, 35, 76, 83, 198–202); yet, insofar as his 'resolution' begins from pure act, which is identified with *esse*, which therefore must exist and must exist separately and uniquely, the identification of this *esse* with God is natural (cf. ibid., 198–208; "La problematica dell' 'esse,'" 109–10). Elsewhere Fabro is explicit about the 'God to Creatures' approach: Fabro, "Elementi per una dottrina tomistica della partecipazione," *Divinitas* 11 (1967): 559–86, repr. in *Esegesi tomistica*, 421–48, at 433; *Introduzione a san Tommaso: La metafisica tomista e il pensiero moderno*, 2nd ed. (Milan: Ares, 1997), 89–90 (the 1st ed. appeared in 1983). Observe, though, that *Participation et causalité* focuses not on the Real Distinction, but on the emergence of '*esse* as act' and on the subsequent dynamic causality and semantics in Aquinas's thought. Fabro's most thorough account of the 'foundation' of the Real Distinction at the final stage of his own development is found in "Notes pour la fondation métaphysique de l'être," where he explicitly does not appeal to God at the moment of the 'foundation,' but only subsequently in completing the causal account; Fabro, "Notes pour la fondation métaphysique de l'être," 291–93, 309–14.

with Dionysius and the Platonic metaphysics of Participation to see all other essences as participating in this intensive act.[91]

Both Gilson and Fabro end by denying that the Real Distinction can be known through proof. But their approach to the Real Distinction leaves it open, again, to the objection that the distinction is a theological or Neoplatonic accretion, unjustifiable on philosophical grounds. As both Gilson and Fabro would admit, the Real Distinction is not per se known: from the understanding alone of essence, substance, or form, on the one hand, and of 'to be,' on the other, it is not obvious that *in reality outside the mind*, 'form' is other than 'to be.' To say otherwise will raise the Question-Begging Objection. The Real Distinction, I conclude, needs to be defended by argument but cannot be deduced from prior principles without assuming 'to be' as an ontological component, without assuming '*esse*' in the Thomist sense. In this situation, it appears that one must resort to indirect argumentation such as through effects or through a *reductio ad absurdum*. Are there any impossible consequences for one who would affirm Aristotelian principles but reject really distinct *esse*? I submit that the Aristotelian Question-Begging Objection *helps* us by leading us to reconsider Aristotle's notions of essence and form, which notions underpin the Real Distinction and without which the distinction cannot be drawn with any philosophical cogency.

---

91. Fabro, *Participation et causalité*, 15, 51, 169, 198, 207–8, 216–19, 229, 537. It does not contradict Fabro's position to add that the 'first moment' of Thomist metaphysics is the Aristotelian concept of act; for the ultimate foundation of the newly emergent *esse ut actus* versus the potency of essence is the Platonic notion of Participation; Fabro, *Introduzione a san Tommaso*, 85, 91. Giacon criticizes Fabro's acceptance of a biblical origin and of a 'God to Creatures' approach in his account of the Real Distinction; Carlo Giacon, "S. Tommaso e l'esistenza come atto: Maritain, Gilson, Fabro," in *Itinerario tomistico* (Rome: La Goliardica, 1983), 137–65, at 162–63. Late Fabro seems to have changed his position, insisting that Aquinas differs from previous Christian thought in that the evidence of the event of creation for him is founded on *esse* as act, rather than vice versa; Fabro, "Intorno al fondamento dell'essere," in *Graceful Reason: Essays in Ancient and Medieval Philosophy Presented to Joseph Owens, C.Ss.R.*, ed. L. Gerson (Toronto: Pontifical Institute for Mediaeval Studies, 1983), 229–37, at 237. In any event, Fabro's account of the Real Distinction turns on his establishing that there is an *esse* as act containing all things *intensively* at a transcendental level, whereas essences at the predicamental level have this act only by Participation. The intensity of *esse* is what makes it possible to establish the Real Distinction, whereas all other accounts take *esse* in a 'logical' or 'formal' sense as containing merely the minimal base of what makes something to be *(existence)*. So thin a notion of *esse* makes the Real Distinction vulnerable to objections such as those of Descoqs or the Question-Begging Objection.

## Aristotle's Conceptual Distinction

The first point that needs to be made, which I cannot defend at length here, is that Aristotle himself maintains a *conceptual* distinction between mere 'to be' and 'that which is.'[92] Thus, Aquinas, insofar as he begins his discussions of the Real Distinction by first establishing a conceptual distinction, as in the *Exposition of Boethius' De hebdomadibus*, follows Aristotle even more than he follows Boethius or Avicenna. It is often observed that Aristotle identifies essence or *to ti ēn einai* with being or *to einai*, as in the formula *to kuklōi einai* (the being of a circle), used for the essence of a circle.[93] Admittedly, *to einai* in the principal sense for Aristotle means essence, a sense that Aquinas himself admits as one of three main senses of *esse*.[94]

---

92. One may find strong defenses of the position—and not merely to favor Aquinas—that there is no hint of an existential notion of 'to be' in Aristotle, that 'to be' always means 'to be so and so,' as in the statement of the principle of non-contradiction; see Joseph Owens, "An Aristotelian Text Related to the Distinction of Being and Essence," *Proceedings of the American Catholic Philosophical Association* 21 (1946): 165–72, at 164; see also G. E. L. Owen, "Aristotle on the Snares of Ontology," in *New Essays on Plato and Aristotle*, ed. R. Bambrough (London: Routledge and Kegan Paul, 1965), 69–95; Alfonso Gomez Lobo, "The So-Called Question of Existence in Aristotle, *An. Post.* 2.1–2," *Review of Metaphysics* 34 (1980): 71–90. Still, many today ascribe to Aristotle propositions that affirm existence; see Milton Munitz, *Existence and Logic* (New York: New York University Press, 1974), 59–62; David Demoss and Daniel Devereux, "Essence, Existence, and Nominal Definition in Aristotle's Posterior Analytics II 8–10," *Phronesis* 33 (1988): 133–54; Thomas D'Andrea, "Essence and Existence in Aristotle's *Posterior Analytics*," in Herrera et al., *Saints and Scholars*, 15–21; Owen Goldin, *Explaining an Eclipse: Aristotle's Posterior Analytics 2.1–10* (Ann Arbor: University of Michigan Press, 1996), 52–71; Jaakko Hintikka, "On Aristotle's Notion of Existence," *Review of Metaphysics* 52 (1999): 779–805, at 785–90; David Charles, *Aristotle on Meaning and Essence* (Oxford: Oxford University Press, 2000), chs. 2–3; and David Charles, "Some Comments on Prof. Enrico Berti's 'Being and Essence in Contemporary Interpretations of Aristotle,'" in *Individuals, Essence and Identity: Themes of Analytic Metaphysics*, ed. A. Bottani et al. (Dordrecht: Reidel, 2002), 109–26. Linguistic studies reveal an existential sense for *einai* in classical Greek and in Aristotle, although Aristotle does not articulate a concept of existence or distinguish it carefully from other senses of *einai*; A. C. Graham, "'Being' in Linguistics and Philosophy: A Preliminary Inquiry," *Foundations of Language* 1 (1965): 223–31, at 223–24, and Charles Kahn, "The Greek Verb 'to Be' and the Concept of Being," *Foundations of Language* 2 (1966): 245–65, at 247–48, 265.

93. Aristotle, *Metaphysics* Z.10, 1036a1–19; for *to ti ēn einai*, see H.3, 1043b1–4.

94. See especially Aquinas, *Sent.* 1, d. 33.1.1 ad 1: "Sed sciendum, quod esse dicitur dupliciter. Uno modo dicitur esse ipsa quidditas vel natura rei, sicut dicitur quod definitio est oratio significans quid est esse; definitio enim quidditatem rei significat. Alio modo dicitur esse ipse actus essentiae; sicut vivere, quod est esse viventibus, est animae actus; non actus secundus, qui est operatio, sed actus primus. Tertio modo dicitur esse quod significat veritatem compositionis in propositionibus, secundum quod est dicitur copula: et secundum hoc est in intellectu componente et dividente quantum ad sui complementum; sed fundatur in esse rei, quod est actus essentiae."

But *Posterior Analytics* 2 holds that the question 'whether *x* is?' is different from and prior to the question 'what is *x*?'; that the 'to be' of a thing in this sense is other than its substance.[95] Accordingly, Aristotle states: "The whatness of a human [*ti estin anthrōpos*] is *other* than that a human is [*to einai anthrōpon*].... 'To be' [*to einai*] is not the substance of anything, since 'a being' [*to on*] is not a genus."[96]

But why, once again, must even Aristotle himself hold that 'to be' is distinct from whatness not only conceptually but also 'in the nature of things,' as Thomas would say?[97] We can ask this question without begging it pre-

95. For Owens, the question 'whether something is' in *Posterior Analytics* 2 in fact asks about a thing's generic or quasi-generic character: Joseph Owens, *The Doctrine of Being in the Aristotelian Metaphysics: A Study in the Greek Background of Mediaeval Thought*, 3rd ed. rev. (Toronto: Pontifical Institute of Mediaeval Studies, 1978), 289–94; or about its logical possibility: Joseph Owens, "The Accidental and Essential Character of Being in the Doctrine of St. Thomas Aquinas," in idem, *St. Thomas Aquinas on the Existence of God*, 52–96, at 59. The work of Graham, Hintikka, Kahn, and Suzanne Mansion helps elucidate the difficulty to which Owens points, even while it admits an existential sense to *einai* in the *Posterior Analytics*. For Graham, "'Being' in Linguistics," 224–25, *einai* in the existential sense in *Posterior Analytics* 2 is a great exception in the *corpus*, and Aristotle must signal its use by adding *haplōs* (2.1–2, 89b33; 90a5, 10–12, 33; *De sophisticis elenchis* 5, 166b37–167a7); elsewhere in *Posterior Analytics* 2, *einai* may include existence but cannot merely be translated by 'exists' since it also may imply a predicate, whether a thing's essence or properties (2.7, 92b20–25). Similarly, Hintikka, "On Aristotle's Notion," 785–87, ascribes to Aristotle the valid inference from 'Homer is human' to 'Homer is' in a jointly existential and essential sense—a fused Aristotelian sense supported by Riek Van Bennekom, "Aristotle and the Copula," *Journal of the History of Philosophy* 24 (1986): 1–18, but opposed by Russell Dancy, "Aristotle and Existence" in *The Logic of Being: Historical Studies*, ed. S. Knuuttila and J. Hintikka (Dordrecht: Reidel, 1986), 49–80, at 59, 64–67; cf. also Richard Ketchum, "Being and Existence in Greek Ontology," *Archiv für Geschichte der Philosophie* 80 (1998): 321–32. Contrary to the suggestion of *Posterior Analytics* 2.1–2, then, Aristotle offers no existential syllogisms—which are impossible since being is not a genus; yet existence can form *part* of the middle term; Jaakko Hintikka and Ilpo Halonen, "Aristotelian Explanations," *Studies in History and Philosophy of Science* 31 (2000): 125–36, at 132. For Kahn, "The Greek Verb 'to Be,'" 248–49, 263–65, although *einai* has an existential sense, there is no universal concept of existence, such as would allow it to be a subject of predication, either in classical Greek or in Aristotle, and such a concept is not found in or required by Aristotle's conceptual scheme, as is indicated by *Metaphysics* Delta 7. By contrast, Suzanne Mansion, *Le Jugement d'existence chez Aristote*, 2nd ed. (Louvain: Éditions de l'Institut supérieur de Philosophie, 1976), 253–74, explains that the question 'whether *x* is' plays a central role in Aristotle's scientific method, since scientific knowledge, though of the universal, attains not merely abstract universals, but real essences of things already judged to be. Yet, Mansion admits that 'that *x* is' in Aristotle's example of geometrical objects really means "that *x* can be constructed based on the principles of geometry" (ibid., 263); whereas for Charles, the point is that a triangle can be proved to exist (Charles, *Aristotle on Meaning and Essence*, 58–75). For an alternative position to Mansion's, see Mario Mignucci, *La teoria aristotelica della scienza* (Firenze: Sansoni, 1965), 58–60.

96. Aristotle, *Posterior Analytics* 2.7, 92b10–13.

97. Aquinas, *In Peryerm.* 2, lect. 2, ll. 35–40.

cisely because of the conceptual distinction between what and whether $x$ is. We may ask, Can the principles of form and matter alone (and their efficient and final causes) 'account for actually *to be*,' that is, explain what it is about $x$ that constitutes $x$'s actually being at all, in addition to explaining what $x$ is? Do form and matter and the causes of becoming alone account for why $x$'s actually being, $x$'s 'actually *to be*,' differs from $x$'s non-being or only potentially being? Notice that this is not Aristotle's question. Aristotle asked only, What brings it about such that $x$ comes to be or ceases to be? whereas the question now is, What is it about $x$ that 'accounts for its actually *to be*' while it is?

## A 'Form-Matter Argument' for the Real Distinction Inspired by *SCG* 2.54

I propose an argument of my own for the Real Distinction based on an examination of Aristotle's notions of form and matter. The inspiration for my argument is Aquinas's dichotomous procedure in *Contra gentiles* 2.54. Aquinas's reasoning there should not be regarded properly as an argument for the Real Distinction, which distinction he presupposes as established two chapters before. Instead, Aquinas argues that the real composition of substance and *esse* that has already been proved cannot be identical to the composition of matter and form. Thomas gives two reasons why matter is not substance, then two reasons why form is not *esse*. I adopt his reasons regarding matter, and I adopt his format, while modifying it to generate the trichotomy required. The Question-Begging Objection must be met ontologically by showing through a *reductio ad absurdum* that neither matter alone, nor form alone, nor matter and form together can 'account for actually *to be*.' Once again, I assume that matter and form are principles of the real, and I argue as follows.

(1) If Aristotle does not need really distinct 'actually *to be*,' then form and matter alone 'account for actually *to be*' (assuming that 'actually *to be*' does not merely name an extrinsic relation).

(2) But, first, matter alone as matter cannot account for 'actually *to be*.'
(2.1) For, matter alone is pure potency; but what is in potency as such is not yet.[98]

---

98. Cf. *SCG* 1.16, n. 7 *(Item. Videmus)*.

(2.2) Also, matter alone does not explain why things come to be, since pure potency, which is not yet, cannot as such act.

(2.3) Also, we do not say that matter alone is, but that the composite is; if matter alone in the genus of substance were to be, then all form would be accidental.[99]

(3) Second, form alone as form cannot account for 'actually *to be*.'

  (3.1) For, although form is actuality, form as form in material things 'is not.'

    (3.1.1) For, otherwise, the form of material things would not need matter to be.

    (3.1.2) Also, just as for Aristotle form does not come to be, but only the composite, so form as such in material things does not have 'actually *to be*,'[100] but only the composite.[101]

  (3.2) Also, form alone does not explain why things come to be. Otherwise, material substances would not need separate moving causes.

  (3.3) Also, even if the cause of coming to be were nothing but the cause of form's being actualized in matter, the source of continuing to be cannot be form alone.

    (3.3.1) For, otherwise, the form of material things would never be destroyed, as in the case of 'separate form,' but would continue to be after the destruction of the composite.[102]

(4) Third, form and matter together cannot alone account for 'actually *to be*.'

  (4.1) For either form and matter account for it insofar as each as such 'actually is,' *contra* Steps (2.1), (2.3), and (3.1).

  (4.2) Or they account for 'actually *to be*' by form's actualizing matter, making one substance.[103] But if so, form alone as form accounts for 'actually *to be*,' contrary to Step (3).

---

99. *SCG* 2.54, nn. 2–3. See also below, nn. 122–23.

100. See below, nn. 122, 124. That the composite alone, unlike matter or form by themselves, is "separate not only in formula *(logos)*, but also absolutely speaking *(haplōs),*" see Aristotle, *Metaphysics* H.1, 1042a29–31; that the composite properly acts, not the soul or intellect, see *De anima* 1.4, 408b13–15; 3.8, 432a1–3.

101. I reverse the argument found in Aquinas; see below n. 122, in addition to Aquinas, *QDDP* 6.3c.

102. See below, nn. 112, 113.

103. Aristotle, *Metaphysics* H.2, 1042b9–11; H.6, 1045a14–33, b16–24; *De anima* 2.1, 412a7–11.

(4.2.1) For only what is actual as such can account for 'actually to be.'
 (4.2.2.1) But the only actuality by which matter as in potency is actualized by form as act is the act of form.[104]
 (4.2.2.2) Also, there is no real distinction between form and 'matter just insofar as it is actualized'; for since nothing can be both in potency and act in the same respect, matter just insofar as it is actualized is solely in act. Consequently, the only actuality in the actuality of matter by form is the actuality of form.
(5) Therefore, form and matter alone do not account for actual 'actually to be.'
(6) But since 'actually to be' must be accounted for, there must be some component that accounts for it that is really distinct from form and matter.

What has been accomplished by this argument? The most compelling 'purely Aristotelian' account of the 'actually to be' of material things may appear to be prima facie that 'actually to be' is nothing but form and matter together, that is, form's actualizing matter thanks to moving and final causes in the case of composite things.[105] The 'Form-Matter Argument' seeks to reduce this third member of the trichotomy to one of the previous two, namely, to the position that form alone accounts for 'actually to be.' First, that matter alone accounts for 'actually to be' seems obviously false: since matter is pure potency, whereas 'actually to be,' whatever it is, is an actuality. But on the same grounds, second, the 'actually to be' of the composite cannot be reduced to the composite itself insofar as it includes matter, which is in potency.[106] The form-matter composite accounts for 'actually to be' only inso-

---

104. This actualization simply results from form as form; see below, nn. 117–20. Cf. Aristotle, *Metaphysics* H.6, 1045a14–33, b16–24.
105. Cf. the reduction of Siger of Brabant, *Quaestiones in Metaphysicam* (Munich and Vienna *reportationes*), ed. W. Dunphy (Louvain-la-Neuve: Éditions de l'Institut Supérieur de Philosophie, 1981), Introduction, q. 7 (Munich), 45.114–20: *esse* is either form, matter, the composite, or an accident. Of course, the Aristotelian would hold that 'actually to be' is form alone in the case of the separate first substances or prime movers—which are not under consideration here.
106. Notice the similarity between this approach and Aristotle's reduction of *ousia* to form, not matter or the composite; Aristotle, *Metaphysics* Z.3, 1029a7–33.

far as the composite is in act. But just insofar as it is in act in the genus of substance, the composite is form: there is no real distinction in composites between form and 'matter just insofar as it is actualized.'[107] Consequently, if 'actually *to be*' is the very actuality of matter by form, this is, again, no other *actuality* than the actuality that is form.[108] Hence, either 'actually *to be*' is reduced to the actuality of form alone,[109] or, if 'actually *to be*' does not merely name a thing's relation to an external cause, the argument reaches its conclusion: 'actually *to be*' is accounted for only by an actuality that is really distinct from both form and matter.

Can form alone, then, in the third place, account for 'actually *to be*'? If so, the Aristotelian finds that form has been substantified or partially Platonized as what 'is' on its own, and that a central Aristotelian tenet has been denied: that form ceases to be upon the destruction of the composite.[110] For if form alone accounts for 'actually *to be*,' why should the form of material things, any less than the form of the immaterial prime movers, ever cease to be?[111] As Aquinas himself argues, any form of a composite that 'is' on its own

---

107. Cf. Aquinas's view that the soul is what makes the body to be a body, and that matter 'is' only because substantial form makes it actually be; Aquinas, *ST* I.76.4c, ad 1; I.76.6c; *De ente* 2, ll. 135–150. See also Christopher Hughes, "Matter and Actuality in Aquinas," in *Thomas Aquinas: Contemporary Philosophical Perspectives,* ed. B. Davies (Oxford: Oxford University Press, 2002), 61–76.

108. It may be thought that this is Aquinas's position, as the following points suggests. (1) Through form, which is the act of matter, matter is made a being in act and 'this something'; Aquinas, *De ente* 2, ll. 31–35; *ST* I.29.2 ad 5; I.66.1c. (2) Thus, form gives *esse* to matter, which receives it; *Sent.* 3, d. 1.1.1 ad 3. (3) Similarly, the soul gives living to the body, that is, 'to be' for what is alive; *QDSC* 1 sc 4, ll. 231–37; 3c, ll. 405–12; 11 ad 14; ll. 421–28. (4) Hence, the only 'to be' that matter or the body has is through form; *De ente* 4, ll. 41–50. (5) Form also gives 'to be' to the *body; QDSC* 3c, ll. 408–9; 6 ad sc 6, ll. 430–31. (6) Thus the soul *makes*—formally, not efficiently—the substance to be, the body to be, and the animated body to be; Thomas Aquinas, *Sentencia libri De anima* 2.1, lect. 1, ll. 265–88, in *Opera omnia*, vol. 45.1; *Quodl.* 1.4.1 ad 2, ll. 111–18. (7) The 'to be' that the body has is the same as the soul's 'to be'; *Sent.* 1, d. 5.5.3c. (8) By being given substantial 'to be' from the soul, the composite is generated, and the body is constituted in the genus of substance; *Sent.* 4, d. 44.1.1 qc 1 ad 4; *ST* I.76.4c. Nonetheless, in other places it is clear that for Aquinas the 'to be' given by form, although only one for form and matter, is really distinct from both form and matter; see *De ente* 4, ll. 185–92. 'To be' is a per se consequent of form, the result of form, just as is a property; see also below, nn. 116, 119, 121. Form as form gives matter its '*esse specificum*'; see below, n. 120. Notice also soul's relation to divine *esse* in human nature hypostatically united to the divine; *ST* III.17.2c.

109. This view can be found among Aquinas scholars. For Hans Meyer, *Thomas von Aquin,* 133, on Aristotelian principles form is so close to *esse* that a Real Distinction is impossible; furthermore, even Thomas and Albert hold that form is *actus essendi*.

110. See, for example, Aristotle, *Metaphysics* H.3, 1043b19–21.

111. For a defense of the view that all form is everlasting, although not without actualizing

Distinguishing Essence from *Esse*  77

right will be everlasting;[112] only if form 'is,' not through itself, but through the distinct 'to be' of the composite, can it cease to be.[113]

In short, in accounting for 'actually *to be*' with Aristotle's principles of substance, it seems necessary to allow for the possibility of ceasing to be without ascribing this to form or matter alone. Accounting for 'actually *to be*' must be detached from form as such—which is really identical to 'form as the actuality of matter'—and cannot be ascribed to matter or to what is

---

the thinnest slice of matter, see James Ross, "Together with the Body That I Love," *Proceedings of the American Catholic Philosophical Association* 75 (2001): 1–20. I owe this argument to the suggestion of Lawrence Dewan. Hints of such reasoning can be found in Dillon, "The Real Distinction," 183; Fabro, "Notes pour la fondation métaphysique de l'être," 293; Giles of Rome, *Theoremata* 12, 68.2–8; 75.23–77.13.

112. Aquinas, *Quodl.* 10.3.2 ad 3, ll. 146–51: "[A]nima [intellectualis] esse suum communicat corpori, quod quidem ita acquiritur anime in corpore ut secundum ipsum subsistere possit, quod non est de aliis formis; et sic ipsum esse anime fit esse compositi, et tamen manet, composito destructo." Thomas Aquinas, *De unitate intellectus* 1, ll. 644–53, in *Opera omnia*, vol. 43: "Forma igitur que habet operationem secundum aliquam sui potentiam uel uirtutem absque communicatione sue materie, ipsa est que habet esse, nec est per esse compositi tantum sicut alie forme, sed magis compositum est per esse eius.... non autem oportet quod destruatur ad destructionem compositi illa forma per cuius esse compositum est, et non ipsa per esse compositi." Cf. also the relation of form and 'to be' in the following. *ST* I.50.5c: "si ipsa forma subsistat in suo esse, sicut est in angelis, ut dictum est, non potest amittere esse." *QDDA* 14c, ll. 179–83: "Si igitur sit aliqua forma que sit habens esse, necesse est illam formam incorruptibilem esse: non enim separatur esse ab aliquo habente esse nisi per hoc quod separatur forma ab eo. Vnde si id quod habet esse sit ipsa forma, impossibile est quod esse separetur ab eo." Notice the objection that if form is the source of 'to be,' then subsistent form cannot be caused; *QDDP* 6.6 ob 4. Given the Real Distinction, Aquinas easily handles the objection without denying that form is a source of 'to be.'

113. *Sent.* 2, d. 19.1.1 ad 2: "Si vero forma non habeat esse absolutum in quo subsistat, sed sit per esse compositi, tunc ex quo compositum desinit esse, oportet quod forma etiam esse amittat, et per accidens corrumpatur." *Sent.* 4, d. 49.2.3 ad 6: "Sed forma quae non est per se subsistens... non habet esse nisi inquantum est actus talis subjecti." *SCG* 2.91, n. 5 *(Item. Si):* "Formae autem quae sunt in materiis, sunt actus imperfecti: quia non habent esse completum. Sunt igitur aliquae formae quae sunt actus completi per se subsistentes, et speciem completam habentes." *QDDA* 14c, ll. 169–79: "Manifestum est autem quod esse per se consequitur formam: unumquodque enim habet esse secundum propriam formam. Vnde esse a forma nullo modo separari potest. Corrumpuntur igitur composita ex materia et forma per hoc quod amittunt formam ad quam consequitur esse; ipsa autem forma per se corrumpi non potest; set per accidens, corrupto composito, corrumpitur in quantum deficit esse compositi quod est per formam, si forma sit talis que non sit habens esse, set sit solum quo compositum est." *De unitate intellectus* 1, ll. 630–50: "Forme igitur que nullam operationem habent sine communicatione sue materie, ipse non operantur, sed compositum est quod operatur per formam; unde huiusmodi forme ipse quidem proprie loquendo non sunt, sed eis aliquid est.... Et similis ratio est de formis substantialibus que nullam operationem habent absque communicatione materie, hoc excepto quod huiusmodi forme sunt principium essendi substantialiter.... Et ideo destructo composito destruitur illa forma que est per esse compositi."

composed of matter as such. Either 'actually *to be*' is a mere relation, accounted for by something entirely extrinsic, as I shall consider in a moment, or it must be a third component, 'given,' so to speak, *through form* to the composite of form and matter under the influence of extrinsic efficient and final causes.[114]

In Aristotelian philosophy it is correct that wherever there is form, there is 'actually *to be*,' and vice versa.[115] For Aquinas, it is correct that *esse always* accompanies form, following it as its principle.[116] Hence, to identify form as that to which 'actually *to be*' is reducible is the 'right mistake' to make. But 'actually *to be*' cannot be reduced to form as such. Certainly, form is not the 'source whence is *to be*' (as if it were *hothen hē archē tou einai*), whether at the outset, at the continuation, or at the cessation of 'actually *to be*.' In what sense, then, is it accountable for 'actually *to be*'? Form as such is the actuality of matter, the source of unity, unity of action, and intelligibility in the body.[117] It is the *formal* cause of the 'to be' of the whole, 'shaping' what is. It is the formal cause of '*to be* in the sense of essence or of what *x* is,'[118] but it is not what *as such* 'accounts for actually *to be*.' As Aquinas puts it in an underused passage, form as form is not non-being but is act; yet, compared to '*esse* in act,' form is a non-being, which 'is' only by participating in *esse*.[119]

114. I am thinking of the Avicennian tag *forma dat esse materiae*, which is not surpassed by Thomas as containing only Aristotle's predicamental notion of being, as is sometimes suggested (Fabro, *Participation et causalité*, 266, 357, 630), but is integral to Aquinas's exposition and refers to 'actually *to be*,' even though it does not express the Real Distinction; see above, n. 108. Notice also that even in Aquinas the efficient 'cause of being' *(causa essendi)* as opposed to the 'cause of becoming' is the cause of form as such, as opposed to the cause of why this matter has this form; Aquinas, *ST* I.104.1–2.

115. *QDDA* 14c, ll. 171–72: "esse a forma nullo modo separari potest."

116. See, for example, *ST* I.90.2 ad 1: "[I]n anima est sicut materiale ipsa simplex essentia, formale autem in ipsa est esse participatum, quod quidem ex necessitate simul est cum essentia animae, quia esse per se consequitur ad formam." *QDDA* 6c, ll. 232–35: "Sic igitur esse consequitur ipsam formam, nec tamen forma est suum esse, cum sit eius principium." See also *In Met.* 4.2, lect 2, n. 11 (558).

117. Note especially the following: "[Q]uia omnes formae, sive accidentales, sive substantiales, quae non sunt per se subsistentes, sunt, quantum est de se, communes multis"; *In Met.* 7.15, lect. 15, n. 13 (1618). "Forma autem per seipsam facit rem esse in actu, cum per essentiam suam sit actus; nec dat esse per aliquod medium. Unde unitas rei compositae ex materia et forma est per ipsam formam, quae secundum seipsam unitur materiae ut actus eius. Nec est aliquid aliud uniens nisi agens, quod facit materiam esse in actu, ut dicitur in VIII *Metaphys.*"; *ST* I. 76. 7c.

118. Aristotle, *Metaphysics* Z.17, 1041a27–32, b12–31; H.2, 1043a2–12.

119. Aquinas, *De sub. sep.* 8, ll. 236–44: "Si igitur per hoc quod dico 'non ens' removeatur solum esse in actu, ipsa forma secundum se considerata est non ens, sed esse participans.

Distinguishing Essence from *Esse* 79

Form tells us not whether *x* is, but what the being of *x* is, what *kind* of 'to be' *x* has.[120] Form is that *through which* a thing has the 'actually *to be*' that it has. Yet, for Aquinas, 'actually *to be*' is the actuality, not of matter, but of the whole substance, a *consequence* of form, the very act of separate form or of the form-matter composite so that it 'is,' just as living is the act of the soul.[121] Thus, insists Thomas, just as neither matter alone nor form alone comes to be, as Aristotle showed,[122] so neither matter alone[123] nor form alone within the composite actually is.[124] The composite alone 'is,' not its principles, by an act distinct from either matter or form, by an act consequent upon form, and therefore by an act distinct also from the form-matter composite itself.

This conclusion, however, rests on excluding an alternative that was mentioned above but not addressed in the 'Form-Matter Argument' prop-

---

Si autem 'non ens' removeat non solum ipsum esse in actu sed etiam actum seu formam per quam aliquid participat esse, sic materia est non ens; forma vero subsistens non est non ens, sed est actus qui est forma participativus ultimi actus, qui est esse."

120. *De unitate intellectus* 1, ll. 493–95: "[A]nima per se ipsam est actus corporis dans corpori esse specificum." *Sent.* 1, d. 49.1.1 qc 1 ad 6: "[L]icet homo ex anima et corpore consistat, tamen esse specificum habet ex anima, non ex corpore, quia forma cujuslibet rei est principium esse ejus specifici." See also *Sent.* 4, d. 36.4 ad 3; d. 44.2.2 qc 1c; d. 44.2.3 qc 1c; *In De an.* 2.1, lect. 1, ll. 285–88; QDDA 9c, ll. 293–95; QDSC 2c, ll. 264–72; 4c, ll. 178–90.

121. See, for example, *Sent.* 1, d. 23.1.1c: "[C]um esse consequitur compositionem materiae et formae, quamvis forma sit principium esse, non tamen denominatur aliquod ens a forma sed a toto" *Quodl.* 9.2.2c, ll. 41–43, 58–63: "Alio modo esse dicitur actus entis in quantum est ens, id est quo denominatur aliquid ens actu in rerum natura. . . . Esse ergo proprie et uere non attribuitur nisi rei per se subsistenti. Huic autem attribuitur esse duplex. Unum scilicet esse resultans ex hiis ex quibus eius unitas integratur, quod est proprium esse suppositi substanciale." *Super Boetium De trinitate* 5.3c, ll. 102–5: "[Ipsum esse rei] quidem resultat ex congregatione principiorum rei in compositis, uel ipsam simplicem naturam rei concomitatur, ut in substantiis simplicibus." See also SCG 2.55, n. 3 *(Amplius. Quod);* ST I.50.5c.

122. Aristotle, *Metaphysics* Z.8, 1033a24–b26; Z.9, 1034b8–16. Aquinas, *ST* I.65.4c: "Sed sicut probat Aristoteles in VII *Metaphys.*, id quod proprie fit, est compositum, formae autem corruptibilium rerum habent ut aliquando sint, aliquando non sint, absque hoc quod ipsae generentur aut corrumpantur, sed compositis generatis aut corruptis, quia etiam formae non habent esse, sed composita habent esse per eas, sic enim alicui competit fieri, sicut et esse." SCG 3.69, n. 21 *(Rationes autem):* "Cum enim ad hoc aliquid fiat ut sit, sicut forma non dicitur ens quasi ipsa habeat esse, sed quia per eam compositum est; ita nec forma proprie fit, sed incipit esse per hoc quod compositum sit reductum de potentia in actum, qui est forma." See also *ST* I.110.2c; QDDP 3.8c; Thomas Aquinas, *Quaestio disputata de caritate* 12 ad 20, in *Quaestiones disputatae*, vol. 2; *De operationibus occultis naturae*, ll. 142–47, in *Opera omnia*, vol. 43; *In Met.* 7.8, lect. 7 (1033b7–8), n. 7 (1423).

123. *Sent.* 3, d. 6.2.2 ad 1: "[F]orma facit esse; non ita quod illud esse sit materiae aut formae, sed subsistentis"; *Sent.* 1, d. 8.5.2c; d. 8.5.3, exp.; *De ente* 2, ll. 51–66; *In Met.* 7.3, lect. 2, n. 23 (1292).

124. In addition to the texts of Aquinas cited in n. 122, see *De ente* 2, ll. 51–66; *Quodl.* 9.2.2c, ll. 51–59; *De unitate intellectus* 1, ll. 633–34.

erly speaking. Why cannot 'actually *to be*' be 'accounted for' by something entirely extrinsic to the form-matter composite, while it itself is the mere relation of a thing to its cause, a relation that belongs to but is not really distinct from the thing caused? This is the alternative put forth shortly after Aquinas's death by Henry of Ghent, in reaction to Giles of Rome. For Henry, no creature has *esse* considered absolutely in itself, but only insofar as it is considered in relation to its ultimate cause—as an effect and as a likeness of the divine *esse*.[125] Therefore, 'to be' is not something added as though to something else that already is, but is simply the creature itself insofar as it is related as an effect to the divine essence in the order of efficient causality, just as essence is the creature itself as related by way of likeness to the divine essence in the order of formal causality. To exist, Henry would say, is simply for a thing to be posited outside its causes. No less than the greatest critic of the Real Distinction, Francisco Suárez, has shown the inadequacy of this alternative, however. To say of a thing 'it is' predicates not something relative but something 'absolute' of the thing, observes Suárez.[126] Otherwise, to say that God is would also be to introduce a relation to a cause. It remains that if we must account for 'actually *to be*' by something other than form, 'actually *to be*' must be a really distinct component intrinsic to things that are.

A Return to the Question-Begging Objection

Unquestionably, the Aristotelian should and will object. Why speak of 'actually *to be*' or 'accounting for actually *to be*' in the first place as if there were something 'real' other than form, form in matter, and their accidents? Does not the very project of the 'Form-Matter Argument' tacitly beg the question, as do all of the other arguments of Aquinas? Why the urgent need to account for 'actually *to be*' as if the reality of form and matter were not enough?

To this point I have presented the Question-Begging Objection as if it were unassailable. The objection helps us see that one cannot prove the real distinction between 'actually *to be*' and essence without showing the real distinction between form and 'actually *to be*,' as Aquinas has not sufficiently done. The objection causes the Thomist to return to first principles. But

125. Henry of Ghent, *Quodlibet* 10.7, ll. 145–59, in *Opera omnia* (Leuven: De Wulf-Mansion Centre, 1979–), vol. 14; *Quodlibet* 1.9, ll. 89–92, in *Opera omnia*, vol. 5.
126. Francisco Suárez, *Disputationes metaphysicae* 31.6.17–18, in *Opera omnia* (Paris: Vives, 1856–77), vol. 26.

should one expect of an argument for the Real Distinction that it exclude altogether from the picture 'actually *to be*,' that it start with form and matter alone and seek to show that they are *not* the exhaustive principles of substance? Under this scenario, an argument for the Real Distinction becomes impossible before it begins. Aquinas would respond, I believe, that 'actually *to be*' has always been in the picture and cannot be excluded, but that this fact, rather than begging, mandates the question, mandates the inquiry into whether form accounts for 'actually *to be*.'

Aquinas cites many times in his own name the Avicennian formula that 'a being' is the first concept that falls into the mind.[127] Admittedly, the temporally first concept, which is also the most universal,[128] contains confusedly all other things within it, unlike the philosopher's systematic formula 'a being qua a being.' Nonetheless, Aquinas is committed to the fact that what first falls into the mind *(ens)* signifies and names something through its *esse* in the primary sense, through its 'actually *to be*,' namely, through its 'to be' in the sense of 'that by which it is versus is not,' 'that by which it actually is versus only potentially is.'[129] Present at the beginning of intellectual life, just as at the beginning of philosophy, is the distinction between what is and what is not.[130] Parmenides mistakenly identified 'a being' with 'that which actually is,' yet even for Aquinas, it is a per se known first principle that 'a being' (in one sense of the word) is.[131] In light of the original intellectual grasp of 'actually *to be*,' even a child can judge that $x$ is or is not. Form is introduced late in the intellectual life, just as it is introduced well after Parmenides by Plato and Aristotle, to account for the unity behind perceptible reality and behind corporeal parts and their action. Form is a highly questionable philosophical principle, as any empiricist knows. Most of those who reject the Real Distinction do so because they do not take form seriously. Given form, however, as has been our procedure from the outset, one must ask, is this 'late arrival' really distinct from 'actually *to be*' which preceded it?

This question does not presuppose the Real Distinction, does not pre-

---

127. E.g., Aquinas, *ST* I.5.1c.
128. *ST* I.85.3.
129. For the meaning of *ens* see *In Peryerm*. 1.3 (16b20–26), lect. 5, ll. 355–76. For the primary sense of *esse*, see ibid., ll. 394–405.
130. *Sent*. 1, d. 24.1.3 ad 2; *In Met*. 4.2, lect. 3, n. 2 (566); 10.3, lect. 4, n. 15 (1998). For the foundation of the principle of non-contradiction, the first judgment, on *ens*, see *In Met*. 4.3, lect. 6, n. 10 (605).
131. *QDDV* 10.12 ad 3. For the multiple senses of *ens*, see *In Met*. 5.7, lect. 9.

suppose an 'actually *to be*' that is *really distinct* from form, does not assume '*esse* in the Thomist sense.' The knowledge of 'human' and 'animal' precedes the knowledge of 'rational.' Once the concept of 'rational' is achieved, one asks, is rationality really distinct from humanity? Aquinas will answer, no, without giving up on the fact that there is something in reality corresponding to both, that each has a foundation in reality.[132] Similarly, to ask whether 'actually *to be*' is really distinct from form is to remain open to the possible answer: no, although each has a foundation in reality. To ask this question does not beg it. I have argued that Aquinas's nine kinds of argument for the Real Distinction fail to remain open to the answer 'no' by assuming without proof 'actually *to be*' as an ontological component that is the act of form, that is, by assuming Thomist *esse*. To this extent I have admitted both the thrust of the Question-Begging Objection and that it has landed a blow. But it would be unwarranted for the objector to exclude all talk of 'actually *to be*.' To assume that 'actually *to be*' has some foundation in reality does not beg the question by assuming Thomist *esse*. It would be odder to deny this foundation because of posterior difficulties than it would be to deny that there is a real foundation for 'humanity' because of difficulties with 'rationality.' Rationality is a highly doubted and dubious concept; the radical empiricist and scientific realist alike even reject humanity. Form (and essence) is far more subject to doubt than rationality; but if form is conceded, the question whether 'actually *to be*' is form (or essence) is precisely what needs to be asked.

At the same time, the ultimacy or primacy of 'actually *to be*' indicates the difficulty faced by the project of 'proving' the Real Distinction. The project rests on a first principle, and first principles cannot be proved, but have to be defended dialectically. To this extent Gilson and Fabro are correct to question the very project of a proof of the Real Distinction. 'Actually *to be*' and that things actually are must be defended dialectically as ontologically and epistemically primary. In drawing attention to 'actually *to be*' as such, the scriptural notion of creation *ex nihilo*, I would argue, has only helped highlight principles that were already obvious.

On the other hand, Aquinas scholarship has been correct to emphasize the essential and central role of the 'God to Creatures' approach in Aquinas. Once form has been *really* distinguished from 'actually *to be*' in mate-

---

132. *Sent.* 1, d. 19.5.1c; *QDDV* 21.1c, ll. 94–110.

rial composites, Aquinas's conclusion that God is 'actually *to be*' itself can take on an ontological significance. As a result, once the Real Distinction is established for *material* things, the 'God to Creatures Argument' can establish cogently that for *all* things except one (whether possible or actual), including for all immaterial beings except one, 'actually *to be*' is really distinct from essence. The universal scope of the 'God to Creatures Argument,' not the evidentness of its starting point, is the reason that Aquinas frequently employs it.

## Résumé

The project of arguing for the Real Distinction begins only after essence and form have been accepted to account for what is. Is form or are form and matter together the same in reality as 'actually *to be*'? The majority of Aquinas's nine kinds of arguments for the Real Distinction are cogent except insofar as they fail to address precisely this question. Form is so close to 'actually *to be*' that Aquinas fails to worry sufficiently about detaching one from another.

I propose an argument that compensates for this lacuna by reducing the alternatives to absurdity. The argument proceeds 'from effects' to their explanation, where the effect to be explained is just the 'actually *to be*' of the form-matter composite, initially understood as conceptually distinct from the composite itself. The question is, what real principle within the composite might account for its 'actually *to be*'? By a process of elimination, the argument shows that the conceptually distinct 'actually *to be*' can be accounted for only by some principle really distinct from form and matter. 'Actually *to be*' cannot be form and matter together; for matter is only in potency, and 'actually *to be*' cannot be matter's actuality—which is nothing but form. It cannot be form because what form brings to the corporeal whole is not needed and is not wanted once that whole ceases to be. What form brings properly *as form* is not 'actually *to be*'—even if wherever there is form there is 'actually *to be*,' and it is only because of form and through form that composites with really distinct matter 'are.' If 'actually *to be*,' then, signifies something 'absolute' and not merely the relation of a thing to its cause, it follows that it must be an intrinsic, really distinct component of a thing. Consequently, if form as a philosophically explanatory principle can be defended and must be restored, 'actually *to be*' will also need to be defended and restored so that we do not lose sight of what came first. This is the lesson that Gilson and Fabro continue to teach us.

I conclude that the real distinction between being and substance, although not drawn by Aristotle, is a natural development required by his philosophical principles weighed against reality. The actuality of form cannot be identified in reality with 'actually *to be*.' Form does not of itself bring 'actually *to be*' to corruptible things. This is not the role of formal causality. Otherwise, the forms of material things should 'be' forever. To protect against this consequence, 'actually *to be*' must be seen as really distinct from form. If things do have Aristotelian essence, it must be really distinct from their 'to be.'

*J. L. A. West*

# The Real Distinction between Supposit and Nature

RECENT SCHOLARSHIP upon Aquinas's metaphysics has given detailed attention to the problem of the real distinction between being and essence. In comparison there has been relatively little study of Aquinas's treatment of the supposit and his argument that the supposit is really distinct from its nature. This is probably due to the fact that many contemporary metaphysicians tend to distance themselves from substance-based theories. In any case, one can hardly expect a clear account of Aquinas's own metaphysics and natural philosophy without coming to terms with his theory of the supposit and its nature.

In this article I will begin by explaining Aquinas's theory of supposit and related concepts (i.e., person, hypostasis, and substance). I will then examine his argument for a real distinction between the supposit and its nature. Finally, I will show how this distinction functions in Aquinas's arguments for divine simplicity, the Trinity, and Christology.

## Substance and Supposit

Before dealing with the philosophical argumentation for this distinction, I will set out Aquinas's theory of the supposit as a complete and subsisting thing. I will begin, as Aquinas does, with a brief summary of terminological

---

I would like to thank E. J. Ashworth and Joseph Novak for helpful comments on an earlier version of this article. Thanks are also due to John Boyle for letting me use his transcription of the Roman Commentary prior to its publication. There is no adequate English term to translate the Latin word *suppositum*, so I have simply anglicized the Latin, using the term 'supposit.'

considerations. I will then discuss St. Thomas's view of the basic characteristics of substance and briefly consider two objections to his view. This will provide the background necessary to understand Aquinas's defense of the real distinction between the created supposit and its nature in the following section.

The first point that requires clarification is a terminological one. Aquinas uses a number of different terms to refer to the supposit. Hypostasis, person, and substance are all used to pick out an individual complete in some nature. Yet, each of these terms varies slightly in connoting a different aspect of the individual. The term 'supposit' is used as a Latin equivalent for the Greek term 'hypostasis.' These terms signify the individual insofar as it is a subsisting entity. Since medieval theologians frequently used these terms interchangeably, I will simply speak of the supposit.

The term 'person' is rather more complex. Aquinas follows Boethius's account of the person as an individual substance of a rational nature.[1] This definition entails a distinction between the notions of supposit and person. The former can be understood as a genus of which the latter is a species.[2] With respect to the theological problems with which I am concerned, the difference between a supposit and a person is largely irrelevant. Accordingly, I will generally use the term 'supposit' rather than 'person' to indicate that the target of attention in this case is the self-subsisting individual, not that individual's rationality. The exception to this will be in the section on the Trinity, where I will follow the usual custom of referring to divine persons rather than supposits.

The term 'supposit' was first discussed in detail by medieval grammarians. Of special importance was the work of Peter Helias, who noted that the term 'supposit' was used in two ways. First, the supposit was a bearer of a name, form, or quality; second, it was the subject of a proposition.[3] Many

---

1. Cf. *Summa theologiae*, 5 vols. (Ottawa: Commissio Piana, 1953) [hereafter *ST*] I, q. 29, a. 1.

2. *Lectura romana in primum Sententiarum Petri Lombardi*, ed. Leonard E. Boyle, O.P., and John F. Boyle (Toronto: Pontifical Institute of Mediaeval Studies, 2006) [hereafter *Roman Commentary*], 67vf–68rf, d. 23, q. 1 c. "Ergo idem est persona in substantiis rationabilibus quod ypostasis in inrationabilibus."

3. Corneille Henri Kneepkens, "'Suppositio' and 'Supponere' in 12th Century Grammar," in *Gilbert de Poitiers et ses contemporains*, ed. Jean Jolivet and Alain de Libera (Naples: Bibliopolis, 1987), 330. Note especially the passage attributed to Peter Helias commenting on Priscian's account of the verb: "Sicut enim nomen repertum est ad significandum quid de aliquo dicitur. Unde nomen nunquam apponitur nisi auxilio verbi substantivi, nec verbum supponitur nisi auxilio nominis substantivi; sed quodlibet nomen per se supponitur, et verbum per se

medieval authors, however, did not clearly distinguish these two uses, and it has been suggested that they would not have seen a significant difference between them.⁴ In any case, Aquinas does not indicate any important difference here. The sense of the term 'supposit' in Aquinas's thought is, however, predominantly metaphysical.

Aquinas often treats the meaning of the term 'supposit' in the context of explaining the different senses of the term 'substance.' Accordingly, 'supposit' is one of the terms that can stand for a substance. When it does so, it signifies a primary substance. "A supposit is a singular in the genus of substance, which we call a hypostasis or prime substance."⁵ A supposit is an individual thing that can have properties predicated of it, and yet cannot be predicated of anything else. Thus, Socrates, considered as a complete thing, is a supposit, but his height or color is not. Further, a supposit is not a part of something, like Socrates' hand or foot.⁶ Rather, a supposit is a whole that subsists through itself.

Nevertheless, Aquinas often uses the term 'supposit' to signify a primary substance in a more specific sense. The term 'supposit' is frequently used when Aquinas wishes to speak about the subject of some form, while 'substance' is used when he wants to indicate that the subject is not separable from its form.⁷ Here he is relying on Aristotle, who writes in the *Metaphys-*

---

apponitur." Kneepkens (ibid., 333) suggests that the absence of these lines from some manuscripts indicates they are an interpolation. However, our concern is not with Helias's thought for its own sake. Whatever its origin, this passage presents what was to become a widely held view, i.e., that supposition was a property of the subject term in a proposition.

4. Stan Ebbesen, "Early Supposition Theory (12th–13th cent.)," *Histoire, Epistémologie, Langage* 3 (1981): 38.

5. *Opera omnia jussu Leonis XIII P. M. edita, t. 25/1: Quaestiones de quolibet. Préface. Quodlibet VII, VIII, IX, X, XI; t. 25/2: Quaestiones de quolibet. Quodlibet I, II, III, VI, IV, V, XII* (Rome-Paris: Commissio Leonina-Éditions du Cerf, 1996) [hereafter *Quodl.*] II, q. 2, a. 2 c. "Suppositum autem est singulare in genere substancie, quod dicitur ypostasis uel substancia prima." Also *Scriptum super Sententiis magistri Petri Lombardi*, t. 1., ed. P. Mandonnet (Paris: Lethielleux, 1929) [hereafter *In Sent.*] I, d. 25, q. 1, a. 1 ad 7; *ST* I, q. 29, a. 1 ad 2; *Roman Commentary*, 69rf–vf, d. 23, q. 4, ad 2.

6. *ST* I, q. 29, a. 1 ad 2.

7. *ST* I, q. 39, a. 2 c.: "et sic natura se habet ut forma, individuum autem ut suppositum formae"; and ad 4: "Ad quartum dicendum quod forma, absolute accepta, consuevit significari ut eius cuius est forma, ut virtus Petri. E converso autem, res habens formam aliquam non consuevit significari ut eius, nisi cum volumus determinare sive designare formam. Et tunc requiruntur duo genitivi, quorum unus significet formam, et alius determinationem formae, ut si dicatur, Petrus est magnae virtutis, vel etiam requiritur unus genitivus habens vim duorum genitivorum, ut cum dicitur, vir sanguinum est iste, idest effusor multi sanguinis." Also *ST* III, q. 2, a. 3 c.: "Tertio, quia tantum hypostasis est cui attribuuntur operationes et proprietates

*ics:* "Substance has two senses, (a) the ultimate substratum, which is no longer predicated of anything else, and (b) that which is a 'this' and separable—and of this nature is the shape or form of each thing."[8] Accordingly, the term 'supposit' tends to highlight two features of substance. First, 'supposit' refers to an individual insofar as it subsists in the genus of substance.[9] Second, 'supposit' signifies a substance insofar as it is a thing having some kind of

---

naturae, et ea etiam quae ad naturae rationem pertinent in concreto, dicimus enim quod hic homo ratiocinatur, et est risibilis, et est animal rationale. Et hac ratione hic homo dicitur esse suppositum, quia scilicet supponitur his quae ad hominem pertinent, eorum praedicationem recipiens." Cf. *ST* I, q. 29, a. 2 ad 5.

8. Aristotle, *Metaphysics*, 1017b26. The Latin text reads "Accidit itaque secundum duos modos substantiam dici: subiectum ultimum, quod non adhuc de alio dicitur: parabile fuerit. Tale vero uniuscuiusque forma et species." Note Aquinas's commentary on this passage, *In duodecim libros Metaphysicorum Aristotelis expositio*, ed. M. R. Cathala and R. M. Spiazzi (Rome: Marietti, 1971) [hereafter *In Metaphys.*], V,10,903: "Deinde cum dicit accidit itaque reducit dictos modos substantiae ad duos; dicens, quod ex praedictis modis considerari potest, quod substantia duobus modis dicitur: quorum unus est secundum quod substantia dicitur id quod ultimo subiicitur in propositionibus, ita quod de alio non praedicetur, sicut substantia prima. Et hoc est, quod est hoc aliquid, quasi per se subsistens, et quod est separabile, quia est ab omnibus distinctum et non communicabile multis. Et quantum ad haec tria differt substantia particularis ab universali. Primo quidem, quia substantia particularis non praedicatur de aliquo inferiori, sicut universalis. Secundo, quia substantia universalis non subsistit nisi ratione singularis quae per se subsistit. Tertio, quia substantia universalis est in multis, non autem singularis, sed est ab omnibus separabilis et distincta." It is also significant that although Aquinas often states that the term 'substance' is used to signify the essence, he claims that such a use is equivocal. *In I Sent.*, d. 23, q. 1, a. 1 ad 5. On these two senses of substance also cf. ibid., corp.: "Si autem accipiatur subsistentia pro eo quod subsistit, sic proprie dicitur illud in quo per prius invenitur talis natura hoc modo essendi. Et cum per prius inveniatur in substantia, secundum quod substantia est; et deinceps in aliis, secundum quod propinquius se habent ad substantiam: constat quod nomen subsistentiae per prius convenit generibus et speciebus in genere substantiae, ut dicit Boetius, et individuis non convenit habere tale esse, nisi inquantum sunt sub tali natura communi. Quamvis enim genera et species non subsistant nisi in individuis, quorum est esse, tamen determinatio essendi fit ex natura vel quidditate superiori. Similiter hypostasis, vel substantia, dicitur dupliciter: vel id quo substatur; et quia primum principium substandi est materia, ideo dicit Boetius in Praedic., quod hypostasis est materia, vel quod substat, et hoc est individuum in genere substantiae per prius. Genera enim et species non substant accidentibus nisi ratione individuorum; et ideo nomen substantiae primo et principaliter convenit particularibus substantiis, secundum philosophum, et secundum Boetium." It is worth noting that Aristotle scholars generally note a difference between the treatment of substance in the *Metaphysics* and the one presented in the *Categories*. In the *Categories* the distinction between primary and secondary substance is fundamental, whereas in the *Metaphysics* it is not. Further, the *Metaphysics* is concerned with the ontological substratum and its properties, while the *Categories* presents more of a logical doctrine, accounting for substance and accidents in terms of predication. Cf. Michael J. Loux, *Primary Ousia* (Ithaca: Cornell University Press, 1991); and Terence Irwin, *Aristotle's First Principles* (Oxford: Clarendon Press, 1988).

9. *ST* I, q. 29, a. 2 c. "Alio modo dicitur substantia subiectum vel suppositum quod subsistit in genere substantiae."

nature.[10] Hence, while the terms 'substance' and 'supposit' refer to the same thing, they focus on different aspects of that thing.

Aquinas's explanation of the notion of substance is relatively well known. It is important, however, to note that he explicitly rejects any simplistic identification of substance with being. This is shown in his rejection of *ens per se* as an adequate definition of substance. While all substances are beings, not every being is a substance. In terms of the categories, substance is the most general genus, while being *(ens)* is not a genus. Consequently, substance cannot be defined as being. In the *De potentia*, for example, Aquinas argues, "As Avicenna says [3 *Metaph.*, c. 8], the definition of substance is not being through itself. For being cannot be the genus of anything as Aristotle proves [III *Metaph.*, c. 10], since nothing can be added to being that does not participate in it; but a difference cannot participate in a genus."[11] Substance is the most general genus, whereas *ens* is not a genus at all. Consequently, it would be erroneous to use 'being' as the genus term in the definition of substance.[12]

In the same text St. Thomas offers his own definition of substance that borrows from Aristotle, who had defined substance as follows: "A substance—that which is called a substance most strictly, primarily and most of all—is that which is *neither said of a subject nor in a subject*, e.g., the individual man or the individual horse."[13] Aquinas, however, adapts Aristot-

10. *In Metaphys.*, V,10, 904. "Sed forma refertur ad materiam, quam facit esse in actu, quidditas autem refertur ad suppositum, quod significatur ut habens talem essentiam." *Roman Commentary*, 67vf–68rf, d. 23, q. 1 ad 1. "Aliquando substantia dicit ipsum suppositum, id est habens naturam." Cf. John F. Wippel, *The Metaphysical Thought of Thomas Aquinas: From Finite to Infinite Being* (Washington, DC: The Catholic University of America Press, 2000), 240.

11. *Quaestiones disputatae, t. 2: Quaestiones disputatae de potentia*, ed. P. M. Pession (Rome: Marietti, 1965) [hereafter *De pot.*], q. 7, a. 3 ad 4. "Ad quartum dicendum, quod ens per se non est definitio substantiae, ut Avicenna dicit. Ens enim non potest esse alicuius genus, ut probat Philosophus, cum nihil possit addi ad ens quod non participet ipsum; differentia vero non debet participare genus."

12. There is a fine article on this point by Étienne Gilson, "Quasi Definitio Substantiae," in *St. Thomas Aquinas: 1274–1974, Commemorative Studies*, ed. Armand A. Maurer, C.S.B., et al. (Toronto: Pontifical Institute of Mediaeval Studies, 1974). Also cf. Wippel, *Metaphysical Thought*, 228–35. Note that the definition of substance in terms of *res* is present in earlier medieval authors. Cf. William of Conches' *Glosule*, where in the course of commenting on Priscian's notion of supposit as a substance William remarks that substance is understood as a *res* existing *per se*, while a supposit is the subject of a locution. "Et nota quod in hac arte dicitur substantia res per se existens et id quod res per se existens dicitur esse, cum queritur quid sit. Et suppositum dicitur actuale quod subiacet locutioni" (MS. Paris, Bibl. Nat. lat. 15130, quoted in Kneepkens, "'Suppositio,'" 341).

13. *Categories*, 2a11–15.

le's definition in order to emphasize the fact that any substance must have a quiddity that is distinct from its being. Accordingly, St. Thomas states: "But if substance could have a definition, notwithstanding that it is the most general genus, its definition would be: a thing to the quiddity of which it belongs not to be in another."[14] According to Aquinas, this definition entails that God is not, properly speaking, a substance.[15] A substance is a thing or quiddity that *has* being. This entails that a substance's essence and being are different, which is not the case in God.

Yet, Aquinas's proposed definition is not a great improvement since he uses res as a genus term, which as a transcendental may be expected to have similar problems to those found with *ens*.[16] The difference of this definition is that in a substance there is a quiddity to which it belongs not to be *in* another, thus the substance subsists *per se*. Accordingly the individual substance is neither in another, nor said of another. Rather, it is a complete thing subsisting through itself. These points are brought out clearly in Aquinas's *Disputed Questions on the Soul,* where Aquinas is arguing that the human soul is a form and a *hoc aliquid* (this something).[17] In this text, Aquinas explains the notion of an individual substance as follows:

14. *De pot.*, q. 7, a. 3 ad 4. "Sed si substantia possit habere definitionem, non obstante quod est genus generalissimum, erit eius definitio: quod substantia est res cuius quidditati debetur esse non in aliquo." Further clarification is offered at Summa Contra Gentiles, ed. C. Pera et al., 3 vols. (Rome: Marietti, 1961) [hereafter *SCG*] I, 25, 236, "Oportet igitur quod ratio substantiae intelligitur hoc modo, quod substantia sit res cui conveniat esse non in subiecto; nomen autem rei a quidditate imponitur, sicut nomen entis ab esse; et sic in ratione substantiae intelligitur quod habeat quidditatem cui conveniat esse non in alio." *In II Sent.,* d. 3, q. 1, a. 6 sol. "Unde Avicenna dicit in sua Metaphysica (tr. II, c. 1, et tr. VI, c. 5), *ad hoc quod aliquid sit proprie in genere substantiae requiritur quod sit res quidditatem habens, qui debeatur esse absolutum,* ut per se esse dicatur vel subsistens. Et ideo duobus modis potest contingere quod aliquid ad substantiae genus pertinens, non sit in genere substantiae sicut species: vel quia res illa non habet quidditatem aliam nisi suum esse; et propter hoc Deus non est in genere substantiae sicut species, ut ipse Avicenna dicit: vel quia res illa non habet esse absolutum, ut ens per se dici possit; et propter hoc materia prima et formae materiales non sunt in genere substantiae sicut species, sed solum sicut principia" (emphasis added). Also cf. *In I Sent.,* d. 8, q. 4, a. 2; *SCG*, I, 25, 235–36; *De pot.*, q. 7, a. 3 ad 4; *ST* I, q. 3 a. 3; and *ST* I, q. 3, a. 5 ad 1.

15. This claim is thoroughly traditional. It is found, for example, in Alexander of Hales, *Quaestiones Disputatae "antequam esset frater,"* vol. 1 (Quaracchi: Collegium S. Bonaventurae, 1960), q. 2, m. 1, n. 5; *Glossa in I Sent.,* d. 8, n. 28; and Bonaventure, *In I Sent.,* d. 23, a. 1, q. 2.

16. The motive for shifting to *res* is surely its association with quiddity, for a quiddity can have *esse*. *In I Sent.*, d. 25, q. 1, a. 4 c. Also cf. *De ver.,* I, q. 1, a. 1 (*Opera omnia iussu Leonis XIII P. M. edita, t. 22: Quaestiones disputatae de veritate* [Rome: Editori di San Tommaso, 1970–1976]).

17. It should be noted that this article is of special interest for Christology, due to the dogma that Christ qua man is a "this something" or *hoc aliquid.* Cf. Wippel, *Metaphysical Thought,* 239.

# Distinction between Supposit and Nature 91

An individual in the genus of substance not only subsists *per se*, but it is something *complete* in some species and in the genus of substance; whence Aristotle also says in the *Categories*, that a hand and a foot and other things of this kind name parts of substances rather than first or second substances: since although they are not in another as in a subject [i.e., they are not accidents], and this is what is proper to a substance, yet they do not share the complete nature of any species; hence they are not in any species or genus except through reduction.[18]

This text reveals that a substance must: (1) subsist *per se*; (2) be a *complete* thing; and (3) be *in some species*. This is entirely in keeping with the previous texts, and also indicates, once again, that God is not, properly speaking, a substance.[19]

This denial that God is a substance might appear to contradict the Christological claim that the hypostatic union takes place in the supposit, as supposit is one of the primary senses of substance. It also seems to create a tension in Trinitarian theology, as Aquinas is committed to the orthodox view that there are three hypostases in God, and that hypostasis is also a synonym for substance and supposit. However, the difficulty is only apparent, as in the case of God the terms 'substance,' 'supposit,' and 'hypostasis' are used slightly differently to signify God's *manner* of existing; namely that he is something that subsists *per se*.[20]

A more significant objection to Aquinas's account has recently been made from the perspective of modern philosophy. Thomas V. Morris has argued that Aquinas's view posits a "hidden" substance or supposit along the lines suggested by Locke, which has been almost universally rejected in light of

18. *Opera omnia iussu Leonis XIII P. M. edita*, t. 24/1: *Quaestiones disputatae de anima*, ed. B. C. Bazán (Rome-Paris: Commissio Leonina-Éditions du Cerf, 1996) [hereafter *Q.D. De an.*], q. 1, a. 1 c. "Individuum autem in genere substantiae non solum habet quod per se possit subsistere, sed quod sit aliquid completum in aliqua specie et genere substantiae; unde Philosophus etiam in Praedicamentis, manum et pedem et huiusmodi nominat partes substantiarum magis quam substantias primas vel secundas: quia, licet non sint in alio sicut in subiecto (quod proprie substantiae est), non tamen participant complete naturam alicuius speciei; unde non sunt in aliqua specie neque in aliquo genere, nisi per reductionem."

19. The view that God is not a substance was widely held. Gilbert of Poitiers, however, maintained that it was necessary to apply the term 'substance' to God. Cf. Marcia L. Colish, "Gilbert, the Early Porretans, and Peter Lombard: Semantics and Theology," in Jolivet and Libera, *Gilbert de Poitiers*, 234–35. The early Porretans significantly qualify Gilbert's view, coming close to Aquinas's own position on this point. Ibid., 241–42.

20. *ST* I, q. 29, a. 3 ad 4. "Substantia vero convenit Deo, secundum quod significat existere per se." *Roman Commentary*, 67vf–68rf, d. 23, q. 1: "Subsistere autem inportat determinatum modum essendi prout aliquid est ens per se, et hoc est proprium substantie, nam accidentia habent esse et non subsistere." In this context, it is worth noting that *Deus* does not, properly speaking, name a person, but a nature. *ST* I, q. 13, a. 8.

Berkeley's criticisms.[21] Although the term 'supposit' is used when Aquinas wants to talk as if there is a substratum, it is clear that he does not limit substance to a hidden "something" *underlying* accidents. Rather, a substance is a *whole* that embraces accidents as well as formal and integral parts.[22]

Indeed, it is true that for St. Thomas, as for Boethius, the substance is something that "stands under," but what a substance primarily stands under is its nature; only secondarily does it stand under its various accidents. Aquinas is explicit on this point: "Persons [i.e., individual substances of a rational nature] are not persons from the fact that they are under properties, but from the fact that they are under an essence."[23] This shifts the terms of the debate significantly, for the sense in which a man, for example, has humanity is quite different from the sense in which he has whiteness, tallness, strength, and the like. There is, of course, nothing to act as a property-bearer at all, unless there is a substance constituted in some species. For Aquinas then, the central feature of a substance is not its "hiddenness," but the fact that it is a whole composed of formal and integral parts.

## The Real Distinction between a Supposit and Its Nature

Having clarified Aquinas's theory of the supposit in relation to substance, it remains to show that it is really distinct from each thing's nature. The claim that there is a real distinction between the supposit and nature in all material things is a central doctrine of Aquinas's philosophy of nature. A real distinction, or a distinction *secundum rem*, is to be understood in contradistinction to a conceptual distinction, or a distinction *secundum rationem*. This means that the supposit and nature pick out two aspects of one and the same thing that are not to be identified ontologically. This is to say that the distinction is an objective one; it is discovered, not imposed, by the intellect.

While it is true that Aquinas uses the phrase "real distinction" only rare-

---

21. Thomas V. Morris, "St. Thomas on the Identity and Unity of the Person of Christ: A Problem of Reference in Christological Discourse," *Scottish Journal of Theology* 35 (1982): 424–25.

22. *ST* III, q. 2, a. 2. Morris recognizes that a supposit is a whole, but does not see the implications of this point for his criticism of Aquinas, cf. "St. Thomas on the Identity and Unity," 423. For more on the difference between Aquinas and Locke, cf. Richard Cross, "Aquinas on Nature, Hypostasis and the Metaphysics of the Incarnation," *Thomist* 60 (1996): 175.

23. *In I Sent.*, d. 34, q. 1, a. 1 c. "Personae non habent quod sint personae ex hoc quod subsunt proprietatibus, sed ex hoc quod subsunt essentiae."

ly,[24] it aptly expresses his account of the relation between both being and essence and supposit and nature as these are developed in many of his texts.[25] It is important to note that when we speak of a "real distinction" what is meant is quite different from the accounts of "real distinction" found in Giles of Rome and Duns Scotus. Giles had asserted that being and essence were really distinct as *res* and *res*.[26] Aquinas would not accept this position. Rather, he holds that being and essence are really distinct aspects of one and the same *res* or thing. Scotus, on the other hand, held that real separability was a necessary and sufficient condition for a real distinction.[27] For Aquinas, however, the claim that being and essence, or supposit and nature, are really distinct in no way implies that the two could ever exist apart from one another: "No nature has being *(esse)* except in its supposit: for humanity can only be in a man. Hence, whatever is existing per se in the genus of substance has the character of a hypostasis, or supposit."[28] A supposit exists at all only insofar as it subsists in some nature or other; likewise, natures exist in reality only insofar as they inform particulars. In a similar way, the smooth texture of my table, for example, is really distinct from its color, which happens to be brown. Nevertheless, it would be foolish to claim that

24. The phrase *distinctio realis* occurs five times in Aquinas: *ST* I, q. 28, a. 3 obj. 2; ibid., obj. 3 and ad 3; I, q. 30 a. 2 c.; q. 39, a. 1 c.

25. There is a tremendous amount of literature on the "real distinction" in the context of the difference between essence and *esse*. There is a considerable consensus that Aquinas holds a doctrine of real distinction, even though he usually expresses it in different terms. Yet, Francis A. Cunningham argues that distinction is by definition conceptual for Aquinas. Cf. "Distinction according to Aquinas," *New Scholasticism* 36 (1962): 279–312. Yet Aquinas does on occasion speak of a real distinction in the context of Trinitarian theology, so the phrase is not unwarranted. In any case, the objection appears to be merely an issue of vocabulary, and it is unclear what difference there is between a real distinction and the alternative he suggests, following Suárez, of a conceptual distinction with a foundation *in re*. Also cf. his work of encyclopedic proportions: Francis A. Cunningham, S.J., *Essence and Existence in Thomism: A Mental vs. the "Real Distinction"?* (Lanham, MD: University Press of America, 1988). Aquinas speaks of a *distinctio rei*, for instance, in *In I Sent.*, d. 34, q. 1, a. 1 and 2: "Omnis distinctio, sive rei sive rationis, fundatur in affirmatione et negatione." The best study of the various arguments in Aquinas that support the real distinction is Wippel, *Metaphysical Thought*, 132–76.

26. Aegidius Romani, *Theoremata de esse et essentia*, ed. E. Hocedez (Louvain: Museum Lessianum, 1930), 1, 34. "Essentia et esse sunt duae res realiter differentes." For a standard summary of Giles's metaphysics, cf. Étienne Gilson, *History of Christian Philosophy in the Middle Ages* (New York: Random House, 1955), 420–25.

27. Richard Cross, *Duns Scotus*, Great Mediaeval Thinkers (Oxford: Oxford University Press, 1999), 149.

28. *In III Sent.*, d. 2, q. 2, a. 3, sol. 1. "Respondeo dicendum, quod nulla natura habet esse nisi in supposito suo: non enim humanitas potest esse nisi in homine: unde quidquid est in genere substantiae per se existens, rationem hypostasis habet, vel suppositi."

the smooth texture of my table could exist without its color, or vice versa. The two are really distinct, but they cannot be separated. Likewise, to claim that the supposit and nature of a material thing are really distinct does not mean that they are separate, or even that they could be separate. Aquinas simply intends to deny that they are merely different terms or concepts for something that is in reality the same.

Aquinas's real distinction needs to be understood in light of his own ontology of the different senses of nature. St. Thomas's most detailed account of the different ways in which we can understand a nature, and the different ways in which a nature can exist, is offered in his early work *De Ente*, 3. This chapter is devoted to the relation between essence and the divisions of genus, species, and difference. The division of nature offered in this text can be presented as follows:

N1. nature signified by an abstract term (e.g., humanity), is signified as a formal part;
N2. nature signified by a concrete term (e.g., man), is signified as a whole.
From a metaphysical perspective N2, that is, nature in the concrete, has three aspects:
N2a. the nature absolutely considered;
N2b. the nature as it exists in the mind; and
N2c. the nature as it exists in individual things.

Each of these needs to be examined in turn. The first way of understanding nature, that is, N1: the specific difference signified by the definition. In this way, the abstract nature, that is, humanity, is taken as a formal part of the thing. To consider human nature in this way is to look at the features that constitute a man as a man. Here we are abstracting or prescinding from all the accidental and individual features that are found in this or that man, in order to focus in on those that belong to him in virtue of being a member of the species. Human nature considered in this way would include rationality and undesignated matter (i.e., since man falls under the genus animal, man must be made up of matter of a general sort). It would exclude features that belong to men as individuals. Thus, human nature understood with precision restricts one's point of view to the formal part of man, excluding any consideration of the particular flesh, bones, color, and height of this or that individual man. Only the fact that a man must be made of up of things of this general sort is included.

Aquinas emphasizes that nature in this sense is not to be identified with the *ratio* of the genus or species. Such a view would undermine our ability to predicate the genus, species, or difference of the individual.[29] Aquinas has in mind the kind of difference that is found between an abstract term such as "humanity" and a concrete term such as "man." It would be erroneous to predicate the formal part, humanity, of an individual man, for a part cannot be predicated of a whole. Hence, "Peter is his humanity" is a false statement. Here Aquinas is following Avicenna. Rationality, for example, cannot be the difference of man; it is, rather, the formal principle of the difference, and likewise humanity is not the species, nor animality the genus. Asserting that kind of identity between the nature understood with precision and the genus, species, or difference would entirely vitiate the ability to predicate these of the individual truthfully.[30]

Yet, the terms we use to refer to a nature can also signify in the mode of a whole. Here we are dealing with the nature as it is signified concretely, for example, "man" or "horse" in contradistinction to "humanity" or "equinity." It is the nature in this sense that is pertinent to genus and species. "And thus it remains that the character of genus or species belongs to the essence insofar as it is signified through the mode of a whole, as the name 'man' or 'animal,' just as it contains implicitly and indistinctly the whole that is in the individual."[31] Turning to the more detailed account of the concrete nature, for example, man, in the *De ente*, St. Thomas distinguishes three ways in which it can be considered. The first of these is nature in its *absolute consideration*. When we view a nature in this way we look at the individual nature signi-

---

29. *Opera omnia iussu Leonis XIII P. M. edita*, t. 43: *De ente et essentia* (Rome: Editori di San Tommaso, 1976) [hereafter *De ente*], 3, ll. 4–9. "Quia autem id cui conuenit ratio generis uel speciei uel differentie predicatur de hoc singulari signato, impossibile est quod ratio uniuersalis, scilicet generis uel speciei, conueniat essentie secundum quod per modum partis significatur, ut nomine humanitatis uel animalitatis."

30. *De ente*, 3, ll. 10–13. "Et ideo dicit Auicenna quod rationalitas non est differentia sed differentie principium; et eadem ratione humanitas non est species, nec animalitas genus." Aquinas seems to be referring to Avicenna, *Metaphysica*, V, c. 6: "Differentia non est talis qualis est rationalitas et sensibilitas.... Conuenientius est ergo ut hec sint principia differentiarum non differentie." For discussion of the Avicennian background to this text, cf. Joseph Owens, "Common Nature: A Point of Comparison between Thomistic and Scotistic Metaphysics," *Mediaeval Studies* 19 (1957): 1–14. On Avicenna's terminology, cf. Deborah L. Black, "Mental Existence in Thomas Aquinas," *Mediaeval Studies* 61 (1999): 48n6.

31. *De ente*, 3, ll. 20–25. "Et ideo relinquitur quod ratio generis uel speciei conueniat essentie secundum quod significatur per modum totius, ut nomine hominis uel animalis, prout implicite et indistincte continet totum hoc quod in indiuiduo est."

fied as a whole, but ignore any of the accidental features that it has in the individual. Thus, we are looking at Socrates insofar as he is a man, without attending to the fact that he is white, bearded, a philosopher, and so on.

The second way of understanding a concrete nature is in terms of the existence it has in the mind, that is, as the concept of that nature. However, since our present concern is with the ontology of nature, this is largely irrelevant.[32] Accordingly, we can turn directly to the third way of considering a nature; namely, as it exists in singular things. It is nature in this sense that is at work when we distinguish it from the supposit and *esse*.

According to Aquinas, a nature embraces only those properties that constitute a thing in its species. Yet, all material things have other properties beyond these essential ones. Obviously, these nonessential properties cannot be included in their nature. It follows from this that in material things the supposit is ontologically distinct from its nature.

The basis for the argument for the real distinction between a supposit and its nature in the *De ente* arises in the context of Aquinas's account of the way matter is included in the essence of composite substances, in chapter two. Of course, for Aquinas the essence of a composite substance includes matter, but only in an undesignated way. It is essential to man as such to have flesh and bones of some sort or other. Anything that lacked flesh and bones would not be human. But it is not essential to having a human nature that a man have this particular bit of flesh and bones. Accordingly, Aquinas argues:

> Since therefore the concept of humanity includes only those things that make a man be man, it is clear that designated matter is excluded or prescinded from its signification. And since a part is not predicated of the whole, hence humanity is not predicated of man nor of Socrates. Hence Avicenna says that the quiddity of a composite is not the composite itself whose quiddity it is, although the quiddity itself is a composite. Just as humanity, although it is a composite, is not a man, rather it must be received in something else, i.e., designated matter.[33]

---

32. It is worth noting that in Aquinas's later works he seems to have focused more upon the intelligible species and attempted to reserve *esse* to refer to real existence outside the mind. Nevertheless, the notion of mental existence continues to play a key role in St. Thomas's refutation of Averroes throughout his career. Black, "Mental Existence," 73–74. For other discussions of mental existence where the notion of intelligible species is taken into account cf. *Sent. de anima*, II, 12, 378–80 and *ST* I, q. 85, a. 2.

33. *De ente*, 2, ll. 262–73. "Cum ergo humanitas in suo intellectu includat tantum ea ex quibus homo habet quod sit homo, patet quod a significatione excluditur vel preciditur materia designata; et quia pars non predicatur de toto, inde est quod humanitas nec de homine nec

This passage lays the basis for the distinction between the supposit and nature. The two are distinct because the supposit, being the complete individual, includes things beyond what is included in the nature qua nature. This point is elaborated upon in chapter four of the *De ente,* where Aquinas is comparing the way essence functions in composite substances to the way it functions in simple substances. Here he notes that because of the presence of designated matter in a composite, its essence can be signified either as a part or as a whole, depending upon whether or not one is prescinding from matter and individuating features. He goes on to make the same point he had made in the passage from chapter two; we cannot attribute the essence of a composite substance in every sense to the individual. For example, we cannot say that a man is his quiddity. This differs from the essence of a simple substance, since in this case the nature is not received into something distinct from it.[34]

The argument that the supposit and its nature are distinct in composite substances, since the individual includes properties that are not included in the nature, is used throughout St. Thomas's career in several contexts, notably in arguments concerning divine and angelic simplicity.[35] Since this principle plays such an important role in Aquinas's thought, it is important to articulate its metaphysical and historical background with some care.

First, it should be noted that unlike the often discussed distinction between *esse* and *essentia,* the distinction between supposit and nature is usually restricted to material beings. This is made clear not only by the difference between supposit and *esse* discussed above, but also by Aquinas's

---

de Sorte predicatur. Vnde dicit Auicenna quod quiditas compositi non est ipsum compositum cuius est quiditas, quamuis etiam ipsa quiditas sit composita; sicut humanitas, licet sit composita, non est homo, immo oportet quod sit recepta in aliquo quod est materia designata."

34. *De ente,* 4, ll. 61–89.

35. See esp. *ST* I, q. 3, a. 3 c. See the discussion of this text in the following section concerning divine simplicity. Also: *In I Sent.,* d. 34, q. 1, a. 1. "Respondeo dicendum, quod persona et essentia omnino re in diuinis non distinguuntur. In illis enim in quibus aliud est essentia quam hypostasis vel suppositum, oportet quod sit aliquid materiale, per quod natura communis individuetur et determinetur ad hoc singulare. Vnde illam determinationem materiae vel alicujus quod loco materiae se habet, addit in creaturis hypostasis supra essentiam et naturam; unde non omnino ista in creaturis idem sunt. In Deo autem non est natura ipsius subsistens per aliquod ad quod determinatur sicut per materiam; sed per seipsam est subsistens, et ipsum suum esse subsistens est; unde natura est ipsum quod subsistit, et esse in quo subsistit: et propter hoc in Deo omnino idem est quo est et quod est." Also cf. *De spiritualibus creaturis,* q. 1, a. 5 ad 9 and *Q.D. De an.,* q. 1, a. 17 ad 10. This point is also held in inauthentic works attributed to St. Thomas: *De natura materiae,* c. 3; *De quatuor oppositis,* c. 4.

argument for the supposit-nature distinction in several texts. In the *De potentia*, for instance, Aquinas argues that a nature, considered precisely as a nature, must be the same in every individual that possesses it, for if there were a difference in the nature, it would change the species. He goes on to note that there can be differences amongst individuals of the same nature insofar as the supposit, which has humanity, can have accidents that are not included in the nature:

> Now the man who has humanity can have something else that is not from the character of humanity, such as whiteness and things of this kind, which are not present in humanity, but in the man. But in any such creature, we find a difference between the one possessing a property and the property possessed. For we find *a two-fold difference* in composite creatures, since the *supposit* or the individual *has the nature of the species*, just as a man has humanity, *and also has being*: for a man is neither his own humanity or his own being; hence some accident can be present in a man, but not in his humanity or his being.[36]

Supposit and nature are distinct in material beings, since each being of this kind includes particular aspects beyond the nature of the species. This raises a problem in the case of immaterial beings, that is, angels. It should be recalled that for Aquinas each individual angel is considered to be a species with only one member. In modern parlance, each angel is a singleton set.[37] Accordingly, his usual position is that there is no distinction between supposit and nature in angels, though there is a difference between their *esse* and their essence. However, in one important text, *Quodlibet* II, q. 2, a. 2, Aquinas does extend the distinction to angels on the basis that they have individual acts of the intellect and will that are proper not to their species, but to the individual.[38]

---

36. *De pot.*, q. 7, a. 4 c. "Homo autem qui habet humanitatem, potest aliquid aliud habere quod non sit de ratione humanitatis, sicut albedinem et huiusmodi, quae non insunt humanitati, sed homini. In qualibet autem creatura invenitur differentia habentis et habiti. In creaturis namque compositis invenitur duplex differentia, quia ipsum suppositum sive individuum habet naturam speciei, sicut homo humanitatem, et habet ulterius esse; homo enim nec est humanitas nec esse suum; unde homini potest inesse aliquod accidens, non autem ipsi humanitati vel eius esse."

37. For further discussion, cf. Wippel, *Metaphysical Thought*, 197–98 and 311–12.

38. *Quodl.* II, q. 2, a. 2 c. "In angelo autem [suppositum et natura] non est omnino idem, quia aliquid accidit ei preter id quod est de ratione sue speciei, quia et ipsum esse angeli est preter eius essenciam seu naturam et alia quedam ei accidunt, que omnia pertinent ad suppositum, non autem ad naturam." Even in *Quodl.* II, q. 2, a. 2, the argument for material beings remains the same. "Secundum hoc igitur, cuicunque potest aliquid accidere quod non sit de ratione sue nature, in eo differt res et quod quid est, siue suppositum et natura: nam in signi-

The historical sources of the real distinction between the supposit and nature are obscure. In most places, Aquinas states it without attributing it to anyone at all.[39] In one text Aquinas makes reference to Aristotle, but the claim does not appear in the text at all. Rather, it is to be found in Aquinas's commentary, where he explicitly states that he is adding this point to a series of arguments given by Aristotle himself.[40] Aquinas is commenting on Aristotle's discussion in the *Metaphysics* of the manner in which the *quod quid erat esse* is related to the thing and the way we use accidental and essential predication to discuss this.[41]

Aristotle argues that there is a difference between what is said accidentally *(per accidens)* and what is said essentially *(secundum se)*. The properties signified by accidental predications are distinct from those that are essential. For example, "white man" is distinct from the essence of man. This is due to the fact that it does not belong to the essence of man to be white; otherwise, every man would be white. To put it another way, being white would be a necessary condition of being a man. In things said *secundum se*, however, the thing and its essence are always the same, for example, a man is rational. In this case, by contrast to the first, rationality is an essential characteristic of being a man and, thus, every man is rational. This provides Aristotle with the grounds for arguing against Plato's theory of Ideas, which allegedly separates the essence from the thing of which it is the essence, and for considering objections to Aristotle's own position.[42]

In most contexts it is essential predications that are of greatest interest,

---

ficatione nature includitur solum id quod est de ratione speciei, suppositum autem non solum habet hec que ad rationem speciei pertinent, set etiam alia que ei accidunt; et ideo suppositum significatur ut totum, natura autem siue quiditas ut pars formalis." For a more detailed examination of this matter, cf. Jacques Winandy, O.S.B., "Le Quodlibet II, art. 4 de Saint Thomas et la notion de suppôt," *Ephemerides theologicae Lovanienses* 2 (1934): 5–29. Philosophically, the argument of *Quodl.* II, q. 2, a. 2 appears to be cogent. For a sense of the scholarly debate on this passage, cf. Wippel, *Metaphysical Thought*, 245–53.

39. Exceptions to this are: (1) *De Unione*, a. 1 ad 4 (*Quaestiones disputatae, t. 2: De unione Verbi incarnati*, ed. M. Calcaterra, T. S. Centi [Rome: Marietti, 1965]): attributed to Aristotle, *Metaphysics*, 7; (2) *De pot.*, q. 7, a. 2, ad 5: attributed to *De Causis*, Prop. 4; and (3) *De pot.*, q. 7, a. 4 c.: attributed to Boethius *De Hebdomadibus*. In light of the discussion of *De ente* 2, we should also note that it has roots in Avicenna's dictum that the quiddity of a composite is not the composite whose quiddity it is.

40. This point is made in lect. V, 1378–80.

41. Cf. *Metaph.*, 1031a15–1032a11.

42. A detailed account of this is also presented in *Quodl.* II, q. 2, a. 2 ad 1. Cf. *De pot.*, q. 7, a. 4 ad 8.

so I will restrict my attention to these. In commenting on Aristotle's arguments against Plato, Aquinas introduces the real distinction between supposit and nature, in the process of adding a further argument to Aristotle's own.[43] He notes that the *quod quid est esse* is what the definition signifies. This entails that when a definition is predicated of the relevant thing, the *quod quid est esse* is as well. Humanity, however, is not the proper definition of man; rather, man is defined as a rational mortal animal. The role of "humanity" is different: "Humanity is taken as the formal principle of [man], which is the *quod quid erat esse*; just as animality is taken as the principle of the genus, and not the genus; rationality, the principle of difference and not as the difference." This difference between the principle of something and thing of which it is a principle leads Aquinas to distinguish different senses of nature in light of the various modes in which a nature can be related to things. Accordingly, he writes:

Now humanity, to this extent, is not entirely the same as man, since humanity implies only the essential principles of man, and excludes all of the accidents. For humanity is that by which a man is man. Now, none of a man's accidents is that by which a man is man, hence all the accidents of a man are excluded from the signification of humanity. Now this very thing that is a man is what has the essential principles, and that in which accidents can be present. Hence, although a man's accidents are not included in the signification of [the term] 'man,' yet 'man' does not signify something separate from accidents; and thus 'man' signifies as a whole, humanity signifies as a part.[44]

In this text, the fact that the term 'humanity' excludes accidents from its signification, which was the very same fact that led Aquinas to posit a real distinction between supposit and nature, is also seen as the underlying difference between the abstract and concrete senses of nature.

## Theological Applications

The previous sections have established the philosophical reasoning behind the claim that the supposit and its nature are really distinct. In the re-

---

43. Thomas explicitly indicates that he is developing the argument found in Aristotle's text. "Sciendum est etiam ad evidentiam eorum, quae dicta sunt."

44. *In Metaphys.*, VII, l.5,1379. "Humanitas autem pro tanto non est omnino idem cum homine, quia importat tantum principia essentialia hominis, et exclusionem omnium accidentium. Est enim humanitas, qua homo est homo: nullum autem accidentium hominis est, quo homo sit homo, unde omnia accidentia hominis excluduntur a significatione humanitatis. Hoc

mainder of this article I would like to demonstrate the importance of this distinction in Aquinas's thought by highlighting a few of its more important theological applications. In fact, this distinction plays an important role in Aquinas's account of divine simplicity, the Trinity, and above all his Christology. The crucial roles that this philosophical distinction plays in such a wide variety of theological contexts demonstrates that this topic warrants much more detailed attention than it has been given by Aquinas scholars thus far.

Since each of these theological problems is treated several times throughout Thomas's career, I will limit my attention to texts from the *Summa Theologiae*. On this issue, the *Summa* is representative of earlier works, insofar as nothing in other parallel texts undermines my arguments here.

*Divine Simplicity*

Discussion of Aquinas's treatment of divine simplicity has tended to focus on the claim in I, q. 3, a. 4, that being and essence are the same in God, but really distinct in creatures. However, it is important to note that in the *Summa* this issue is engaged only after Aquinas has shown in a. 3 that God is the same as his nature. This article demonstrates that God is the same as his nature by showing that a supposit is distinct from its nature only in substances composed of matter and form. This is proven making use of the philosophical argumentation we have discussed above. Arguing that God is the same as his essence or nature, Aquinas states:

In order to understand this we must note that in things composed of matter and form, it is necessary that the nature or essence differ from the supposit. Since essence or nature includes in itself only those things that fall under the definition of the species, just as humanity includes in itself those things that fall under the definition of man; for by these man is man, and this is what humanity signifies, that by which man is man. But individual matter, with all its individuating accidents, does not fall under the definition of the species. For this flesh and these bones, or whiteness or blackness, or anything of this sort does not fall under the definition of man. Hence this flesh and these bones, and accidents designating this particular matter, are not included in humanity. Yet they are included in the thing that is a man. Hence, the thing that is a man has in itself something that humanity does not have. On account of this, man and humanity are not entirely the same.[45]

---

autem ipsum quod est homo, est quod habet principia essentialia, et cui possunt accidentia inesse. Unde, licet in significatione hominis non includantur accidentia eius, non tamen homo significat aliquid separatum ab accidentibus; et ideo homo significat ut totum, humanitas significat ut pars."

45. *ST* I, q. 3, a. 3 c. "Ad cuius intellectum sciendum est, quod in rebus compositis ex ma-

Aquinas goes on to argue that in substances that are not composed of matter and form, the forms are, obviously enough, not individuated by matter. Rather, in such substances the forms themselves are *supposita subsistentia*, subsisting supposits. Consequently, in these cases the supposit and the nature do not differ.

In the overall context of Aquinas's defense of simplicity the real distinction between supposit and nature plays an important role. In *Prima pars* q. 3, Aquinas moves from the merely negative conclusion that God is not a body to argue that he is not composite in any way. After showing that God is not composed of matter and form, Aquinas then argues that God is his essence. It is at this point that the distinction between supposit and nature in creatures, and the lack of such a distinction in God, comes on the scene. Only once this has been proven is Aquinas in a position to deal with the fundamental metaphysical question of the identity of being and essence in God. Consequently, the argument from the real distinction between supposit and nature in *Prima pars* q. 3 plays a transitional role in the move from the comparison between God and material substances to the consideration of the divine *esse* as such.

The Trinity

While the distinction between a supposit and its nature can be applied to God's simplicity in straightforward manner by affirming their identity in simple substances, the application to the Trinity is not so easy. Indeed, the Trinity is problematic in this respect because the divine persons or supposits are multiplied, but the divine essence is not. On the standard orthodox position that Aquinas holds, God is three persons, but retains one unified essence or nature. Aquinas points out that some resolved this difficulty by asserting a distinction between God's essence and the divine person. Given the discussion of simplicity above, it is no surprise that Aquinas does not

---

teria et forma, necesse est quod differant natura vel essentia et suppositum. Quia essentia vel natura comprehendit in se illa tantum quae cadunt in definitione speciei, sicut humanitas comprehendit in se ea quae cadunt in definitione hominis, his enim homo est homo, et hoc significat humanitas, hoc scilicet quo homo est homo. Sed materia individualis, cum accidentibus omnibus individuantibus ipsam, non cadit in definitione speciei, non enim cadunt in definitione hominis hae carnes et haec ossa, aut albedo vel nigredo, vel aliquid huiusmodi. Unde hae carnes et haec ossa, et accidentia designantia hanc materiam, non concluduntur in humanitate. Et tamen in eo quod est homo, includuntur, unde id quod est homo, habet in se aliquid quod non habet humanitas. Et propter hoc non est totaliter idem homo et humanitas." Cf. *SCG*, I, 21; *Comp. Th.*, c. 10.

## Distinction between Supposit and Nature 103

adopt this solution. Rather, he tries to resolve the tension through a closer analysis of relations. Relations in creatures are merely accidental. However, in God the relations that constitute the divine persons are "the divine essence itself." Accordingly, there is no distinction between nature and the person or supposit in God. Yet, there is a real distinction between the three persons:

> For person, as was said above, signifies a relation as subsisting in the Divine nature. Now relation as compared to essence does not differ in reality, but only by reason; but as compared to an opposed relation, it possesses a real distinction *(realem distinctionem)* in virtue of that opposition. And thus one essence remains, and three persons.[46]

Consequently, each of the divine persons is really identical with the divine essence and in this manner divine simplicity is preserved, while each of the persons is really distinct from the others because of their mutually opposing relations.

What is interesting about this use of the distinction is that it enters into Aquinas's Trinitarian theology not as a solution, but as a problem. In this case the real distinction between a supposit and its nature in creatures, and their consequent identity in God, highlights the need to find a way to reconcile God's simplicity with the Trinity. As we have seen, Aquinas carries out this project through an analysis of the relations that constitute the divine persons.

### Christology

Aquinas's Christology is rooted in the declaration of the Council of Chalcedon (c. AD 451).[47] With respect to Christ, the decree of Chalcedon requires at least two things. First, it demands that the *integrity* of the both the human and divine natures after the union be respected. The union can-

---

46. *ST* q. 39, a. 1 c. "Persona enim, ut dictum est supra, significat relationem, prout est subsistens in natura divina. Relatio autem, ad essentiam comparata, non differt re, sed ratione tantum, comparata autem ad oppositam relationem, habet, virtute oppositionis, realem distinctionem. Et sic remanet una essentia, et tres personae." Cf. *In I Sent.*, d. 34, q. 1, a. 1.

47. "The Chalcedonian Decree," in *Christology of the Later Fathers*, ed. Edward Rochie Hardy (Philadelphia: Westminster Press, 1954), 373. Also important is Cyril of Alexandria's third letter to Nestorius (ibid., 349–54). On St. Thomas's knowledge and use of Chalcedon, cf. G. Geenen, "En marge du Concile de Chalcédoine. Les textes du Quatrième Concile dans les oeuvres de Saint Thomas," *Angelicum* 29 (1952): 43–59. On the historical circumstances of the council and the accuracy of Cyril's interpretation of Nestorius, cf. Aloys Grillmeier, *Christ in the Christian Tradition*, vol. 2, trans. James Bowden (Atlanta: John Knox Press, 1975).

not come about through any mingling or confusion of the human and divine natures. Each remains what they are. Second, Chalcedon requires that there be a *unity* of these two natures, such that they are natures of one and the same thing, that is, the divine person or supposit.

St. Thomas's Christology strives to preserve both these features coherently. In medieval terminology this problem is often referred to as the problem of the "mode of union." As the more recent phrase "hypostatic union" suggests, the difficulty is presented in terms of the supposit or hypostasis in which the two natures are united.

In his attempt to show that Jesus Christ retained fully human and divine natures in the unity of the divine supposit or person, Aquinas bases his explanation on the real distinction between nature and supposit in material beings. The central text is worth quoting at length:

> 'Person' signifies something other than 'nature.' For nature signifies the essence of the species, which the definition signifies. If nothing could be found added to those things that pertain to the character of the species, it would not be necessary to distinguish the nature from the supposit of the nature (which is the individual subsisting in that nature), because every individual subsisting in the nature would be entirely the same as its nature. But in some subsisting things it happens that something is found that does not pertain to the character of the species, namely accidents and individuating principles: just as appears most clearly in things composed from matter and form. *And thus, in such things nature and supposit differ in reality, not as though they are something entirely separate, but because in the supposit the very nature of the species is included, and some other things are added that are beyond the character of the species. Hence the supposit is signified as a whole, having the nature as a formal part perfective of it.* And on account of this, 'nature' is not predicated of a supposit in things composed of matter and form: for we do not say: "this man is his humanity." But if there is a thing in which there is entirely nothing else beyond the character of the species or its nature, just as in God, there supposit and nature do not differ in reality, but only according to our manner of understanding; since we say 'nature' insofar as there is a certain kind of essence; but we say 'supposit' insofar as there is a subsisting thing. And what was said of the supposit, must be understood of the person in a rational or intellectual creature, since person is nothing other than an individual substance of a rational nature, according to Boethius.[48]

---

48. *ST* III, q. 2, a. 2 c. "Respondeo dicendum quod persona aliud significat quam natura. Natura enim significat essentiam speciei, quam significat definitio. Et si quidem his quae ad rationem speciei pertinent nihil aliud adiunctum inveniri posset, nulla necessitas esset distinguendi naturam a supposito naturae, quod est individuum subsistens in natura illa: quia unumquodque individuum subsistens in natura aliqua esset omnino idem cum sua natura. Contingit autem in quibusdam rebus subsistentibus inveniri aliquid quod non pertinet ad rationem speciei, scilicet accidentia et principia individuantia: sicut maxime apparet in his quae

The article has the following structure:

(1) Definition of nature as a thing's essence or the specific difference (from a. 1);
(2) Principle: There is no distinction between the supposit and nature in a thing that has nothing added to it beyond the species;
   (a) Some subsisting things have something beyond the species (e.g., composites of matter and form). In such things, supposit and nature do differ *secundum rem*, though not as if they were entirely separate. Rather, the supposit includes both the nature and other things (e.g., accidents) not determined by the nature; and
   (b) In cases such as 2a the supposit is taken as a whole and the nature as a formal part perfective of it;
(3) Therefore, the nature is not predicated of the supposit in these cases; i.e., we do not say 'Peter is his humanity.'

In this argument the real distinction between the supposit and its nature applies, since Christ qua man is a material being: a real individual man with a human body and soul. Like any other man his supposit is really distinct from his nature. Indeed, it is this distinction that allows Aquinas to maintain both the *integrity* of the two natures and their *unity* as demanded by the Chalcedonian decree. Since the nature and the supposit are really distinct, Aquinas can hold that Christ's human nature is genuinely human and not divinized by some intermingling with the divine nature. The distinction also allows him to hold that it is the divine supposit, the person of the Son, that has the human nature, for this nature remains really distinct from the person. Thus, Aquinas is able to present a coherent Christology precisely because of the philosophical distinction between a supposit and its nature.

---

sunt ex materia et forma composita. Et ideo in talibus etiam secundum rem differt natura et suppositum, non quasi omnino aliqua separata: sed quia in supposito includitur ipsa natura speciei, et supradduntur quaedam alia quae sunt praeter rationem speciei. Unde suppositum significatur ut totum, habens naturam sicut partem formalem et perfectivam sui. Et propter hoc in compositis ex materia et forma natura non praedicatur de supposito, non enim dicimus quod hic homo sit sua humanitas. Si qua vero res est in qua omnino nihil est aliud praeter rationem speciei vel naturae suae, sicut est in Deo, ibi non est aliud secundum rem suppositum et natura, sed solum secundum rationem intelligendi, quia natura dicitur secundum quod est essentia quaedam; eadem vero dicitur suppositum secundum quod est subsistens. Et quod est dictum de supposito, intelligendum est de persona in creatura rationali vel intellectuali, quia nihil aliud est persona quam rationalis naturae individua substantia, secundum Boetium."

## Conclusion

In this article I have argued that Aquinas holds that there is a real distinction between the supposit and its nature in all composite substances. This distinction is established through a philosophical argument that points to the fact that any individual material substance will have attributes beyond those that are included in the principles of its nature. Moreover, I have shown that this distinction plays a central role in Aquinas's arguments for divine simplicity, the Trinity, and the union of the human and divine natures in Christ. In light of this evidence, it seems clear that this is an issue that warrants much more attention than it has received to date. If we are to reach a clear understanding of Aquinas's philosophy and his approach to these key theological issues, it is necessary to recover a full understanding of this theory of the real distinction between the supposit and its nature in composite substances.

PART II

# NATURAL THEOLOGY

*Ralph McInerny*

# From Shadows and Images to the Truth

IN HIS ENCYCLICAL *The Gospel of Life,* John Paul II wrote that "a new cultural climate is developing and taking hold, which gives crimes against life a *new and—if possible—even more sinister character*" (n. 4). Later in the same letter, having documented this claim, he said the following: "This reality is characterized by the emergence of a culture which denies solidarity and in many cases takes the form of a veritable "culture of death." This culture is actively fostered by powerful cultural, economic and political currents which encourage an idea of society excessively concerned with efficiency" (n. 12). Elsewhere, the pope has pointed to the paradoxical fact that there is a false humanism that leads to the inhuman treatment of others, a notion of freedom that leads to slavery. Only a true humanism, one that sees man as made in the image and likeness of God, provides a stay against the developments here condemned. That is, the root of the problem is atheism.

Is the pope alone in this dire estimate of the culture in which we live?

## Read My Apocalypse

There is of course a vast literature of apocalyptic estimates of where modern culture was taking us. Contemporary with the excesses of the French Revolution, wise heads saw where it was heading; Joseph de Maistre, Chateaubriand, Alessandro Manzoni, Edmund Burke, and the later Tocqueville come to mind. In recent years, recognition of the failure of the Enlightenment has become commonplace. T. S. Eliot, George Steiner and, of course, Alasdair MacIntyre have driven this lesson home.

Eliot's postwar essay *Notes on A Definition of Culture* lent its name to the lectures in which George Steiner's *In Bluebeard's Castle* (1971) and John Carey's *The Intellectuals and The Masses* (1992) have been prominent entries. And Northrop Frye revisited Oswald Spengler in a 1974 essay.[1] People my age will remember the many years during which Toynbee's *A Study of History* was a premium for joining the Book of the Month Club. Not unlike Spengler, Toynbee sought a kind of law for the rise and fall of civilizations. Recently, Jacques Barzun proved to be a cautious Cassandra in *From Dawn to Decadence*, whereas E. Michael Jones in his *Libido Dominandi* was anything but a timid Torquemada. But John Paul II has pointed to the basic cause of the culture of death: the absence of God, atheism.

While ideas have consequences, it would be difficult to establish a strict causal relation between developments in philosophy and the shape of culture. Doubtless the traffic between them goes in both directions. Nonetheless, it is not daring to see the way in which developments in philosophy have fostered what the pope calls the culture of death. Seemingly abstruse developments in moral philosophy soon voided ethical judgments of objectivity or truth value, save as reports on the state of mind of the speaker.

A century ago, G. E. Moore in *Principia Ethica* argued that value judgments are unmoored in any true facts about ourselves and the world. They float free of the describable world in an autonomous realm, and it is simply fallacious to think that our evaluations are underwritten by factual truths. Since previous moral philosophers had held that when we say of a book that it is good it is facts about the book that are taken to justify the judgment, Moore's divorce of fact and value was widely considered to consign all prior moral philosophy to the trash bin of history. Of course he had his predecessors, but it has been de rigueur in philosophy since Descartes to earn one's spurs by parricide, dismissing the past as irrelevant. It was not only the aesthetes of Bloomsbury who found the alleged naturalistic fallacy attractive. A case can be made that it haunted twentieth-century moral philosophy, certainly of the dominant Anglo-American kind. By the time Peter Geach pointed out the relevance of the distinction between attributive and predicative adjectives, thereby convicting Moore *et sequaces ejus* of what might be called the grammatical fallacy, the influence of Moore was entrenched. But it was A. J. Ayer in his sassy little book *Language, Truth and Logic* who linked moral and theological statements under the rubric of meaningless

---

1. Northrop Frye, "Spengler Revisited," in *Spiritus Mundi* (Markham, Ontario: Fitzhenry and Whiteside, 1991), 179–98.

propositions devoid of truth or falsity. Judgments of good and evil were at best expressions of the emotions of the speaker. What MacIntyre has called universal emotivism became a cultural fact, a mainstay not only of academics but of most pundits and writers of letters to the editor. Any suggestion that one's moral judgments had a claim on others was regularly taken to be incipient tyranny, as indeed it is—if emotivism is true.

The marriage of emotivism as a metaethical theory and atheism found its best expression in Jean-Paul Sartre's little postwar essay *Existentialism Is a Humanism*. It is worthwhile to recall how Sartre compared theism and the atheism he himself embraced. For the theist, man is a creature of God endowed by his maker with a nature or essence that is antecedent to his moral decisions. Moral judgments, for the theist, are grounded in human nature, which functions as the source of criteria for human flourishing, for what is permissible and what is forbidden. In Sartre's lapidary phrase, for the theist, *essence precedes existence*. That is, what we are provides a measure of what we ought to do. There have been atheists who thought that God and religion could be set aside and things would go on pretty much as before, morally and politically speaking. Sartre dismisses this. If God is denied, if there is no creator, there is no human nature. There is no antecedent source for judgments of what I ought do or not do. There are no given limits on my freedom. Atheism is encapsulated in the complementary phrase: *existence precedes essence*. Moral guidelines are freely chosen, and none of them can claim to be rooted in what we are. That is, none of them is true.

More recently, the implications of the epistemological and linguistic turns have been clearly drawn. It is not only moral judgments that are said to have no basis in the way things are; descriptive judgments too are unanchored in the world, the way things are being unreachable by thought or language. We are urged to become strong poets, recognizing that ontological claims are impositions of subjectivity.

Forgive this barefoot trip through the twentieth century. It has been meant to show that dominant trends in philosophy underwrite what the pope calls the culture of death. That culture has its root in atheism.

Of the sixteen documents of Vatican II, the one most often cited by John Paul II is *Gaudium et Spes*, the Pastoral Constitution on the Church in the Modern World. In a first part, the fathers of the council attempt a sketch of the modern mind, which they seek to address. In doing this, they provide what might be called a little treatise on the varieties and causes of atheism. What is the point of the exercise? It is impossible to have a true understanding of the dignity of the human person without a recognition that he is God's creature. In paragraph 19 there is a phrase that fairly lifts off the page. *Atheismus enim, integre consideratus, non est quid originarium.* I suggest this translation: Atheism, taken all in all, is not the default position. Theism is. It is this sentence that provides the text for what follows.

## How Natural Is Belief?

Sarah Miles in Graham Greene's *The End of the Affair* is confirmed in her faith by the arguments of a rationalist intended to show the absurdity of theism. Greene has some fun with arguments for and against the existence of God, and the suggestion is that they matter little either way. Maurice Bendrix tells poor Henry that he has seen a three-legged man on the Common.

"You're joking."

"But prove I am, Henry. You can't disprove my story any more than I can disprove God. But I just know he's a lie, just as you know my story's a lie."

"Of course there are arguments."

"Oh, I could invent a philosophic argument for my story, I daresay, based on Aristotle."

In the novel, arguments have little to do with the great shifts that take place. Miracles provide the motive.

Of course, this is one of Greene's Catholic novels, and it is conversion to Catholicism that is the theme. This suggests a need to distinguish between arguments that play a dispositive role to the grace of faith, on the one hand, and arguments on behalf of the truth of such statements as "There is a God," on the other. There is a fashionable tendency to ridicule both kinds of argument, but if they are ridiculous they must be ridiculous in different ways.

It is the rare religious believer who describes what he believes as nonsense. Sarah Miles ends the affair because she has come to believe in God. *"But what's the good, Maurice? I believe there's a God—I believe the whole bag of tricks; there's nothing I don't believe; they could subdivide the Trinity into a dozen parts and I'd believe. They could dig up records that proved Christ had been invented by Pilate to get himself promoted, and I'd believe just the same. I've caught belief like a disease. I've fallen into belief like I fell in love."*

Faith as *amour fou*. One shouldn't go to novels for theology, of course, nor to theologians for fiction, though Sarah may remind you of some. For one thing, you can't refute a novel.

Trusting others for the truth of things, believing one another, is an ineradicable feature of human life, however annoying it is to a certain kind of philosopher. You couldn't get through the day without accepting the word of others for lots of things, and, given this, it seems reasonable to believe and unreasonable not to. Trying not to believe is one of those philosophical projects that have gotten us into so much trouble. It's not that the project could be carried out and we don't have the heart for it, but that it is madness to undertake the impossible. Of course it would be wrong simply to segue from this into a discussion of religious faith. Why? How does religious faith differ from the garden-variety belief that characterizes our lives?

Content, for one thing. I take others' word for where I was born, who my godparents were, the location of Paris and the cost of a meal in Manila, and the like. Such claims can be checked out, some more easily than others, but there is nothing in what I am told that requires that I accept another's word for it.

Of course there are difficulties here. If you tell me you have a headache and I believe you, that seems unlike taking your word on the location of a bookstore in Niles. I can go to Niles and see for myself, but how could I say you have a headache otherwise than because I believe you? Frowns, groans, bloodshot eyes, a bottle of Advil clutched in your hand? Such signs are an adequate basis for believing you, but of course you could be faking. Epistemologists wary of buying bridges in Brooklyn seize upon this as if faking were the default position. But sometimes one feigns being well, and the symptoms belie the claim. When someone tells you she has a headache, it matters a lot whether you are an intern in ER or an eavesdropper on the bus. Or the spouse of the speaker.

What if you told me that you loved me? This stretches credulity, of course, but it underscores the fact that some things that we believe matter more than others. Why? The price of a Big Yak in Helsinki—or a Big Smack in Oslo—is unlikely to matter much to me one way or the other. That is why, over and above the content of beliefs, we would doubtless want to mention personal involvement or the lack of it in what is accepted. Finding the location of the bookstore in Niles means you need no longer take anyone's word for it. Lovers like to be told, but is their confidence in the other's love just taking his word for it? Unlikely.

One could go on. Let us say that with beliefs of the kind mentioned—those without which human life would be impossible—any one of them could be turned into knowledge, however differently in the case of personal and impersonal beliefs. While it would be madness to want to replace the totality of such beliefs with knowledge, no one of them is such that it *must* be believed. It is the assumption of what is called natural theology that "There is a God" is like the location of a bookstore in Niles and quite unlike accepting as true that Christ is both human and divine and that there are three persons in the divine nature. The difference between the deliverances of natural theology and religious faith is frequently blurred. There are extenuating reasons for this blurring, but for now it is the difference on which I wish to insist.

## Is God Proof-Proof?

A sign of their difference is that pagan thinkers argued for the existence of God but of course had no inkling of the mysteries of the faith. Their arguments may be good or bad, but they seek to lead to knowledge and thus to the replacement of taking God's existence on trust. This is not something that could be said of those arguments meant to commend the credibility of Christianity. The articles of the Creed can only be believed. As Kierkegaard said of Christianity, the simple man does not understand it and the wise man understands that he does not understand it. Like marriage, faith is terminated only by death. Of course the living can lose it, or gain it, but as Greene's characters suggest, neither the gaining nor the losing of it is like taking a trip to Niles to locate that bookstore. One can come to think that an argument previously accepted for God's existence is flawed, or that a supposed flaw in it is not really such, but this is not the same as deconversion from or conversion to Christianity.

It is an oddity of the philosophical turns that I reviewed at the outset that the efforts of only a generation or so ago to disprove theism have given way to a kind of permissiveness. This was one of the things I tried to show in *Characters in Search of Their Author*.[2] Maurice Bendrix in the novel contrasts the passionate disproofs of the old rationalists with the blasé dismissals of Russell and Ayer.

In short, there has been a general devaluation of the range of reason,

2. *Characters in Search of Their Author*, Gifford Lectures Glasgow 1999–2000 (Notre Dame: Notre Dame University Press, 2001).

and this has affected both natural and supernatural theology in unfortunate ways. Believers, relieved that the rationalist siege has been lifted, find it tempting to say that their beliefs are no more false than physics, but of course this means they are no truer either. Such muddleheaded welcoming of the recent loss of trust in reason is not shared by Pope John Paul II in *Fides et ratio*. It is noteworthy that the Holy Father finds it important to come to the defense of reason against the current widespread loss of confidence in it. This tells us something worth remembering about the relationship between reason and religious beliefs. The Church has always been the defender of natural theology, and this defense is essential to discussions of the mysteries of faith.

All the more reason why the loss of confidence in natural theology by Catholic thinkers is a momentous development. Even Thomists have advanced theories that have the doubtless unintended effect of undermining the project of natural theology. Some versions of Christian philosophy also have this effect.[3]

## Two Kinds of Truth about God

I said above that the tendency to identify natural theology and religious faith is understandable. When Thomas Aquinas distinguishes two kinds of truth about God,[4] those that can be arrived at by the normal discourse of reason and those that are accepted on the basis of revelation, it occurs to the reader that the former are a subset of the latter. If the philosopher can prove that there is a God, that there is only one God, that God is intelligent and the cause of all else, he arrives at truths that are embedded in Christian belief. The God of Abraham swallows up the God of the philosopher. If this is so, there seems to be no reason why the believer should be interested in natural theology. He has nothing to gain from it—or so it would seem.

Thomas Aquinas dubbed those truths about God that are naturally knowable the "preambles of faith" and called those accepted only on the ba-

---

3. I develop this in the sequel to my Gifford Lectures, *Praeambula Fidei: Thomism and the God of the Philosophers* (Washington, DC: The Catholic University of America Press, 2006).
4. As in *Summa contra gentiles* I, 3: "Est autem in his quae de Deo confitemur duplex veritatis modus. Quaedam namque vera sunt de Deo quae omnem facultatem humanae rationis excedunt, ut Deum esse trinum et unum. Quaedam vero sunt ad quae etiam ratio naturalis pertingere potest, sicut est Deum esse, Deum est unum, et alia huiusmodi; quae etiam philosophi demonstrative de Deo probaverunt, ducti naturalis lumine rationis."

sis of revelation "mysteries of faith." But the believer can hold both sets on the basis of faith. When you instruct your children in the faith you are unlikely to make this distinction. Religious faith does not repose on arguments of the kind the philosopher constructs. This was Gilson's powerful reminder in *The Philosopher and Theology*. And yet among the things the believer believes is that man can from the things that are made come to knowledge of the invisible things of God. That is, it is a truth of faith that God can be known apart from faith. Is this a contradiction or merely paradoxical?

In commenting on the second verse of Psalm 18 ("The heavens declare the glory of God, and the firmament proclaims the works of his hands."), St. Thomas has this to say: "In the first place God is commended for the teaching whereby he instructs us. There is one that is common and addressed equally to all, and this is manifested by his works. Rom 1,20: *The invisible things of God are known through what is understood.* There is a second that is special, through the law, which is addressed only to the faithful."[5] The reference to Romans is to a text that has played a key role from time immemorial and is cited by Vatican I, which declared the mind's natural capacity to know God to be *de fide*.[6] Thomas in commenting on this text stresses that we are incapable of knowing God in his essence, which is why Paul speaks of the invisible things of God.[7] Man has a natural capacity *(ex lumine intrinseco)* to know God—indeed this is the ultimate point of his existence—yet he is incapable of comprehending the nature of God. He cannot know *what* God is, only *that* he is. Why? Because judgments that God exists are

---

5. "In prima enim commendatur Deus ex sua eruditione, qua nos instruit. Et hoc dupliciter. Una communi, quae se habet aequaliter ad omnes: et haec per opera sua manifestatur: Rom. 1, 20: *Invisibilia Dei per ea quae facta sunt intellecta conspiciuuntur.* Alia speciali, per legislationem, quae est solum ad fideles."

6. "Eadem sancta mater Ecclesia tenet et docet, Deum rerum omnium principium et finem, naturali humanae rationis lumine e rebus creatis certo cognosci posse; 'invisibilia enim ipsius, a creatura mundi, per ea quae facta sunt, conspiciuntur' (Rom. 1, 20)." Denzinger-Schoenmetzer, *Enchiridion Symbolorum Definitionum et Declarationem de rebus fidei et morum*, 36th ed. (Rome: Herder, 1976), n. 3004.

7. "Dicit autem pluraliter *invisibilia* quia Dei essentia non est nobis cognita secundum illud quod est, scilicet prout in se est una. Sic erit nobis in patria cognita, et tunc *erit Dominus unus et nomen eius unum*, ut dicitur Zac. xiii, 17. Est autem manifesta nobis per quadam similitudines in creaturis repertas, quae id quod in Deo unum est, multipliciter participant, et secundum hoc intellectus noster considerat unitatem divinae essentiae sub ratione bonitatis, sapientiae, virtutis et huiusmodi, quae in Deo unum sunt. Haec ergo *invisibilia Dei* dixit, quia illud unum quod his nominibus, seu rationibus, in Deo respondent, non videtur a nobis."—*Super Epistolam ad Romanos Lectura*, lectio 1, n. 117, in *Super Epistolas sancti Pauli lectura*, ed. P. Raphaelis Cai, O.P. (Turin/Rome: Maritetti, 1953).

grounded in created perfections that are incommensurate with their cause. Only if some creature, or the whole of creation, exhausted the divine causality could it provide a means of knowing God in himself.

This is not the place to mount a defense of natural theology, however essential that defense is. Let us say that I had world enough and time to make that defense. After your applause died away, an uneasiness would likely set in. You might think of your Uncle George, who hasn't a philosophical bone in his body. You might think of yourself on most days. If theism depends on one's being a philosopher, the mass of mankind seems placed on the margin of the discussion. That sentence I cited from *Gaudium et Spes*, indeed Paul's remark in Romans, does not seem relevant only to the class of professional philosophers and the subclass among them who have retained confidence in natural theology. They do not marginalize Uncle George.

## Is Theism Elitist?

Proofs of God's existence and the analysis of the divine attributes of the kind that we find in the writings of St. Thomas Aquinas are not the sort of thing often overheard down at McDonald's—unless of course you and your beloved are ensconced in a booth there. Thomas sees the whole of philosophy—for him an umbrella term covering a plurality of disciplines—aiming at theology as its telos and culminating goal. The wisdom that defines philosophy is its ultimate end and philosophical wisdom is preeminently knowledge of God. But this entails that the vast range of human sciences are prerequisites for it, and since in this vale of tears not everyone successfully reaches that term, and they only after long effort, the achievement seems restricted to a few. But that seems to make that text from Romans applicable not to everyone, but only to some.

It is this realization that led Thomas to argue for the fittingness of the preambles of faith—naturally knowable truths about God—being included in revelation. The believer has certainty from his mother's knee of truths philosophers reach only with difficulty and when hoary with age. It is fitting that even these truths be objects of his faith because nothing is more important for human life than certainty that God exists. We need to lead our lives when young as well as middle-aged or old in the light of our dependence upon God.

That undoubted consolation, however, is available only to believers. But what of all those who have not the faith and are not philosophers? Is it possible to hold that there is a garden variety of certainty that God exists, short of philosophical proofs and independent of faith? John Henry Newman and Jacques Maritain gave an affirmative answer to that question. But how could such natural knowledge be described?

Jacques Maritain devoted a number of works to the problem of atheism in the modern world, and in *Approches de Dieu*, before considering philosophical proofs he writes of a natural pre-philosophical knowledge of God. At the heart of his suggestion is what he calls the intuition of being, which can be read as a version of that wonder which is the trigger of philosophizing. But Maritain dwells on wonder in its pre-philosophical form, which he calls virtually metaphysical. He speaks of the sudden awareness that comes to all sooner or later of existence, one's own and that of the world in which one is. In being overwhelmed by the existence of a thing I become aware of my own, and, Maritain suggests, there is a natural transition, virtually argumentative, to the cause of it all. And Maritain further suggests that this is what Paul meant in Romans 1:20, a realization that is common to all.

Well, that is a large topic. Thomas Aquinas once said that nothing is easier to know than that God exists, but he added immediately that such a realization is compatible with thinking that God is a tree or the sun or, as might be said nowadays, the Force. Newman's approach was through conscience and is in many ways more appealing than Maritain's. The intuition of being may seem recherché, but every person acts, deciding between this or that, looking for the right thing to do. Newman is interested in conscience here not in terms of judgments that this or that is right or wrong but rather as the sense of answerability, of responsibility, that is lodged in moral decision. Answerability to whom? Reflection on this question leads, Newman suggests, to the recognition of God.

However one describes it, there seems something right in these efforts to recognize a common pre-philosophical awareness of God's existence. Surely Maritain is right in saying that Paul was not restricting his claim to philosophers. And *Gaudium et Spes*, as I indicated, makes a similar assumption.

## Christian Philosophy

Secular philosophers, whether nonbelievers or believers who feel they must put their faith in escrow when they think, have often claimed that any influence of religious faith on philosophizing turns it into something other than philosophizing of the standard sort. I have dealt with this accusation on a number of occasions and do not propose to do so again now. But robust believers often adopt a complementary accusation, claiming that for a believer the whole project of natural philosophy is rendered otiose. For a believer, the question of God's existence is definitively settled, and any effort to prove it is taken to involve a fundamental misunderstanding, if not the assumption that religious faith as such can be derived from philosophical arguments. To attempt to cross the chasm from sinful man to God smacks of Pelagianism or worse.[8] Standing athwart this incipient fideism is the clear teaching of Romans 1:20. It is possible for natural and sinful man to come to knowledge of God from the things that are made.

I mentioned earlier Thomas's view that the preambles of faith, naturally knowable truths about God, are part of the package of revelation, however embedded in the distinctive mysteries proposed for belief. Of course, this could be taken to mean that while pagans, unaided by revelation, can arrive at knowledge of those truths, the believer who holds them on the authority of God revealing no longer needs to engage in natural theology. Of course it is true that certainty about these naturally knowable truths about God is had by the believer from his faith. It is not as if he is required first to do natural theology and, on that basis, accept the mysteries of faith. Surely the task of natural theology is not incumbent on every believer; still every

---

8. Interestingly, Thomas Aquinas, in a passage to which Russell Hittinger draws attention in *The First Grace: Rediscovering the Natural Law in a Post-Christian World* (Wilmington, DE: ISI Books, 2002), seems to share this misgiving. Commenting on Romans 2:14, in which St. Paul speaks of the Gentiles doing naturally what is of the law, Thomas says this: "Secundo commendat in eis legis observantiam, cum dicit *naturaliter faciunt quae sunt legis,* id est, quae lex mandat, scilicet quantum ad praecepta moralia, quae sunt de dictamine rationis naturalis... [n. 215]. Sed quod dicit *naturaliter,* dubitationem habet. Videtur quod patiocinari Pelagianis, qui dicebant quod homo per sua naturalia poterat omnia praecepta legis servare. Unde est exponendum est *naturaliter,* id est per naturam gratiam reformatam. Loquitur enim de Gentilibus ad fidem conversis, qui auxilio gratiae Christi coeperant moralia legis servare.—Vel potest dicit *naturaliter,* id est per legem naturalem ostendendum eis quid sit agendum, secundum illus Ps. iv, 7 s. *Multi dicunt: Quis ostendit nobis bona? Signatum, etc.,* quod est lumen rationis naturalis, in qua est imago Dei. Et tamen non excluditur quin necessaria sit gratia ad movendum affectum, sictu etiam *per legem* est *cognitio peccati,* ut dicitur infra 3, 20, et tamen ulterius requiritur gratia ad movendum affectum." The passage concerns the moral order and says that, when it comes to *observing* (not when it comes to knowing) the natural law, the will must be moved by grace. Knowledge of the precepts of natural law is a matter of nature, not of grace—though the reception of grace can buttress this knowledge. *A fortiori,* natural knowledge of God is independent of grace.

believer must hold that such truths about God are naturally knowable. And, if that is so, the believer has a powerful incentive to show that such truths about God can be known, and the successful outcome of that inquiry is important for showing that the acceptance of truths about God that cannot be proved is a reasonable thing to do. How is this shown?

If some of the things that God has revealed about himself can be known to be true, and thus are intelligible, it is reasonable to hold that the mysteries of faith too are intelligible in themselves, however obscure to us. This is not of course an argument for the truth of the mysteries of faith, such truths as the Trinity, the union of natures in Christ, and so forth. But however pious it may seem to be, the suggestion that the mysteries of faith bear no relation to what can be known leads to fideism. In its most outré form, fideism would hold that nothing naturally knowable counts for or against the acceptance of the mysteries of faith or even that what we know is in conflict with what we believe.

It is when there is such a conflation of preambles and mysteries that the project of natural theology will be denied. The believer rightly rejects the suggestion that what he believes, that is, the mysteries of faith, could be established on the basis of arguments of the usual sort. But if not everything that has been revealed is a mystery and some revealed truths about God can be known, they are not of faith *(de fide)*, certainly not in the same sense. It was St. Thomas's conviction that pagan philosophers had proved such truths about God that led him to ask why such knowable truths had been revealed. We have already mentioned his argument for the fittingness of this.

## Envoi

There are many reasons for the loss of confidence in reason and in the project of natural theology, the culminating achievement of philosophy. I will end by considering merely one of them. In repudiating natural theology the objector often deplores the suggestion that God can be reached by syllogisms, and "syllogisms" becomes almost a sneer. The suggestion is of an austere, bloodless, impersonal use of reason that could not possibly engage the wellsprings of human assent and action. The thinking that enters into the lives of human beings involves more than logical connectives and may seem to lack all formal elegance. This is an objection worth reflecting on.

No doubt it is true that there are arguments in which the arguer does not figure as an element, and proofs for the existence of God are like that. For all that, arguments are fashioned by flesh-and-blood human beings and are elements in their biography. That Euclid fashioned a given proof may seem the very paradigm of a *per accidens* truth. Nonetheless, he is the author of the *Elements* every bit as much as Shakespeare—or the Earl of Oxford—is the author of the plays, and, hidden as it may be from us, the biographical underpinning of such efforts is essential to their getting done. Are proofs for the existence of God any different? Surely, the defining desire to know what it's all about, a desire that is personal as well as merely intellectual, is the motor for the search for the prime mover. Perhaps we are too influenced by the exiguous description many contemporary philosophers give of their task. It is almost as if disembodied minds were engaged in activities that bear no relation to the hopes and dreams of those whose minds they are. But syllogisms float on a sea of presuppositions which do not enter formally into them but without which they would never be fashioned.

Arguments are disparaged in *The End of the Affair*, but even one who runs as he reads will be struck by the large role that arguments play in the novel, in the dialogue, in Maurice Bendrix's thoughts. Arguing against arguments reveals the inescapable human setting of intellectual activity. And after all, natural theology, as the telos of philosophy, is the wisdom the love of which keeps the philosopher at his desk. The love that moves the sun and all the stars moves his fingers across the keyboard of his computer, and if he is successful he will come to know that.

John Paul II reminded us that without the recognition that there is a God our difficulties are insoluble. For us that question, through no merit of our own, is settled by the faith we have received. But among the tenets of that faith is that God's existence can be known from the things he has made. Natural theology is a difficult business in which our reach must seem to exceed our grasp. For all that, God is inescapable. Flee him as we might, the Hound of Heaven is on our trail. I am not given to invoking Kant, but there is for everyone the reminder of the moral law within and the starry heavens above. Let the psalmist have the last word. *Caeli enarrant gloriam Dei, et opera manuum eius annuntiat firmamentum.* "The heavens declare the glory of God, and the firmament proclaims the work of his hands" (Psalm 18:2).

*Leslie Armour*

# Re-thinking the Infinite

IN MANY WAYS, though not in all, the high points in Western natural theology remain the works of Thomas Aquinas and John Duns Scotus. St. Thomas defined the task of natural theology, and Duns Scotus exposed much of its logic. Aquinas's philosophy was provoked by a number of developments that put great strains on the Platonic thought that had been the vehicle for Christian theology almost from the beginning. Arab science and the philosophy of Aristotle came into the West together and provoked a major crisis in thought. A new kind of concern with the natural world was thus one ingredient. Philosophers talk less about it, but the flourishing economy of the high Middle Ages provided another ingredient.

From Augustine to Bonaventure (who was Thomas's contemporary) the Platonic tradition in Western thought emphasized a kind of otherworldliness—a concern with the eternal against the temporal, with the truths of reason rather than the data of the senses, and with the next world rather than this. Without abandoning the notion that human destiny is tied to God, that this world leads on to the next, and that the overindulgence of the senses may lead to damnation, Christian theology had to cope by

---

This chapter began life as my St. Thomas Lecture at St. Thomas University in Fredericton, New Brunswick, given on January 26, 1995. Since that time it has been extensively revised but never published. Conversations with Lawrence Dewan, several about early versions of this paper, have sustained my interest in St Thomas over the years. This paper is a small tribute to him in recognition of a valued friendship and of his ability to keep these important questions alive and interesting. But he bears no responsibility for the opinions here. Much of the research was done under a grant from the Social Sciences and Humanities Research Council of Canada. I am grateful to Ms. Suzie Johnston not only for her research work under that grant, but also for many long discussions. No doubt important ideas originated with her, though she is not responsible for either my opinions or my mistakes.

Augustine's time with the new concern with the present world. From the perspective of my enquiry here, Thomas's most important thought had to do with the transformation of the all-transcendent infinite into a series of precisely defined and unlimited powers of God and with the attempt to tie our knowledge of God to our knowledge of this world. These developments became the foundation of most subsequent natural theology. They remain a major intellectual concern in our own time, but they do so in a special kind of intellectual tension. This tension, I shall argue—though not everyone would agree with me—was in any case present from the beginning in St. Thomas's thought.

## The Debate about the Infinite

In the period leading up to 1250 there was a dispute as to whether God could be infinite by nature, that is, in essence, or only in his powers. Some took the view that he could not be infinite in essence because then finite beings could not grasp the essence in the beatific vision. Aquinas and Bonaventure both believed that God could and must be infinite in the traditional sense of being by nature beyond all categories, but they also took the view that his infinite nature is expressed through unlimited powers, especially omnipotence and by extension omniscience. Perfection perhaps belongs to his essence.

Aquinas insisted that one begins with the infinite nature of God and infers his powers. We do not grasp the divine essence, but we do understand that God is infinite and we can see how this infinity can be expressed in the divine powers. Bonaventure worked the other way around, inferring the infinity of the nature of God from the divine powers. He explains in his *Itinerarium* how the soul's journey to God leads us along a path of explanation.

Thus in many ways the question of God and the world was as central and as puzzling as it is today. Indeed, it may help to clarify the issues if we begin by asking how the situation appears now. In the philosophy journals, natural theology is alive and well. It is even living in Paris and enjoying what Dominique Janicaud has called "le tournant théologique."[1] But, though it

---

1. See Dominique Janicaud, *Le tournant théologique de la phénoménologie française* (Paris: Éditions de l'Éclat, 1991). The leading figures are probably Emmanuel Lévinas and Jean-Luc Marion. Janicaud thinks they jump too quickly into theological explanations, but the movement is a strong one, and it continues.

may thrive in the seminar rooms (and perhaps even in a few cafes where the more serious young philosophers gather), it struggles for existence in the larger world. Certainly among people in the streets, in North America and in Europe, there are believers, but they are found more and more often in the pews of fundamentalist churches whose overseers place little stock in the search for answers to our most fundamental problems by purely natural means.

It is certainly not true that people have given up on all kinds of natural knowledge. Philosophers know that there is always a case for skepticism, but in fact ours is an age of credulity. Just now we cannot make ourselves immortal, or find a rational economic system or halt the headlong plunge of much of the world into war, ever-greater poverty, and chaos. Some discouragement is evident, yet plenty of people in white coats expect that solutions are just around the corner. Apart from a few physicists like Paul Davies,[2] though, they do not expect to come home from a day in the laboratory or the observatory with fresh news about the divine.

The reasons for the problems people find with natural theology are more subtle than one might think, but I suggest that the situation is a serious one. For, despite the declining strength of the older and larger religious denominations in Europe and North America, over the globe as a whole people do not seem to be getting less religious. And every day people die because, when they can't reason together about what divides them and often matters most to them, they are very likely to fight.

This is to say that, when knowledge—or rather the conceptual structure within which it is used—and our fundamental intuitions and basic emotions clash, the result tends to be an emotion-driven fundamentalism. It shows itself not only in religion but also in politics. Eric Voegelin's writings are laced with warnings about what he calls the new gnosticism—the thesis that one has some inner knowledge that will solve all problems.[3] Nazism and Fascism were (are?) emotion-driven gnostic fundamentalisms as much as the Islamic republic of the late Ayatollah Khomeini and still fighting Taliban of Afghanistan. But the gnostics include not just the people denounced

---

2. See Paul Davies, *The Edge of Infinity* (London: Penguin, 1981); *God and the New Physics* (New York: Simon and Schuster, 1983); *The Mind of God* (New York: Simon and Schuster, 1992); and Paul Davies and John Gribbin, *The Matter Myth* (London: Penguin, 1992).

3. See Eric Voegelin, *From Enlightenment to Revolution* (Durham, NC: Duke University Press, 1975).

hourly by the newspaper editorialists. There are free market fundamentalists, people who think that a market economy solves all problems (and who have not been to Eastern Europe or to Watts lately).

This is nothing new. Aquinas, Bonaventure, and Scotus, too, lived at a moment of increasing worldliness and a period when, despite our popular beliefs about the Middle Ages, there was a strange mixture of credulous superstition and crass ecclesiastical politics that encouraged worldly men and even women to buy their way into heaven. Many deeply religious men and women sought refuge in orders as clearly separated from the world as possible and consecrated themselves to lives of prayer and contemplation. By contrast, the Franciscan and Dominican orders (to which Aquinas, Bonaventure, and Duns Scotus belonged) were founded to go out into the world and preach. But they took it as axiomatic that they must reintroduce rationality into religion if they were to overcome a world of emotional indulgence without falling back solely on the inner life of prayer and contemplation. Only reason, they surmised, could respond to emotion, and their rallying points were the great universities, especially Oxford and Paris.

## Concepts of God

I shall argue that the trouble then and now was and is not so much with knowledge as with our concept of God and with our willingness to avoid certain issues that are, at bottom, logical. In particular it is my argument that we need (as they did) to think through very carefully the concept of the infinite and its relation to the finite. If we are to piece together the shattered bits of our notions of science and theology, we must see the finite and infinite as indissolubly interrelated.

One must concede at the beginning that in the monotheist traditions of the Near East and Europe, religious sentiment and rational natural theology exist only in tension. Religious sentiment tends to emphasize the distinctness of God. Rational natural theology must always look for the connections between God and the world.

The possibility of natural knowledge of God is invariably puzzling. Such knowledge must be unlike knowledge of rock formations in New Zealand or the dimensions of the planet Neptune. It seems to many people that knowledge of God is positively incommensurate with knowledge of these mundane kinds. One does not discover God with the microscope, the telescope or the stethoscope. Does the fact that most of the universe consists of cold empty space and that the rest of it is frequently too hot for intelligent life make it less likely that God exists? Does the fact that many cosmologists think they cannot see beyond an initial event in the history of the universe that has been dubbed the "big bang" make it any more likely that God exists?

A logically complete separation of our idea of God from our ideas about the world makes natural theology ultimately unintelligible. The clues to a workable natural theology must lie, if they exist at all, in the relation between the finite and the infinite. I shall claim that, if one gets the problem about the infinite straight, many difficulties disappear, and natural theology becomes a possible enterprise.

The blockage in our thought is not, it turns out, in our scientific pictures of the world, but in the logic of our accounts of the relation between God and the world. As they were often understood, the most popular cluster of arguments from nature to God produced a logical impasse and a moral disaster.[4] For their proponents mostly regarded the incommensurability of the two kinds of knowledge as an advantage. They held that the existence of God was demonstrated precisely by the finitude and inadequacy of our natural knowledge. Natural theology was used to plug the holes when ordinary knowledge ran out. Thus, when philosophers and theologians with a taste for reasoning saw that scientific explanations tended to run backward through an unintelligible infinity of causes and effects, they argued that this weakness could be made good by a God who sustained the whole chain of causes and who, therefore, must stand outside them.

## God and the World

What they missed was the connection between the world and God. Unless there is a relation of logical necessity between the truth of some propositions about the existence of God and the truth of some propositions about the world, the argument proves nothing.[5] But how can one get from the

---

4. Such arguments are commonly called "cosmological" to distinguish them from purely logical arguments.

5. Notice, however, that it is not required that the propositions expressing facts about the world should be logically necessary. That would produce a disaster for both science and theology. It is required, though, that there be some propositions such that if they express a fact about the world then some proposition expressing a fact about God also must be true.

facts about the world to such a logical necessity if God is quite other than the world and stands outside it?

A mysterious God unconnected to the world explains nothing—sometimes because such a God explains too much. Those who thought that one could use God to plug the holes in our natural knowledge wanted to say that God is so unlike the other components of reality that, whereas any ordinary thing or event can be used to explain only a special selection in the world, God can explain everything. Ordinary things, since they have only a limited subset of the properties that the world can exhibit, can explain only those other things to which they have special connections. But the infinity ascribed to God enables God to be the explanation for everything. Infinite means unlimited in one way or another, and the kind of infinity ascribed to God is having a nature from which the possession of properties that imply unlimited powers follows necessarily.[6] Omniscience, omnipotence, and perfection form a trio. Omnipotence is the power to do anything or at least anything possible. Omniscience is unlimited knowledge. To have perfection is to lack nothing.

Inevitably, such unlimited powers produce paradoxes. If God is omnipotent, then he is free, since freedom is a possible power. But if God is omniscient he knows what he will do for ever and ever. If he knows what he will do, can he be free to do something else?

These are problems. But the most shattering truth that traditional practitioners of natural theology tend to forget is that whatever can explain everything explains nothing. If the ultimate explanation for everything is that God wills it, then there is no explanation for what God wills. But unless one knows that God wills some things according to a principle and knows what the principle is, the words "God wills it" have no more meaning than that "it happens." There is no advantage in replacing a mysterious infinite regress with an equally mysterious reference to the will of God. An infinite regress may be vicious, but an unprincipled will is unintelligible.[7]

If one does know the principle, then the explanation is in that principle. God wills it perhaps because it is good, but then it is the good that explains the world—as Plato and Iris Murdoch thought.[8] Admittedly, if God is so

---

6. This is not to say that infinity is, as Locke thought, a negative concept. But one must be careful to say just how the unlimited expresses itself.
7. Thus St. Thomas holds that will and intellect are inseparable in God (*Summa theologiae* [hereafter *ST*] I, 19, 1) and never wholly unrelated in us—a position that compels him to face up to the problems I am outlining here.
8. See *Metaphysics as a Guide to Morals* (London: Chatto and Windus, 1992).

powerful that everything that happens is necessarily due to him and is necessarily the way it is—if he is the only possible explanation and he does everything he does because it is his nature to do it—then "God wills it" does add something to "it happens," for then it seems that what happens is necessary.

## A Moral Disaster

But either way, we have a moral disaster. If everything can be explained by reference to what God decides (whether he decides necessarily or not), then God must answer for everything. Such a God, since he is all-powerful, must be what George Holmes Howison called a "moral monster."[9] Things happen either because God wants them to or because he lets them. The mere existence of a God who explains everything and is therefore responsible for everything makes us all puppets in a horror play in which a Calvinistic God juggles with the meaningless lives of those whom he has already saved or damned. Such a God is somehow beyond the world, but some of his properties are imagined to be in it, and the proponents of such views thought they could establish a hierarchy of things by determining the extent to which created beings were like God. The relative places of angels and men was a disputed matter—giving Milton the plot for *Paradise Lost,* in which angels rebelled in the name of the principle of seniority after a man was given pride of place over them—but human beings, especially male ones, came next, and animals well after them. Plants were better than dirt and grime mainly because they were useful.

The Calvinistic horror story has been with us for a long time,[10] but recent events have conspired to make the idea of a God who controls everything and orders everything hierarchically seem (if possible) even more shocking. If a God who really controls everything exists and yet permitted the Holocaust or the atom bombing of Hiroshima (and still more of Nagasaki, which many people believe to have been an event designed only to see if the dif-

---

9. In fact it was the Absolute of Josiah Royce—God deliberately de-anthropomorphized and rendered as friendly to science as possible—that Howison was concerned about. See his notes entitled "Steps in My Critique of Royce," University of California, Berkeley, Bancroft Library, C-B 1037, typescript, 7.

10. John Calvin's *Institutes* appeared in 1536. His is the name usually associated with the most deterministic account of "predestination," though Martin Luther held much the same view and expressed it a few years earlier.

ferent, bigger bomb worked), must not the universe truly be run by a moral monster? And if human beings are created in the image of God and yet can commit mass murder, trample animals into oblivion, and turn rainforests into rivers of mud, must not the image of God be either a truly evil thing or else completely inefficacious? Admittedly we may have been corrupted by original sin, but if the image of God is consistent with such obvious corruption, how trustworthy is the God whose image we bear?

Such considerations must certainly give us pause for thought. Even if we can get matters straight, has not the concept of God been so muddied and muddled by philosophers and theologians that it should be abandoned?

St. Thomas never wanted any part of the Calvinistic horror story, but many people would blame him for an important part of these muddles, especially for the separation of God from the world in a way that finally makes natural theology unintelligible, and for a kind of hierarchicalism that follows from convictions about a God who orders everything and needs no cooperation from the world.

## A Different Thomas?

I shall argue that we can find in St. Thomas's writings the seeds of a position that will rescue us from these muddles. Admittedly, we always find him struggling with the balance between religious sentiment and rational natural theology, and not all the answers or even all the clues are in his writings, but there are few issues that he fails to illumine.[11]

One may conclude that either his critics or his conservative defenders are right. Or one may conclude that the foreshadowings of what I think are the solutions are to be found in St. Thomas. But everyone should begin any inquiry into natural theology by looking at St. Thomas's work. About the need for natural theology he was blunt: "Faith presupposes natural knowledge even as grace presupposes nature, and perfection presupposes something to be perfected."[12]

There are many claims to divine revelation, and they cannot all be true. The claims that they are true must be among those consistent with our natures in the sense of our potentialities as knowers, they must be intelligible,

---

11. Feminists think he is usually wrong about women, but he does make a point of insisting that the risen Jesus chose to appear first to a woman, Mary Magdalene: see *ST* III, 55, 1 ad 3.
12. *ST* I, 2, 2 (Reply to Obj. 1).

and they must lead us beyond our ordinary knowledge by some path we can follow. To be intelligible a doctrine has to be consistent with natural reason. If it contains a formal contradiction, then it is useless. For from P and not-P one can deduce the truth of Q, whatever Q might be. Everything is either P or not-P, so if they are both true, all propositions are true. If both P and not-P, then I am the king of New York. And there is no king of New York.[13] What is more, genuine revelation, if it exists, must lead us from what we know in a direction that we can actually follow and understand.[14]

Could it be that God exists, but that no natural knowledge of him is possible? It could be so if, as Calvin thought, our reason is so deficient that we can really know nothing without divine assistance; or perhaps we could have no knowledge of God if God turned out to be like Lewis Carroll's Boojums. Calvin thought that the fall of man had so damaged all our faculties that we could no longer reason our way to any knowledge, but his claims about the deficiency of reason would imply that no particular beliefs are ever more soundly based than others.[15] This would include beliefs that we have received by divine revelation, and Calvin could not accept such a view.

13. It could be asserted, of course, that the principle of non-contradiction does not hold. Graham Priest has argued that it does not; he says that the argument that everything follows from "P and not-P" is "no better than an appeal to received semantics." But to assert both P and not-P is pointless; if one does, then any assertion one makes can be countered by another assertion, denying it, and the counter-proposition will have exactly equal weight. François de le Mothe le Vayer held that such skepticisms offer a good defense of religion, for they leave one free to believe what one chooses. But one can do that anyway. There are, of course, other difficulties with Priest's thesis. Chief among them, perhaps, is that we get our terms into discourse by assigning them some predicates and withholding others. This process seems to break down if we deny the principle of non-contradiction. Certainly, many apparent contradictions are not really contradictions, and one can explore other kinds of logical tension. Priest gives credit to "Hegel and some of his intellectual descendants" for exploring this line of thought. But he quickly gives up trying to follow it. I have explored this idea myself in *Logic and Reality: An Investigation into the Idea of a Dialectical System* (Assen/New York: Royal Vangorcum and Humanities Press, 1971). Priest is mainly concerned with particular issues, the apparent contradictions that emerge as we approach and pass beyond the "limits of thought."

14. These universal truths—"not both P and not-P" for instance—are only skeletons on which actual reasoning hangs. Actual reasoning brings to bear the complexities of experiences. The experiences themselves have complexities and ambiguities that the "universal forms" do not necessarily capture. See Armour, *Logic and Reality*. Any argument that has bite must finally return to the particularities of experience.

15. Alvin Plantinga claims that the denial of the need for rational natural theology was one of the great forward steps of the Reformation. Plantinga specifically says that Calvin and others abandoned the doctrine that there was or could be adequate evidence for the existence of God, and held instead that such a belief required no evidence. Thus the heirs of the reformers have been freed from tiresome arguments with people like Bertrand Russell. Plantinga specifi-

Could God be a Boojum? Boojums, you will recall, are a special sort of Snark. The trouble with Boojums is that if you meet one you disappear. There is, therefore, in principle, no knowledge of Boojums. But even this does not quite suffice. For knowledge to be impossible it would also have to be true that God, or the Boojum, made no difference to the world. We cannot see electrons, much less quarks, but we can see their traces in bubble chambers. We cannot, perhaps, see God, but could God leave no trace? God must make a difference to the world. Whether God must have created a world is a much harder question, but if there is a world, God cannot both play a role in reality and make no difference to it. That is part of what is meant by "God," and it is also part of what is meant by "electron." If electrons made no difference to anything else, they could not exist. Whatever has a role in reality has some properties and lacks others.

"Exists" comes from a Latin verb that means "to stand out." In various senses electrons "stand out"—that is, they play a fundamental role in certain sorts of explanations. But "exists" in English seems to imply a thing among things. I shall argue that there cannot be a God who is a thing among things. At this point in the argument "plays a role in reality" is the best we can do.[16] In so doing, it prevents anything else from having just those properties in just that way—for if any two things are really different, they must differ, and that means they must not have all their properties in common.[17]

---

cally mentions Russell and, of course, W. K. Clifford, who thought that it was immoral to believe what one has no evidence for. But among beliefs that require no evidence, one is as good as the other. Plantinga admits that we might thus come to believe in the Great Pumpkin, but he says we have no "natural inclination" to believe in it. People do, however, have natural inclinations to believe in gods who seem to tell them to go out and kill people with differing beliefs. See Plantinga's essay "On Taking Belief in God as Basic" in *Classical and Contemporary Readings in the Philosophy of Religion*, ed. John Hick (Englewood Cliffs, NJ: Prentice Hall, 1990), 484–99, reprinted from *Religious Experience and Religious Belief*, ed. Joseph Runzo and Craig Ihara (New York: University Press of America, 1986).

16. "Exists" in English seems to imply a thing among things. I shall argue that there cannot be a God who is a thing among things. At this point in the argument "plays a role in reality" is the best we can do.

17. The argument shows that one of four propositions is true: (1) Some being is necessary; (2) the range of possibilities is finite; (3) the number of moments of lapsed time is less than aleph null (the smallest infinite number); or (4) the theory that holds that any possibility always has a probability of greater than zero but less than one is false. One must be careful, too, just how one talks about the necessity of diversity. Leibniz spoke of the "identity of indiscernibles" but, as McTaggart pointed out, he should have spoken of the "dissimilarity of the diverse." The first makes it seem as if two things we can't tell apart from each other must be the same thing. But anyone who dates twins will suspect that this is false. If we do find that two things are diverse, though, we can be sure that they differ in some way.

How, then, does St. Thomas see our problem? According to one view—which I shall question—the Thomistic natural world forms a single, connected causal chain that leads us back either to an infinity of similar causes or to a first cause. Since infinities in this sense are vicious, Aquinas believes that natural reason leads us to opt for the notion of a first cause. Remember that I am expounding a view that is thought to be St. Thomas's yet that is inadequate to his writings. But, even now, it is true that everyone would admit that there are two reasons for the viciousness of such infinities. One is that they suppose that something—call it a causal impulse—has passed through an infinity of points in space and time to get to us. But nothing can traverse an infinite series. You cannot count from one to aleph null. The other reason for thinking that infinite regresses of this sort are vicious is logically even more troubling: such infinite explanations get you nowhere. However far back you go you still need another event, and so all your explanations are hollow. It is as if there were ten men roped together climbing a mountain—only no one has his pick in the rock. On the same kind of reading, St. Thomas rounds up the remaining logical issues in his presentation in two neat little arguments, the second and third "ways" of proving the existence of God. The second way reminds us that it is not just the causal impulse in time that should trouble us but also the question of the dependence of contemporaneous things on one another. Efficient causes cannot be infinite in number at a moment of time either. The third way introduces us to something very important, the idea of an infinity of possibilities or of a world with the potentiality for an infinity of events, and suggests that if everything were contingent and there was an infinity of time, then nothing would exist. One of the possible states of affairs is one in which nothing exists. In an infinite series every possible state of affairs must turn up at least once. For to be possible is to have a probability of greater than zero. So sooner or later the possibility that represents emptiness will turn up.[18]

18. The notion of possibilities as independent logical entities plays a more important role in modern philosophy than it generally did in the thirteenth century. St. Thomas usually talks of potentialities in the Aristotelian sense, in which something is possible if it is a potential state of something that already exists. But St. Thomas clearly uses the notion of possibility in *ST* I, 25, 3, where he says, "a thing is called possible or impossible absolutely according to the relation in which the very terms stand to one another—possible if the predicate is not incompatible with the subject." In *ST* I, 2, 3, the celebrated "third way" of demonstrating the existence of God comes very close to using the modern notion—if we take "possible" to mean "absolutely possible" in the sense of I, 25, 3. If we do, St. Thomas's proposal can be read with the aid of modal logic as a powerful argument.

Therefore, on this view, St. Thomas paints his first cause as the pickax in the rock, the boundary to infinite dependence, and the one absolute necessity in a world with many contingencies.[19] This may not be—is not really, I shall argue—the view of St. Thomas, but if it is, then it is just this puzzling representation of the relation between necessity and contingency that, I argue, gives rise to the problem. The rock on which everything hangs has to be perfectly stable, unmoving, and capable of explaining everything. This is God conceived as infinite in one sense of infinite, the God of unlimited powers.

Here it seems the world depends on God and God does not depend on the world. Certainly it is often true that P implies Q while Q does not imply P. To be a professor, I hope, implies literacy, while, luckily, not all literate people are professors. But the problem here is that the God of unlimited powers belongs to a wholly different realm or order of things and also has no apparent logical connection to the world. If such a God exists and created the world, the creation of the world seems purely fortuitous. It is a piece of good luck—or bad luck if you think the world isn't up to much.[20] But good luck and bad luck are not explanations. We usually explain our good luck or bad luck by reference to probabilities. We know the odds on getting snakes eyes in the next throw in a crap game. We could use the God who is supposed to emerge from this argument as an explanation only if we knew that such a being had a tendency to create worlds, and we could learn something about the world only if we knew that such a God was likely to create a world of a certain kind. But if God belongs to a wholly different mode of being, beyond all natural knowledge, we cannot have any such knowledge unless we get it by special revelation.

## Digging Deeper into Thomistic Thought

If we read a little further into the *Summa theologiae*—as far as question 7—we find that St. Thomas does find himself more deeply involved with the question of the infinite. Just how is the infinite related to the finite? He then

---

19. Of course there are many different kinds of "necessities," some of which arise only in a created world. But these are necessary relative to the world that exists.

20. G. H. Hardy, the Cambridge mathematician, is said to have envisaged a God who was troubled to learn that, while all the rest of the universe was clean and sterile, our planet had a curious fungoid phenomenon called life.

tells us that being has two forms: finite and infinite. And he says that it is the forms on which we should concentrate. The infinite is the only contrary of the finite.

There is a vital logical issue here that must give us pause. Suppose you wonder what words like "red," "yellow," "blue," and "green" mean. Someone might point at things that are yellow and say "yellow" each time. But that wouldn't teach you the meaning. For you would have to know the nature of the thing pointed at. The things pointed at successively might add up to some geometrical shape, say a dodecahedron. Or the things might be ordered in space so as form a curve and you might think "yellow" was the name of the curve. To get the meaning you would have to know that yellow was what W. E. Johnson called a "determinate" of the "determinable" coloredness and that being colored was one of the ways of occupying a spatial surface.[21] Spatial surfaces in turn are determinate forms of the determinable spatiality (and perhaps of others as well). As one mounts the determinate-determinable ladder, one arrives at more and more general properties.

Being is one of the limiting points in all sets of determinate-determinable hierarchies, for every characterizable mode of reality has being. Now St. Thomas says that in *one* dimension or way of ordering the world, there are two and only two forms of being: finite and infinite.[22] Notice that every determinable has more than one determinate. Not everything can be "red." If everything were red, then being red and being colored would be the same thing and "redness" (as opposed to coloredness) would be a redundant term.

No characterizable mode of reality can be both infinite and finite or neither. St. Thomas puts it this way: matter, for example, cannot be infinite, for it must have some form, which in giving it shape, puts a limit on it. So it is with all the things we can imagine.[23] The source of these limits is the infi-

---

21. W. E. Johnson, *Logic*, Part 1 (Cambridge: University Press, 1921).

22. There are many dimensions of being, and it is St. Thomas's view that being, like other divine predicates or properties, is, in a sense, shared with the world: the being we have is not the being God has, though it is not unrelated to it either. This is St. Thomas's way of—amongst other things—dealing with the problem of how God is related to the world. He is thus able to establish a relation while keeping the two separate. Duns Scotus thought that this wouldn't work—that one doesn't really get God into the world in a way that makes natural theology possible. But it depends on how one develops the metaphysics of analogy.

23. And not just "things." The infinite is a characterizable mode of reality but not another thing. St. Thomas does not say it is a thing at all.

nite. God is Infinite Being in this sense.[24] When we were talking about the impossible infinite causal chain, we might have been tempted to ask, "What caused God?" But now we see that we can't pose this question. For the infinite, in this sense, can have no cause. Otherwise it would be finite.

Notice, though, that the infinite can be spoken of only insofar as it does limit the finite. St. Thomas says "a thing is called infinite because it is not finite."[25] The two are inextricably intertwined. Understanding the infinite is thus an essential part of understanding the finite—and vice versa.

Many people would want to read St. Thomas as holding that the infinite might have existed alone. God, they think, did not need to create the world even though there is no way in which there could be any manifest divine activity if there were no world.

But what St. Thomas insists upon in the passage I cited is that it is the form of the infinite that gives rise to finitude. If he is right, it could not otherwise exhibit itself as a form—even to itself. In his discussion of life in God (a fascinating topic that deserves an essay to itself) St. Thomas says both that "Life is in the highest degree properly in God"[26] and that "to live is nothing less than to exist in this or that nature."[27] But to exist in a particular nature is, of course, to be manifest in some world, ours or another. Either it is necessarily true that God is manifested in some world or it is not necessarily true that God has life. St. Thomas does not tell us which, but I rather think he believed that life was a necessary property of God and not just something that God chose to have. Assuming that this is true, it does not mean, of course, that Thomas thinks that God had to create *our world* or *any* particular world, but only that life is intrinsic to God and must be manifested.

Can we put the case more simply? If there are determinates of any determinable, there have to be two. Without the finite there would be only being, but not infinite being, for infinite being and being would be the same thing. God is the infinite that emerges as determinate in the created world.

---

24. *ST* I, 7, 1. To put it in St. Thomas's own words: "Form is not made perfect by matter, but rather is contracted by matter; and hence the infinite, regarded on the part of the form not determined by matter, has the nature of something perfect. Now being is the most formal of all things, as appears from what is shown above (I, 4, 1, Obj. 3). Since therefore the divine being is not a being received in anything, but He is His own subsistent being as was shown above (I, 3, 4) it is clear that God Himself is infinite and perfect."

25. *ST* I, 7, 1. Again this does not imply that infinity is a negative concept.

26. *ST* I, 18, 3.   27. *ST* I, 18, 2.

Notice that this account of the infinite provides us with an argument for the existence of God, but one quite different from those that at any rate form the first two of the "five ways" as they are usually read.

This argument, though, gives us a clue about how they might be read. What is being urged is that nothing can be a thing in the world—a material object for instance—unless it is limited. One finite thing can limit another, of course, but what can limit all finite things? Only an infinite. This infinite must be quite different from the one we imagined as the infinity of a God with literally unlimited powers. It turns out, indeed, that such an idea is only an imprecise approximation. We now have an infinity that cannot be expressed as the sum of any set of finite predicates whatever. The logic of the argument is given a new sense, too. What is being claimed here is that the concept of limited things is unintelligible without a concept of what limits them but has no limits itself. The claim is that, if one principle has application, the other does too. But beware. This infinity is not expressible in terms of the traditional predicates assigned to God. Omnipotence and omniscience are particular forms. The infinite that is the nature of God is beyond all that. Notice that this makes sense of St. Thomas's insistence that the infinity of God is not simply an infinite of predicates but an infinity that belongs to the nature that is expressed through those predicates. This is the central burden of question 7, article I, of the *Summa theologiae*.

An obvious logical problem arises here. Is not being infinite just another predicate? If not, how are we to understand it? Notice that there are always three issues involved in the analysis of standard propositional forms such as "All Xs are Ys and if anything is an X, then it is a Y" or "Some Xs are Ys" and "There is an X such that X is Y." There is the question of the assigned predicates (the Ys), the question of the subject to which the predicate is assigned (the Xs), and the question of how X has Y (is it contingently, possibly, or necessarily?).

## Noticing a Key to St. Thomas and Duns Scotus

A way of summarizing St. Thomas's position is this: he thinks that the ultimate subject (X) is God. In general all other Xs are creatures of God, and so they can be analyzed out into predicate sets. There is an exception for human beings because they are capable of knowledge, and in a sense the whole world can be replicated within their knowledge. So we are like God—created in the image of God—in the sense that creation can be expressed in and through us, and so there is a spark of real subjectivity within us. The limit is that we cannot grasp the infinite essence of God. God has at least certain of his predicates—those that best express his infinity—by necessity, and there are other necessities in the world, although creation generally expresses the contingency that comes from being creatures of God.

The infinite must also work through us. Crucially, James H. Robb says: "There seems to be something even contradictory in speaking about spirit as finite."[28] He associates the agent intellect, whose role it is "to make the species [of things] actually intelligible," with the infinite. Intelligible being that is the object of any intellect and the infinite is not merely the sum of finite elements.

Robb admits though that there are many texts in which St. Thomas speaks of the human being as finite. And in some sense we are, or at least we have a finite aspect. But St. Thomas insists that forms that are not embedded in matter are in a qualified sense infinite even though only God is infinite without qualification.[29] As Norah Willis Michener notes: "Man can through his intellect know—and hence intentionally become—all things."[30]

The argument I suggested about how finitude and infinity imply one another actually follows a form developed a little later by Duns Scotus, an argument that depends on a principle that is called, if you like impressive names, the reciprocity of the disjunctive transcendentals.[31] This principle in turn has its roots in the work of a thirteenth-century philosopher who was both St. Thomas's coworker and his opponent, St. Bonaventure. This way of looking at things also has roots, of course, in the work of John the Scot, who held, as we saw, that God is involved in all possible categories and that all the categories of being are mutually implying.[32]

These problems came to fruition in the work of another Franciscan, Duns Scotus, and what Duns Scotus said was that there are some properties that characterize everything. But some of them are not simple but complex properties that come in pairs. Every characterizable mode of reality is either

---

28. *Man as Infinite Spirit* (Milwaukee: Marquette University Press, 1974), 4.
29. See *ST* I, 7, 2 objections 2 and ad 2.
30. *Maritain on the Nature of Man* (Hull: Éditions L'Éclair, 1955), 53.
31. In *Ordinatio* I, 39.
32. For a discussion see Ewert H. Cousins, *Bonaventure and the Coincidence of Opposites* (Chicago: Franciscan Herald Press, 1978). John the Scot's *Periphyseon* has been translated by I. P. Sheldon-Williams (Montréal: Bellarmin, 1987).

finite or infinite, for instance. Nothing can have the property that we know about directly (finitude) unless there is some other mode of reality—unless, that is, something is infinite. This enables us to infer from our experience of the finite to the reality of the infinite. But, as a matter of logic, it also works the other way given certain premises.

Duns Scotus believed strongly in the univocity of being. There is one kind of being though it appears in many forms.[33] So what appears as finite being must also be an expression of the infinite being. If there must be two determinates of being, they must share the same being. St. Thomas generally did not want to have the divine being shared literally, and so he held that our being is only an analogy of God's being. But the form that the infinite gives to things—the form that comes from the power of the infinite to limit—is in some sense the divine form.[34]

Thus he goes as close as he can to telling us how what is a principle in God will be a principle in the world. In *Summa contra gentiles* he says, "In willing himself, God also wills other things," though he hesitates to take this position in the *Summa theologiae* where he backs over the line and says, "He understands things apart from Himself by understanding his own essence" and "the will of God is not moved by another but itself alone."[35] Between the connections of God to the world envisaged by Duns Scotus and those envisaged by St. Thomas there is a fine line.

St. Thomas hesitates to entangle God in the world in any way that would seem to limit the divine independence, but the expressions of God un-

---

33. *Ordinatio*, I, 3.

34. Thus he says, "God exists . . . in all things . . . as agent." But he also says, "God is in all things innermostly." *ST* I, 8, 1. For God to be in all things "innermostly" and "according to its mode of being" the doctrine of analogy has to admit that there is some likeness of forms.

35. *Summa contra gentiles* [hereafter SCG] I, 75, 1; *ST* I, 19, 2 (Reply to Obj. 2) and I, 19, 1 (Reply to Obj. 3). Still, I am inclined to believe that when one puts together the whole of St. Thomas's philosophy the tension tends to be resolved in favor of the view that the divine principle leads necessarily to some natural world that is good. Father Lawrence Dewan disagrees. Like me he thinks that St. Thomas moved to resolve the tension between the needs of natural theology and the religious sentiments of Western monotheism, but he thinks Aquinas is finally satisfied with the independence of God. He and I would certainly agree that St. Thomas stops short of making any particular act of creation necessary to God. I simply think St. Thomas might finally agree that there is something in the divine nature that must be manifest in some world or other, for he would certainly oppose the notion of an unprincipled will. What I want to argue in this paper, though, is just that St. Thomas clearly exposed the problems that surround this question and set in train a line of thought that St. Bonaventure, Nicholas of Cusa, and others pursued and that leads to the conclusion I think is right. I am grateful to Fr. Dewan for extended discussions of the question.

der determinate forms are not limitations on God. The logic of the case is, again, that a God quite apart from the world must fail to function as its explanation. The existence of God will explain too little if we think that the separation is truly complete, or it will explain too much if we offer the divinity as a kind of supervenient cause that overrules all other causes and is radically different in kind from those in the natural order of things. If it is offered as something that can fill any explanatory gap whatever, then it can be used whenever we want, and God explains both everything and nothing. "God wills it" becomes "it happens."

St. Thomas is, it seems to me (though not to everyone), edging away from this intellectual disaster—the final shipwreck of natural theology. He still says that God explains the finite world because his infinite being is the limit to the finite. What God allows therefore will be. God is, however, involved with the world. It is an expression of divinity, and God would be quite different without a world. For God would lack an element in the divine self-expression. Yet the finite things in the world have their own being. Each has shape and takes on an explanatory power of its own.[36]

Even so, it has still been tempting for readers of St. Thomas to conclude that this God is responsible in a Calvinistic way for the whole of creation, and in the sixteenth century "Calvinist" became a term of abuse that Jesuits hurled at their Dominican opponents. (The Dominicans in turn threw "Pelagian" at the Jesuit friends of Suárez and Molina.)

## There Is No Mold for God

Let us be careful, however. The infinite being is not just the obverse of the totality of finite beings; the infinite God, the form of forms, can be fitted into no mold. Aquinas puts it starkly enough. When he talks about how the universal properties that shape the world get into existence he talks about the forms as "being received" by something that is informed. But he says, "The divine being is not a being received in anything."[37]

This overflowing infinite plays a vital role in the thought of Nicholas of Cusa, who envisions that the finite and the infinite are truly incommensurate but that each must figure in the other in a union of the opposites. It was

36. "There does not fall under the scope of God's omnipotence anything that implies a contradiction." *ST* I, 25, 4. He adds: "some things are not subject to His power" (Reply to Obj. 2).
37. *ST* I, 7, 1.

not perhaps until Descartes's *Third Meditation* that the infinite as whatever it is whose description overflows all possible predicates is suddenly (and without any explanation on the part of Descartes)[38] contrasted with the infinite that simply possesses specifiable powers in an unlimited form. Aquinas does want to talk about God as simple, immutable, eternal, and unified, but each time he explores one of these properties he brings us back to the notion that these are the properties of a being who fits no mold. Thus he says "the expression simultaneously-whole is used to remove the idea of time and the word perfect is used to exclude the now of time."[39] God thus is not a specially powerful and intelligent thing in the world—not a sort of celestial Pierre Trudeau with a Turing machine, the computer that can compute everything.

Such a God is rather an unlimited source, a fountain of being that both feeds and responds to the world, for the argument is that finite and infinite are inseparable and unintelligible without one another. Because the infinite can never be encompassed by the world and each finite thing has a kind of distinctness that the infinite does not have, the world acquires a measure of independence.[40]

But the world gets this independence only through the action of an infinite that is always expressed through particular things. St. Thomas is aware of the fine lines one must draw in talking about such matters, but he reminds us that some things even God does by the necessity of his nature. "He [God] wills something of absolute necessity. The divine will has a necessary relation to the divine goodness."[41] *He adds that God does not will everything by necessity.*

---

38. Most of Descartes's readers do not yet seem have grasped that there are four infinities mentioned in the *Third Meditation*.

39. *ST* I, 10, 1 (Reply to Obj. 5).

40. Thus Duns Scotus worried about *haecceitas*, the "thisness" of things that is not a property of the infinite but only, as Nicholas of Cusa might say, the dialectical outcome of the formation of the finite by the infinite. The independence of the world is especially marked by St. Thomas's notion of the relation between the infinite and the "removal of time," something that makes clear that the infinite cannot be another thing among things.

41. *ST* I, 19, 3. Here is another tricky issue. We can again see St. Thomas struggling, trying to sustain as much as he can of the magisterial independence of God—and yet doing justice to the God who must be involved in the world. Lawrence Dewan has pointed out ("St. Thomas, God's Goodness, and God's Morality," *Modern Schoolman* 70 [1992]: 45–51) that we can hardly know that God has a duty to the world, for this implies a kind of relation that could not exist, at least in St. Thomas's picture of the world. But we can say, of course, that God does invariably what is suitable, and that he does it because it is his nature to do so. Father Dewan would resist

Such a view accords well with a scientific picture that now allows for uncertainty principles and stochastic processes and enables us to explore the complex interconnections between knowledge and reality. We should remember that the mechanical efficient causes (which form the chain that runs from the mysterious first cause, through all time, and down to us on the usual reading of St. Thomas's "first way") have been replaced, interestingly, in our science, by what should properly be called formal causes. We no longer think of nature as a push-pull affair. Rather we think of nature as unfolding against a background of probabilities that give form to events. We admit, now, that nature is changed by our knowing it, and cannot be understood apart from us.

As our view of the infinite changes, the hierarchical elements begin to fade. The origins of this shift are deeply rooted in the writings of John the Scot and St. Bonaventure, who believed that women and men are equal, and in the Franciscan tradition that animals are not merely something to be manipulated by us. If a God emerges from a sensible view of the infinite, it is not a tyrant God who orders things in an arbitrary way.

As we develop this notion of the infinite, are we parting company with St. Thomas? Perhaps, but let us hear what he has to say. First, about necessity and contingency, he is very clear. When he comes to talk about divine providence, he says, "Divine providence imposes necessity upon some things; but not upon all as some formerly believed.... The effect of divine providence is not only that things should happen somehow, but that they should happen either by necessity or by contingency."[42] God knows, in some sense, everything that will happen. God does predestine men and women. But St. Thomas explains that he means by predestination the direction of "things towards their end"[43] and that "free will is not destroyed."[44] He insists that God does know how many are saved, but he tells a curious story about this: he says it is like the affairs of kings. Though one may lose the crown, we know that another will gain it, so we always know there is a king. So it is, he says, with God and the saved. The divine plan requires that there be saved

---

the conclusion that there is a logical necessity involved, but it would seem to be a contradiction to say that God acts contrary to his own nature—for what it is to be God is to have a nature that acts in a certain way. St. Thomas does not think God can evade logic, but he is inclined to emphasize the uniqueness of the divine nature. But see the discussion that follows.

42. *ST* I, 22, 4.  43. *ST* I, 23, 1.
44. *ST* I, 23, 6.

men and women just as political plans require that there will be a king. But God can intervene by adding new characters to the cast, so that if some are lost, others are added.[45]

Attention to his actual words calls into question the whole way in which his various remarks about the hierarchy of the universe have usually been understood. This questioning becomes overwhelming if we take seriously a passage from his other *Summa*, the *Summa contra gentiles*. The important section is headed: "That the perfection of the universe required the existence of some intellectual creatures."[46] The theme he expounds is Neoplatonic, but it is not at odds with the main thrust of his work. He thinks all intellectual creatures are very close to God. And they are important because they can know things, and through their knowledge the things of the world are transformed so that, as he puts it, they can return to God. Things known are intelligible and thus can form part of the divine mind.

It may puzzle us that St. Thomas thinks such creatures are necessary to God. But he says: "The existence of some creatures endowed with intelligence was necessary in order that the universe of created things might be perfect." It would seem contrary to the nature of God to deliberately create imperfection. Though he could of course have chosen different modes of the perfection of the world, creatures with intellects must necessarily figure because they alone, having been created, can return to God. But things are not returned to God unchanged. For, in knowing, we enable ourselves to act, and in acting we once again replicate a power that is God's.

In knowing things, we transform them in a way that makes them capable of playing a role in the working out of the divine plan for the world. Knowledge therefore changes the world, and, through it, things have a different perfection. St. Thomas calls it a second perfection, which things can attain insofar as they are known. "Each and every creature returns to its source in so far as it bears a likeness to its source, according to its being and its nature."[47] And he reminds us that "God's intellect is the principle of the production of creatures."

Surely, we must think, God could do this without any help from us. But not so. For what becomes intelligible through our knowledge is the existence

---

45. *ST* I, 23, 6.
46. *SCG*, II, 46.
47. It is important to notice that being and nature are both involved and mentioned. The nature of the thing is given in its properties. But it is the particular mode of being of intellectual entities that gives them their creative power.

of things in and of themselves, as distinct from God. In creating them, God knows them as a principle of the divine nature. In sharing in our knowledge God knows them as distinct. The world, if it is to have objective existence, requires the cooperative activity of a community. People are not known by God without knowing themselves.

## Perfecting the Universe

One may well want to separate two questions. One is: given that God decided to create a universe at all, what was needed to perfect it? The other is: did God need to create a universe at all? But they are not really separate questions because we can see from this account of intellectual creatures that God would have failed to bring into reality one of the divine capacities—the capacity to understand things as distinct pluralities—if there had not been a created world. But it is presumably contradictory to say that God might have been in any way less than the God we know, though a different world could have been realized (even, Aquinas thinks, a better one) had God wanted one. Notice that the idea of perfection is the idea of completeness. The perfection of any world is attained when there is nothing missing from it, but the best world—if that means with most good and least evil—might have been one in which there was no freedom. Then it would have lacked something, freedom. Some things, like freedom, may be desirable for the completeness of the universe even if there is a risk of some evil as a consequence.

The Christian God, at any rate, has always been seen as a God in the world, and, despite Peter Geach, it is St. Thomas's position that the world can be perfected only with our cooperation, for the creation of intellectual beings, if not necessary in some other sense, is, Aquinas says, necessary to the perfection of the world.[48] We must know and share our knowledge. The

---

48. Geach claims St. Thomas agrees with him that God doesn't need us. But in *Providence and Evil* (Cambridge: Cambridge University Press, 1977), 124–27, he draws on an argument that he claims to be Spinozist. He says that since God does not change he cannot possibly need us; indeed, we cannot be expected to be loved by him. But this is a confusion. Spinoza's God is "expressed" (a favorite word of Spinoza's) in the world. God has an idea of each of us *sub specie aeternitatis*, and this is the idea of each of us as having as much perfection as we are capable of. The intellectual love of God enables us to understand this, and, as Spinoza says, we do not expect to be loved by a God conceived as an eternal, unchanging being. But we are not complete until we have brought ourselves *sub specie temporis* to the perfection God knows, and God, too, is expressed through the world and thus through us. *Sub specie aeternitatis* God

world has the potentiality for many orders and perspectives, and this aspect of it, logically, can be known only as a plurality.

Having created a world, God needs us in order to achieve its perfection, and the perfected community of human spirits will share in all the expressions of the form of the good. It is this form of the good that St. Thomas calls "the sun of Plato." He says "in our faith, this is God himself."[49]

Lo, the monster god is gone. And you will recall that St. Thomas assures us that God actually lives, by which he means that God partakes in the process of knowing, which St. Thomas likens to the arts.[50] God shares creativity with us and shares in our creativity. We are related to God evidently, then, not as an arrow is related to a bow, but as another subject in our experience with whom we share in a creative activity. Thus Aquinas says: "If natural things, insofar as they are perfect, communicate their good to others, much more does it appertain to the divine will to communicate by likeness its own good to others as much as possible."[51] (Notice the "insofar as they are perfect" which in the case of our communication with God refers to the "second perfection" of things.) The difference between us and God is now one of degree: "Our intellect moves itself to some things, yet others are supplied by nature," whereas God is "that being whose act of understanding is its very nature." Here one finds, I think, the final definition of God that Aquinas is willing to give—"that being whose act of understanding is its very nature."[52] Our understanding always has an object that is apart from us.

---

lacks nothing whatever and needs nothing, but God, too, can be considered *sub specie temporis* (through his expressions that are the world), and in this mode he does need us. In his expressions in the world he becomes, as Whitehead says, "our fellow pilgrim." See Leslie Armour, *Being and Idea: Developments of Some Themes in Spinoza and Hegel* (Hildesheim: Georg Olms, 1992), and "Knowledge, Idea, and Spinoza's Notion of Immortality," in *Spinoza, the Enduring Questions,* ed. Graeme Hunter (Toronto: University of Toronto Press, 1994).

49. *ST* I, 79, 4.      50. *ST* I, 18, 3.
51. *ST* I, 19, 2.
52. *ST* I, 18, 3. Father Dewan, who, as I noted earlier, believes that St. Thomas did not go so far as *I* think he did to tie God to the world, cites the definition that Aquinas gives in I, 2, 3: "a definite kind of thing which for all beings is the cause of being and goodness and of every sort of perfection." I am going to argue that the God of I, 2, 3, is God seen from a human perspective that focuses on sequences of efficient causes in the natural world. God must really transcend this perspective, and the later definition seems to me to make this clear. But, once again, the argument is really that there are in St. Thomas the seeds of a position that is more rational than the one usually ascribed to him. Insofar as philosophers rarely explore the full logical consequences of their positions, they very often see further than they know—for better or for worse.

## Divine Understanding, the Ultimate Causal Force

For God to understand things, of course, is equally for them to be. The ultimate causal forces in the universe are the divine understandings, often represented in St. Thomas as "exemplary causes." Still, because there are other intellectual beings, the world acquires a certain objective distance from God, and that objective distance is what gives us our footing.

We can therefore begin to see how this line of argument may really be associated with the famous lines of argument in the first three of the five ways of demonstrating the existence of God. And when we look at the central meaning of them, we will see, I think, how it all begins to tie in.

We are human beings, and we must start where we are, St. Thomas thinks. We find ourselves in a sensory world in which one of the certainties is that something moves. If nothing moved we couldn't think. We would be stuck in one thought forever.

Furthermore, this movement is distinct from us. We cannot stop all movement, or we can only do so perhaps on pain of death. We therefore begin to look at the world as a chain of movements that we find not to be self-explanatory. It is this that begins to take us out of ourselves.

But we begin to notice that there is a world and that it contains form and content—that is, its potentialities include properties waiting in the wings to be instantiated. If you like to give the idea a modern turn, possibility outruns actuality. Then we see that this objectivity is only relative and that we have a closer relation with the once distant first cause than we originally thought. After all, it takes Aquinas nearly a hundred thousand words to work his way through the thickets of objections between Question 2, in which the five ways appear, and Question 18, in which something is at last said about the living God.

## The Obverse of All the Limiting Finitudes

The hierarchical notion is finally dissolved—it seems to me—when we learn that God appears in our experience as the obverse of all the limiting finitudes and not simply as a master. Insofar as our intelligence extends through the whole of human reason, we are our own masters, for the reason that guides is our own, and there has to be a particular element in it that differs for each of us at least in the sense that it is the nature of providence (or so St. Thomas says) that each of us has a part to play in the universe.[53] Of course our understanding does not run to everything. The infinite of God is beyond our full comprehension.

But though I think St. Thomas did not believe in the moral monster God, we must be careful that this view does not obscure things that, though they may make difficulties for his philosophy, were important to him. It would appear, from what I have been saying, that the human perspective on the world is a localized and temporary one. According to St. Thomas, God does not see the world as a hierarchical system of objects independent of his being. We see it so because we do not fully understand it. But what is the ontological status of this separate objective world in which we live?

St. Bonaventure took seriously what I have been hinting at. For him the objective world is just symbolic. The soul in its journey to God overcomes it.[54] For St. Thomas, the objectified external world is real and has an order and structure that does tell us much about God's priorities. It is not merely to be taken as symbolic.[55] This has serious consequences. If the natural world is symbolic we can understand how the infinite can manifest itself in the finite, just as we can represent infinity in language and in mathematics. If it is not symbolic it is hard to see how finite material objects, taken as ultimately real, can be related to the infinite.

Some of the consequences are more practical. Women and men have different bodies. Did God therefore intend them ultimately for different ends? St. Thomas himself, when he is talking about intellectual beings per se, makes no distinction. John the Scot, who saw the natural world as a complex projection of underlying principles that wrongly created the impression of a separate material world, thought that the difference between the sexes was temporary. In the next world such differences will disappear.[56] St. Bonaventure believed that such differences are only symbolic: gender difference can be overcome, and he insisted on the absolute equality of wom-

53. *SCG* II, 45.
54. For the text see *Tria Opuscula Seraphici Doctoris S. Bonaventurae* (Quaracchi: Typographia Collegii S. Bonaventurae, 1911), 289–364.
55. One commentator, Matthew M. de Benedictis, insists that for Bonaventure all created things should be looked on only as "symbols of something higher and more real." See *The Social Thought of Saint Bonaventure* (Washington, DC: The Catholic University of America Press, 1946; repr. Westport, CT: Greenwood, 1972), 42.
56. *Periphyseon*, 800–807 (in which the physical and spiritual bodies are discussed) and 855D–856A (in which Eriugena sees the masculine and feminine principles coming finally together in a natural union).

en.⁵⁷ The particular form of the body is interesting only insofar as it figures in the story. Bonaventure can make allowances for the illusions of difference that different bodies may present to us, and for the limits of bodily capacity, but this is as far as he will go in departing from claims to equal treatment. St. Thomas believes that such differences in bodies are permanent and eternal and that God intends there to be a distinction.⁵⁸

## A Symbolic World

There are logical and moral advantages to the view that the natural world is symbolic in nature, but one must look carefully at what happens when one develops it. The picture I am suggesting—one close to Bonaventure and Nicholas of Cusa and a foundation for a certain kind of modern objective idealism but farther from St. Thomas's—is the picture of a finite structure whose meaning leads us beyond itself to an infinite that we can know only through these symbolic expressions.

Notice that this is not a subjectivist world. Nicholas of Cusa devotes much of his writing to mathematics. The symbolic structures of mathematics are not subjective inventions. You cannot abolish the number 2. Language is also not subjective. It must meet very stringent objective conditions in order to function at all.

On this view, it is the very nature of reality to be an infinity that is expressible through the finite.⁵⁹ In mathematical terms the series of integers cannot be confined to a finitude, but the infinity they express must always be understood thorough a series of finite expressions.

It is true that on this view God appears in and through the finite world—a view consistent enough with the Christian notion of the Incarnation and

---

57. See Emma Thérèse Healy, *Woman according to Bonaventure* (Erie, PA: Congregation of the Sisters of St. Joseph, 1956). Sister Healy has assembled most of the relevant texts. She does all she can to reconcile Bonaventure and Aquinas but it is still clear that there is a difference between them. Bonaventure was not uninterested in the differences between men and women. He thought that the relative frailty of women might make them more clearly aware of the image of God, for instance. In dealing with these differences he has lapses that every reader will notice, but in the main he takes a stand for the equality of women (cf. de Benedictis, *Social Thought of St. Bonaventure*, 138).

58. *ST* I, 92, 1.

59. "Expressible through the finite" is meant to be taken literally and not suggest that the infinite is something apart from its expressions. For this only leads back to the moral monster God. Just as a word is something that can be understood only through its expressed meanings, so the infinite can be understood only through its expressions.

the workings of divine providence. Yet as Nicholas of Cusa recognized, such a view leaves us very much on our own. There is not a God who is a sort of spaceman who may land tomorrow in Salt Lake City and solve all our problems. If God returns tomorrow it will be, as Pascal grasped, probably in the way that God appeared before—as a human being. God might appear in any guise, but in this world God must appear as a being with a place in this world. Whether God appears as a peasant woman in Mexico, or a male Chechen on a horse, or a woman brain surgeon in Boston, or a Jesuit philosophy professor at the Gregorian, or, for that matter, as a transcendent tachyon,[60] we will still have to understand the divine mission for ourselves.

Nicholas of Cusa understood that what we have by way of a guide to the infinite is language.[61] Our language is infinite, something lately demonstrated in linguistic theory.[62] One can also use Richard's paradox and Gödel's theorem to show how even our knowledge outruns finite formulations.[63] But one hardly needs anything so complex. The ordinary exchange

---

60. See Blaise Pascal, *Pensées* (Lafuma-Delmas 344; Brunschvicg 231; Lafuma-Luxembourg 420). For detailed references to the various editions and *Pensée* numbers see Leslie Armour, *"Infini Rien": Pascal's Wager and the Human Paradox* (Carbondale, IL: Southern Illinois University Press for the *Journal of the History of Philosophy*, 1993), xv–xvi. Pascal supposed that there could be a point that traveled at infinite speed and that this might be God in the world. Recently, physicists have developed a theory of "tachyons"—particles that travel faster than light and that need force to slow them down. Pascal says: "Croyez-vous qu'il soit impossible que Dieu soit infini, sans parties? Oui. Je vous veux donc faire voir [une image de Dieu en son immensité] une chose infinie et indivisible: C'est un point [remuant] se mouvant partout d'une vitesse infinie. Car il est—*un*—en tous lieux et est tout entier en chaque endroit." ("Do you believe that it would be impossible for God to be infinite and without parts? Yes. I want to let you see [an image of the immensity of God]: something both infinite and indivisible. It is a [moving] point which moves everywhere at an infinite speed. Because it is—*one*—everywhere and it is complete in each place.") The words in brackets are not included in most modern texts, but they are in the MS. BN 9202 (see Tourneur's "paleographic edition," 312).

61. Cusa's *Idiota de Mente* is devoted to an account of how the human mind unfolds a world of its own creation through language and other symbolism. In paralleling the divine process, it comes to grasp the infinite. See also *Trialogus de Possest* 27. Cusa's use of language is explored fruitfully in Nancy M. Struever, *The Language of History in the Renaissance* (Princeton: University Press, 1970), and Ronald Levao, *Renaissance Minds and Their Fictions* (Berkeley: University of California Press, 1985). There is a good summary of the thesis that in language we are creators like God in Pauline Moffitt Watts, *Nicolaus Cusanus: A Fifteenth Century Vision of Man* (Leiden: E. J. Brill, 1982), 136–39.

62. See D. Terrence Langendoen and Paul M. Postal, *The Vastness of Natural Language* (Oxford: Blackwell, 1984).

63. The essence of Kurt Gödel's theorem is a proof that we cannot include everything we know in the set of propositions whose truth we can prove. We always know the truth of one more proposition than we can prove. It shows that we always know more than we can prove

of meanings requires a potentially unlimited discourse. Each use of a word changes its meaning. The situation is like that in the law: each conviction adds or subtracts something from the law of larceny. Language must be indefinitely malleable and beyond any limit. We thus become creative forces in the world. The infinite is expressed through us. None of us is a full expression of the infinite, but the infinite is not "another thing" out there waiting to be expressed, either. Rather, nothing can be finite without participating in the infinite and vice-versa. So what is not expressed through one of us must be expressed in the end through another. Discerning the divine in the other may well be the business of religion, as Christians and many others have thought. But what is discerned is fully in this world, and what is not in this world must be expressed in another finite world, too. If there is a divine expression, we must all participate in it or it will fail.

By means of language we can begin to plumb the depths of our own experience. We are not confined to the present, for language enables us to link the past and future. So linked, we know at once that we are always at the center of a pool of experience that, while it fades toward its edges in space and time, nevertheless goes on indefinitely. You cannot come to the end of it.

In addition we know that we can never plumb the depths of our experience. Look closely at a leaf, a painting, a piece of cloth, and you will notice that you can go on indefinitely distinguishing more and more things.

It is only because we have language that we can do this, for we must have language to link the successive experiences in a creative unity. But notice also that we must choose between saying either that the experiences we so generate just pop into existence *ex nihilo* or else that they are already parts of a larger experience. But we can make the identification with ourselves only by a linguistic device. The first-person pronoun works only by contrast to second- or third-person pronouns. Every experience field in which you can find yourself is one in principle in which you can find another subject. There is, indeed, a second subject, as Newman thought, and this sub-

---

or that, if you like, we are always one step ahead of our proofs. In 1905 Jules Richard, a French mathematician, proved that one could always divide any set of numbers into two sets such that one knew that one set had some members whose existence one could not prove. A quarter century later Gödel generalized the proof. But the genesis of such ideas is to be found in the paradox of the map. Suppose you are in Florence and you ask for a complete map. The whereabouts of the map you get should be shown on any complete map. But this map will have to show another map and so on to infinity. There is no "complete" map. Language is like this in that it can describe itself—so we are always one step beyond any system we build.

ject shares in our experience.[64] Whenever we can give it a name, it is always another of us, and so Christianity has it that to love God is also to love your neighbor—for the "other" in the end embraces all others.

## The Second Subject in Experience

Again, just as it is language that enables us to link ourselves to others, so it is language that allows us to link ourselves to the second subject in our experience. (This is one sense of what Emmanuel Lévinas has called "the other.")

There is a creative element in all this, as St. Thomas suggests, and there is a sense in which the infinite transcends everything that we can know. Jean-Luc Marion has emphasized this elusive quality of the overflowing infinite of Descartes's *Third Meditation*,[65] but Lévinas has emphasized that the infinite appears always through "the other." The other is another of us.[66] I would emphasize that it always appears as a community. The infinite draws us beyond ourselves into a world that we must share with others if we are to have any sense at all of its potentiality. The infinite is constitutive of our language and born into cultures. We are led naturally into cooperation, but it is only through a plurality of expressions that we can rise above our limitations. The infinite is infinite, and, indeed, no finite world can exhaust it. No doubt there is an infinity of other worlds in which we can come to share.

The story, then, goes like this: As we assess our relation to nature we come to realize that the finite does not suffice. Once we realize that the finite and the infinite are intertwined we begin to see that the infinite will manifest itself in just the kind of world that we find around us—a world that is intelligible, available to language, rational in the sense of probabilistic, and capable of development through the interaction of the finite and the infinite.

---

64. See John Henry Newman, *The Philosophical Notebook*, ed. Edward J. Sillem, rev. A. J. Boekraad (Louvain: Nauwelaerts, 1970); and A. J. Boekraad and Henry Tristram, *The Argument from Conscience to the Existence of God* (Louvain: Nauwelaerts, 1961). See also Leslie Armour, "Newman, Anselm and Proof of the Existence of God," *International Journal for Philosophy of Religion* 19 (1986): 87–93.

65. See especially *L'Idole et la distance* (Paris: Grasset, 1977) and *Dieu sans l'être* (Paris: Fayard, 1982). Marion also sees St. Thomas as pointing the way toward his own views, though it seems to me that he does not give enough weight to the world and the infinite's involvement in it.

66. *Totalité et Infini*, 5th ed. (Paris: Kluwer, 1992), and *Autrement qu'être* (The Hague: Martinus Nijhoff, 1974).

The way in which this happens is fairly exactly paralleled by the way in which we create worlds through language, and through these worlds that we create we can begin to mirror the structure and the openness of the infinite. Our sciences and our arts go together.

When we examine our own experience we find that the infinite lodges there in structures that always take us beyond ourselves, and this suggests what Newman called "conscience" and what Lévinas calls "responsibility for the other," the germ of a community from which moral responsibility emerges.

There is a clear sense in which we can tie recognition of this other to the traditions of Western (Christian, Judaic, and Islamic) natural theology. Should one claim that this is the right concept of God? Bonaventure, Cusa, and many of the seventeenth- and eighteenth-century philosophers—Yves de Paris, Bérulle, Descartes, and Locke—would, I suppose, say "yes." All of them could at least find much with which they would be at home. In some of his moods Pascal might welcome the ideas I have been expressing here; in others he would ask if this is the philosopher's God and not the God of Abraham and Isaac. In the nineteenth century Newman and Matthew Arnold were both at home with ideas like those I have been expressing. Kierkegaard smelled the heavy breath of Hegel in all such notions, though Hegel himself would have found such a God not grand enough to be the Absolute.

There is after all something to be said for the thought that we ought to be careful about naming "the other"—or even giving it capital letters. Natural theology is possible, but it can carry us only so far. Perhaps it will not carry us far enough to sustain St. Thomas's own religious sentiments. Nietzsche would not have been surprised to see God revived, but he would have noticed that even if our science allows such speculations, the mechanical nature of our technological world may still render such a God irrelevant. One cannot in the end, I am sure, have a natural theology that argues successfully for a God who is totally beyond our world and who could have chosen to avoid involvement with us. I hope St. Thomas did not think we could have such a natural theology. His quarrel with what I have been saying would more likely have had to do with the Bonaventurian notion of a natural world that is through and through symbolic. But now that we know from our enquiries in physics how closely knower and known are tied in the world and how much we are involved in making the world we know, it is hard to avoid the conclusion that the physics Aquinas hoped for cannot be, and he would have been among the first to rethink his science.

The upshot of these arguments is that the infinite surely is among us not as another thing but as something that constitutes the nature of each of us and yet that transcends each of our momentary expressions. We are still much on our own. There is comfort in an infinite that sustains our world in the sense that the finite can be only in relation to the infinite. There is thus more to things than meets the eye, and everything may be much better than our momentary myopias and stumbling expressions suggest. But then, again, there is an infinity of dark possibilities—as there must be if we are free. There are no guarantees that we will not perpetrate on ourselves horrors even greater than those that we have known. As Pascal thought, we still have to bet. What is certain is that reality cannot be confined to any simple categories.

Gregory T. Doolan

# Is Thomas's Doctrine of Divine Ideas Thomistic?

THROUGHOUT HIS CAREER, dating back to his earliest works, Thomas Aquinas presents an account of ideas existing in the mind of God. For Thomas, these divine ideas serve two distinct although interrelated roles: one as cognitive principles accounting for God's knowledge of things other than himself, the other as ontological or causal principles involved in God's creative activity.[1] Although this Neoplatonic theme is seemingly straightforward in its presentation, its significance in Thomas's writings has prompted much debate among scholars, principally concerning the question of how a multiplicity of ideas could be reconciled with the simplicity of the divine essence.

Most of the debate in recent years has been stimulated by an article in which James Ross argues against what he terms a "photo-exemplarist" reading of Thomas Aquinas's doctrine of divine ideas. Attributing such a reading to Etienne Gilson, Armand Maurer, and John F. Wippel, Ross explains that photo-exemplarism holds that God has a multiplicity of ideas, each acting like a photograph or blueprint for both actual and possible things. Ross argues not only that this is a philosophically problematic account, but also that it is a misreading of Thomas: "For [1] there is only *one* divine idea, the *same* no matter what God does; [2] 'possibles' have no status at all prior to

---

1. Thomas's *ex professo* treatments of the divine ideas appear in *Scriptum super libros Sententiarum* I, d. 36, q. 2 [hereafter *In I Sent.*]; *De veritate*, q. 3 [hereafter *De ver.*]; *In librum beati Dionysii De divinis nominibus expositio* V, Lect. 3 [hereafter *In De div. nom.*]; *Responsio de 108 articulis*, 66; *Summa theologiae* I, q. 15 [hereafter *ST*]; *Quodlibet* 4, q. 1, a. 1. See John F. Wippel, *Thomas Aquinas on the Divine Ideas*, Etienne Gilson Series, no. 16 (Toronto: Pontifical Institute of Mediaeval Studies, 1993), 1.

creation."[2] It is the former claim that I am interested in here, the latter having received sufficient attention from several authors, including Lawrence Dewan himself.[3]

In responding to Ross's latter claim, Dewan effectively refutes the former as well, showing that Thomas does indeed defend a multiplicity of ideas in the mind of God. As he explains, "The multiplication of divine ideas by denomination from creatures is *not* from *actual* creatures, or even from creatables which have been 'tagged' *to be created*, but from creatables themselves, prior to the intention of the divine choice to create. And such items known by God are infinite in multitude."[4]

Given these thorough responses to Ross as regards his interpretation of Thomas's theory, my aim here will be to examine some of the consequences of adopting his position. For in denying the multiplicity of divine ideas, Ross is denying not merely that multiplicity but also, I would contend, the very doctrine of divine ideas. Thus, we find him stating that "I say Aquinas explains the plurality of ideas as a multiplicity from the vantage of things made, but says, strictly speaking, there is only one divine idea; thus, there is little left of Augustine's doctrine, except for the words."[5] In short, Ross's position is that Thomas's doctrine of divine ideas (at least as it has been traditionally understood) is not a Thomistic one. This conclusion is one that was reached earlier by none other than Gilson. In his response to Ross, Maurer has shown that despite Ross's description of Gilson as a "photo-exemplarist," the two authors in fact have much in common with each other on this topic.[6] For this reason, it is worth our while to consider what Gilson also has to say about Thomas's doctrine of the divine ideas.

---

2. James F. Ross, "Aquinas's Exemplarism; Aquinas's Voluntarism," *American Catholic Philosophical Quarterly* 64 (1990): 173–74.

3. See Armand A. Maurer, "James Ross on the Divine Ideas: A Reply," *American Catholic Philosophical Quarterly* 65 (1991): 213–20; Lawrence Dewan, "St. Thomas, James Ross, and Exemplarism: A Reply," *American Catholic Philosophical Quarterly* 65 (1991): 221–34. For Ross's reply to these two articles, see James F. Ross, "Response to Maurer and Dewan," *American Catholic Philosophical Quarterly* 65 (1991): 213–20. For a more recent response to Ross, see Aaron Martin, "Reckoning with Ross: Possibles, Divine Ideas, and Virtual Practical Knowledge," *Proceedings of the American Catholic Philosophical Association* 78 (2004): 193–208.

4. Dewan, "St. Thomas, James Ross, and Exemplarism," 222.

5. Ross, "Response," 235.

6. See Maurer, "James Ross," 213ff. This is a point that Ross comes to acknowledge in a future article. See, "Response," 235.

In one of his later works, Gilson observes that "it is hardly an exaggeration to say that at bottom everything St. Thomas said about the Ideas was in his view one more concession made to the language of a philosophy that was not really his own. No doubt it was also the recognition of St. Augustine's authority in theology."[7] If this is so, one might wonder why Thomas would bother to discuss the divine ideas to the extent that he does. According to Gilson, it is not because Thomas is "adding one more piece to a sort of philosophical mosaic." Indeed, Gilson does not even consider Thomas's doctrine of the divine ideas to be a philosophical one at all; rather, he concludes, it is a theological effort to reconcile an otherwise Augustinian doctrine with the "strictest philosophical truth." To speak of a multiplicity of ideas, he argues, is to employ a Platonic language that is foreign to the Aristotelianism of Thomas's theology. If we must use the language of ideas, Gilson maintains that we should say instead that there is only *one* idea and that that idea is nothing other than God himself, the very view expressed by Ross. As absolute existence, Gilson explains, God is the exemplar of all created things, while created things, in turn, are but "finite and deficient approximations of the pure act of *esse*."[8]

As evidence that Thomas's philosophy does not require divine ideas, Gilson points to Book I of the *Summa contra gentiles*. In that work, Thomas provides a consideration of the divine cognition as he does in the *Commentary on the Sentences, De veritate,* and *Summa theologiae*. But unlike those other works, where this consideration is followed by a discussion of the divine ideas, there is no such discussion in the *Summa contra gentiles*. If Thomas were to have directly addressed the divine ideas in there, cc. 53 and 54 would have been the most logical place for him to have done so. In these chapters, however, the very word "idea" is noticeably absent from this discussion, at least until the final sentence of c. 54, and then only in reference to Plato. The absence of the divine ideas in these chapters lends to the impression that Thomas found it unnecessary to speak about ideas in order to address the divine cognition.[9] Further lending to this impression is that

---

7. Étienne Gilson, *Christian Philosophy: An Introduction*, trans. Armand Maurer (Toronto: Pontifical Institute of Mediaeval Studies, 1993), 103–4. For Maurer's exposition of this text, see "James Ross," 217–20.

8. Gilson, *Christian Philosophy: An Introduction*, 106–8.

9. Louis B. Geiger, "Les idées divines dans l'oeuvre de s. Thomas," in *St. Thomas Aquinas: Commemorative Studies*, vol. 1 (Toronto: Pontifical Institute of Mediaeval Studies, 1974), 197–98.

Thomas in fact suppressed earlier redactions of these chapters in which he *had* explicitly referred to the divine ideas.[10]

Nevertheless, we are still faced with the fact that in works both prior and subsequent to the *Summa contra gentiles*, Thomas not only advances a doctrine of divine ideas, but expressly defends the existence of a *multiplicity* of such ideas. Before considering the consequences of Ross and Gilson's position on the divine ideas, then, it is worth examining (1) Thomas's defense of a multiplicity of divine ideas elsewhere and, then, (2) the reasons for this discussion's absence from the *Summa contra gentiles*.

Thomas offers a philosophical defense of the multiplicity of ideas in each of his *ex professo* treatments of the divine ideas, and his general approach to examining this topic varies little from work to work. Rather than summarize his treatments in each work, therefore, I will instead simply present here his treatment in the *prima pars* of the *Summa theologiae* (1266–68) as representative of his general conclusions regarding the question of how a multiplicity of divine ideas can be reconciled with the simplicity of the divine essence. Although Thomas does not offer in this work the same detail as he does in the earlier *De veritate* (1256–59), his account in the *prima pars* will be of particular interest to us here because it is one of his latest considerations of this topic, and also because it was written after the *Summa contra gentiles* (1259–64).[11]

Thomas addresses the issue of the multiplicity of ideas in question 15, article 2, beginning the article with an argument to prove their multiplicity. In any effect, he explains, the ultimate end is the proper intention of the principal agent, just as the order of an army is intended by its general. Now, the order of the universe is likewise the proper intention of God: it is not merely accidental, as if God had created only the first creature, which created the second, and so forth, resulting in the multitude of things. If this model presented an accurate account of the order of things, then God would have

---

10. For a consideration of the development of these redactions, see Louis B. Geiger, "Les rédactions successives de *Contra Gentiles*, I, 53 d'après l'autographe," in *Saint Thomas d'Aquin aujourd'hui*, ed. R. Jolivet et al., Recherches de Philosophie 6 (Paris: Desclée de Brouwer, 1963), 221–40. Cf. René-Antoine Gauthier, *Somme contre les gentils*, Introduction (Paris: Éditions Universitaires, 1993), 109ff.

11. Dating of Thomas's texts follows Jean-Pierre Torrell's *Saint Thomas Aquinas*, vol. 1, *The Person and His Works*, trans. Robert Royal (Washington, DC: The Catholic University of America Press, 1996).

only one idea, namely, an idea of the first creature, for that is all that he would have intended. But since God does intend the order of the whole universe (insofar as the whole universe has been created by him), he must have an idea of how the universe is ordered.

Now, God could not have a proper understanding *(ratio)* of the whole unless he had proper understandings *(rationes)* of those things that constitute the whole, just as the builder would be unable to conceive the nature of a house unless he had a proper understanding of each of its parts. Hence, in the divine mind there must exist the proper understandings for all things, as Augustine notes in *83 Different Questions*. Thus, Thomas concludes that there must exist a multiplicity of ideas within the divine mind.[12]

Having demonstrated the plurality of divine ideas, Thomas then proceeds to consider how such a plurality is possible without compromising the simplicity of the divine essence. He observes that the idea of something produced does not exist in the mind of the producer as a species *by which* something is understood since an intelligible species actualizes the intellect. Rather, an idea exists in the mind of the producer as *that which* is understood. Thus, for example, the form of a house in the mind of the builder is something that is understood by him, and in likeness to this he forms a house in matter. In light of this distinction between an intelligible species and an idea, Thomas observes that—although it would be contrary to the simplicity of the divine intellect to be informed by many species—it is not contrary to its simplicity that it *understand* many things. In short, the plurality of ideas does not compromise the simplicity of the divine mind because the ideas are not really many things *by which* God understands, but rather are many *as understood* by him.[13]

Thomas then proceeds to explain how the divine mind can be possessed of many such understandings. Since God knows his essence perfectly, he knows every way in which it can be known. Now, it can be known not only as it is in itself, but also inasmuch as it can be participated by creatures according to any manner of likeness. Every single creature has a proper nature *(speciem)* according to which it participates in a likeness of the divine es-

---

12. *ST* I, q. 15, a. 2 (Leon. ed., vol. 4.201–2). See Wippel, *Divine Ideas*, 34. Regarding the reference to Augustine, see question 46 of Augustine's *De diversis quaestionibus LXXXIII*, ed. Almut Mutzenbecher, in *Aurelii Augustini opera*, Corpus Christianorum, Series Latina vol. 50.1 (Turnhout: Brepols, 1975).

13. *ST* I, q. 15, a. 2 (Leon. ed., vol. 4.201–2): "Et sic patet quod Deus intelligit plures rationes proprias plurium rerum; quae sunt plures ideae."

sence in some respect. Thus, since God knows his essence inasmuch as it is imitable by a creature, he knows his essence as the proper reason and idea of that particular creature. And so it is as regards each and every creature. In this way, Thomas concludes, it is clear that God has many proper understandings of many things and, consequently, that there are many ideas.[14]

Thomas's conclusion is further developed in his replies to the article's objections. In the first objection it is argued that since the divine essence is only one, there is only one idea. As we have seen, this is precisely the position taken by both Ross and Gilson. Thomas replies, however, by noting that an idea is called such not simply inasmuch as it is the divine essence but rather inasmuch as it is the likeness or reason of this or that thing. Since there are several understood reasons from the one divine essence, there are also said to be several ideas.[15]

Thomas's reply to the second objection complements the first by further refining the meaning of what constitutes an idea. In the objection it is argued that just as there are not several arts or wisdoms in God, so too there are not many ideas. In response, Thomas repeats his distinction from the corpus of the article, noting that wisdom and art signify *that by which* God understands, whereas an idea is *that which* he understands. Now, God not only understands many things by his essence, Thomas explains, but he understands *that* he understands through his essence. And it is this understanding that constitutes an idea. Since such an understanding, however, is of many things, there must be many ideas as things that are understood by God.[16]

In the remaining replies to objections, Thomas goes on to explain that although the ideas are many because of their relationships to created things, these relationships are caused not by those things but rather by the divine intellect comparing itself with them. Thus, these relationships exist in God and not in creatures; but they do not exist in God as real relationships like those among the Divine Persons; rather, they exist in him only as *understood*.[17]

14. Ibid.; cf. *ST* I, q. 47, a. 1, ad 2 (Leon. ed., vol. 4.486).
15. *ST* I, q. 15, a. 2, ad 1 (Leon. ed., vol. 4.202). In the prior article, Thomas had noted that although God knows both himself and other things through his essence, his essence is the operative principle only as regards other things, not for himself. For this reason, Thomas concludes that the divine essence has the nature *(ratio)* of an idea only with respect to other things. Thus, while God has knowledge of himself, he does not have an *idea* of himself (*ST* I, q. 15, a. 1, ad 2 [Leon. ed., vol. 4.199]).
16. *ST* I, q. 15, a. 2, ad 2 (Leon. ed., vol. 4.202).
17. Ibid., ad 3 and 4 (Leon. ed., vol. 4.202).

We see in this article that the crux of Thomas's argument defending the plurality of divine ideas lies in the distinction that he makes between a form taken as the first principle of an act of understanding (an intelligible species) and form taken as the terminus of such an act (an idea).[18] Since God is pure act, nothing other than his own essence can actualize his intellect as the first principle of understanding. Thus, there can be only one such principle. Since that essence is imitable in a variety of ways, however, God can have many ideas as the termini of his act of understanding. In this way, his unity is not compromised, for even though these ideas constitute a multiplicity of things *that* he understands, the medium *by which* he understands them is the one divine essence. In short, the multiplicity of the divine ideas is a logical multiplicity, not a real one.[19]

Given that the multiplicity of divine ideas is not a real one, it might be tempting to dismiss it as *merely* logical: a multiplicity according to our reason but not God's. But this is not Thomas's position. To understand why, it is helpful to consider the different types of logical multiplicity. In the *De veritate,* Thomas explains that sometimes a logical multiplicity is reduced to some diversity of the thing. Thus, there is a logical difference between Socrates and Socrates sitting, which is reduced to the difference between a substance and an accident; similarly, there is a logical difference between "man" and "animal," which is reduced to the difference between form and matter since a genus is taken from the matter, whereas the specific difference is taken from the form. The multiplicity that results from this sort of logical difference, Thomas notes, is repugnant to the highest unity and simplicity that is found in God.

In contrast to this sort of logical diversity, there is another sort that is not reduced to a diversity in the thing but, rather, to the *truth* of the thing, which is intelligible in diverse ways. In this sense, Thomas concludes, we can posit a plurality of notions in God, for this is not repugnant either to his unity or to his simplicity.[20] It is in this sense that there is a logical diver-

---

18. This is a distinction that first appears in *De ver.*, q. 3, a. 2 (Leon. ed., vol. 22.1.104:158–200).

19. As Wippel observes, "the plurality of divine ideas joins with the ontological unity of the divine essence to form two essential parts of Thomas's effort to account for the derivation of the many (creatures) from the one (their divine source)" (*Divine Ideas*, 19–20).

20. *De ver.*, q. 3, a. 2, ad 3 (Leon. ed., vol. 22.1.105:244–59): "Pluralitas rationis quandoque reducitur ad aliquam diversitatem rei, sicut Socrates et Socrates sedens differunt ratione, et hoc reducitur ad diversitatem substantiae et accidentis, et similiter homo et animal ratione dif-

sity of divine ideas, and not only according to our understanding since this diversity is reduced to the truth of the divine essence. Thomas would reject the contention that there is an arbitrariness to positing such a multiplicity precisely because the divine essence is itself intelligible in diverse ways. As Vincent Branick observes, "It is not up to us to choose the multiplicity or not. There is a structure of reality which precedes our intellection and which forces us to consider God in a multiplicity of ideas, as long as we are working with ideas."[21] This is why Thomas concludes that "although the relationships of God to creature are really founded in the creature, nevertheless according to reason and intellect they also exist in God; and, I say, *not only the human intellect, but also the angelic and divine.*"[22]

Nevertheless, despite Thomas's insistence here and elsewhere on this multiplicity, we are still faced with the fact that reference to the divine ideas is noticeably absent in the *Summa contra gentiles*. The question we will need to address next is whether this absence is evidence, as Gilson suggests, that the doctrine of divine ideas is an unnecessary appendage in Thomas's system.

Like those works of Thomas that contain *ex professo* treatments of the divine ideas, the *Summa contra gentiles* provides an account of the divine understanding. But unlike those other works, as we have seen, it does not contain a distinct consideration of the divine ideas following this account. Nevertheless, there is still a defense of the existence of a plurality of divine reasons *(rationes)* for individual creatures. And rather than focusing his attention on the absence of the term "idea," Gilson ought to have focused it instead on the presence of this defense.

---

ferunt, et haec differentia reducitur ad diversitatem formae et materiae quia genus sumitur a materia, differentia vero specifica a forma: unde talis differentia secundum rationem repugnat maxime unitati vel simplicitati; quandoque vero differentia secundum rationem non reducitur ad aliquam rei diversitatem sed ad veritatem rei quae est diversimode intelligibilis, et sic ponimus pluralitatem rationum in Deo: unde hoc non repugnat maximae unitati vel simplicitati."

21. Vincent P. Branick, "The Unity of the Divine Ideas," *New Scholasticism* 42 (1968): 171n1. Branick is here commenting on a passage concerning the divine attributes: *In I Sent.*, d. 2, q. 1, a. 3 (Mandonnet ed., vol. 1.70–71).

22. *In I Sent.*, d. 36, q. 2, a. 2, ad 2 (Mandonnet ed., vol. 1.842): "Quamvis relationes quae sunt Dei ad creaturam, realiter in creatura fundentur, tamen secundum rationem et intellectum in Deo etiam sunt; intellectum autem dico non tantum humanum, sed etiam angelicum et divinum" (emphasis added in translation). Cf. *De potentia*, q. 3, a. 16, ad 14 (Marietti ed., vol. 2.90 [hereafter *De pot.*]); *De ver.*, q. 3, a. 2, ad 8 (Leon. ed., vol. 22.1.107:58–64).

In Book I, c. 54, Thomas shows that God does not merely have a general or universal understanding of things but that he has a proper understanding of them as well. To this end, Thomas draws an analogy from human understanding. He explains that our intellect is able to consider in a distinct way things that are not separated in reality. Thus, in considering the number ten, the mind can grasp the proper reason *(ratio)* of the number nine by subtracting one unit; similarly, from the notion of "man" it can grasp the proper reason of "irrational animal" by "subtracting" the specific difference "rational" and considering only that which is included in sensible being.[23]

Turning his attention next to God's understanding, Thomas explains that the divine essence comprises within itself the perfections *(nobilitates)* of all beings—not in a composite manner but in a perfect one.[24] Now every form, whether proper or common, is a certain perfection and includes imperfection only insofar as it falls short of true being *(esse)*. Hence, the divine intellect can grasp what is proper to every single thing by understanding both the way in which that thing imitates his essence and the way in which it falls short of the perfection of his essence. In this way, Thomas explains, God grasps the proper form of plant in understanding his essence as imitable in respect to life but not cognition; he grasps the proper form of animal in understanding his essence as imitable in respect to cognition but not intellect; and so forth. Inasmuch as the divine essence is absolutely perfect, therefore, it can be viewed as the proper reason *(ratio)* for individual things. And in this way, God can have a proper knowledge of all things.[25]

This account of God's understanding not only preserves the integrity of the divine simplicity, but it also simultaneously affirms the plurality of his notions. As Thomas proceeds to explain, the proper reason of one thing is distinct from the proper reason of another; but distinction, he notes, is the principle of plurality (this is because distinction occurs between things that are not the same and, hence, not one).[26] Thus, there must be a certain distinction and plurality of understood reasons in the divine intellect inasmuch as that which is in the intellect serves as the proper reason for differ-

---

23. *SCG* I, c. 54 (Leon. ed., vol. 13.154); Wippel, *Divine Ideas*, 26. For a consideration of the Aristotelian influences in Thomas's mathematical example, see Mark D. Jordan, "The Intelligibility of the World and the Divine Ideas in Aquinas," *Review of Metaphysics* 38 (1984): 25–26.
24. See *SCG* I, c. 30 (Leon. ed., vol. 13.92).
25. *SCG* I, c. 54 (Leon. ed., vol. 13.154–55); Wippel, Divine Ideas, 26.
26. On Thomas's views regarding distinction and plurality or multitude, see, e.g., *De pot.*, q. 9, a. 7 where he examines whether numeral terms can be predicated of the divine persons.

ent things. However, since this plurality of reasons follows from the fact that God understands the particular relationship of imitation that each creature bears to himself, these reasons do not exist in the divine intellect as many or diverse except insofar as God knows that things are (or may be) like himself according to many and diverse ways. Thomas explains that it is in this sense that Augustine says God has made a man and a horse according to different reasons and, furthermore, that there are many reasons for things in the divine mind. And thus, Thomas concludes, in this qualified sense Plato's theory of Ideas can be saved.[27]

We see in this passage that the language of ideas is indeed absent, save for the last line of the chapter. Nevertheless, if we compare this consideration with his discussion of the divine ideas in the *Summa theologiae* and other works, we discover that c. 54 is equivalent to a defense of a plurality of divine ideas. As evidence, we can point to Thomas's reference to question 46 of Augustine *83 Different Questions*, a question entitled *De ideis* in which Augustine himself defends the existence of divine ideas. In short, the difference between the *Summa contra gentiles* and other texts is not a matter of doctrine but one of semantics: what Thomas terms "ideas" elsewhere, here he terms *rationes*.[28] That Thomas does not himself see a discrepancy between the two terms is confirmed by his concluding observation that Plato's theory of Ideas can, in a certain respect, be saved. Thus, it is no surprise when in the later *Summa theologiae*, as we have seen, Thomas identifies the *rationes* with the divine ideas.[29]

If the substance of this passage in the *Summa contra gentiles* is the same as that found in other works that address the divine ideas, we are still left with the question, why does Thomas not employ the language of ideas here

---

27. *SCG* I, c. 54 (Leon. ed., vol. 13.155): "Quia vero propria ratio unius distinguitur a propria ratione alterius; distinctio autem est pluralitatis principium: oportet in intellectu divino distinctionem quandam et pluralitatem rationum intellectarum considerare, secundum quod id quod est in intellectu divino est propria ratio diversorum. Unde, cum hoc sit secundum quod Deus intelligit proprium respectum assimilationis quam habet unaquaeque creatura ad ipsum, relinquitur quod rationes rerum in intellectu divino non sint plures vel distinctae nisi secundum quod Deus cognoscit res pluribus et diversis modis esse assimilabiles sibi. Et secundum hoc Augustinus dicit quod Deus alia ratione facit hominem et alia equum; et *rationes rerum* pluraliter in mente divina esse dicit. In quo etiam aliqualiter salvatur Platonis opinio ponentis *ideas*, secundum quas formarentur omnia quae in rebus materialibus existunt." See Wippel, *Divine Ideas*, 26.
28. See Wippel, *Divine Ideas*, 28.
29. *ST* I, q. 15, a. 2, ad 1 (Leon. ed., vol. 4.202): "Et sic patet quod Deus intelligit plures rationes proprias plurium rerum; *quae sunt plures ideae.*" Emphasis added.

Thomas's Doctrine of Divine Ideas 163

as well? Here we need to recall that for Thomas, the divine ideas serve two distinct although interrelated roles: one as cognitive principles accounting for God's knowledge of things other than himself, the other as ontological or causal principles involved in God's creative activity. Nevertheless, Thomas tends to place a greater emphasis on their latter role. Thus, as Wippel observes, in those texts where Thomas explicitly addresses the divine ideas, his emphasis is on the theme of exemplar causality. His concern in those texts is to show how God, who is perfectly one and simple, can produce a diversity of creatures; in contrast, in the *Summa contra gentiles* his concern is to show how God can *know* a diversity of creatures. Without an emphasis on the ontological issue of the production of creatures, there is less need for the language of ideas.[30]

Following this thesis, we can see why Thomas would return to a discussion of the divine ideas in the *Summa theologiae*. Gilson's contention is that their presence in the *Summa* is merely as a useless appendage. But, as one author asks, "Is it likely that so soon into a work whose aim was to avoid useless questions, Saint Thomas would include just such a useless question?"[31] Indeed, a close examination of question 15 in the *prima pars* reveals that the consideration there of the divine ideas is not merely a reiteration of the preceding articles on God's knowledge in question 14.[32] Thomas himself clearly sees a use in asking this question, explicitly noting to the reader that he is including it because everything that is known is in the knower, and in God we call these reasons *(rationes)* "ideas."[33]

But what role does this doctrine play in Thomas's system? Certainly, Thomas attributes a theological significance to it, as Gilson himself observes.[34] M.-D. Chenu argues that the theological intelligibility of the *Summa theologiae* necessarily leads Thomas to consider this doctrine. According to Chenu,

---

30. See Wippel, *Divine Ideas*, 28, 38–39. Cf. John L. Farthing, "The Problem of Divine Exemplarity," *Thomist* 49 (1985): 214.

31. Vivian Boland, *Ideas in God According to Saint Thomas Aquinas* (New York: Brill, 1996), 213–14.

32. See Geiger, "Les idées divines," 204.

33. ST I, q. 14, *prologus*: "Quia omne cognitum in cognoscente est, rationes autem rerum secundum quod sunt in Deo cognoscente, ideae vocantur, cum consideratione scientiae erit etiam adiungenda consideratio de ideis" (Leon. ed., vol. 4.166).

34. Although, of course, he sees the doctrine as unnecessary (Gilson, *Christian Philosophy: An Introduction*, 106–8). For a consideration of the theological implications of Thomas's doctrine of divine exemplarism, see David L. Greenstock, "Exemplar Causality and the Supernatural Order," *Thomist* 16 (1953): 18–31.

the full intelligibility of the work requires such a consideration because the doctrine of divine ideas provides a religious account of the destiny of created things.[35] Thus, Thomas notes that there must be exemplar ideas of individuals because providence extends not only to species but to individuals as well.[36]

Nevertheless, despite the theological significance of the divine ideas, Thomas's doctrine is at heart a philosophical one. And contrary to Gilson's claim (and Ross's implication), it is a necessary part of Thomas's metaphysical thought.

Given the dual role of the divine ideas as cognitive and ontological principles, we can consider the philosophical significance of Thomas's doctrine of ideas from both of these perspectives. First of all, as regards its cognitive significance, we can observe that his doctrine has the benefit of emphasizing the complex philosophical issues concerning the divine understanding. One reason that Thomas preserves the ideas is precisely to draw our attention to the apparent contradiction between the divine simplicity and God's knowledge of a multiplicity of objects.[37] What is more important, the doctrine enables Thomas to resolve a problem that was not even posed by Aristotle.[38] The apparent contradiction between God's simplicity and his multiplicity of ideas is further emphasized by Thomas's tendency over time to place a greater emphasis on the nature of mind as analytic in order to account for God's understanding of a diversity of things. As Dewan observes, "Thomas is doing all he can do to introduce actual consideration of distinction into the content of divine knowledge."[39] Thomas is able to account for this distinction in God's knowledge precisely inasmuch as he posits (logically) distinct ideas as present in the divine mind. Whereas Gilson's claim that "the plurality of ideas known by God is only a plurality of natures in things" (a claim made by Ross as well), Thomas is insistent that it is the other way around—there is a plurality of natures in things only inasmuch as there is first a plurality of ideas *in* God.[40]

---

35. M.-D. Chenu, O.P., *Introduction à l'étude de saint Thomas d'Aquin* (Montreal: Université de Montréal, 1954), 267–68.
36. *ST* I, q. 15, a. 3, ad 4 (Leon. ed., vol. 4.204); ST I-II, q. 93, a. 1 (Leon. ed., vol. 7.162–63). For a consideration of the role that Thomas attributes to the divine ideas in God's providence, see Boland, *Ideas in God*, 262–70.
37. See Geiger, "Les idées divines," 179.
38. Ibid., 182.
39. Dewan, "St. Thomas, James Ross, and Exemplarism," 226.
40. Gilson, *Christian Philosophy: An Introduction*, 109.

The cognitive significance of Thomas's doctrine thus implies the ontological significance: to dismiss the multiplicity of divine ideas is to dismiss the diversity of finite beings. Gilson's solution is to focus instead on the finite and deficient approximations that creatures have to the divine essence as a sufficient account of divine exemplarism, noting that "If you wish, you can call this essential exemplarity of God an idea; it will not remain less identical with the divine essence itself."[41]

No doubt both Gilson and Ross are correct to identify the divine essence as itself being the exemplar of all created things, but in dismissing a true doctrine of ideas, they also end up dismissing a key distinction regarding the different ways that things imitate the divine essence. As Thomas explains in his *Commentary on the Sentences*, the exemplar of things exists in God in two ways. In one way the exemplar of things is in God as that which is in his intellect. And, thus, his ideas are the exemplars of all the things that he makes, just as the exemplars of works of art exist in the mind of the artisan. In another way, however, the exemplar of things is in God as that which is in his nature *(in natura sua)*, as his goodness is the exemplar of everything that is good.[42] Thus, we see that God is the exemplar form of things both as regards his ideas *(rationes ideales)* and as regards his attributes *(attributa)*.[43] Unlike the divine ideas, which signify God's knowledge of his essence inasmuch as it is imitable, the divine attributes signify the divine essence itself. Hence, Thomas explains in the *De veritate*, the divine attributes signify only one thing (although they are conceptually distinct), whereas the divine ideas according to their proper meaning signify a multiplicity of things, namely, the different proportions that creatures have to the divine essence.[44]

We again find this distinction between these two modes of causality in the *prima pars* of the *Summa theologiae*. In an article considering whether

---

41. Ibid.

42. *In I Sent.*, d. 19, q. 5, a. 2, ad 4 (Mandonnet ed., vol. 1.493). In the objection, it is argued that if we say that the exemplar form that makes all things true exists in God, we are presented with an absurdity: just as the exemplar of truth would be in God, so too would the exemplar of color. Hence, if all things should be called true because they are exemplified by a form that is in God, it would seem that all things should also be colored, which is clearly false (Mandonnet ed., vol. 1.491).

43. *In I Sent.*, d. 2, q. 1, a. 2 (Mandonnet ed., vol. 1.62–63). For a detailed consideration of the distinction between these two modes of divine exemplarism, see Federico Balmaceda, "La doble causalidad ejemplar divina en Santo Tomás de Aquino," *Philosophica* 9–10 (1986–87): 155–66.

44. *De ver.*, q. 3, a. 2, ad 2 (Leon. ed., vol. 22.1.105:229–43).

the image of God is to be found in irrational creatures, Thomas responds to an objection (citing Boethius) that the entire world is made in the image of God. In reply, he explains that the word "image" *(imago)* can be used in two respects. According to the first respect, "image" refers to the likeness by which a work of art imitates the species in the mind of the artisan. It is in this sense that Boethius is speaking, and in this sense every creature is an image of an exemplar *(imago rationis exemplaris)* that is in the mind of God. According to the second respect, "image" refers to a likeness in nature *(similitudinem in natura)*. And, in this respect, Thomas explains, "all things are alike to the First Being inasmuch as they are beings; and to the first Life inasmuch as they are living things; and to the Highest Wisdom inasmuch as they are intelligent beings."[45] Here, then, Thomas again draws a distinction between the divine ideas and the divine attributes, but this time considered from the perspective of the image rather than of the archetype itself.

To grasp the significance of this distinction between the two modes of divine exemplarism, we first need to consider the limited nature of finite beings. Unlike God, a finite being is not its *esse* but rather participates *esse*. Hence, while a finite being is good, goodness does not belong to it essentially but only by participation, inasmuch as it has an act of being. Thus, Thomas explains that humanity does not have the formality (the *ratio*) of goodness except inasmuch as it has *esse*.[46] Now, a finite being *is* a being and is good inasmuch as it imitates the divine essence taken as such (rather than the divine ideas).[47] In short, the perfections involved in this sort of imita-

45. *ST* I, q. 93, a. 2, ad 4 (Leonine ed., vol. 5.403): "[I]mago accipitur a Boetio secundum rationem similitudinis qua artificiatum imitatur speciem artis quae est in mente artificis: sic autem quaelibet creatura est imago rationis exemplaris quam habet in mente divina. Sic autem non loquimur nunc de imagine: sed secundum quod attenditur secundum similitudinem in natura; prout scilicet primo enti assimilantur omnia, inquantum sunt entia; et primae vitae, inquantum sunt viventia; et summae sapientiae, inquantum sunt intelligentia." In the body of the article, Thomas observes that, following this threefold manner by which things can be likened to God by nature (viz., according to being, life, and wisdom) there is a hierarchy involving degrees of similitude: the first is the most common, the last is the most specific. Thus, according to the second sense of the word "image," only intellectual creatures are properly said to be made in the image of God (ibid., c.).

46. *De ver.*, q. 21, a. 5 (Leon. ed., vol. 22.1.606:133–41): "Essentialis enim bonitas non attenditur secundum considerationem naturae absolutam sed secundum esse ipsius; humanitas enim non habet rationem boni vel bonitatis nisi in quantum esse habet. Ipsa autem natura vel essentia divina est eius esse; natura autem vel essentia cuiuslibet rei creatae non est suum esse sed est esse participans ab alio." Cf. *De ver.*, q. 21, a. 5, ad and 6 (Leon. ed., vol. 22.1.607:192–209).

47. *De pot.*, q. 3, a. 4, ad 9 (Marietti ed., vol. 2.48): "Quamvis inter Deum et creaturam non possit esse similitudo generis vel speciei; potest tamen esse similitudo quaedam analogiae, si-

tion are the transcendental perfections that a finite being participates in inasmuch as it receives an act of being. Thus, for example, Socrates receives his total being as an *ens* by imitating the divine nature, for he is thereby imitating the absolute perfection that is being itself *(ipsum esse)*; however, he receives merely his essence by imitating his respective divine idea, for he is thereby imitating merely one *mode* of being. This distinction forms the foundation of the essence-*esse* distinction in any finite being. In short, whereas a finite being receives its essence from the exemplarism of the divine ideas, it receives its total being *(entitas)* from the exemplarism of the divine nature, including its essence *and* its act of being.

The two modes of divine exemplarism thus entail two moments within the structure of participation. The first moment is constituted by what Cornelio Fabro terms the "diremption" of the divine essence in the formal order such that it comprises the multiplicity of divine ideas that are the exemplars of created things.[48] Because of this diremption, every real created formality is referred to its respective exemplar according to its mode of being. This constitutes the derivation of the created essence. Then there is the derivation of all the transcendental perfections that follow from the divine essence that embraces *esse* in all of its intensity.[49] And this double exemplarism is founded before all on that very act of intensive *esse* that *is* the divine essence.[50] In dismissing Thomas's doctrine of the divine ideas, then, Gilson and Ross are also implicitly rejecting this important distinction between these two modes of divine exemplarism, altering and even compromising Thomas's metaphysical system.

Their rejection of the divine ideas also results in another difficulty. In limiting divine exemplarism simply to the finite and deficient approximations that creatures have to the divine essence, they unwittingly rob both the creature and the creator's act of some of their dignity. Gilson and Ross's position is quite right as regards Thomas's description of the exemplarism of the divine attributes: since no created being is goodness, truth, or being

---

cut inter potentiam et actum, et substantiam et accidens. Et hoc dicitur uno modo in quantum res creatae imitantur suo modo ideam divinae mentis, sicut artificiata formam quae est in mente artificis. Alio modo secundum quod res creatae ipsi naturae divinae quodammodo similantur, prout a primo ente alia sunt entia, et a bono bona, et sic de aliis."

48. Cornelio Fabro, *Participation et causalité selon S. Thomas d'Aquin* (Louvain: Publications Universitaires, 1961), 435.
49. Ibid., 518–19.
50. Ibid., 435.

itself, all created beings are merely deficient imitations of the divine essence. Thomas presents a different picture, however, as regards the exemplarism of the divine ideas.

Unlike the exemplarism of the divine attributes, the exemplarism of the divine ideas includes the notion of God's intentionality. Thus, even though Socrates' imitation of the divine essence is itself deficient, this does not reflect a deficiency on the part of God's intention. As Thomas explains, "The likeness of a creature to God is accounted for in this way: that the creature corresponds to that which is in the intellect and will of God regarding it."[51] In creating Socrates or any other creature, then, God does not fall short of what he intends, for whatever he wills and whatever he makes corresponds to what is in his intellect. And what the creature corresponds to in God's intellect is its exemplar idea.[52]

Thus, neither Socrates nor any other creature is a deficiency in its essence because every creature lives up to its respective divine idea. Commenting on an observation by Boethius, Thomas observes that material forms are images of immaterial ones, that is, images "of the ideal reasons existing in the mind of God from which [material forms] arise *according to a perfect likeness.*"[53] Thus, although Socrates falls short of imitating the divine

---

51. *De pot.*, q. 3, a. 16, ad 5 (Marietti ed., vol. 2.89): "Appropriatio causae ad effectum attenditur secundum assimilationem effectus ad causam. Assimilatio autem creaturae ad Deum attenditur secundum hoc quod creatura implet id quod de ipsa est in intellectu et voluntate Dei; sicut artificiata similantur artifici in quantum in eis exprimitur forma artis, et ostenditur voluntas artificis de eorum constitutione."

52. As Dewan shows in response to Ross, God's knowledge is prior to his willing: "It is true that God never wills to produce the never-createds (of which he *does* have ideas, Thomas insists). Nevertheless he wills 'that he himself be able to produce them, and he *wills* that he have knowledge of what is involved in their production.' That is why Pseudo-Dionysius does *not* say that for one to speak of an 'exemplar,' there must be pre-defin*ing* and effect*ing* will. He rather says 'definit*ive* and effect*ive.*' Thomas thus shifts Pseudo-Dionysius's references to will to the level of God's will vis-à-vis his own nature, power, and knowledge. This is a *concomitant* willing, not a *causal* willing. It is not a *choice to create*, nor the choice of which creatables to create. The determinate ideas of creatables pertain to a divine 'survey' and 'approbation,' we might say, of God's own *creative potential*. I believe we have said enough to indicate that Professor Ross is going against the evident intention of St. Thomas" (Dewan, "St. Thomas, James Ross, and Exemplarism," 233).

53. *De ver.*, q. 10, a. 7, ad 11 (Leon. ed., vol. 22.2.318:327–32): "Boetius formas materiales ponit esse imagines non Dei, sed formarum immaterialium, idest rationum idealium in mente divina existentium a quibus secundum perfectam similitudinem oriuntur" (emphasis added in translation). See Boethius, *De Trinitate*, II, ll. 51–56, in *The Theological Tractates with an English Translation: The Consolation of Philosophy*, new ed., trans. H. F. Stewart, E. K. Rand, and S. J. Tester, Loeb Classical Library (Cambridge: Harvard University Press, 1973), 12–13. I

essence itself, he does not fall short of imitating the divine idea of man or that of Socrates; unlike transcendental and pure perfections, predicamental perfections do not admit of more or less. Socrates is Socrates precisely because that is what God intends according to his divine idea of Socrates. Gilson's focus on the creature's deficient imitation of the divine essence loses sight of the perfection with which the creature imitates its proper *ratio*. In contrast, Thomas's doctrine of the divine ideas has the benefit of accounting for such imitation by positing distinct ideas for everything that God can or does create.

We see, then, that Thomas's doctrine of the divine ideas is more than a mere theological concession to the authority of Augustine. Contrary to Gilson's claim, the divine ideas do indeed form another piece in Thomas's "philosophical mosaic," and an integral one at that. And contrary to Ross's claim, there must be a multiplicity of such ideas. Geiger observes that if one were to consider how Thomas's doctrine of the divine ideas differs in content or function from his predecessors' doctrines, it is true that one could logically conclude it to be unnecessary to preserve the word "idea." Nevertheless, one could *not* conclude that the doctrine itself is useless, or unnecessary, or only a faithfulness to the vocabulary of a certain tradition. Rather, what we have seen is that Thomas preserves this vocabulary for positive and systematic reasons.[54]

---

read Thomas to be saying that this "perfect likeness" is in the creature. In support of this reading stands a passage in the *Sentences* commentary where Thomas, citing the same line of Boethius, explicitly says that "every single thing attains a perfect likeness of that which is in the divine intellect," i.e., its respective divine idea. *In II Sent.*, d. 16, q. 1, a. 2, ad 2 (Mandonnet ed., vol. 2.400): "[S]imilitudo operis potest dici ad operantem dupliciter: aut quantum ad id quod habet in natura sua, sicut homo generat hominem; aut quantum ad id quod habet in intellectu suo, sicut artificiatum ab artifice in similitudinem artis suae procedit. Utroque modo procedit creatura a Deo in similitudinem ejus. Primo modo, quia ab ente sunt entia, et a vivo viventia. Secundo modo, quia procedunt a rationibus idealibus. Cum ergo unaquaeque res pertingat ad perfectam imitationem ejus quod est in intellectu divino, quia talis est qualem eam esse disposuit; ideo quantum ad hunc modum similitudinis quaelibet creatura potest dici imago ideae in mente divina existentis; unde dicit Boetius, in lib. *De Trinit.* cap. II, quod formae quae sunt in materia possunt dici imagines, eo quod ab his formis venerunt quae sine materia sunt; sed quantum ad alium modum sola intellectualis natura pertingit ad ultimum gradum imitationis, ut dictum est; et ideo ipsa sola dicitur imago Dei."

54. See Geiger, "Les idées divines," 179–80.

PART III

# PHILOSOPHY OF NATURE

*Christopher A. Decaen*

# The Impossibility of Action at a Distance

ALBERT EINSTEIN AND ISAAC NEWTON are not famous for their agreements. Historically speaking, Einstein proposed his theory of relativity in direct opposition to the absolutism underlying Newton's theory of gravitation. Absolute space, time, velocity, mass, and so on were thereby reduced to quantities contingent upon the relative state of the reference-frame of the observer, and force itself seemed to fade into energy potentials expressing the non-Euclidean "curvature" of space-time itself.

So finding the two emphatically agreeing about nontrivial matters gives one pause, and perhaps in no other context is this pause more pregnant than in the matter of action at a distance. For in spite of the fact that Einstein and Newton are sometimes *thought* to demand action at a distance in their respective accounts of nature—the latter quite often[1]—both never-

---

I am greatly indebted to wiser men than I from whom I have learned much over the years in thinking about action at a distance, the first among whom are John F. Nieto, Glen Coughlin, and Peter Orlowski. I thank Dr. Nieto in particular for his careful reading of an earlier draft of this essay. And I thank Rose Decaen for making the whole more readable.

1. The positing of action at a distance has been regularly attributed to Newton, first by his contemporaries, and ever since then by philosophers, physicists, and amateur historians of science. On the former, see Alexander Koyré, *Newtonian Studies* (Chicago: University of Chicago Press, 1965), 115, 139, 149–63, and William Berkson, *Fields of Force: The Development of a World View from Faraday to Einstein* (London: Routledge, 1974), 19–21. Examples of the latter group are commonplace, but two may be mentioned: John Wheeler and Richard Feynman (quoted in Mary B. Hesse, *Forces and Fields: The Concept of Action at a Distance in the History of Physics* [New York: Dover, 2005; originally published in 1962], 270), and Einstein himself (*Sidelights on Relativity* [New York: Dover, 1983], 4). A specialist in the history of action at a distance theories, Francis J. Kovach claims—oddly, as I will show—that Newton holds that we cannot know that action at a distance is impossible because "efficient causes are unknown to us ... empirically" speaking ("The Enduring Question of Action at a Distance in Saint Albert the Great," in

theless reject action at a distance outright. Indeed, they both seem to think that, regardless of the apparent compatibility between the mathematics of physics and action at a distance, the *natural philosophy* of physics requires the impossibility of action at a distance to be taken as a principle or starting point for natural science itself.

Thus, although his *Principia mathematica philosophiae naturalis* is notorious for offering no hypothesis about the proximate agent cause of the gravitational attraction of distant bodies—recall the oft-quoted *hypotheses non fingo*[2]—Newton insists in the same work that there must *be* a proximate agent cause, something over and above the forces two bodies somehow exert upon each other. This cause simply remains to be found, he says, and his *Principia* is just that: the *"principles* of natural philosophy," the necessary foundation for making such a future discovery.[3] To explain gravitation by action at a distance, according to Newton, is not truly to explain it but to despair of explanation. Thus, in a letter Newton gives his most explicit repudiation of action at a distance and a scathing assessment of those who endorse it:

It is inconceivable that inanimate brute matter should, without the mediation of something else which is not material, operate upon and affect other matter without mutual contact, as it must be if gravitation, in the sense of Epicurus, be essential and inherent in it. And this is one reason why I desired you would not ascribe innate gravity to me. That gravity should be innate, inherent, and essential to matter, so that

---

*Albert the Great: Commemorative Essays*, ed. Francis J. Kovach and Robert W. Shahan [Tulsa, OK: University of Oklahoma Press, 1980], 164). Kovach lists Einstein as believing that the very question of the possibility of action at a distance is "unreasonable or meaningless," because Einstein believes that "there are no causes" (ibid., 163). Moreover, Henry Margenau claims that, by doing away with the luminiferous ether, Einstein's relativity required science to "acknowledge the possibility of 'action at a distance'" (*Open Vistas: Philosophical Perspectives of Modern Science* [Woodbridge, CT: Ox Bow Press, 1983], 114–15).

2. See, for example, the General Scholium to the *Principia*. Koyré argues that Newton is himself to blame for the fact that so many have misinterpreted him to be endorsing action at a distance; see *Newtonian Studies*, 149–50. Ironically, John Locke was a victim of this myth about Newtonian action at a distance. In the fourth edition of his *Essay Concerning Human Understanding* (1700), Locke modified his earlier absolute rejection of action at a distance to accommodate his belief that Newton's gravitation requires such; see Koyré, *Newtonian Studies*, 155, and Hesse, *Forces and Fields*, 166–68.

3. Again, see the General Scholium, and also Hesse, *Forces and Fields*, 149–52. To what extent this matter of the agent cause of gravitation has since been pinpointed, as Newton hoped, I leave to the discernment of any reader of popular science articles in which the latest wildly named theoretical entities (from gravitons to superstrings to energy "branes") are so often proposed as "the" explanation of gravitation.

one body may act upon another at a distance through a vacuum, without the mediation of anything else, by and through which their action and force may be conveyed from one to another, is to me so great an absurdity that I believe no man who has in philosophical matters a competent faculty of thinking can ever fall into it.[4]

Clearly Newton is not claiming that action at a distance should be only a last-resort option for the natural scientist. His intolerance for action at a distance here is not merely a working hypothesis, for Newton feigns no hypotheses: action at a distance is impossible because it is unthinkable.

Einstein is similarly unambiguous. First, according to the principles of the theory of relativity, a body cannot act upon or even in some way be spatio-temporally related to another distant body except after a delay that is a function of the speed of light in a vacuum. Between the sudden annihilation of the sun and the subsequent liberation of the earth from its orbit would be a delay of about 8 minutes (measured from the sun's frame of reference), and this appears to imply that the sun's gravitational agency on distant objects is neither instantaneous nor unmediated. It is not immediate action on a distant body because the efficacy of the action is dependent on distance and time, being propagated over distance and at a definite speed.[5]

Likewise, in general relativity, gravitational attraction is explained by the degree of space-time curvature in a given region; here the surrounding "medium" determines the motion of the attracted body. Distant agents are active only through the proximate space-time medium. Thus, in spite of special relativity's refutation of the mechanical luminiferous ether of nineteenth-century electromagnetism,[6] according to general relativity a sort of massless relativistic "ether" has

---

4. Newton, "Third Letter to Richard Bentley, 02-25-1692/3," in *Newton's Philosophy of Nature: Selections from His Writings*, ed. H. S. Thayer (New York: Haffner Press, 1953), 54. Note, however, that some have claimed Newton made an about-face on this matter in his *Opticks* (1717); see Francis J. Kovach, "Action at a Distance in Duns Scotus and Modern Science," *Regnum hominis et regnum Dei: Acta Quarti Congressus Scotistici Internationalis*, tom. 1, ed. Camille Bérubé (Rome: Societas Internationalis Scotistica, 1978), 486–88. Kovach, however, seems to be assuming that one of Newton's questions (query 31) about action at a distance is really an assertion about the possibility of it.

5. It is true, however, that the medium here, space-time itself, is not a material agent (or a substance) in the ordinary sense; this is perhaps part of the reason why relativity is often thought to posit action at a distance.

6. This rejection of a certain kind of ether has, in another myth perpetuated in popular histories of science, been commonly taken to mean that Einstein rejected ether as such; see Ludwik Kostro, *Einstein and the Ether* (Montreal: Apeiron, 2000).

a role in the causal nexus of physics, ... [and relativity, therefore,] employs an ether hypothesis. This ether would be a physical reality, as good as matter.... [Ernst Mach's rejection of ether, on the other hand, had tried to explain] inertia in terms of the immediate interaction between the piece of matter under investigation and all other matter in the universe. This idea is logically possible, but, as a theory involving action-at-a-distance, it does not today merit serious consideration.... [T]he general theory of relativity, whose basic points of view physicists will surely always maintain, excludes direct distant action.[7]

Elsewhere Einstein reiterates that "the modern physicist does not believe that he may accept this action at a distance, [so] he comes back once more ... to the ether."[8]

So both Newton and Einstein insist that the natural scientist *as such* should not entertain any theory positing action at a distance, apparently because of the philosophical principles that underlie natural science itself. In other words, neither feels the need to *prove*, either by empirical, mathematical, or philosophical argument, that action at a distance is impossible. To the natural scientist—indeed, according to Newton, to any thoughtful man—its impossibility is a given. So what makes the impossibility of action at a distance so obvious? The question becomes even more puzzling considering that, historically speaking, most physicists and natural philosophers— even those with radically divergent views about the nature of things—reject action at a distance, in some cases tentatively and in others without qualification. Here one finds that philosophy makes for strange bedfellows. For the unanimity stretches from dualists (e.g., Descartes) to monists (Leibniz), and from materialists who border on atheism (Democritus and Hobbes) to those who see the primacy of mind and form in nature (Aristotle, Anaxagoras, and St. Thomas Aquinas).[9]

---

7. Albert Einstein, "On the Ether," originally published in 1924 but reprinted in *The Philosophy of Vacuum*, ed. Simon Saunders and Harvey R. Brown (Oxford: Oxford University Press, 1991), 13–15, and 20. See also *Sidelights on Relativity*, 4–6.

8. Einstein, *Sidelights on Relativity*, 17–18; see also *Relativity: The Special and General Theory*, trans. Robert W. Lawson (New York: Bonanza, 1961), 63.

9. It is worth noting that philosophers better known for their proficiency in metaphysics than for work in the empirical study of nature, or natural philosophy in general, tend to be more open to action at a distance, especially if these philosophers exhibit an overriding interest in mathematics and/or theology; see, for example, Plotinus, Duns Scotus, William of Ockham, Immanuel Kant, and Robert Boscovich. For a thorough enumeration of the different schools of thought about the possibility of action at a distance, see Hesse, Forces and Fields. Kovach is the only historian I have encountered who seems to think that the reality of action at a distance is the majority view of contemporary philosophers and scientists; see "Action at a Distance in

Indeed, even some who *claim* to employ action at a distance in their account of natural phenomena, for example, those who use the notion of fields in electromagnetic theory, embrace only a quasi-action at a distance.[10] For the field, which admittedly is not physical in the sense of a massive, particulate substance, acts locally and extends continuously from the distant agent to the patient. Whether the field is understood to be the effect of an emanation that travels from its source with a finite speed or instantaneously, the field is itself a mediating agent in contact with both mover and moved, so this is not action at a distance.[11] Moreover, for all the so-called fundamental forces—namely, gravitational attraction, electromagnetic attraction and repulsion, and the strong and weak nuclear forces—physicists find them decreasing with distance. Thus, the distance between an agent and a patient is not irrelevant; indeed, it suggests that the force is somehow effected through the medium. For if, for example, the magnet were acting on the iron filings at a distance, that is, at the iron itself, then one is at a loss to explain exactly why the distance between the magnet and the iron filings makes any difference as to how the magnet acts upon them. Rather, the magnet should be equally *at* the iron filings *wherever they are*. But if the magnet acts *through* the distance, perhaps as an emanation that propagates as an ever-expanding sphere centered on the magnet, the decrease of the force with distance would make

---

Duns Scotus and Modern Science," 488. Compare also his puzzling claim that "as science progresses, more and more natural forces seem to act at a distance," and that no one can claim that empirical study supports a rejection of action at a distance "unless one prefers to ignore all the specific findings of modern times" (Francis Kovach, *Scholastic Challenges to Some Mediaeval and Modern Ideas* [Stillwater, OK: Western, 1987], 164, note 64).

10. I have in mind in particular Michael Faraday in certain phases of his work; in his later work he seems to have been convinced that the field concept is more accurately seen as opposed to action at a distance; see Berkson, *Fields of Force*, 33, 72–93, and Hesse, *Forces and Fields*, 198–222. Note also that, like Newton and Einstein, Faraday finally thought the rejection of action at a distance should be regarded "as a first principle" of natural science (Berkson, *Fields of Force*, 93).

11. Since the advent of relativity, most physicists have taken as a principle that the speed of light is the limiting speed with which physical agency can be effected over space, so one sometimes finds histories of science claiming that only with relativity was action at a distance finally refuted; see, for example, David Lindley, *The End of Physics: The Myth of a Unified Theory* (New York: Basic Books, 1993), 78–79. While this is not simply false, the impossibility of action at a distance does not take its origin merely from the delay in causal agency. One recalls Aristotle's belief that light is communicated through the medium, but instantly (see *De anima* II, 7). It is not at all inconceivable that an agent can act upon a distant patient through a rigid medium without any lag time, just as the movement of my arm seems to be simultaneous with the motion of the cue stick and the cue ball. (Whether there are in fact such perfectly rigid bodies is a different question, of course; relativity implies that there are not.)

sense.[12] Thus, an implicit rejection of action at a distance seems unavoidable to the modern physicist.

But then along comes the quantum theory of the early twentieth century, part of which seems to require action at a distance between correlated particles. It would take us too far afield to explain the "quantum strangeness" of so-called EPR phenomena that are so often commented upon and wondered about in both popular and philosophy of science literature.[13] Nevertheless, we may say in brief that quantum theory requires that a pair of, for example, electrons simultaneously emitted from an atom cannot have a determinate "spin," or angular momentum, until measured, and thus they must be taken as existing in a state of potentiality, or "superposition," with respect to their spin. Admitting that this is where much of the paradoxical in quantum theory comes from, and simply taking it as a given, we can readily see how action at a distance is thought to be part and parcel of the theory. For as soon as one of these electrons is measured, say as having an "up" spin, the state of superposition immediately disappears, and, according to the theory, the other electron must instantaneously snap into a correlative "down" spin. Now, experiment confirms this prediction, and since the theory makes no restrictions about how far apart the electrons can be when the measurement is made, many quantum theorists have taken this to mean that the one electron effects the determination of the other at an "infinite speed" and at any distance. Naturally, then, Einstein was quick to dismiss quantum theory as absurd; as he famously quipped, it explains by using "spooky actions at a distance," and thereby amounts to "the abandonment of the concept of reality in physics."[14] Nevertheless, with the universal experimental success of

---

12. A similar argument is made by Glen Coughlin in his commentary on Aristotle's *Physics, or Natural Hearing*, trans. idem (South Bend, IN: St. Augustine's Press, 2005), 278–79. As Gauss has pointed out, if we imagine a force being propagated as an expanding sphere, because of the geometric property of the spheres—the area of their surfaces are as the square of their radii—we can predict the inverse-square force law one finds in so many forms of energy. St. Thomas himself intimates such a notion of agency effected through a medium when he claims that the efficacy of an agent weakens with distance because the power itself becomes spread out over more space; see *In De anima* II, lect. 15, nn. 8–9; III, lect. 6, n. 10.

13. EPR phenomena are named for Einstein, Boris Podolsky, and Nathan Rosen, who together published one of the first papers critiquing quantum theory in light of such phenomena, entitled, "Can Quantum-Mechanical Description of Physical Reality Be Considered Complete?" *Physical Review* 47 (1935): 777–80.

14. Respectively, *The Born-Einstein Letters*, trans. Irene Born (New York: Walker, 1971), 158, and Max Jammer, *The Philosophy of Quantum Mechanics: The Interpretations of Quantum Mechanics in Historical Perspective* (New York: Wiley-Interscience, 1974), 187.

quantum theory, this quantum action at a distance, which has come to be called "nonlocality," among scientists is now almost universally accepted, or at least tolerated. So it appears that the tide may be changing in the general methodological repudiation of action at a distance.

Such a shift of the consensus, however, only makes all the more perplexing the conviction of Einstein and Newton that action at a distance is bad science. Are Einstein and Newton simply being dogmatic (as some have implied),[15] or are these geniuses seeing something that perhaps the average physicist or philosopher nowadays overlooks, something without which recent physics will reach a philosophically dead end? And if the latter, why do they not spell out this insight? Although Einstein and Newton may not offer much help in answering these questions, perhaps Aristotle and St. Thomas Aquinas, vestiges of whose influence on science have sometimes been suggested as the source of our instinctive abhorrence of action at a distance, can.[16] For, while equally explicit in rejecting action at a distance, Aristotle and St. Thomas offer us an account of why they do so.[17] However, their position, and especially that of St. Thomas, has its own obscurity. For although the impossibility of distant action is a manifest corollary of their claim that all agency is by contact, it is unclear whether the induction they offer in support of this claim is exhaustive.[18] Thus, it would seem that their generalization could be only probable.

Although this might seem prima facie a reasonable way to take St. Thomas and Aristotle's intention, in the following I will argue otherwise, presenting what I take to be St. Thomas's rather subtle position about the impossibility of physical action at a distance. In one sense, and principally, he holds this impossibility to be derived from an induction terminating in intuition of the universal. But it is also true for St. Thomas that this intuition

---

15. Saunders and Brown, for example, describe Einstein's rigidity about action at a distance as an "article of faith"; see *The Philosophy of Vacuum*, 54.
16. See, e.g., Margenau, *Open Vistas*, 104; Francis Kovach, "Action at a Distance in St. Thomas Aquinas," in *Thomistic Papers II*, ed. L. Kennedy and J. Marler (Houston, TX: Center for Thomistic Studies, 1986), 110; and idem, "Action at a Distance in Duns Scotus and Modern Science," 484. Note that Kovach believes that, just as the residual influence of Aristotle and St. Thomas is why many reject action at a distance, so also Scotus is the inspiration for many scientists who tolerate or endorse action at a distance; see ibid., 488–90.
17. See Aristotle, Physics VII, 2, and St. Thomas, In Phys. VII, lects. 3 and 4.
18. Kovach, for example, claims that St. Thomas's use of induction here "constitutes the most fundamental weakness" of his position. See Kovach, "Action at a Distance in St. Thomas Aquinas," 88.

of the nature of physical agency is itself susceptible to a deeper explanation through a metaphysician's consideration of physical agent causality, which explanation the physicist sees in a confused way when he has the aforementioned intuition. In short, while the physicist can be certain, based merely on experience, that physical action at a distance is impossible—and therefore he need not (indeed, should not) try to demonstrate it—nevertheless, after ascending to metaphysics he can offer something like the *propter quid* of this certainty, and thereby render it more certain.

## Action at a Distance and *Physics* VII, 2

In this section I will present first a clarification of the issue, followed by a summary of the reasoning in *Physics* VII, 2, and finally some observations on the force and nature of this reasoning. Now, in order to appreciate the induction in this chapter we need to see more explicitly what is being considered. Action at a distance is itself being treated here only by negation; Aristotle's chief aim is to show that that "whence is the beginning of motion is together with what is moving" (243a4, 243a33),[19] that is, there is always an agent in contact with all bodies that are being moved from without.

Now, this last bit—"moved from without"—is crucial, and because of this Aristotle begins the inquiry into the principle by distinguishing: "Everything in motion, then, is moved either by itself or by something different [*ē hyph' autou ē hyp' allou*]. In the case of things which are moved by themselves, then, it is apparent that in these the moved and the mover are together [*hama*]. For the first mover is present in these, so that nothing is between them" (243a11–15, 243a21–23). After noting this, the rest of the chapter is aimed at manifesting the principle of things that are moved "by another." Thus, because he later in the *Physics* tends to apply the title "self-mover" to animals most of all, and to plants in a less perfect sense,[20] Aristotle is not primarily looking for an extrinsic agent cause in contact with an ox as it walks about, or one moving a flower to grow, for in these cases the proxi-

---

19. Aristotle, *Physics, or Natural Hearing*, trans. Coughlin, 146, 200; I will be using this translation throughout. The two Bekker citations designate what Ross calls the principal and alternative manuscript traditions. Note that I will be following principally what Ross calls the alternative text; the two are substantially the same, however; see note 27 below.

20. See *Phys.* VIII, 2, 252b18–25, and VIII, 4, 254b15–255a6. Since self-motion forms the foundation of what it means to be alive, the highest forms of soul—and therefore of life—would possess self-motion in the highest sense; see St. Thomas, *STh* I, q. 78, a. 1.

## Impossibility of Action at a Distance 181

mate mover is already "together" with the moved; the agent "touches" the patient as intimately as is possible, for they are as one as form and matter. Rather, as the division Aristotle immediately makes of motions from without manifests, Aristotle's chief interest is in externally coerced motions, motions *para physin*—motions opposed to a thing's nature.

Now, this puts us in an odd situation with regard to the natural motion of an inanimate substance, such as the falling of a rock: Is this to be understood as motion from within or motion from without? Aristotle is not explicit here,[21] but it is likely that he intends us to see this as a middle case, in some way partaking of both extremes. For it is more like self-motion than violent motion, inasmuch as it stems from the nature of the mobile, and thus we say that it happens "naturally." But it is also more from without than is the motion of an animal, nor can we say that an inanimate natural mobile possesses life in even a minimal way, and therefore neither does it possess self-motion. Indeed, the only sense in which we can say that there is a per se agent cause of the falling of the rock, Aristotle says, is in the sense that there is an agent cause of the rock's heavy nature, which cause he calls the generator (and he probably has in mind the heavenly bodies).[22] This universal causality of the generator makes the rock to be heavy, that is, to be the sort of thing that goes down; so there *is* an extrinsic agent cause of the

---

21. Rather, it is not until *Phys.* VIII, 4, that Aristotle thinks it necessary to distinguish explicitly between the natural motions of inanimate things and those of animate things, when he is trying to identify the mover behind the former. There he puts greater emphasis on falling's likeness to violent motion than on its likeness to self-motion, perhaps because we more readily notice the opposite: recognizing that both are uncoerced, and by nature, and so from within, one tends to class falling rocks with the growth of plants and the peregrinations of animals.

22. *Phys.* VIII, 4, 256a1. See St. Thomas, *In Phys.* VII, lect. 3, n. 7; VIII, lect. 8, nn. 3–8; and *STh* I, q. 105, aa. 2 and 5, and I-II, q. 26, a. 2. On universal and equivocal causes in general, see *STh* I, q. 45, aa. 1 and 5; q. 104, a. 1; q. 112, a. 1. On the heavens as universal causes, see *STh* I, q. 13, a. 2, and q. 44, a. 2; I-II, q. 9, a. 6. Newton, Einstein, and modern physicists in general would probably agree that there would be no question of action at a distance for natural motions, but would simply add that there are no natural motions. Witness the fact that all nonuniform motions are now assumed to be due to force, i.e., they are from without. Once one admits this, it is difficult to avoid admitting some version of Newtonian physics or its modern heirs. It is also difficult to avoid reaching Newton's frustrated puzzlement about gravity: there should be a proximate agent cause—and, as he notes at the end of the *Principia*, it somehow must act not at the surface of the mobile (like bodies that push or pull from the outside), but throughout its volume (since the mass of the mobile is a part of the proportion measuring this force)—*but what is it?* Perhaps we were wrong to assume that falling is not a natural motion. Again, causality that acts through the volume of the patient is suggestive of universal causality and the distinction between physical contact (i.e., surface to surface) and virtual contact (i.e., presence by power).

downward motion (inasmuch as there is a cause of the nature of the rock and so of the rock itself), but not one that acts according to particular and univocal causality. Thus, to the extent that the natural motion of the rock should be explained by a likeness to the motion of living things, there is no obstacle to admitting that the mover is always in contact with the moved, but to the extent that it should also be explained by a likeness with violent motion, Aristotle would be intending that the consideration of violent motions in this chapter be sufficient. Thus in *Physics* VII, 2, Aristotle is arguing through the more manifest case to what in some measure falls away from it; as he will say in VIII, 4, "it is most apparent in things moving beside nature [*para physin*] that what is moving is moved by something . . . [but] the remaining division [namely, inanimate natural motions] is the most doubtful" (254b25, b34).[23]

Allusion to the universal cause that effects inanimate natural motions brings us to a second distinction we should make more explicit before going further: Besides physical contact, there is a broader notion of contact that Aristotle and St. Thomas often employ in their rejection of action at a distance. Because of the principle established in *Physics* III, 3, that the act of every agent is in its patient, an agent as such must be understood to be present to its patient, even if the latter is moved by the former only by way of an intermediate instrument. This presence of the agency, and therefore of the *power* of the agent, is usually described by St. Thomas as "presence by power," or "virtual contact."[24] This notion that every agent is wherever its effect is, is itself broader than presence by physical contact both because it allows an agent to be "touching" even what it cannot be in physical contact with and because it thereby can be attributed to immaterial agents as well as material ones. Thus a writer is virtually touching the paper when he writes upon it with his pencil, although he is not physically touching it, the way his pencil is; likewise angels can be virtually present on the tip of a needle because that is where the pulsation of their tap-dancing is occurring. Whence, just as in *Physics* VII, 2, Aristotle and St. Thomas are not attending to inanimate natural motion first, so the principal sort of contact Aristotle and St. Thomas have under consideration is physical, not virtual, contact. One grasps the latter only through first grasping the former, and by way of

23. *Physics, or Natural Hearing*, 167.
24. See St. Thomas, *ScG* II, ch. 56, nn. 3–6; *Quodlibet* I, q. 3, aa. 1 and 2; *STh* I, q. 8, a. 2, and q. 52, a. 1.

the likeness between the orders of agent causality (i.e., the particular and the universal, the instrumental and the principal agents). A sign that virtual contact is not the chief notion of contact here is that even if St. Thomas and Aristotle were to grant action at a (physical) distance, one would still have to grant virtual contact between the agent and patient. For even if one were to posit a void or a simply incidental medium between agent and patient, obviously agency itself would still be admitted, and from this alone follows virtual contact.[25]

The issue having been so specified, we turn to *Physics* VII, 2, and its context. The issue of whether all motions require agents in contact with the mobile comes up for two reasons. First, although the first six books of the *Physics* discuss motion and the mobile and their various measures (place, time, and magnitude), the seventh book is the first extended treatment of the agent cause as such—that is, in its relation to the patient or the mobile—and thus it is worth seeing in what this relationship consists in light of the principles laid out in the foregoing books. Second, the study of nature in general, and of the relationship of the agent and the patient in particular, culminates in the demonstration of the existence of a first unmoved mover, and Aristotle fortifies the presentation of this demonstration in VII, 1, by taking as a supposition that "what is moving primarily according to place and bodily motion [must] be touched by or continuous with the mover" (242b24–25; 242b59–60).[26] Thus, in the second chapter he offers a *probatio mediae*.[27]

Although Aristotle begins the chapter by noting that what he intends to show is "common in the case of all movers and things moved" (243a5; 243a35), in the remainder of it he treats separately each species of motion: local motion, alteration, and growth (with only brief consideration of the

---

25. However, it is equally clear that virtual contact must be implicit in the discussion of *Phys.* VII, 2, for later in VIII, 5 and 10, Aristotle assumes that the first unmoved mover must "touch" the first mobile, which contact obviously cannot be physical. Likewise St. Thomas takes the treatment in *Phys.* VII, 2, as sufficient foundation for saying that spiritual beings can be in (virtual) contact with physical bodies; see *STh* I, q. 8, a. 2.

26. Aristotle, *Physics, or Natural Hearing*, 145, 199.

27. What follows does not pretend to be a detailed study of chapter 2; for such exegesis I recommend St. Thomas's commentary, lects. 3 and 4, and for a careful study of the differences in the dual manuscript tradition of the first three chapters of book VII, see David Ross, ed. and trans., *Aristotle's Physics* (Oxford: Oxford University Press, 1936), 11–15, 18–19, 671–74. Rather, I intend to give what I take to be essence of the chapter; my reasons for this approach should become apparent from the interpretation I will offer.

last). Aristotle approaches local motion by distinguishing what he takes to be the four fundamental ways one thing moves another, saying that all others reduce to these four: pushing, pulling, carrying, and whirling. One might see that this division is exhaustive by considering that agency is always either (1) *toward* the agent (pulling); (2) *away from* the agent (pushing); neither, but (3) *around* the agent (whirling); or (4) in any of these ways, but *per accidens* (carrying). Aristotle then contracts this list by noting that carrying and whirling themselves reduce to or are based upon pushing and pulling: on the one hand, whirling is evidently composed of a pulling (toward the center) and a pushing (circularly, around the center), and on the other, an agent that acts by carrying the patient does so merely by being itself in motion and being attached to the patient, so the agent itself is in turn being either pushed, pulled, or whirled. He then concludes that "it is apparent [*phaneron*], then, that nothing is between the moved and the mover," that is, that the latter touches the former, "since the one pushing and the one pulling are together with what is being pulled and what is being pushed" (244a15–19; 244a4–7).[28] In short, action occurs only by contact because the two fundamental sorts of action, of which all others are special or complex cases, themselves occur evidently only by contact. Then for most of the second half of the chapter Aristotle aims to show the same thing with respect to alteration, and this is done principally by comparison with the quasi-alteration involved in sensation: since in every sensation the quality sensed is made to be present to, and therefore together with, the sense (be that through a medium or directly), likewise in every alteration the agent is in contact with the patient. Let that suffice as an outline of VII, 2.

This is a difficult chapter, as it is sometimes unclear what the arguments are intended to be, and often they appear flimsy. But what is perhaps most striking about it is Aristotle's (and, we should add, St. Thomas's) conviction that the conclusion is certain: Aristotle ends the chapter with, "It is *apparent*, then, that nothing is between the extreme mover and the first thing moved" (245b15–16; b1).[29] Indeed, Aristotle had introduced the claim as something both "necessary" *(anagkē)* and something "we see [*horōmen*] happening in

---

28. Aristotle, *Physics, or Natural Hearing*, 147, 201. In what Ross treats as the principal manuscript, the corresponding section of the text ends by saying that moving something by pushing or pulling is "impossible [*adunaton*] . . . without touching" (244a14–15).

29. Ibid., 148, 202. Aristotle says calls this conclusion "apparent" *(phaneron)* or "clear" *(delon)* no fewer than six times in this chapter (244a17, 19, 24, 26, 245a23, and b16). St. Thomas likewise says countless times in lects. 3 and 4 that Aristotle "proves" *(probat)* or "shows" *(ostendit)*,

## Impossibility of Action at a Distance 185

all cases" (242b26; b61). Aristotle wants the claim that no agent acts at a distance to be transparent both "from induction" (*ex epagōgēs*, 244a26; b4) and "from the definitions" of the things under consideration (*ex tōn horismōn*, 244a7; a18).[30] Unless we assume that Aristotle and St. Thomas are merely trying to bully us into agreement, the only plausible reading of the chapter is that they believe the impossibility of action at a distance is something one can gather through the appropriate survey of our experience. In short, Aristotle's mode of argument and St. Thomas's interpretation of it suggest that they see this proposition as more than a probable opinion.[31] Rather, they think that the attentive mind can become intuitively certain that action is effected only by contact. That is, VII, 2, is a *manuductio*, a leading by the hand, through sensible examples—especially the reduction of agent causes to the very concrete notion of pushes and pulls, which are inconceivable without an agent in contact, and the appeal to our certainty of the union between the knower and the thing known in sensation[32]—aimed at an insight into the nature of physical agent causality.

Confirmations of this interpretation are manifold. First, because (as we saw above) Aristotle and St. Thomas use this proposition—that the proximate agent is in contact with its patient—in their proofs for the first unmoved mover,[33] their arguments would be severely handicapped if their premise were dubious, and we see no sign that they think their proofs are tentative.[34] Second, we find both Aristotle and St. Thomas always willing to

---

and therefore "it is evident" (*patet*) and "manifest" (*manifestum*), that the mover and the moved are together. Later he calls the principle "necessary" (*In Phys.* VIII, lect. 9, n. 8).

30. *Horismos* could also be translated as "determination" or "distinction," in which case Aristotle could be referring to the distinctions he has presented as already enough to make the proposition evident.

31. There are of course many inductions in Aristotle's corpus that are merely *ut nunc*, i.e., accepted tentatively, contingent on new or better observations; they are most common in the more particular considerations of natural philosophy as found in *De caelo*, *Meteorology*, and *De generatione et corruptione*, among others. However, where the conviction Aristotle claims to offer is only tentative, he will frequently indicate this by calling his conclusion *pistis*, "faith," or something equivalent—language absent from *Phys.* VII, 2. *De caelo*, for example, is peppered with such language: 269b14-20, 274a30-34, 277a9-13, 283b26-28, 287b29-288a2, 291b24-28, 292a14-18, and 293a25-30 (by no means a complete list).

32. On *manuductio*, see *STh* II-II, q. 174, a. 2, and Marie I. George, "Mind Forming and Manuductio in Aquinas," *Thomist* 57 (1993): 201-13.

33. See also *Phys.* VIII, 5, 256b15-23, and VIII, 10, 266b25-267b9; and *In Phys.* VIII, lect. 9, n. 8, lect. 22, *in toto*, and lect. 23, nn. 4-8.

34. Indeed, St. Thomas speaks of it as demonstrative, especially in the *ScG* I, ch. 10, where he is most obviously restating Aristotle's arguments in *Phys.* VII-VIII.

dismiss any case that appears to be action at a distance by saying that there is in fact always something intermediate that one has not noticed.[35] Thus, for example, neither of them hesitates before the agency of magnets, the perennial instance of an apparent action at a distance.[36] There seems less concern with identifying precisely how the medium carries the efficacy of the agent than with insisting that there is always such a medium.[37] Likewise, when in *De anima* (II, 7, 419a18–b3) Aristotle tries to show that each sense has a medium that transmits the sensible species—a premise that, as we saw, is assumed in *Physics* VII, 2—his strategy is again merely to survey the senses and suggest what seems to be a plausible medium for each; no explicit demonstration is offered. Again it is as though it should have by now become *obvious* that action at a distance is impossible, so each sense *must* employ a medium. And finally, the principle is assumed as early as III, 2 (202a5–7), where Aristotle is showing that usually the mover is moved in return by what it moves; making this assumption before VII, 2, suggests that Aristotle thinks that it can be seen in a vague and confused way at or near the beginning of the study of nature, but that it becomes clearer still the deeper one's study of nature becomes.

To develop this reading it may be helpful to recall the distinction St. Thom-

---

35. At 244a22–25 Aristotle offers a brief presentation of his notoriously problematic account of projectile motion in response to the quite natural objection that there appears to be no conjoined mover; likewise in the principal manuscript of VII, 1–3, Aristotle is not troubled by the fact that heated wood appears to draw fire from a flame when they are brought near but are not yet touching (244a12–14). Similarly, in response to an objection in the commentary on this chapter (*In Phys.* VII, lect. 4, n. 1), St. Thomas simply states that when the sun heats the earth without heating the intermediate orbs, or the torpedo fish numbs the hand without affecting the net in which it is caught, these are not actions at a distance, but actions through media that carry the agent's efficacy in accord with their peculiar natures (the former via its transparency, and the latter via its nonsensitive nature).

36. Aristotle refers to the magnet as being able to move the air, which in turn moves the iron, at *Phys.* VIII, 10, 267a1; St. Thomas, at least in one place, seems to think that the magnet so alters the iron (through the medium) that the latter's motion toward the magnet becomes effectively a natural motion; see *In Phys.* VII, lect. 3, n. 7; *ScG* II, 68.

37. Recall that VII, 2, is after IV, 6–9, which shows that there is no void—i.e., there is always a medium. This is a key principle for the entire matter of action at a distance, for those who argue for action at a distance usually assert that there is no continuous medium to communicate a distant agent's effects (and so often merely try to refute a particle-emission theory). Seeing the impossibility of void, Aristotle and St. Thomas are in a better position to assert that there is always a proximate body that is in fact the proximate agent. All careful studies of the idea of action at a distance recognize that how one answers the question about the possibility of a void is of fundamental importance. See, for example, Margenau, *Open Vistas*, 104–5, and Hesse, *Forces and Fields*, 67, 82–86.

Impossibility of Action at a Distance 187

as borrows from Boethius between propositions *per se nota quoad omnes* and ones *per se nota quoad sapientem*.[38] For although a proposition is known through itself if one grasps the nature of the subject and predicate well enough to see the latter as implied in the former—St. Thomas's examples include "man is an animal," "if equals are subtracted from equals, the remainders are equal," and "every whole is greater than its part"—nevertheless not all propositions that are self-evident, or known through themselves, are so to all men:

> If, however, the "what it is" of the predicate and subject is not known among some men, the proposition in itself will indeed be known through itself, and yet it will not be so for those who are ignorant about the predicate and subject of the proposition. And therefore it happens that, as Boethius says in the book *De hebdomadibus*, some conceptions of the mind are common and known through themselves among only the wise [*quaedam sunt communes animi conceptiones et per se notae, apud sapientes tantum*], such as that incorporeal things are not in place.[39]

He explains, in his commentary on Boethius's words in *De hebdomadibus*, both this example and why there are different "measures" *(modi)* according to which propositions can be known through themselves:

> The reason for this distinction is that when a common conception of the mind, or a principle known through itself, is a proposition of the sort that the predicate is of the notion of the subject, then if that same thing that is signified by the subject and predicate falls into the cognition of all men, consequently the proposition of this sort is known through itself for all men [*per se nota omnibus*].... But only the intellect of wise men rises up to the apprehending of incorporeal reality [*Sed ad apprehendendam rem incorpoream solus intellectus sapientum consurgit*], for the intellect of common men [*vulgarium hominum intellectus*] does not transcend the imagination, which is of only corporeal things. Thus, the intellect of wise men right away withdraws from incorporeal things those things that are properties of bodies, such as to exist in place circumscriptively [*circumscriptive*], which the common man is unable to do.[40]

Thus, some propositions that are most knowable in themselves are not clearly known to us, and because of the feebleness of our intellects, some of these propositions will never, *in via*, become self-evident. We can only (at

---

38. This distinction is implied in Aristotle's distinction between the two kinds of immediate first principles of science called "axioms" and "theses" in *Post. An.* I, 2, 72a15–25, and I, 10; see St. Thomas, *In Post. An.* I, lect. 5, nn. 6–9, and lects. 18–19.
39. *STh* I, q. 2, a. 1. All translations of St. Thomas will be my own.
40. *In De hebd.*, proem.

best!) prove them to be so by an effect-to-cause demonstration: Such propositions range from things as close to us as the definition of the soul as the form of an organism[41] to ones as transcendent as the existence and attributes of God. But St. Thomas is emphasizing here that perhaps a few other propositions knowable in themselves *can become so to us as well;* this sort of proposition "is a common conception of the mind only to those who have been taught [*solum doctis*], [and] is derived [*derivatur*] from the first conceptions of the mind that are common to all men."[42] These propositions are seen to be true not by coercing the mind to assent through a demonstrative syllogism—although St. Thomas clearly indicates above that there is indeed a sort of movement of the mind from the more patently and universally self-evident propositions[43]—but rather in a more subtle and more penetrating way: such propositions become manifest when the teacher leads us by the hand, often by way of concrete and particularly illustrative examples and analogies, toward a new or deeper understanding of what something is, which understanding is "even more accurate than science,"[44] because it is an unmediated apprehension of a nature.

Likewise, then, our interpretation of *Physics* VII, 2, is that the claim that all physical agency is effected by contact (and, implicitly, that action at a distance is impossible) is self-evident to the wise. Aristotle's goal here is not to demonstrate this proposition, but to dispose the student's mind to grasp the truth of it—indeed, it is to render the student, in this respect, *sapiens* and *doctus*. The structure of the chapter, then, is merely a review of our basic experience of the clearest examples of physical agency in which our intellect's attention is artfully directed, by a series of divisions, reductions, and comparisons, toward seeing more explicitly that the proposition in question is

---

41. I refer to the demonstration in *De anima* II, 2, which begins from the effect that the soul is the principle of living. As Aristotle puts it there, from "unclear but more apparent things," namely, those things that are *per se nota* to all, or perhaps only to the wise, we can see what is "clear and more knowable according to its notion" (II, 2, 413a12).

42. *In De hebd.*, proem.

43. This *discursus*, or reasoning, would materially belong to the third operation of the intellect, but the induction in which it terminates is not simply reducible to the third operation the way knowledge of the conclusion of a syllogism is, but formally belongs to the first operation of the intellect. On intuition *(intellectus)* sometimes being the result of a discourse of the mind, see St. Thomas, *In Sent.* III, d. 35, q. 2, a. 2, sol. 1, and d. 14. art. 1, sol. 2, and the little read but still unsurpassed essay by Thomas McGovern, "The Logic of the First Operation," *Laval théologique et philosophique* 12 (1956): 52–74.

44. Aristotle, *Post. An.* II, 19, 100b8.

in fact a principle.⁴⁵ In short, the impossibility of action at a distance is not self-evident to all, but it is self-evident to the well-formed natural philosopher.

## Manifesting the *per se notum*

Is there, then, no possibility of discussion about the intelligibility of action at a distance? In other words, is this merely a case in which, according to St. Thomas, either one sees it or one does not, and if one finds no illumination from the considerations in *Physics* VII, 2, then nothing can be done with such a student? And are we to expect that even the *sapiens* who sees that action at a distance is impossible will be intellectually satisfied after VII, 2? I think the answer to both questions is no. For St. Thomas says that even an immediate principle that is self-evident to the wise man, what Aristotle calls a "thesis," "can be strengthened by external reasoning, that is, by some argument."⁴⁶ In the same way that whether, or how well, something is known through itself is always contingent on the disposition of the learner, so also a proposition might be self-evident to someone and yet become *more so* at a later time, particularly when it is studied under a different or brighter light. The question is merely whether our eyes have adjusted to that light.

To see how this is possible we should recall one of the less well-known but nevertheless principal purposes of dialectic: although dialectic usually

---

45. It is perhaps worth noting that book VII comes on the heels of extremely abstract considerations of motion and its measures in the preceding books, especially book VI; in VII we are presented with a vivid array of common examples, from art to violence, from eating and drinking to tossing objects in the air. Experience is here most obviously the starting point of our ruminations. Nevertheless, the preceding books are crucial as a foundation for the induction, as seeing the need for a contiguous agent presupposes a solid grasp of motion in its relation to place and time (book IV), the continuous (VI), and most especially to act and potency (III), which latter leads to the nature of agency. Often inductions must be made in a particular order (which is further evidence that the impossibility of action at a distance is not *per se notum quoad omnes*). Kovach faults the particularity of the experiences in this chapter, saying that it renders the induction insufficiently universal, and that this fact alone makes it clear that what Aristotle offers is "a generically and/or specifically . . . incomplete induction" (*Scholastic Challenges*, 164); in response, I would suggest that the human intellect can sometimes see more in a few well-known examples than in a complete enumeration of all the most puzzling cases. An apt comparison can be drawn with the biologist trying to define life looking at clear instances (such as animals) while ignoring obscure cases (such as viruses). See Charles De Koninck, *The Hollow Universe* (Quebec: Le Presses de l'Université Laval, 1964), 79–114.

46. *In Post. An.* I, lect. 19, n. 3.

starts and ends only in mere opinion, sometimes dialectic can lead one to an insight into the starting points of a science. As Aristotle says, dialectic

> is also useful for [discerning] the first things of every science. For it is impossible, in whatever science is put forth, to say anything about these [first things] from the proper principles because the first things are the principles of all the others; so it is necessary to come near to them [*anagkē peri autōn dielthein*] through the reputable opinions [*dia tōn endoxōn*] in reference to each [science]. And this is a property of, and most of all belongs to dialectic. For itself being skillful at scrutinizing things, [dialectic] bears the path [*hodon*] toward the principles of all subsequent paths [*methodōn*].[47]

Generalizing this, then, the philosopher may employ dialectic *before* beginning a science in order to give the well-disposed student a vague but certain grasp of the principles of the science; or he may use it *within* the science, when the student has acquired sufficient (and sufficiently ordered) experience of the subject to be capable of intuiting another principle; or the philosopher may wait until the student has reached metaphysics, where he may now use dialectic to manifest more deeply a previously grasped principle through more universal considerations. In all three employments the principles of a science become more evident to the student. As St. Thomas puts it, although we have knowledge *(notitia)* of and believe *(credere)* the principles of a science, and therefore these things are givens *(suppositiones)* for that science, in metaphysics these same principles "are made more fully known."[48] Fortunately, then, when one asks whether the impossibility of action at a distance is itself susceptible to a metaphysical manifestation of the sort described, we can look to an illuminating passage in the *Summa theologiae.*

Toward the end of the *prima pars,* St. Thomas begins the question on the action of bodily creatures by asking whether any body is active. Having answered that it is obvious that some bodies are active, he goes on to explain why people often do not think they see this by addressing three errors: Avicebron's opinion that no body acts upon another, all physical changes being the effects only of separated substances; the more moderate error of Plato and Avicenna that material agents effect only accidental changes, substan-

---

47. Aristotle, *Topics* I, 2, 101a36–b4.
48. St. Thomas, *In De Trin.* q. 3, a. 1. Note that here *credere* is being opposed to *opinari* insofar as the latter contains *dubitatio;* although St. Thomas calls it belief, he is not saying that it is merely probable or in any way uncertain.

tial changes being due to the separated forms alone; and Democritus's opinion that bodies act upon each other, but only by the emission of atoms. St. Thomas notes that the latter two errors have been adequately explained and critiqued elsewhere,[49] so he spends most of his time on the first, which he notes is an extension of the Platonic position:

> For Plato posited that all forms that are in bodily matter are participated, determined, and contracted to this matter, but the separated forms are absolutes and, as it were, universals, and therefore he said that those forms are the causes of the forms that are in matter. Following this, then, that a form that is in bodily matter has been determined to this matter individuated through quantity, Avicebron posited that bodily form is held back and confined by quantity [*a quantitate... retinetur et arcetur*], insofar as it is the principle of individuation, lest [the form] be able to extend itself into other matter through action; rather, [Avicebron posited that] only a spiritual and immaterial form, which has not been confined by quantity, can flow forth into another through action.[50]

This being the position and its origin, St. Thomas critiques the implied inference by distinguishing two orders of agent causality:

> But this reasoning does not conclude that a bodily form is not an agent, but that it is not a universal agent. For insofar as something is participated, so far is it necessary that what is proper to it is participated [as well], just as to the degree that something of light is participated, so much of the notion of the visible is participated. To act upon something, however, which is nothing other than to make something to be in actuality, is a *per se* property of actuality as actuality [*Agere autem, quod nihil est aliud quam facere aliquid actu, est per se proprium actus, inquantum est actus*], and whence also every agent makes something be like itself. So then from this, that something is a form not determined through matter subjected to quantity, one has it that it is an indeterminate and universal agent—but from this, that it has been determined to this matter, one has it that it is a contracted and particular agent. Whence if there were a separated form of fire, as the Platonists posited, it would be in some manner the cause of every combustion. But this form of fire which is in this bodily matter is the cause of this combustion which is from this body into that body.[51]

Then St. Thomas adds what appears to be merely a corollary to the foregoing, but which is most important for our discussion: "This is also why such action [of a bodily agent] comes to be through the contact of the two bodies."[52]

---

49. The former was treated in the *Summa* itself (I, q. 45, a. 8), whereas the latter was treated by Aristotle in *De gen. et corr.* I, 8.
50. *STh* I, q. 115, a. 1.
51. Ibid.
52. "*Unde et fit talis actio per contactum duorum corporum*" (ibid.).

Now, it would be difficult to try to offer here a thorough account of this article, dealing as it does not only with the aforementioned distinction between universal and particular causality, but also with the principle of individuation and the nature of Plato's errors about the forms. Nevertheless, a few things must be said about the argument above pertaining to the first distinction, given that St. Thomas clearly is saying that it manifests not merely *that* physical agent causality occurs only by contact, but also *why* it does so.

Avicebron's argument is that whatever form is participated, contracted, and individuated by matter cannot in any way extend itself to other matter—which extension Avicebron understands to be the same thing as agent causality—so he concludes that material forms are not active. Implicitly rejecting both premises, but more properly the former, St. Thomas responds by saying that Avicebron's legitimate conclusion is narrower than the latter realizes: The argument really rules out only corporeal forms being strictly *universal* agents. To make this clear St. Thomas lays down what appears to be a more fundamental pair of premises: First, to have a participated and individuated form is to have some measure of what is proper to that form, the measure being determined by the degree of the participation possible to a given sort of matter. This is really nothing more than the principle that everything received is received according to the mode of the receiver. And second, it is proper to bodily forms as forms, that is, as actualities, to act upon another—that is, to share that actuality. Again, this is little more than the complementary principle that an agent's action follows upon its mode of being, its actuality.[53] The consequence, then, is that all forms participated and individuated by matter possess some measure of the actuality of forms that are not participated and individuated by matter, that is, pure actualities, and therefore all bodies have some measure of agent causality. Just as universal forms as such act universally and immaterially, so particular or corporeal forms as such act—but particularly, according to the limitations of the nature of body.

53. Hence the body of the article concludes by more or less summarizing those two principles: "It ought to be said, therefore, that a body acts according as it is in actuality, [and it acts] on the other body insofar as it [i.e., the patient] is in potency." To put the first principle in a converse manner: Whatever is actual as such is capable of action, i.e., of communicating actuality. Just as actuality makes agency possible, whatever agency arises is limited by that actuality. One might manifest this principle by noting that if agency does not follow the agent's actuality, it would follow its potency; but only an *active* potency is a principle of agency, and a potency acquires its activity only via form, i.e., actuality. Hence, although our first imposition of the word "power," or "potency," signifies active powers, the purest sense of potency would be found only in passive potency.

It is from this last point that St. Thomas says it follows that material agents act only by contact. The implied argument is, then, that (1) a thing acts according to the way it exists, and (2) a body exists localized, so a body acts according to its locale. Spelling it out more explicitly: being a materially individuated substance—that is, one having a form that is distinguished from others principally in virtue of matter subject to quantity, and therefore having the corollary characteristic of being in an individual place—causes that substance also to act according to that individuation and localization.[54]

The minor premise is obvious to sense and to common sense, although more could be said to unpack it insofar as it implies that bodies are measured by their places. For place and time are the principal external measures of bodies,[55] and just as time is an external measure of the being of a mobile according to the priority and posteriority in its motion,[56] so place is an external measure of the same—one more directly connected with its quantity than is time—closely connected with its agency and patiency with respect to other mobiles. Recalling that place is the innermost surface of the containing body,[57] we conclude that a body can act immediately only at the surface of what contains it, or it contains, or it touches and shares a place with.

The major premise, however—which is equivalent to the medieval dictum *agere sequitur esse*—does the real work of St. Thomas's article, and in its most perfect form the premise belongs to the science of metaphysics. For St. Thomas here takes the principle in its full generality, applying it to both material and immaterial forms, as his argument assumes that the idea

---

54. On the connection between signate matter as the principle of individuation and *situs*, see *In De Trin.* q. 4, a. 2, ad 3, and a. 3. I should note that my presentation of the argument in q. 105 differs greatly from that of Kovach, who presents and critiques the inference in terms of participation and finitude; see *Scholastic Challenges*, 154, 166–67. As this is a misreading, Kovach's objections are irrelevant.

55. See St. Thomas, *In Phys.* III, lect. 5, n. 15; *In Metaph.* V, lect. 9, n. 8, and lect. 15, nn. 8–10; *In De Trin.* q. 4, a. 3.

56. See Aristotle, *Phys.* IV, 11–12, especially 220a25. We could add that, just as being localized results in the togetherness in place that restricts the agent causality of bodies, so too being time-bound results in the togetherness in time (or simultaneity) that restricts that same agency. That is, only bodies in the same place (by which I mean "in contact") at the same time can act upon each other. Likewise, the order of places and of time periods measures and restricts the order of causality. The imaginative science-fiction enthusiast would find this conclusion disappointing, for it means that both the future causing the past and time travel in general are metaphysically impossible. (Perhaps it is noteworthy that those who accept the possibility of action at a distance are—quite consistently—inclined to accept the possibility of time travel; see Hesse, *Forces and Fields*, 279–89.)

57. See Aristotle, *Phys.* IV, 4, 212a20.

of an immaterial form is intelligible, something possible only for one who has seen that being as such is not the same as material being. The physicist might grasp the principle in the more limited manner appropriate to his science—such that it would effectively be "physical agency follows from how a physical substance exists"—and perhaps still (after noting that a body's existence requires that it exist *somewhere*) draw the conclusion that a physical substance must act *at* and *in virtue of* that "somewhere." However, he would not be seeing the truth in its commensurate universality, nor would he be proceeding as St. Thomas does here, from the vantage point of the metaphysician or natural theologian, who sees the principle as applying to material as well as immaterial being.

Now, this interpretation of the relationship between *Physics* VII, 2, and the article in the *Summa* might superficially appear to imply a vicious circle in the relationship between physics and metaphysics. For we will have a problem if physics grounds metaphysics (such as by establishing the existence of immaterial being), while physics also needs metaphysics to establish its own principles. St. Thomas, in his commentary on Boethius's *De Trinitate*, addresses just such an objection to the kind of position we are taking, saying that when

one science supposes those things that are proved in the others, while it also proves the principles of those others, it is not necessary that there be a circle. For the principles that another science, such as physics, receives from first philosophy do not prove those things that the same first philosopher receives from the physicist; rather, they are proved through other principles known through themselves. Similarly, the first philosopher does not prove the principles that he hands on to the physicist through the principles that he receives from the latter, but through other principles known through themselves.[58]

Apply this to our situation: Metaphysics may manifest and render more certain physics' principle that action at a distance is impossible—and thus, the latter may be said to receive the principle from the former—but this manifestation is not itself deduced from the impossibility of action at a distance, nor from any other proposition that is deduced from this principle. Rather, the metaphysician argues from the principle that action follows being, a principle that is *per se notum*, clearly so to himself but less clearly to others. To be more explicit, St. Thomas continues:

---

58. *In De Trin.* q. 5, a. 1, ad 9.

Impossibility of Action at a Distance    195

And besides this, sensible effects, from which physical demonstrations proceed, are the more known with respect to us in the beginning. But when we will have come through them to the cognition of the first causes, due to these [first causes] the why [*propter quid*] of the effects—from which they were proved by demonstration of the fact [*quia*]—will become apparent to us. And thus natural science hands on something to divine science, and nevertheless through the latter its own principles are made known.[59]

Thus, although experience of nature can make one certain *that* action occurs only by contact (and this *demonstratio ad sensum* can be treated as a special sort of *demonstratio quia*), the higher light of metaphysics can help one see *why* action occurs only by contact (and this, likewise, can be treated as a special sort of *demonstratio propter quid*).[60] Thus the metaphysician's inference is superior to, and in a way supersedes, the physicist's induction from sensible effects.[61]

Thus, when we have spoken of major and minor premises, or said that St. Thomas is presenting us with something like the *propter quid* of a proposition, we should not be taken to imply that the *Summa* argument is a demonstration that we need in order to grant the principle. For St. Thomas indicates that the proposition that all agency occurs through contact can be seen well before this argument is offered, inasmuch as he himself assumes it

---

59. Ibid.
60. Demonstration *quia* is properly speaking syllogistic, whereas the *manuductio* Aristotle employs in *Phys.* VII, 2, is not, so the parallel is not perfect; see St. Thomas, *In Post. An.* II, lect. 4, n. 8. But just as "proof" and "demonstration" can be taken broadly, and in their original meanings, as equivalent to "manifestation," I doubt that St. Thomas here means to exclude cases of this sort. (Aristotle himself uses *apodeixis* so as to include inductions in *Post. An.* I, 31, 88a4, and II, 7, 92a34–37.) Thus, note that in the *In De Trinitate* passage St. Thomas cites and summarizes approvingly the beginning of Avicenna's *Metaphysics* commentary, in which the latter explains how "a physical principle can be manifest through itself, and can also be manifested in first philosophy" (*In I Metaph.*, c. 3, f. 71va); his account is indistinguishable from that of St. Thomas. See also St. Thomas, *In Post. An.* II, lects. 7–8, on arguments that are syllogistic and manifestative of what something is and even its *propter quid*, and yet are not demonstrative, properly speaking, although they might be called quasi-demonstrations.
61. Are there any other propositions that are readily induced in one science, and yet seen again through their causes in a pedagogically posterior science? Let me briefly mention two examples: (1) that nature acts for an end, and (2) that in physics the more known is the more universal. Aristotle (and St. Thomas in his commentary) argues for the former in *Phys.* II, 8, largely by means of analogies with art and by focusing on the clear case of unintelligent animals doing intelligent things; however, in a natural theological context St. Thomas argues for this again, this time from a more metaphysical perspective (*ScG* II, 2 and 3). The latter Aristotle states in *Phys.* I, 1, giving examples or signs that are sufficient to manifest it, whereas St. Thomas, in his commentary on the same (*In Phys.* I, lect. 1, n. 7), gives an argument through the cause (the potentiality of the intellect with respect to its objects); this aspect of intellect

many times in earlier questions of the *Summa*;[62] thus, the proposition was sufficiently transparent at those points to be taken as given. Indeed, in those places St. Thomas simply references *Physics* VII, 2, saying that there "it was shown that the mover and moved must be together."[63] In confirmation of this reading, we see that here in q. 115, a. 1, the matter of physical agency being by contact comes up in the form of an after-thought—it is not St. Thomas's main point. This, then, suggests that St. Thomas believes he is here manifesting the cause of something that need not be taken up in its own right, for *that* it is so has been evident all along. The proposition in question, then, is being taken as sufficiently evident at the beginning of the *Summa* to serve as a foundation for much of the science of natural theology, and yet its evidence can be illuminated further, as is done at the appropriate time when the theologian considers the order and relationships among bodily creatures, at the end of the *prima pars*.

Looking back, we might even notice one final sign that the conclusion of the argument in q. 115 was already certain. Consider St. Thomas and Boethius's aforementioned example of a proposition that is *per se notum quoad sapientem*: namely, that immaterial substances are not in place. St. Thomas says that we see this when we truly apprehend (however inadequately) what an immaterial substance is; in that moment we immediately know that such creatures cannot have their being measured by place. But in this same thought we must have already seen that material substances *do* have their being so measured. And since the being *secundum quid* of any substance follows on the being *simpliciter* of that substance, any recognition of the localized character of material being entails an implicit (if not fully conscious) recognition of the localized character of its agency. This grasp of the nature of material substance, then, contains in fact the indistinct grasp of the proposition that material substances act only by contact. The argument in q. 115 is, then, nothing more than the unfolding of this insight.

---

(and apprehensive powers in general) is not formally considered until the physicist has descended to study of soul (*De anima* II, 5, and III, 4–6), but here this movement from induction to propter quid could be understood to occur entirely within natural science.

62. For explicit instances, see *STh* I, q. 8, a. 1, and a. 2; q. 45, a. 5; and q. 112, a. 1.

63. *STh* I, q. 8, a. 1. St. Thomas employs the principle that action occurs only by contact throughout his philosophical and theological opera, often merely assuming that the principle is readily admissible—e.g., *De ver.*, q. 5, a. 9, objs. 16 and 17; *ScG* III, ch. 68; *De pot.*, q. 6, a. 7, objs. 11–12, and ad 15; *Quodlibet* XI, q. 1, a. 1; *STh* I, q. 45, a. 5—or, on other occasions, again simply citing *Physics* VII, 2, as having settled the matter—*STh* I, q. 8, a. 1; *In Sent I.*, d. 37, q. 1, a. 1; *De malo*, q. 16, a. 10, obj. 4; *Quodlibet* VI, q. 2, a. 1, ad 1.

## Concluding Remarks

A good refutation of any error should also be able to show the source of the error. And although few philosophers and scientists—some quantum theorists excepted, as we mentioned in the introduction—believe that action at a distance actually occurs, many claim not to see that it is inherently impossible. Now, although I think St. Thomas and Aristotle help us to see this impossibility as implied in the notion of physical agency, we should still offer an explanation of why we often do not see (or *think* we do not see) this impossibility.

The cause of this error is the same one St. Thomas mentioned when explaining why things are sometimes self-evident only to the wise: namely, the common man's habitual inability to rise above the imagination. One can imagine one body acting on another at a distance;[64] thus, while making the common mistake of assuming that everything imaginable is logically possible, one concludes that action at a distance is too. A sign that imagination is at the heart of the matter lies in the fact that the most vocal proponents of action at a distance these days, the quantum theorists, are those most at home in the most abstract parts of mathematical physics. For in spite of this abstraction, mathematics always resolves to the imagination, and the mathematical formalism of quantum mechanics, largely because of its complete dependence upon symbolic equations, is almost entirely conducted on the "mental chalkboard" of the imagination.[65] A further sign that the intellectual custom of the mathematician is the source of this interest in action at a distance lies in the two principal kinds of relations—those between quantities (e.g., double and half) and those between agents and patients (e.g., father and son). For the mathematical physicist, being preoccu-

---

64. Of course, this is also speaking loosely, as the image of A acting on B at a distance is no different from that of A changing and then B changing (or even B changing simultaneously). That is, causality is not strictly speaking imagined any more than is any *per accidens* object of sense. That is part of what makes the imagination such an impoverished starting point for speculating about causality. In the imagination anything can happen, even the unthinkable.

65. This imagination is of course different from that in, e.g., geometry, in which the imagined continuum is the matter and locale of the object. For although in quantum mechanics the objects—the wave equations—are straightforward images, insofar as their symbolic elements all have a functionally well-defined meaning and can therefore be consistently manipulated, nevertheless the waves described by the equations are themselves not perfectly imaginable. For they "exist" in an abstract sort of "space" containing complex numbers (quantities that are the sums of real numbers and multiples of i, the root of negative one). Thus, even the quantum theorist's tie to the *intellect* via the imagination is somewhat tenuous.

pied with quantitative relations—and rightly so, as mathematics abstracts from the end, and therefore also the agent cause[66]—tends to reduce causal relations to quantitative ones, which in turn leads the physicist to think that the connection between agent and patient is like that between double and half. Now, an orange the same size as a lemon might later grow to be twice the size of that lemon, thereby simultaneously changing their respective relations, and this regardless of the distance or medium between them; the mathematical physicist then wonders why something similar is not possible in all physical relationships. But the potencies of the mathematical object are based upon an abstraction from the potencies of the physical object, so the characteristics of the former are often an inadequate indication of those of the latter. The mathematical physicist is being too mathematical and insufficiently physical.[67]

What then do St. Thomas and Aristotle have to say to the modern physicist who is nervous that the impossibility of action at a distance will render a well-tested theory such as quantum theory unsound? Or conversely, what is to prevent a scientist from dismissing St. Thomas's "a priori" rejection of action at a distance as incompatible with well-established science, and calling it just one more instance of a philosopher's unwillingness to look in the proverbial telescope? Is there a necessary tension between the philosopher and the physicist here? To begin a response, first a word of caution is in order regarding quantum theory in particular: The jury is still out on how to interpret quantum theory as a whole.[68] But to offer a more determinate response, one might recall that St. Thomas and Aristotle also thought that the notion of a void, a space that is literally empty, is also absurd,[69] and so posited the existence of a subtle body pervading the heavens and filling apparent voids. Now, although the "luminiferous ether" of nineteenth-century elec-

66. See Aristotle, *Metaph.* III, 2, 996a29–32, and St. Thomas, *In De Trin.* q. 5, a. 4, ad 7.
67. See St. Thomas, *In De Trin.* q. 4, a. 3, and q. 5, a. 3.
68. For an excellent recent review of the physicist's situation vis-à-vis making sense of quantum theory, see F. Laloë, "Do We Really Understand Quantum Mechanics? Strange Correlations, Paradoxes, and Theorems," *American Journal of Physics* 69 (2001): 655–701. "It is probably safe to say that we understand its [quantum mechanics'] machinery pretty well; in other words, we know how to use its formalism to make predictions in an extremely large number of situations . . . Conceptually, the situation is less clear" (ibid., 691). Hesse, for example, argues that quantum phenomena that are sometimes taken to imply action at a distance really "cannot be described as actions at all, since . . . [this would] presuppose that some energy passes from one end-point to the other" (*Forces and Fields*, 271–72).
69. See note 37, above.

tromagnetism has been thoroughly discredited, the general ether concept has not, and both Einstein and many quantum theorists have seen a need to understand their work in light of an ether of some sort.[70] But if quantum theory is not inherently inimical to ether, then what superficially looks like action at a distance in that theory may be action through a quantum ether.[71] So one can accept "nonlocality" as consistent with requiring all agency to be effected locally and through contiguous media, and the apparent opposition between the substance of modern physical theory and the perennial philosophy evanesces.

Thus, not only did Einstein and Newton, for instance, see no incongruity between physics and philosophy, they even thought that the two are in some way one, and likewise took as a principle of natural philosophy that things do not act at a distance. In this, we have shown, they agree with St. Thomas and Aristotle. Being natural philosophers by profession, however, Newton and Einstein took the matter no further, nor should they have. St. Thomas and Aristotle, however, being not only natural philosophers but also *first* philosophers, further thought that how clearly this principle is seen admits of degrees, degrees that can be obtained both over the course of pursuing natural philosophy and, more so, in metaphysics. For one's knowledge, even of what one already knows—and even of what one sometimes does not *know* that one knows—can always become sharper, more profound, and in this sense, more certain,[72] and this is especially the case when one sees a proposition to be true through grasping its cause. Thus, the most rudimentary understanding of what body is—which understanding is common to all men—latently contains the basic principles about how bodies can and cannot act, and the abstraction of these principles can become more explicit by way of examples carefully chosen and presented in a strategic order (as Aristotle does in *Physics* VII, 2), and more explicit still by an inference of the same from more universal principles (as St. Thomas does in *Summa theologiae* I, q. 115, a. 1).

I do not pretend that this reading of St. Thomas and Aristotle on the

---

70. See Hesse, Forces and Fields, 274–75, and Christopher A. Decaen, "Aristotle's Aether and Contemporary Science," *Thomist* 68 (2004): 375–429.

71. This agency through a quantum medium appears to be either instantaneous or at least faster than the speed of light, neither of which is a problem for action through a medium as such (as I argued in note 11, above), although it is for relativity.

72. Thus, St. Thomas says that the more certain *(certior)* is the same as the "more fully grasped by the mind" (*STh* II-II, q. 4, a. 8).

matter of action at a distance is particularly novel.[73] However, I hope that such an account might help resolve a perennial bone of contention not only between Aristotle and modern science, but even among modern scientists themselves. At minimum perhaps it is a little clearer how what is evident to wise men, such as Newton and Einstein, may become even more so when they are guided by even wiser men, such as St. Thomas and Aristotle.

73. Hesse, for example, agrees with my claim that Aristotle regards the impossibility of action at a distance as "self-evident" and that in *Phys.* VII, 2, he intends to be presenting "a list of phenomena in common experience" to lead the student to an "intuition . . . [of] the necessary first principles of the science" (Hesse, *Forces and Fields*, 67–68).

*Jude P. Dougherty*

# Physics and Philosophy

THERE CAN BE NO CONFLICT between philosophy and the natural sciences any more than between theology and the natural sciences as long as both remain true to their methods. Conflicts do arise between physicists and philosophers or biologists and theologians, largely because of misunderstanding, sometimes aided and abetted by the propensity of some to "publish in the *New York Times.*" The sciences thus reported come laden with metaphor. We hear of "anti-matter," "drops of electricity," "black holes," "right- or left-handed spin of a K-meson," and I haven't even mentioned relativity and indeterminacy. In the early 1950s when someone at the University of California introduced the concept of "anti-matter," one of my graduate student classmates, in trying to elucidate the term for a newspaper reporter, ended up being presented as refuting an eminent physicist at Berkeley. He was merely trying to unpack the metaphor. Burnt once, he accepted the advice of another classmate: "When you see a reporter, you run, not walk, the other way." My classmate and lifelong friend survived some mild ridicule, and after earning his Ph.D. at the Catholic University of America, within little more than a decade became chairman of the Physics Department at Vanderbilt University.

Of course, there is the well-known case of Galileo, who tried to teach biblical scholars how to interpret Scripture and whose work in return was subjected to scrutiny. As you know, he got caught teaching a likely hypothesis as if it were demonstrated fact. We all know that Darwin was supposed to have done away with a creative God, whether he said so or not. And Einstein removed moral constraint with his theory of relativity. Both Einstein and Heisenberg must have been amused by the misuse made of terms associated with their names. Then there is the more recent episode of James

Watson and Francis Crick, the discoverers of the double-helix structure of DNA. Crick, reflecting on his landmark work in human genetics, asserted, "The God hypothesis is rather discredited." Watson similarly concluded, "Only with the discovery of the double helix and the ensuing genetic revolution have we had grounds for thinking that the power held traditionally to be the exclusive property of the gods might one day be ours."

Journalists on both sides of the Atlantic are only too willing to seize upon an ambiguous metaphor to undermine Christian belief in a benevolent God or to discard biblical standards of morality. And we have come to expect that of them. But when physicists and other natural scientists transfer their authority from their legitimate domain to areas that are philosophical and theological, their motives become suspect.

Of course, the physicist, chemist, or biologist is a product of his early education, wherein he has likely incurred a critique of the Western intellectual tradition in the Enlightenment manner. John Dewey's educational philosophy that has long prevailed in academic circles can be summed up in one sentence: "The function of education is not to transmit an inherited intellectual tradition but to subject it to criticism." When it came to morality, however, Dewey was cautious. Biblical morality was not to be rejected outright, but a proper or secular rationale was to be sought for those values retained after the sifting takes place.

The necessity of providing the modern mind with an adequate interpretation of natural science is a task inherited from the eighteenth century, wherein Locke and Hume challenged the notions of "substance" and "causality" and thereby undermined a classical understanding of science. The awakened Kant accepted Hume's psychological account of causality and went on to develop a theory of knowledge with repercussions in the philosophical world and beyond. The emphasis Kant placed on the categories as mental structures whose function consisted mainly in organizing data received by the senses had a profound effect on the common understanding of science. Karl Popper's later questioning of the value of induction may be regarded as a logical consequence.

Ancient notions of science presupposed through the Renaissance, certainly by Copernicus, Galileo, and Kepler as well as their contemporaries, assumed the intelligibility of nature and the power of mind to ferret out the secrets of nature. With roots in Plato, Aristotle, and the Scholastics, philosophical realism was the coin of the day, but with the advent of British empiricism, our understanding of the nature of science was transformed. When Kant asked how science is possible whereas metaphysics is not, his answer was no help. Having acquiesced to Locke and Hume, he was led not to skepticism but to a peculiar kind of faith wherein the assumption of postulates provided the foundation of both physics and belief in God. Old ideas—God, nature, soul—were not to be dismissed but to be reinterpreted and retained for their regulative value.

The positivism spawned by eighteenth-century empiricism in effect reduced knowledge to sensory experience. Given its premises, we can believe only what we sensorially encounter. On the basis of what we observe we can make predictions—assuming the accuracy of our description and the adequacy of our mathematics—about what may happen in the future. What things are in themselves, *noumena*, is beyond us. On this account, description replaces definition in the Aristotelian sense. Some theorist went so far as to say that all we know is the reaction of natural phenomena to our instruments, in extreme cases the readings on a dial. An explanation for someone such as Carl Hempel (1905–97) or Ernest Nagel (1901–85) becomes a hypothesis to be tested for adequacy.[1] A hypothesis is a conceptual scheme that not only enables data to be correlated but signals certain results when the integration of its components is established.

An amusing account may illustrate the point being made here. Wolfgang Pauli in 1930 postulated the existence of an undetected particle to account for phenomena he could not otherwise explain. Perhaps tongue in cheek, he apologized in the atmosphere of the academic zeitgeist, writing to a colleague, "I have done a terrible thing. I have postulated a particle that cannot be detected." Supporting Pauli, Enrico Fermi baptized the hypothetical particle "neutrino," or "little neutral one," but his paper was rejected by the prestigious journal *Nature* as "too speculative and remote from reality." The first experiment to hunt for the neutrino was called "Project Poltergeist." In 1956 Clyde Cowan and Fred Reines found a definite trace of the elusive neutrino as a result of experiments performed with a newly commissioned reactor at Los Alamos. Pauli, in an Aristotelian manner, was seeking an expla-

---

1. Cf. Carl G. Hempel and Paul Oppenheim, "Studies in the Logic of Explanation," *Philosophy of Science* 15 (1948): 135–75; Carl G. Hempel, "Studies in the Logic of Confirmation," *Mind* 54 (1945): 1–26, 97–121, reprinted in *Aspects of Scientific Explanation*, ed. idem (New York: Free Press, 1965), 3–46; Ernest Nagel, *The Structure of Science* (New York: Harcourt, Brace, and World, 1961).

nation, reasoning from effect to unseen cause, but clearly he was out of line as judged by positivistic canons.[2]

It is my contention that the eighteenth-century British empiricism as found in Locke and Hume is incompatible with contemporary science. From an Aristotelian point of view the object of scientific inquiry is the essence or nature of material things as inferred from their behavior. Things are what their natures' activity discloses them to be. Nature is understood as the whatness or quiddity of a thing, the source of its activity, both active and passive. It is a synonym for essence considered dynamically.

The empiricist is right when he affirms that essence or nature is not given sensorially. But there is more in the sense report than the senses themselves are able to appreciate. The sense report of a common element is a report of its accidental features, such as color, resistance to pressure, relative weight, and perhaps odor. Locke declared that what we call a "substance" is nothing more than the name we give to our mental collation of these properties. The substance itself remains an unknown substrate. Shades of Ockham!

Couple Locke's account of substance with Hume's account of causality and you have the repudiation of science in the Aristotelian sense. For Aristotle the aim of scientific inquiry is to explain something that is unintelligible taken by itself. To have scientific knowledge is to know why things are the way they are or behave the way they do. The basis of explanation is the principle of sufficient reason. To know the *propter quid* is a mark of success, the end of a quest. Given the complexity of nature, the quest is apt to be open ended in the sense that there is always more to know. A provisional explanation may give way to a fuller one without the repudiation of a previous one. Thus, a prescientific knowledge of materials or processes can lead to a scientific one. The ancients well knew the properties of copper, its malleability, its relative softness, and in a vague way its melting point and its ability to form compounds with other metals. The molecular structure responsible for these properties, of course, eluded them.

In this presentation I focus on two related notions that play an important role in an Aristotelian account of science. The first is the notion of "potentiality"; the second, the concept of nature or, in contemporary epistemology, its more or less equivalent, "structure," and our mental representation

---

2. As reported in a feature article, "Annals of Science," by K. C. Cole, *New Yorker*, June 2, 2003.

of such. I then discuss the role of models in our attempt to capture structure mentally. From an Aristotelian point of view, contemporary attempts to model are attempts to grasp by means of equations or visual aids the structure responsible for behavior, the locus of potentiality. Although Aristotle was convinced that there is no intellection without accompanying sensation, he did not use the term "model."

It is the Aristotelian notion of "potentiality" and its related notions of capacity, power, and possibility that first command our present attention. In particular we are interested in the way these notions are handled by representative contemporary authors working from radically different positions. We argue that only a realism will enable one to deal successfully with the notions of potentiality and possibility, that purely logical accounts are inadequate, that nothing less than a metaphysical scrutiny of structure will enable us to tie possibility to potentiality, and that a doctrine of potentiality is essential if we are to understand the work of the natural sciences.

Under the influence of Gilbert Ryle (1900–1976), statements about disposition have come to be treated as hypothetical or conditional statements or as conjunctions of such statements.[3] "He is intelligent" is taken to mean that if he is presented with a problem, he will quickly produce a solution. It is easy to transform a declarative sentence about what is into a modal assertion about what may be expected. "The vase is fragile" becomes "If dropped, it will break." Avoided is the ascription of an inherent property or the recognition of a real capacity. The common-sense recognition that capacities imply a subject, the ontological grounding of possibility, is put aside.

From an Aristotelian point of view, the problem of what the ascription of a power or disposition to a thing means when it is not exercising that power is not solved by transforming sentences from the indicative to the subjunctive mood. To claim that "brittleness predicated of glass is to make a prediction about how a piece of glass will behave if certain conditions are fulfilled" is not enough. Both common sense and natural science tell us that things and materials have powers even when they are not exercising them. That, in fact, is the way they are differentiated from other things.

The ability to deal with the concept of "potentiality" is a major test for any philosophy of science. Few will deny that capacities, dispositions, pro-

---

3. Gilbert Ryle, *The Concept of Mind*, first published 1949; numerous editions. See the recent edition that contains a valuable introduction by Daniel C. Dennett (Chicago: University of Chicago Press, 2002).

pensities, and tendencies are real. It is how these are to be understood that divides philosophers into camps. Alfred North Whitehead's (1861–1947) use of the term "potentiality" and its correlative "actuality" is not Aristotle's, and it answers to a uniquely Whiteheadean problem.[4] Locke's constellation-of-events metaphysics differs from Nicholas Rescher's conceptual idealism.[5] One's answer to the question, "In what sense are potentialities real?" indicates one's intellectual bent if not indeed one's whole philosophy. How the issue is treated divides not only idealist from realist but metaphysician from logician. There is ample evidence that those who write about possible worlds tend to blur, if not confuse, logical and material possibility. Logicians by trade are inclined to pay no attention to the way premises are obtained. Logic deals with judgments as it finds them; its subject matter is the given. Since logical and mathematical truths are universal and necessary, it is tempting to think of them as eternal and to relate them to the actual as if the relation were that of the determinable to the determinate. The logician is tempted to speak of existence as a determination that happens to a possible essence. Thus conceptually whatever is possible may be instantiated.

The careful logician will, of course, avoid the trap. He is aware that the manifold of merely possible things is an intellectual construct and that the starting point of this construct is an informed view of the real world as provided by the sciences. The realist recognizes that intellectual construction is subject to the implicit constraint of the given. One must acknowledge the distinction between real or physical possibility and the strictly hypothetical. The physically possible is governed by the laws of nature. Even from a logical point of view, the really possible is that which is consistent with a certain body of stipulated fact. But how determine that consistency? Is all that is not intrinsically self-contradictory possible? As long as we remain in the order of abstract possibility, whatever is not blatantly self-contradictory can be said to be possible. But as soon as we enter the order of existence, impossibilities begin to multiply. If existence is imparted to any one structure, some others become impossible.

This can be illustrated by the difference between the artist and the art critic. Artists, painters, sculptors, musicians always function in an existential situation. The "form" is either found in marble or dictated by material

---

4. Cf. Alfred North Whitehead, *Process and Reality* (New York: Harper and Row, 1960).

5. Rescher's theory is set forth in *Conceptual Idealism* (Oxford: Basil Blackwell, 1973) and in *A Theory of Possibility* (Pittsburgh: University of Pittsburgh Press, 1975).

contingencies. The critic, not so constrained, is free to imagine possibilities contrary to the structures available to the artist. Who has not experienced the critic, who, in the light of ideals inappropriate or impossible to attain, nevertheless finds fault with the artifact before him. Something like this occurs in the political order, where the ideal frequently drives out the good. In human experience there are no such things as fully determined essences prior to their actual instantiation. They cannot be what they are unless they first become it. The key word from a realist perspective is "finding," not "supposition."[6]

From a realist perspective, if we talk about possibilities, we do not ordinarily concern ourselves with logical possibility. Logical and mathematical truths are universal and necessary possibilities, and about them we do not deliberate. Nor do we normally deliberate about the content of a creative imagination at play. Such imagination feeds on intelligible factors drawn from experience.

From the realist perspective, it is capacity, tendency, and disposition on the part of physical objects that is at once the ground of logical possibility, artistic imagination, and the object of scientific inquiry. In determining what is materially possible, reference, of necessity, is made to empirical laws, that is, to laws of nature or to statistical evidence pertaining to what has been observed to be the case. The potentialities recognized in things are permanent features of those things. They are predicated of those things whether or not they are acting or being stimulated. We utilize copper tubing because of its resistance to corrosion and because of its ability to conduct heat effectively, and similarly copper wire because it is capable of conducting electricity. We mark "Fragile" on packages because we know something about the structure of glass and its inherent properties. The capacity to break does not consist in the occurrence of the event. It seems forced to construe fragility in modal terms such that we say or imply something like "A fragile piece of glass is one which would break in some possible world in which, unlike the present world, it is actually being dropped."

The reason we believe that a certain disposition can be asserted of a subject is that we know that it currently has such and such power. Thus to as-

---

6. Foremost among those who advocate a realist interpretation of science is William A. Wallace. See, e.g., *The Modeling of Nature* (Washington, DC: The Catholic University of America Press, 1996). See also *Causality and Scientific Explanation,* 2 vols. (Ann Arbor: University of Michigan Press, 1972–74).

cribe a power to a thing or material is to say something about what it can or will do. To merely specify external conditions is not enough. Circumstances may change without affecting the thing itself. To ascribe a power is to ascribe a disposition to a specific subject because we have some insight into the nature or structure of the thing.

The term "magnetic" is another example of a disposition term. It designates not a directly observable characteristic but rather a disposition on the part of some physical object to display a specific reaction under certain circumstances. The vocabulary of natural science abounds in dispositional terms, such as "malleable," "elastic," "conductor of heat," "fissionable," "recessive trait," and the like. Are these features not as real as any empirically discernable property we may predicate? Does not structure as disclosed through previous behavior manifest real disposition? Unavoidable is the inclination to form some sort of a conceptual aid as we attempt to understand the mechanism responsible for the activity under consideration. Those who favor a contextual approach merely describe, not explain. The subjunctive conditional, while not inaccurate, nevertheless flies in the face of the way we normally think and speak about things. Only by recognizing a physical connection between the nature of a thing and the way it acts do we find the root of conceptual connections employed in talk of material and logical possibility.

We need not suppose that every capacity or disposition of magnesium that we have identified requires the attribution of a power. There is reason to argue that diverse dispositions may be manifestations of the same power. In fact, dispositions attributed to a thing may be nothing more than structure viewed from several vantage points. On the other hand, as we move from atom to molecule, to compound, to organism, powers are more easily discerned, particularly when the subject is animate. Since antiquity, cognitive and appetitive powers have been distinguished, and both distinguished from the purely vegetative. The list has never been very long, and always where encountered, identification is thought to follow empirically ascertained evidence. "Powers are specified by behavior, behavior by object," is an old Scholastic maxim. Unless demanded by the evidence, nothing is inferred, nothing is predicated of a subject. The processes of attribution and, negatively, of elimination are by no means simple. The lower the order, the more constant or invariable the nature. The more sophisticated our knowledge of things becomes, the more we understand their mechanism to confer and receive. In dealing with relatively simple structures at the atomic or molecular level, the identification of the molecular structure may be simply the identification of the power. Molecular structure may itself be the only capacity we need to recognize in order to account for an element's physical or chemical behavior. Structure itself is, after all, a disposition of parts. The more we know about those parts and their relation to each other, the more we can determine (predict) what is possible. To say this is not to subscribe to a mechanistic interpretation but to recognize that powers are closely related to natures that manifest them. J. L. Mackie would banish altogether the notion of "power" and settle for a purely descriptive account.[7] The metaphysician, he thinks, is affected with double vision. But to the realist, the distinctions between thing and disposition, between disposition and activity, are real and when acknowledged assist in rendering intelligible the phenomena that require explanation.

As Rom Harré has argued, scientific knowledge consists primarily in a knowledge of the internal structures of persisting things and materials; secondarily in the knowledge of the statistics of events, of the behavior of such things and materials, wherein one discerns patterns among these events through certain types of change and not through other kinds. Emphasis is placed on structures and their persistence.[8] The recognition of such units and their differentiation is the recognition of natural kinds. The chemical analysis of a material, the genes inherited from a parent, the structure of a crystal, the electronic configuration of an atom, point to real natures or essences. In them reside the powers of generation and production; it is through their operation that the flux of events results. On this account, a scientific explanation consists principally in accounting for the second type of information in terms of the first. A scientific explanation shows how the patterns discerned amidst the flux of events are produced by the persisting natures and constitutions of things.

There are many ways in which we mentally capture and communicate our knowledge of the structures under consideration. We use sentences to represent and communicate linguistically, but linguistic vehicles are not the only vehicles of thought. Pictures, models, and diagrams are also vehicles of

7. John Leslie Mackie, *Cement of the Universe: A Study of Causation* (Oxford: Clarendon Press, 1974).
8. Rom Harré, *The Principles of Scientific Thinking*, ch. 4, "Laws of Nature" (Chicago: University of Chicago Press, 1970), 92–126.

thought. To draw a diagram or to make a model is to think. To construct a diagram, a picture, or a model is to attempt to get at the inner structure or constitution of a thing. The twentieth-century preoccupation with linguistic vehicles such as declarative sentences and hypothetical propositions has blinded us to the structural picture from which they have been abstracted. Conditional statements are more apt to call attention to the possibilities of change, to the successive states of things, than to the structure of the things themselves. The two approaches, needless to say, are complementary; structure may be presented diagrammatically by means of pictures and models; the possibilities of change may be presented sententiously as conditional statements.

Pictures, models, and diagrams are metaphors or forms of analogy not unlike those we employ in ordinary discourse. In scientific as well as in ordinary speech, analogy functions to make available the less known in terms of the better known. Natural science is so permeated with metaphor that its use goes almost unnoticed. Lord Kelvin once said that he could not understand anything except insofar as he could construct a model. In physics, we speak of light *waves*, talk about heat as *fluid*, gases as if they consisted of plastic *particles*, electricity as a *current*, *drops* of electricity, *anti-matter*, *right-handed* and *left-handed spin* on a K meson; we talk of Faraday's *strained space*, electron quantum *jumps*, and star *creation*. In spite of the widespread employment of metaphor in the sciences, one encounters few theories of their function.

Parenthetically it may be noted that theories of analogy first came into being in an attempt to understand how metaphysics could speak of things divine and not slip into either agnosticism or anthropomorphism. This is not to suggest that common metaphors in the sciences function in exactly the same way as they do in theological discourse. In ordinary prescientific knowledge, just as in scientific knowledge, metaphor plays a heuristic role, revealing semidisclosed aspects of things and suggesting new ways to look at things. Or perhaps I should put it the other way around. The scientific employment of metaphors, analogies, and models is not unlike their use in everyday coming-to-know. The value of a prescientific knowledge of things tends to be underacknowledged. Overlooked is the continuity between the two types of prescientific and scientific knowledge. Things and processes that form the object of scientific knowledge are known in a vague or imprecise manner before they become objects of the controlled and system-

Physics and Philosophy 211

atic knowledge, which is science. One of the unfortunate effects of certain nineteenth-century theories of science was to place the emphasis upon mathematics and experiment divorced from our personal contributions in using them, thus creating a gulf between science and life.

Natural scientists in much of their theoretical activity are, in fact, trying to form a mental picture of the mechanisms of nature that are responsible for the phenomena they observe. The forming of a mental picture, in effect, is the making of models. Models may be sentential or iconic. A model may be nothing more than a tentative analogue for the real but as yet unknown mechanism or structure. The model itself may be fashioned on things we know or understand only imperfectly. When theory construction is successful, that which is presented as a model of an unknown mechanism in one generation may in another generation be seen to approximate the physical structure of the object in question. In the lifetime of our fathers, if not in our own lifetime, the molecular structure of a solid was a mere postulate, a crude analogue to represent what was thought ought to be the case on the basis of the evidence at hand. Today an electron microscope can take directly interpretable pictures of atoms within solids. Now we can understand why some solids behave as insulators, others as semiconductors, and still others as metals. To use another example, with nuclear magnetic resonance imaging we are able to determine sodium or phosphorus concentrations in compounds such as fats and carbohydrates in the living tissues of the human body. Various nineteenth-century models of the cell and its components turned out in the twentieth century to be a close approximation of the postulated structure.

Models approximate structure when adequate. We had a visual model of the cell long before we saw it with a microscope. The double-helix structure responsible for the inheritance of genetic traits was an iconic model long before the electron microscope confirmed it. The inference to many chemical and subatomic structures has been supported in a plurality of ways as our instruments have become more sophisticated. As our knowledge of the structures of things becomes more refined, we can understand why things behave as they do. But no matter how revealing structure may be, it is not metaphysically ultimate from an Aristotelian point of view.

Considerations of our knowledge of nature, I am arguing, lead to the recognition of natural structures. But those structures are not ultimate; they presuppose a nature that is structured. The question regarding ultimacy is obviously a question of a different order. To answer it, it is necessary to go back to Aristotle's analysis of change and to the metaphysical structure that analysis reveals. A theory of being is unavoidable as one attempts to explain change. For Aristotle, structure is a proper accident, the manifestation of a composite essence, an essence composed of matter and form. The many distinctions he introduces in his attempt to account for becoming not only give him a theory of reality but contribute to his theory of knowledge.

George Santayana, commenting on the view of substance entertained by Locke and Hume, wrote: "When modern philosophers deny material substance, they make substances out of the sensations or ideas which they regard as ultimate facts.... They deny substances in favor of phenomena which are hypostatized because phenomena are individually wholly open to intuition."[9] Santayana had his own reasons for dismissing Hume; in part they are not unlike the reasons that have been given here. Santayana himself thought that substance as a category is needed to understand the flux of events.

I have suggested with Harré and others that models, pictures, and diagrams are created in an attempt to understand the natures of things. In some instances they may be little more than visual aids, but more often than not they express insights into natures that exist independently of the mind. Since the accumulation of knowledge is an ongoing process, no model is ever likely to be complete. The ontological richness of even the simplest structure is apt to require revision after revision. We can never plumb the depths of the beings that we encounter. If biography after biography is sometimes required to fathom the personality of a great man, so too the science accumulated over century after century may be required to intellectually approximate nature's structures. Model supplants model, each incorporating preceding discoveries. It is rare that the false is supplanted with the true; rather the less adequate account is usually enriched or replaced by the more adequate.

For those schooled in the realist tradition, permit me now to make a distinction, lest it be supposed that I have been identifying structure with the Aristotelian concept of essence. Structure is not a synonym for essence. Structure is in the order of accident; it is an arrangement of parts outside of

---

9. This quotation is authentic Santayana, but I have not been able to trace the quotation to its original source.

parts in space. Ontologically structure presupposes the parts that are structured. Aristotle's doctrine of form and matter accounts for the nature of that which is determined in a given way structurally. In one sense, structure may be called a proper accident since structure follows nature. But structure *can* be modified without changing the thing fundamentally. Electron orbits can change without destroying the atom; isotopes are a good example of two forms of the same structure. Legs and limbs can be amputated, organs be removed, without destroying the organism. Perhaps there is a note of equivocation here. Implicit seems to be a distinction between essential structure and accidental structure. Pruning a tree in some sense alters the structure of the tree but does not affect the specific nature of the tree. The nature of the thing and its concomitant structure permit only so much and no more change in the arrangement of, or loss of, parts. The arrangement must still conform to a specific structure, or the thing will pass out of existence or be transformed into something else—for example, a log can be burned to become ashes.

In sum, if anything is to be gained from this discussion it is this: beware the metaphor; it can be misleading. Yet we cannot think without accompanying images. A model, as distinct from a metaphor, is an attempt to form an image of what we have not experienced sensorially but have reasoned to as the source of something experienced. From effects we grasp something of their cause. The hidden something is not made up or imposed but discovered by inference. We may represent the hidden or semidisclosed cause iconically by models or sententially by equations. It is my contention that neither Hume nor Locke can satisfactorily account for the activity of the theoretical physicist. Kant's postulates and Hegel's imposition of categories fail also, for reasons I have not given. Why then do so many hold to an outmoded empiricism? That may be a moral question beyond the scope of this inquiry.

Ralph Nelson

# Two Masters, Two Perspectives

## Maritain and Gilson on the Philosophy of Nature

WHEN TWO IMPORTANT TREATISES by leading Thomist philosophers were published just after the end of the Second World War, during the ascendancy of existentialism in Europe, Maritain's *Court traité de l'existence et l'existant* and *L'être et l'essence* by Étienne Gilson,[1] it was reasonable to see a basic similarity between them. Of course Gilson was a well-known historian of philosophy and his research followed a historical order, while Maritain followed a doctrinal order. But the end result of both is a defense of a philosophy of being.

However, with time, more attention has been paid to differences between them. The epistemological differences that first surfaced in the 1930s have been the subject of a recent essay by Ray Dennehy.[2] There are also obvious differences palpable in their respective approaches to the philosophy of art. There may also be differences concerning ethics, but since Gilson usually wrote about Thomistic ethics, while Maritain was more innovative, that comparison does not seem particularly fruitful.

---

1. Jacques Maritain, *Court traité de l'existence et l'existant* (Paris: Paul Hartmann, 1947); trans. Lewis Galantiere and Gerald B. Phelan as *Existence and the Existent* (Garden City, NY: Doubleday, 1956). Étienne Gilson, *L'être et l'essence* (Paris: J. Vrin, 1948); in English, *Being and Some Philosophers* (Toronto: Pontifical Institute of Mediaeval Studies, 1949). Father Dewan has written a number of papers on Maritain and Gilson. He has also discussed the differences between Bergson and Einstein. Hence a paper that covers these three philosophers seems a fitting tribute to him.

2. Ray Dennehy, "Maritain's Reply to Gilson's Rejection of Critical Realism," in *A Thomistic Tapestry: Essays in Memory of Etienne Gilson*, ed. Peter A. Redpath (Amsterdam: Rodopi, 2003), 57–80.

But there is one contrast that is striking, and has not been examined to my knowledge, and that is the development of both a metaphysics and a philosophy of nature in Maritain, and the absence of much, if any, attention to the philosophy of nature in Gilson, at least until relatively late in his life. This absence is remarkable given Gilson's fidelity to the writings of Thomas Aquinas, and the latter's recognition of the philosophy of nature as a branch of theoretical inquiry. It may be noted that one of Gilson's friends, Mortimer Adler, raised an objection to what might be called Gilson's metaphysical imperialism at the time when he published *The Unity of Philosophical Experience*.[3]

The purpose of this paper is to try to explain why Maritain spent so much time and effort on the philosophy of nature, while Gilson, in effect, ignores this kind of inquiry. I shall begin by looking at their views of Bergson's philosophy, their common teacher and the great influence of their youth. For each of them had much to say about Bergson, and they came to frequently opposing assessments on the significance of his oeuvre. Once I have presented these views, and the variant interpretations of Bergson's philosophy, the situation in regard to the philosophy of nature will become clearer.

Given the fact that Thomas Aquinas discusses the three degrees of abstraction, the distinction between physics and metaphysics in terms of the respective objects of each, and the way in which concepts are resolved, in his commentary on Boethius's work *On the Trinity* as well as in his *Commentary on Aristotle's Physics*, it would not be a stretch to see this as standard Thomistic doctrine. However, it is left to interpretation to decide what to make of physics once Aristotle's general account has been discarded. If there seems to be no place for the philosophy of nature in Gilson's account of theoretical knowledge, we want to know why this is so. There are those who see it as part of what they call Gilson's anti-Aristotelian stance, or it is alleged that he simply misunderstood the subject matter of the field.[4] I am not convinced by this interpretation, for we have to include the late work

---

3. "Throughout the book and especially in the last and summary chapter you *seem* to identify philosophy with metaphysics, you *seem* to ignore the philosophy of nature as a quite separate division of philosophical knowledge.... In short, the error with which you might be charged is metaphysicism, and this I am sure you would say is just as bad an error as any of the others." Cited by Laurence K. Shook, *Etienne Gilson* (Toronto: Pontifical Institute of Mediaeval Studies, 1984), 231.

4. Ralph McInerny, *Boethius and Aquinas* (Washington, DC: The Catholic University of America Press, 1990), 158. See also the same author's *Being and Predication: Thomistic Interpretations* (Washington, DC: The Catholic University of America Press, 1986), 174–213.

*From Aristotle to Darwin and Back Again*[5] in any thorough examination of Gilson's position.

Of course we could say that he was not interested in this domain, but the precise point here is to understand why he was not interested. Did he think that the development of modern science had rendered much of Aristotle's physical speculation no longer relevant? Thus what we now had was a philosophy of science, analogous to the philosophy of art, in that it was primarily dependent on the practitioners (scientists or artists) and an attempt to recognize what they had discovered or done. To support this contention I would refer to his foreword to the English translation of a book by Gaston Bachelard.[6]

## Maritain on Bergson

The structure of Maritain's first book is brought out in the English title, *Bergsonian Philosophy and Thomism*.[7] For it compares and contrasts the "new" philosophy of Bergson and the "scholastic" philosophy of Thomas Aquinas. It is unfortunate that Maritain uses the term "scholastic" so often when he is solely concerned with Thomism. I won't go into the reasons why this usage is misleading, but suffice it to say that it suggests a doctrinal unity that does not exist in historical Scholasticism. Furthermore, Maritain is not concerned only with the philosophical aspects of the new philosophy, but also with its influence on Roman Catholics, more specifically on Catholic thought.

Though part of the book is exposition, its critical tone is pervasive. Though occasionally he does acknowledge positive Bergsonian contributions, the critical cast predominates. He accuses Bergson of anti-intellectualism for having rejected the intellect as incapable of dealing with life and reality. The concept of duration is taken to be promoted in place of being, and is identified with becoming. Maritain speaks of Bergson's mobilism and maintains that it is change without anything that changes.[8] He character-

---

5. Étienne Gilson, *From Aristotle to Darwin and Back Again: A Journey in Final Causality, Species, and Evolution*, trans. John Lyon (Notre Dame: University of Notre Dame Press, 1984).

6. In a foreword to Gaston Bachelard, *The Poetics of Space*, trans. Maria Jolas (New York: Orion Press, 1964), vii–x.

7. Jacques Maritain, *Bergsonian Philosophy and Thomism*, trans. Mabelle L. Andison, with J. Gordon Andison (New York: Philosophical Library, 1955).

8. Ibid., 128.

izes Bergson's freedom as a kind of spontaneity, not free choice in the full sense. His misgivings about the notion of a higher being are stated when he says that "Bergsonian metaphysics, in spite of itself, falls a prey to pantheism . . . a pantheism of creation, through self-production or self increase of the absolute in 'real duration,' in substantial and creative time."[9] These are only some of the critical notes in Maritain's study. At the end there is a distinction between the Bergsonism of fact and of intention—a way of praising Bergson for his intentions, his aspirations, while taking issue with the objective system that he had produced. In spite of Maritain's rather harsh criticisms, he admired Bergson for his rejection of mechanism, determinism, and scientism, however Bergson may have failed in his own doctrine.

Commentators then and now have taken Maritain to task for the first book. Gilson's remark was recorded in the Shook biography: "Still there is one thing that cannot be done: to condone his book on Bergson. . . . There would be no problem if Maritain didn't wield Thomism like a bludgeon."[10] Not so long ago the Polish philosopher Kolakowski brought up Maritain's book in a little study of Bergson, a rather unusual reference to a work that has largely disappeared from the Bergson bibliography, where he suggests a kind of bigotry on Maritain's part. "Maritain sums up his strictures in a magnificent statement reminiscent of Savonarola: 'a poor peasant who believes that God created Heaven and Earth and who believes in the Holy Sacrament of the Altar knows more about truth, Being, and substance, than Plotinus, Spinoza and the whole of Bergsonism.'"[11] He goes on to say, "why it is St. Thomas, rather than Bergson, who is a possessor of truth is a different dispute."[12] The offending passage is not to be found in the English translation.

In the introduction to the second edition of *Bergsonian Philosophy and Thomism*, there is an admission that there was a harshness that he wants to overcome in the new edition. "Of my first book, I have explained above that I regret its excessively severe and often unjust tone; but that I believe the doctrinal substance still to be sound."[13] In the previous edition he had spoken of Bergson's metaphysics; now he clarifies this remark by noting that

---

9. Ibid., 200.
10. Shook, *Gilson*, 346.
11. Leszek Kolakowski, *Bergson* (Oxford: Oxford University Press, 1985), 97.
12. Ibid.
13. Maritain, *Bergsonian Philosophy*, 60.

"it had been possible to believe for a moment that he would undertake to construct a metaphysics; all he sought to do was to introduce us to the subject."[14] But this pertains to the main theme of this paper. Maritain tells us that he criticizes the Bergsonian philosophy of nature and the Bergsonian metaphysics,[15] yet Bergson never made a distinction between the two, nor does Maritain give us any indication of how to draw the line between them, except by imposing on Bergson a scheme of the sciences that he never accepted. The point is that there is still some doubt in our minds, even after this very helpful introduction, as to how to characterize in an exact way what Bergson is doing.

The essay on Bergson's metaphysics does not answer this question, though it is a philosophical review of Bergson's philosophy in its own terms. Of course it is a perusal of the author from a point of view, the philosophy of being, but it looks at the coherence of Bergson's treatment as well as a way in which a disciple of Aristotle and Thomas Aquinas would evaluate the main Bergsonian themes. For instance, the notion of intuition in Bergson is corrected by the assertion of an intellectual intuition.

When Maritain attended Bergson's course, he says, "what we looked for was the revelation of a new metaphysics, and it was that the lecturer himself seemed to promise us."[16] But he was disappointed because he did not receive what he believed Bergson had promised. It is always possible that Maritain was mistaken in this regard. Rather than what Maritain desired, Bergson sought "a metaphysics of modern physics."[17] This means both a criticism of some of the limitations of modern science and a continuation of it. What Bergson produced, according to his commentator, may be described as "a singularly bold declaration of integral empiricism."[18] The result is "the metaphysics of pure change."[19] Maritain clarifies his earlier allegation of pantheism with a distinction between Bergson's intentions that rejected pantheism and the fact that "one cannot see how a certain pantheism is not in line with the internal logic of those concepts through which in fact the Bergsonian system finds expression."[20] We recognize here the distinction between the two Bergsonisms articulated earlier: the Bergsonism of intention and

14. Ibid., 48.
15. Ibid., 45.
16. Jacques Maritain, "The Metaphysics of Bergson," in *Ransoming the Time*, trans. Harry Lorin Binsse (New York: Gordian Press, 1972), 53.
17. Ibid., 62.                          18. Ibid., 54.
19. Ibid., 74.                          20. Ibid., 77.

the Bergsonism of fact. There is no mention in the essay about the distinction between a philosophy of nature and a metaphysics. Gradually a change in Maritain's interpretation of Bergson's philosophy occurs. In a footnote in *Science and Wisdom*, he remarks: "With regard to Bergson it should be added that his direct objective was perhaps more in the order of the philosophy of nature than of metaphysics."[21] This insight is fully developed only in *The Philosophy of Nature*, and because the argument is rather complex, I will quote Maritain extensively. Observing that Bergson sought a metaphysics of modern science, "a philosophy or metaphysics of the experimental sciences," he goes on: "Bergson's intention is not to construct a psychological philosophy but rather to embrace physics so closely that he will discover at its heart a metaphysics that is unknown to the physicist himself."[22] In spite of the realist tendency of Bergson's approach, it is an illusion to rely on this procedure, for the sole result is to find reality in change itself.

From the fact that this is an effort to attain philosophically to the sensible real, this attempt approaches the philosophy of nature. It is an effort to penetrate philosophically (by means of intuition, which for Bergson is the reverse of scientific analysis) the realm of the natural sciences itself. So from the noetic point of view, this does approach the philosophy of nature.[23]

He believes this is why Bergson had a certain influence on the development of the sciences. Yet it is only one side of the picture, for Maritain now argues why it resembles metaphysics.

But actually it is not yet a philosophy of nature; this conception remains a metaphysics, for its interest in the science of the physical world springs from the desire to find within it and by its means a metaphysical absolute which would be the absolutely last reality. To tell the truth, what this philosophy thinks it finds in this sub-soil of physics whereto physics itself cannot penetrate, is something which it has itself placed there: a reality derived from psychological intuition and introspection.[24]

And then Maritain's conclusion:

So that while this pseudo-philosophy of nature tries to be a philosophy of physics, it nevertheless remains dependent upon the modern spiritualist tradition which began with Descartes and Leibniz and which seeks in introspection the means of the

---

21. Jacques Maritain, *Science and Wisdom*, trans. Bernard Wall (New York: Charles Scribner's Sons, 1940), 48n1.
22. Jacques Maritain, *Philosophy of Nature*, trans. Imelda C. Byrne (New York: Philosophical Library, 1951), 58.
23. Ibid., 59.           24. Ibid.

mechanism of the natural sciences. In effect what we have here is a philosophy of nature which is really a metaphysics and an erroneous one at that.[25]

Those who want a clear-cut answer to the question whether Bergson is offering a philosophy of nature or a metaphysics will not be satisfied with Maritain's solution that Bergson's philosophy is both at the same time. Those who search for a disjunction will find a strange combination. Still this is where Maritain's musings lead him.

When Bergson's book on morality and religion was published in 1932, Maritain says, "we had for a long time been aware that Bergson was preparing a moral philosophy and that he even intended to enter upon questions of theodicy."[26] He calls it a "a classic from the day it appeared."[27] To relate it to his previous research, it is termed cosmic: "Bergson has linked the destinies of the philosophy of human action to a philosophy of the universe."[28] In contrast to Aquinas it is cosmic irrational rather than cosmic rational; Maritain has not left aside his previous conclusions of the shortcomings of Bergson's philosophy.

As in *Time and Free Will* with the distinction of space and duration, in *Matter and Memory* that between pure perception and pure memory, in *Creative Evolution* between instinct and intelligence, there is a dualism in *The Two Sources of Morality and Religion:* on one hand, between the morality of pressure and that of aspiration, on the other; between the closed and open religion. He took over the notion of social obligation as based on pressure from Emile Durkheim, on a social pressure. But this was counterposed by the morality of aspiration, based on the call of the hero. However

---

25. Ibid., 59–60.
26. Jacques Maritain, "The Bergsonian Philosophy of Morality and Religion," 84. Yves Simon recalls the day Bergson's book came out: "I remember very well the day when I was told 'Bergson's book of ethics is out.' Bergson had not published any important book since 1907. It was known that he was working on a book of ethics and it was feared that he might very well die without having completed it. I was about to give a lecture and to catch a train. I gave the lecture and before I jumped into a streetcar to catch my train, I first ran into a bookshop to buy the book and I was already flipping the leaves as I was entering the streetcar. What struck me first was that this book was obviously written by a disciple of the man who had written *Creative Evolution*. That was the first impression, but perhaps not the most profound. Whether Bergsonism finally remains a philosophy of universal mobility is not so sure: perhaps it does not. It strikes me that some aspects of Bergsonism as the philosophy of universal mobility are corrected in this last book of his." *The Great Dialogue of Nature and Space*, ed. Gerard J. Dalcourt (Albany: Magi Books, 1970), 72–73.
27. Ibid., 86.
28. Ibid., 91. The word order has been altered.

Maritain and Gilson 221

he will later suggest that the hero acts as the instrument of God rather than being the ultimate source. Are there, then, two notions of obligation? This has been a problem for the interpreters of Bergson. Obligation seems to be a general force, similar to necessity. The essence of our obligation to society is to cultivate a social ego, which means submitting to rules and regulations, so as to achieve social cohesion.

The question then is whether there is another kind of obligation above and beyond social pressure, which he ordinarily calls aspiration. In contrast to pressure, it is not considered to be a form of obligation. So we might conclude that there is in fact only one source of obligation. The assumption here is that obligation properly speaking is pressure. Yet Bergson insists that "complete and perfect morality has the effect of an appeal."[29] Now without going into some of the difficulties of his position, let us simply say that there ultimately seem to be two moralities.

Now Maritain observes that while one morality is infra-rational and the other morality is supra-rational, there is no place for a simply rational morality. Or in another formulation, there is a morality stemming from society, and another morality whose source is in the divine; there is none of purely human provenance. At least one critic questioned whether Bergson has any morality at all. "Because having two moralities is to risk not having any at all, the first disappearing in sociology, and the second in religion."[30] Maritain, after having defended the intellect against Bergson's attempt to reduce it to being a faculty for working on matter or for making tools, now defends the role of reason in ethics. "The most captivating thing about Bergsonian ethics is precisely that morality in the strictest sense of the word, has been eliminated."[31]

If Bergson "passes by authentic moral obligation,"[32] Maritain once again takes the occasion, as he had earlier in *An Introduction to the Problems of Moral Philosophy*,[33] to expound his own account of moral obligation. This

29. Henri Bergson, *The Two Sources of Morality and Religion*, trans. R. Ashley Audra, Cloudesley Brereton, and W. Horsefall Carter (Garden City, NY: Doubleday, 1956), 34.
30. Madelaine Barthélemy Madaule, *Bergson adversaire de Kant* (Paris: Presses Universitaires de France, 1966), 163.
31. Maritain, *Ransoming the Time*, 93.
32. Jacques Maritain, *Moral Philosophy: An Historical and Critical Survey of the Great Systems*, ed. Joseph W. Evans (New York: Charles Scribner's Sons, 1964), 430.
33. Jacques Maritain, *An Introduction to the Problems of Moral Philosophy*, trans. Cornelia N. Borgerhoff (Albany: Magi Books, 1990), 172–80.

involves an important distinction between two aspects of the conception of
moral good, value and end, and an interpretation of the relation between
the intellect and the will. Obligation is not constraint in any physical sense.
Maritain says we can discern good in the order of specification, which he
calls value, and good in the order of exercise, or the end. "Moral obligation
is based on value."[34] Suffice it to say, without going into a complete explanation, that this account offers a reasonable alternative to Bergson's lack of a
rational version of obligation.

It is remarkable that Bergson spoke of the mystics, and especially of
the Christian mystics, from a purely philosophical viewpoint, for this subject clearly transcends philosophy. Maritain has high praise for the way in
which he has done this. "Outside of the analysis by proper causes, which the
instruments of theology alone allow us to carry out, by informing philosophers of those realities which are grace, the theological virtues, and the gifts
of the Holy Spirit, it is impossible to speak of mystical experience with more
depth, and with a more intense far-sighted sympathy than the author of *The
Two Sources* has done."[35] This is a rare tribute from the author of *The Degrees
of Knowledge*.

Finally, to illustrate how Maritain always kept Bergson in mind, he once
again returns to the issue of intuition in an essay entitled "No Knowledge
without Intuitivity" in which after having examined Descartes, Hegel, and
Heidegger, he concludes:

> Not a single one of the three philosophers I just spoke of experienced either formally
> or virtually the metaphysical intuition of being. Bergson had it in a virtual manner
> ... it was an effort of the entire soul toward this intuitivity, and its beginning. This is
> why Bergson was truly a metaphysician, and this is why we are indebted to him for
> having cried out for all to hear, in the metaphysical desert of our time, the call for
> that basic renewal which philosophy had been awaiting for three centuries.[36]

## Gilson on Bergson

Gilson has told in memorable terms what Bergson meant to him, as
well as the reasons why he lost interest in the latter's philosophy. In what,
I believe, is Gilson's earliest venture in the philosophy of art, "Art et mé-

---

34. Ibid., 91.  35. Maritain, *Moral Philosophy*, 435.
36. Jacques Maritain, *Untrammeled Approaches*, trans. Bernard Doering (Notre Dame, IN:
University of Notre Dame Press, 1997), 325–26.

Maritain and Gilson    223

taphysique," which appeared in 1916,[37] one finds pervasive references to intuitions, be they metaphysical or aesthetic, terminology completely foreign to what we may call the later or definitive Gilson. Compare this to what he says of Bergson's doctrine in *The Unity of Philosophical Experience*, "with its criticism of intellectual knowledge in the name of intuition, it was a revival of old philosophical mysticisms."[38] Yet Gilson, as we indicated earlier, was severely critical of Maritain's treatment of their common teacher. What is clear from this work is that Gilson situates Bergson in a long line of thinkers that may be traced back to Democritus, the metaphysicians. As Adler observed, this could be seen as an illustration of Gilson's tendency to leave the philosophy of nature out of consideration.

During the centenary of Bergson in 1959, Gilson had the opportunity to deal at length with his first master in "A Recollection of Bergson." "We have admired him, loved him, he dwelled in us, and does so still."[39] For the young Gilson, "he was philosophy itself."[40] It was an encounter with a real philosopher, and such experiences are rare. "What I experienced formerly in hearing Bergson, this internal upheaval, immediate and comparable to the most lively musical emotion, that one feels in contact with pure metaphysical thought."[41] He was only to experience this once again, with Martin Heidegger, whom he heard in 1957 in Freiburg-im-Breisgau. Gilson said the experience he had reminded him of those who heard Socrates. It reminded him of fifty years before with Bergson. "It was indeed wisdom in person."[42]

As a historian of philosophy, Gilson relates Bergson to his predecessors, going so far as to see in him the last word of Maine de Biran's spiritualism. More recently, he compares him to a trio of philosophers, finding some of his themes in their writings, but indicating why Bergson made such an impact. The limit of Boutroux, Lachalier, and Ravaisson was their inability to go beyond scientism, for they sought from science what it could not supply.[43]

---

37. Étienne Gilson, "Art et métaphysique," *Revue du métaphysique et de morale* 23 (1916): 243–67.
38. Étienne Gilson, *The Unity of Philosophical Experience* (New York: Charles Scribner's Sons, 1937), 292.
39. Étienne Gilson, "Souvenir de Bergson," *Revue du métaphysique et de morale* 63 (1959): 129–40.
40. Ibid., 129.                              41. Ibid., 130.
42. Ibid., 131.
43. For a more complete survey of the three philosophers, see Étienne Gilson, "French and Italian Philosophy," in *Recent Philosophy: Hegel to the Present*, ed. idem, Thomas Langan, and Armand A. Maurer (New York: Random House, 1962), part 2, ch. 10, 290–317.

In an academic atmosphere in which metaphysics was not considered to be knowledge, Bergson's approach was liberating. If one wants to see an instance of the latent neopositivism of the time, of someone who adopted the regnant scientism, one might well examine the novel *Jean Barois* by Roger Martin du Gard, published in 1913.[44]

In order to find a way into metaphysics, after his famous criticism of mathematical reason, Bergson appeals to an "essentially ineffable intuition."[45] It is following the critique of a bad use of reason, of a "certain abstract rationalism" that Bergson found his alternative.[46] Gilson was never one of those, like Maritain, for instance, who took issue with Bergson's alleged anti-intellectualism. He believed that Bergson opened "the path of renewal" to metaphysics.[47]

One of the difficulties in understanding Bergson is his precise use of scientific information in his major works, thus building on a solid basis of scientific fact, just as *The Two Sources* includes an extensive inquiry into spiritual experiences, "religious reality empirically given," as the sciences represent natural reality for him.[48] Gilson notes significantly that Bergson "recalls metaphysics to its tradition which is to come after physics and is based on it."[49] This was essential for him. Later the similarity of Aristotle and Bergson is observed on this point, each treating the physics of his time. Bergson sought the possibility of a concrete metaphysics. "We have asked of Bergson, and received from him, a philosophy centered on problems other than those of which science speaks, but which as science had a content."[50]

The critique of the immobility of "the natural Platonism of the intellect,"[51] is that the real is the fixed, and Gilson refers to the conclusion of *Creative Evolution* and what Bergson has to say about the Greeks. But he considers how much Bergson remained a Greek, "the whole question being for him to know what choice to make between being and becoming."[52] Remember the great division expressed in Plato's *Timaeus* between eternal being and becoming. And, in contrast to Gilson's own philosophy, being has no prominent role in the philosophy of evolution, as if being and becoming were

---

44. Roger Martin du Gard, *Jean Barois* (Paris: Gallimard, 1913). For a commentary, see M. J. Taylor, Martin du Gard: Jean Barois (London: Edward Arnold, 1974).
45. Gilson, "Souvenir de Bergson," 134.
46. Ibid.
47. Ibid.
48. Ibid., 133.
49. Ibid.
50. Ibid., 134.
51. Ibid., 137.
52. Ibid., 139.

contraries. Gilson speaks of a "metaphysical region transcending the antinomy of the static and the moving, between being and becoming."[53] However, he states that he does not propose to criticize Bergson since the philosophy of being was not something that he knew.

Now to some extent we come to grips with our main problem only in the book that was published the following year, *The Philosopher and Theology*. So we now have an account of Bergson in a quite different context. Maritain had, as the English title of his first book expresses it, a Thomistic critique of Bergson's philosophy. I suppose the method followed by Gilson was to understand Bergson's philosophy in its own terms, though inevitably even that hardly precludes any criticism. In many respects it is the most biographical of his works, with the emphasis on the intellectual life. The portion on Bergson begins with a chapter entitled "The Bergson Affair." Once again Gilson remarks on the significance of Bergson's arrival at the university. "For the first time since Descartes and Malebranche, France then had the good fortune to possess that rare being, a great metaphysician."[54] He refers to Bergson as "the man whose first philosophical career ended, so to speak, with *Creative Evolution*."[55] What his students were exposed to was his vision of the universe. At the time, Gilson believed that Bergson had then given all that he had to give. There is a curious statement to the effect that "his philosophy of nature had been for us a liberation."[56] I say curious because it might be an attempt to distinguish between the Bergsonian metaphysics and a philosophy of nature. While it could be taken to be another way of describing his metaphysics as a kind of naturalism, I have previously noted this problem with Maritain, who suggests just such a distinction without clearly articulating in what the difference consists. Bergson's writings indicate respect for scientific research, even while recognizing its limitations, as in his famous analysis of time and duration. His love of empirical knowledge meant that philosophy itself was an extension of empirical knowledge. So Bergson, "starting from what was the accepted notion of intelligence, undertook the task of submitting it to a much needed critique."[57] What he criticized was "the bad use men made of intelligence when, pretending to

---

53. Ibid., 140.
54. Étienne Gilson, *The Philosopher and Theology*, trans. Cécile Gilson (New York: Random House, 1962), 107.
55. Ibid., 108.      56. Ibid.
57. Ibid., 114.

speak in the name of science, they take advantage of this pretension to deny the possibility of metaphysics."[58] Thus "Bergson wanted to revive metaphysics as a science, and since intelligence had disqualified itself to this end, it was necessary for the metaphysician to look elsewhere."[59] Despite this position, we are indebted to Bergson for his criticism of scientism, materialism, and determinism. And in this its liberating potential consisted.

Gilson enters into a critical interpretation of Aristotle, as well as a comparison of Aristotle's and Bergson's philosophies that explains, I am convinced, the main reason for the absence of a philosophy of nature in Gilson's philosophy until the remarkable development in *From Aristotle to Darwin and Back Again*. Gilson recognizes that there still remain truths in Aristotle's *Physics*. Aristotle based his philosophy on the state of physics in his time. The later differentiation of physics and the philosophy of nature is foreign to him. Gilson maintains that in the universe of Aristotle leading to the Pure Immovable Mover, "nothing new ever happens."[60] And contrary to what Francesca Murphy says in her study of Gilson, there is no confusion of Aristotle and Bergson.[61] Rather there is an analogy. Just as Aristotle relied on the physics of his time, so Bergson relied on the physics of his time. And so those Thomists, like Maritain, who make of the philosophy of nature "a sort of intermediary wisdom and, so to speak, a halfway house between science and metaphysics, something that Aristotle himself did not do."[62] I find this interpretation reinforced by Gilson's remarks on Gaston Bachelard.[63] Of course, a most significant issue, which we need not address here, is precisely the view that Thomas Aquinas held on the status of the philosophy of nature. One supposes at this stage that Gilson believed that the truths of Aristotle's physics can be somehow absorbed in metaphysics.

Gilson had no illusions about Bergson's book on *Duration and Simultaneity*, with its critique of Einstein. He thinks "the philosophy of Bergson itself lost its breath trying to catch up with the world of Einstein."[64] His conclusion on Bergson's thought: "Whatever one may think of it, one can hardly

---

58. Ibid.  
59. Ibid.  
60. Ibid., 127.  
61. Francesca Aran Murphy, *Art and Intellect in the Philosophy of Etienne Gilson* (Columbia: University of Missouri Press, 2004), 5.  
62. Gilson, *The Philosopher and Theology*, 127.  
63. Gilson, foreword to *The Poetics of Space*.  
64. Gilson, *The Philosopher and Theology*, 129. Cf. Henri Bergson, *Duration and Simultaneity*, trans. Leon Jacobson (Indianapolis: Bobbs-Merrill, 1965).

Maritain and Gilson    227

deny that with its insistence on change, becoming, duration—in short, creative evolution—Bergson's philosophy truly was that of the science of our own time."[65]

As to *The Two Sources of Morality and Religion*, Gilson reveals deep misgivings. He admits that he had the book, had it bound, but for a long time it remained on his shelf, unread.[66] His apprehension was that he had his religion; Bergson was searching for his own. But as Gilson's own religion did not depend on philosophy, which came only later, he interpreted Bergson's project as an attempt to draw out a religion from his philosophy. "One does not find the source of religion at the term of any philosophy, but beyond it."[67] When he finally read the book, he says, "my worst fears proved more than justified.... [T]he whole book was out of focus. The author had established himself outside the focus of his subject and remained there."[68] As he will say later, "the method did not fit the object,"[69] and the method is empiricism.

It is remarkable how different are the attitudes of the two masters to *The Two Sources*. Maritain, who had been an intransigent critic of Bergson, and still was critical of certain aspects of Bergsonian ethics, was, however, surely impressed by the treatment of the mystics—see his own treatment of the topic in *The Degrees of Knowledge*—enough to quote certain passages at length. Was it not notable that a great philosopher would examine the experiences of the mystics of the Catholic tradition? Gilson, on the contrary, tended to stress the disparity between the project and the inevitable results of a non-theological account of the mystics.

A subsidiary consideration brought up by Gilson concerned the task that Catholic theologians had to do with Bergson's philosophy just as St. Thomas had done with Aristotle. He was convinced that none of the theologians who considered Bergson's philosophy, and there were surely a fair number, had successfully carried out this task.

Sometimes we have the impression that Gilson was by force of his own philosophy quite adverse to the great Bergsonian themes, although he was always critical of Maritain's early heavy-handed approach to the philoso-

65. Ibid.
66. In a letter written in 1958, Gilson made the rather startling remark that "I have never read The Two Sources." See "Lettres d'Etienne Gilson à Henri Gouhier," in *Revue Thomiste* 94 (1994): 470.
67. Gilson, *The Philosopher and Theology*, 109.
68. Ibid., 110.                69. Ibid., 165.

pher. He wanted very much to accentuate the positive in dealing with Bergson, but in the final analysis was he any more indulgent toward him than Maritain?

If *The Philosopher and Theology* had been the last word on the philosophy of nature and Bergson, we would be rather puzzled by propositions to the extent that "*Creative Evolution* is essentially a philosophy, and even in the Aristotelian sense of the word, a physics."[70] However, this remark does not justify a division of theoretical philosophy into metaphysics and the philosophy of nature. But with Gilson's book on evolution, the whole situation changes. Now, whatever the ambiguities expressed before, there is a forthright treatment of the philosophy of nature or, more precisely, of biophilosophy. And more surprisingly for someone known to often take Aristotle to task—he refers to the god of Aristotle as "a sluggard god"[71]—he now offers a very positive presentation of Aristotle's approach to the subject. Gilson was once taxed for failing to understand what the philosophy of nature was all about; he now writes the most Aristotelian of his books. We are not sure how this change in direction came about. Whatever the explanation may be, it is clear that any attempt to deal with a modern scientific movement that had become a belief system for many could not ignore Aristotle's biological philosophy. Two books that were planned or published during the last years of Gilson's life have one feature in common. *Constantes métaphysiques de l'être*,[72] composed of a number of essays written by Gilson between 1952 and 1967, published posthumously in 1978, and *From Aristotle to Darwin and Back Again*, published in 1971, both deal with constant features of two disciplines, the former metaphysics, the latter what Gilson called biophilosophy. Among the constants of biophilosophy are the distinction between the homogeneous and the heterogeneous, the problem of final causality, or teleology, the problem of species, the scale of beings, the inadequacy of mechanistic accounts, and the recognition that chance is not an explanation, any more than mechanism in some circumstances. Heterogeneity of parts is important for defining what is peculiar to organic beings. The second of these features we can take as the main theme of the book. Granted that Descartes and Bacon, to begin with, and later biologists, such as Darwin, Huxley, Claude Bernard, Jean Rostand, and Jacques Monod, have excluded final

70. Ibid., 145.
71. Ibid., 147.
72. Etienne Gilson, *Constantes métaphysiques de l'être* (Paris: J. Vrin, 1983).

causes from science, what should be the stance of the biophilosopher in the light of this exclusion? And yet there is "the finalist biology of Aristotle"[73] with its articulation of substantial forms and natural teleology that seemed so evident in the study of nature. But the early moderns, such as Descartes, had no use for substantial forms, any more than Bergson did. "But," Gilson says, "if there is really final causality in nature, it is then still necessary to take it into consideration."[74] Correspondingly, "living things are inexplicable in terms of the efficient or motor cause alone."[75] Hence the inadequacy of purely mechanistic accounts.

Gilson has a great deal to say about the problem of species, with particular reference to the discussion challenging Linnaeus's conclusion "that no new species are produced nowadays."[76] Transformism maintains the change of species in the passage of time. This, of course, was Darwin's position, along with the notion of natural selection that Gilson critically examines, while explaining how Darwin finally adopted the term "evolution," taken from Spencer. This means pointing out "the analogy between the results of natural selection and those of domestication." It was "as if there had been choice in the matter,"[77] although the word might imply a selector. Gilson believes that Darwin "never completely exorcised the phantom of teleology,"[78] in spite of all his efforts to do so.

Bergson takes up the issue of the evolution of species and, like Spencer, identified evolution and progress. He rejected both radical mechanism and radical finalism. Yet there is a role for teleology in his philosophy. "Far from having held teleology to be a peripheral notion, Bergson, then, sought to revive it under a purer form, and in a sense he succeeded, but not completely."[79] So he offers a new version of finalism. And although he too had no place for substantial forms, "it was he however who opened the way to a renovation of finalism."[80]

Finally, some of Gilson's conclusions vindicate Aristotle's approach to biology. First, "the very existence of the biological is not susceptible of a mechanist explanation. The facts that Aristotle's biology wished to explain are still there."[81] And he signals the inevitability of the notions of organization and teleology invoked by Aristotle.

73. Gilson, *From Aristotle to Darwin*, 5.
74. Ibid., 24.
75. Ibid., 25.
76. Ibid., 35.
77. Ibid., 83.
78. Ibid., 86.
79. Ibid., 100.
80. Ibid., 101.
81. Ibid., 118.

Gilson seems to have identified the philosophy of nature and biophilosophy, as if the study of the infra-biological should be left to science. Nor is the biophilosopher in any way a theologian. Furthermore, "it is not necessary to the biophilosopher that natural teleology be perfect in order to authorize him to say that it exists."[82] He concludes on a point he has made throughout the book. Supposing that science, as its many followers contend, "has no need for final causes, but it is no less true that what we call final causality exists in reality."[83] So it is the case that what the scientist ignores or denies, the philosopher asserts in his own investigation. And Bergson as well as Aristotle may assist him in this effort.

In our day, in which evolution is once again much discussed and much contested, whether in the name of creationism or of intelligent design, Gilson has drawn a limit to bioscience, one its imposes on itself, but there is no reason that the limits of bioscience should be those of biophilosophy, for the latter asserts what the former denies, that is, teleology.

## A Third Approach to Bergson

After the Thomistic reading and the Aristotelian reading, there is still another way to approach Bergson. Perhaps this may throw a new light on Bergson's philosophy and address the two issues with which we started: the meaning of the philosophy of nature and the interpretation of Bergson's philosophical achievements. The approach I have in mind is that of the historian, who is primarily concerned with understanding and elucidating the philosophical text by bringing out relevant factors about its genesis, showing connections between different works, and in general helping us to penetrate the meaning of a work that may not easily reveal its message to the uninitiated. In this genre, there are the writings of Henri Gouhier, particularly when he interprets Bergson's thought as he did in *Bergson et le Christ des Evangiles* and in *Bergson dans l'histoire de la pensée occidentale*.[84] And then there were a series of books and essays where he has important commentaries on various aspects of Bergsonian philosophy, as in his introduction to the centenary edition of the *Oeuvres de Bergson*.[85] For unlike the work of

---

82. Ibid., 121.   83. Ibid., 124.
84. Henri Gouhier, *Bergson et le Christ des Evangiles* (Paris: Fayard, 1961), and *Bergson dans l'histoire de la pensée occidentale* (Paris: J. Vrin, 1989).
85. Henri Gouhier, "Introduction," in *Oeuvres de Bergson, edition du centenaire* (Paris:

Maritain and Gilson 231

the two masters of Thomism, his treatment cannot be accused of an ulterior motive. As a recent essay states it, Gouhier "was a historian and never presented his own philosophy."[86]

In a series of treatises beginning in the 1920s, Gouhier wrote on Descartes, Pascal, Malebranche, Rousseau, Comte, and Maine de Biran, and subsequently on Bergson. He also wrote several volumes in his chosen field, philosophy and history, with special attention, as is evident, to the history of French philosophy. Among his concerns is the affective history of philosophy. He was a student and later a friend of Gilson. We have already referred to the extensive correspondence between the two. But Gouhier's approach to the study of philosophers differs from Gilson's as expressed in *The Unity of Philosophical Experience*. Let us say that Gouhier was interested in individual philosophers and consequently shows a concern in the diversity of the philosophical spirit. At least this is the conclusion one draws from Gouhier's reflections on Gilson's important work.[87]

We follow Bergson's itinerary, in which he thought he had found in Spencer's philosophy of evolution "a philosophy of nature in agreement with the progress of biology,"[88] until he came to the conclusion that Spencer's theory of evolution had left out evolution itself, that is, the continuum of becoming, and presented us with the fragments of change. Again Gouhier states in "Le bergsonisme dans l'histoire de la philosophie française," that *Creative Evolution* is essentially a philosophy of nature.[89] Now occasionally Gouhier will also refer to Bergson's metaphysics, but it is certainly not the way he characterizes *Creative Evolution*.

There are other places in his writings in which Gouhier emphasizes this interpretation of *Creative Evolution*. In *Les grandes avenues de la pensée phi-*

---

Presses Universitaires de France, 1959), vii–xxx. To mark the centenary of Bergson, Gouhier wrote "Le bergsonisme dans l'histoire de la philosophie française," *Revue des travaux de l'academie des sciences morales et politiques*, 4th series (1959): 184–93. Bergson is also discussed in the following works: *La philosophie et son histoire* (Paris: J. Vrin, 1948), 20–21; *L'histoire et sa philosophie* (Paris: J. Vrin, 1952), 67–90; *Les grandes avenues de la pensée philosophique en France depuis Descartes* (Louvain: Publications Universitaires de Louvain, 1966), 166–68; *Maine de Biran par lui-même* (Paris: Editions du Seuil, 1990); and *Etudes d'histoire de la philosophie* (Hildesheim: Georg Olms Verlag, 1976), 259–70.

86. Richard J. Fafara, "Gilson and Gouhier: Approaches to Malebranche," in *A Thomistic Tapestry*, 147.
87. Gouhier, *La philosophie et son histoire*, 127–34.
88. Gouhier, "Introduction," xxiii.
89. Gouhier, "Le bergsonisme," 184.

*losophique en France depuis Descartes*, he says of the self: "However, in Bergsonian spiritualism, being is only given with its participation in the being of the vital impetus [*élan vital*] and the conscious, free, and creative subject emerges, in a way, from a philosophy of nature: it is 'the universe which is a machine for the making of gods.'"[90]

In comparing Maine de Biran and Bergson, Gouhier observes that "the religious psychology of Biran is the final stage of a philosophy of spirit, that of Bergson, the final stage of a philosophy of nature."[91] To correct a rather common viewpoint of the relation of psychology to the other parts of Bergson's philosophy, Gouhier argues "that it is not in going from psychology to the philosophy of nature, as a hasty reading of his books could make one believe, but a movement from the philosophy of nature to psychology."[92] I believe an explanation of this assertion is to be found in the fundamental importance and priority that Gouhier gives to the repeated refutation of Zeno's sophistries on motion in Bergson's works, for surely an emphasis on the reality of motion is basic to the study of the philosophy of nature.

Sometimes Gouhier speaks of the cosmology of Bergson, and that usage has become problematic, even equivocal, at a time when the term is more often used to denote a certain aspect of science, the study of the birth, structure, and dynamics of the universe, than a philosophical study of the physical world. The two-sided aspect of the word "cosmology" is brought out in the *Encyclopedia of Philosophy*: "The term 'cosmology' stands for a family of related inquiries, all in some sense concerned with the world at large. Two main subgroups of uses may be distinguished: those belonging to philosophy and those belonging to science."[93] All well and good until we find that cosmology in the philosophical sense is identified with Christian Wolff and his notorious confusion of the philosophy of nature and metaphysics, all too common in a number of dictionaries, both ordinary and technical. Among recent books on cosmology, Jacques Merleau-Ponty's study *Cosmologie du xx$^e$ siècle*, in both the text and the bibliography, is completely concerned with contemporary science, not with philosophy. Clearly Stephen Toulmin's *The Return to Cosmology* is broader in scope, dealing with science and natural theology. Jean E. Charon's *L'esprit, cet inconnu*, gives us a definition of contemporary cosmology as constituting "the branch of physics

90. Gouhier, *Les grandes avenues*, 60–61.   91. Gouhier, *Maine de Biran*, 169.
92. Gouhier, "Introduction," xxi.
93. Paul Edwards, ed., *Encyclopedia of Philosophy* (New York: MacMillan, 1967), 2:237.

which tries to tell us the history of space-time, and what it contains, from the beginning up to the 'end' of time."[94] All of this is to support our contention that Gouhier is speaking of a philosophical account, not a scientific theory, when he refers to Bergson's cosmology. For instance, I think we capture Gouhier's intended meaning in the phrase "we would seek in vain reminiscences of Genesis in the cosmology of *Creative Evolution*,"[95] which appears in his last, and most complete, examination of Bergson's philosophy, *Bergson dans l'histoire de la pensée occidentale*. So in view of his considered judgments elsewhere, it is clear that for him cosmology is a synonym for the philosophy of nature.

One cannot reflect on these issues without a regret that what Maritain understood as the philosophy of nature, or what Gilson preferred to call biophilosophy, has been in eclipse in philosophical circles for a very long time. If one is to follow Maritain's prescription, its practitioners must have a good understanding of contemporary science as well as a philosophical mind, and that combination is probably quite rare. So the perusal of these issues is tinged with a feeling of nostalgia for a time when they were of a burning actuality.

94. Jean E. Charon, *L'esprit, cet inconnu* (Paris: Albin Michel, 1977), 196; Jacques Merleau-Ponty, *Cosmologie du xx$^e$ siècle: Etude épistemologique et historique des théories de la cosmologie contemporaine* (Paris: Gallimard, 1965); Stephen Toulmin, *Return to Cosmology* (Berkeley: University of California, 1982).

95. Gouhier, *Bergson dans l'histoire*, 54.

PART IV

# ETHICS AND SPIRITUALITY

Kevin L. Flannery, S.J.

# Moral Taxonomy and Moral Absolutes

IN *SUMMA THEOLOGIAE* 1–2.18.10, Thomas Aquinas asks whether a circumstance might put a moral act into the species of good or evil. His answer is yes. "Whenever," he says, "a circumstance concerns a special order of reason, either for it or against, it is necessary that the circumstance give species to the moral act, whether the act be good or evil." This reply may strike some as incompatible with the rest of Thomas's ethics. Is not one of his governing principles the pseudo-Dionysian dictum, "Good comes of a single and perfect cause, evil from many and particular defects"?[1] As usually interpreted, this means that, in the analysis of an act, as soon as we find one aspect of it that is morally bad, whether it be object, intention or whatever, our work is done: that act can never be good since an act is good only if it is "single and perfect." How then could a circumstance make an act already tainted by evil, good?

The simple—and correct—answer to this question is that in *ST* 1–2.18.10 Thomas is not speaking about concrete acts that contain evil which is somehow taken away or obliterated by overriding circumstances. He is speaking

---

I am grateful for their comments on an earlier version of this essay to Frs. Stephen Brock and Lawrence Dewan, O.P., and to Michael Pakaluk.

1. "Bonum procedit ex una et perfecta causa, malum autem procedit ex multis particularibus defectibus" (*De div. nom.* §572). See Pseudo-Dionysius the Areopagite, *De divinis nominibus*, vol. 1 of *Corpus Dionysiacum* 4.30 175.10–11 (PG 3 729C) (Berlin: De Gruyter, 1990): Τὸ ἀγαθὸν ἐκ μιᾶς καὶ τῆς ὅλης αἰτίας, τὸ δὲ κακὸν ἐκ πολλῶν καὶ μερικῶν ἐλλείψεων. Other uses of the dictum by Thomas can be found, for instance, at *ST* 1–2.18.4 ad 3; 18.11 obj. 3; 19.6 ad 1; 19.7 ad 3; 71.5 ad 1; 72.9 obj. 1; at *De ma.*: 2.4 ad 2; 2.7 obj. 3; 2.9 obj. 12; 4.1 ad 13; 8.1 obj. 12 et c; 10.1c; 16.6 ad 11; and *Sententia libri Ethicorum* (Rome: Commissio Leonina, 1969), vol. 47 of *Opera Omnia* 2.7.9–12 (§320). Abbreviations for the various works of Aquinas are standard ones; the symbol '§' always precedes a reference to one of the Marietti editions. Where especially useful, I give a precise line reference to the Leonine edition.

rather about the classification of acts and saying that although a type of act might at first appear to belong in the species of bad acts, certain circumstances might put that type into the species of the good. But this leaves one with another question, How then does *this* work? How in the process of classification can a type of act be shifted from the species of evil to the species of good? Fr. Lawrence Dewan, with typical clarity, candor, and incisiveness, says that it all depends on reason. He uses the example of capital punishment: "That the man executed is a criminal adds a circumstance of the sort which constitutes a new and good rational order. To shy from this is simply to doubt reason's ability to recognize good order for human life. Thus, people who fail to recognize the difference of the two species might be suffering from a blindness as regards the primacy of the common good."[2]

The present essay takes this remark of Fr. Dewan's as its starting point. It attempts to show how the task of classifying some acts as prohibited and other acts as nonprohibited can be assigned to reason without eliminating true moral absolutes: that is, types of acts that are never moral. It proceeds by way of a study of a number of texts in both Aristotle and Thomas; it presupposes, therefore, a certain unity of approach between these two authors. We find in neither Thomas nor Aristotle a systematic treatment of this theme, that is, how reason might effect the taxonomy of human acts. But we do find in them a number of remarks that, interpreted in the light of one another, give us the basic lineaments of such a theory.

## *Summa theologiae* 1–2.18.10

Before getting to Aristotle, it would be best to expound more fully the argument of *ST* 1–2.18.10. As already remarked, the issue here is whether a circumstance might put a moral act into either the species of good or the species of bad. Such a switch of species could not happen among natural things, Thomas says, since the natural world is much more stable: natural substances, as he puts it, are "determined toward one," that is, toward the forms that they are. But the practical sphere, depending as it does solely upon reason, is much more fluid. The forms of acts *come* from reason, so that, if a circumstance is tied up with whether that type of act conforms to reason or does not, that circumstance gives the form. "And thus," says

2. Lawrence Dewan, "St. Thomas and Moral Taxonomy," *Maritain Studies/Études maritainiennes* 15 (1999): 153.

Thomas, "what in one act is accepted as a circumstance added to the object determining the species of the act can again be accepted, by reason which orders, as the principal condition of the object determining the species of the act."[3] It is clear here that Thomas is speaking about the classification of types of acts since he speaks about "that which in one act" might have one species and in another act another. A bit later he speaks of the place where a theft occurs, first as a true circumstance, accidental to the characterization of the act, then as a "principal condition of the object, repugnant to reason." Whether one steals from this house or that, the act remains simply theft; but if one steals from a church, one commits sacrilege. He is clearly referring to different places here—and so to distinct acts. We can be sure, therefore, that he is talking about the classification of acts.

As we have seen, Thomas says in ST 1–2.18.10, "whenever a circumstance concerns a special order of reason, either for it or against, it is necessary that the circumstance give species to the moral act, whether the act be good or evil."[4] What is a "special order of reason [*specialem ordinem rationis*]?" Whenever Thomas uses the expression "special order," it is within a context in which a larger group is broken down into smaller groups, as when a genus is broken down into its species, or at least a specific member of a larger class is singled out. In *Sent.* 4.48.1.4c obj. 3, for instance, he speaks, first, of all the angels standing before the throne of judgment, and then he notes that among the angels "the powers" signifies a "special order."[5] And in ST 1–2.113.1 ad 2, he says that the terms 'faith' and 'charity' refer to a "special order" of the human mind to God, whereas 'justice' refers more generally to the "whole rectitude of order."[6] So, although the word 'special' in the phrase "special order of reason" bears the familiar connotation of 'extraordinary'

---

3. "Et ideo quod in uno actu accipitur ut circumstantia superaddita obiecto quod determinat speciem actus, potest iterum accipi a ratione ordinante ut principalis conditio obiecti determinantis speciem actus."

4. "Et per hunc modum, quandocumque aliqua circumstantia respicit specialem ordinem rationis vel pro vel contra, oportet quod circumstantia det speciem actui morali vel bono vel malo" (ST 1–2.18.10c).

5. "Praeterea, omnes angeli astabunt divino judicio; unde *Apocal.* vii,11: 'et omnes angeli stabant in circuitu throni.' Sed virtutes nominant unum specialem ordinem in angelis."

6. "Ad secundum dicendum quod fides et caritas dicunt ordinem specialem mentis humanae ad deum secundum intellectum vel affectum. Sed iustitia importat generaliter totam rectitudinem ordinis." See also Thomas Aquinas, *Quaestiones disputatae De anima* (Rome/Paris: Commissio Leonina/Les Éditions du CERF, 1996), vol. 24.1 of *Opera omnia* 20c.328-32: "Sed tamen huiusmodi species influxae determinantur in ipsa anima ad cognitionem aliquorum singularium, ad quae anima habet aliquem ordinem specialem vel inclinationem."

or 'unique,' it bears also an additional connotation more closely tied to its etymological root, the word *species*. If in some instances circumstances give acts their species, this is because in these instances there is present a special—or 'species-giving'—order with respect to reason. Similarly, when in *ST* 1-2.18.10, a couple of sentences before the remark about the "special order of reason," Thomas says that "taking the property of another from a holy place adds a special repugnance in relation to the order of reason," he means not just that the repugnance is a distinctive addition to the moral character of the act but also that it gives species to the act, so that it is no longer just an act of theft but is an act of sacrilegious theft.

As Fr. Dewan reminds us, we ought not to ignore that this placing of an act in a species—this moral taxonomy—depends on reason. This is particularly apparent in this argument about sacrilege. The pervasive mention of reason is difficult to render into English; in the Latin it is more apparent:

> Sicut tollere alienum habet speciem ex *ratione* alieni, ex hoc enim constituitur in specie furti, et si consideretur super hoc *ratio* loci vel temporis, se habebit in *ratione* circumstantiae. Sed quia *ratio* etiam de loco vel de tempore, et aliis huiusmodi, ordinare potest, contingit conditionem loci circa obiectum accipi ut contrariam ordini *rationis;* puta quod *ratio* ordinat non esse iniuriam faciendam loco sacro. Unde tollere aliquid alienum de loco sacro addit specialem repugnantiam ad ordinem *rationis.* Et ideo locus, qui prius considerabatur ut circumstantia, nunc consideratur ut principalis conditio obiecti *rationi* repugnans. (*ST* 1-2.18.10c)[7]

## *Nicomachean Ethics* ii,6: Moral Absolutes

The example of an act's "changing species" used in *ST* 1-2.18.10 is not particularly controversial: most people would accept the idea that a bad act such as stealing might be made even worse by the presence of morally significant circumstances, such as the location of the thing stolen. It is easy too to come up with uncontroversial examples of basically good acts "become"

---

[7]. "For instance, taking the property of another has its species by reason of its being another's and is thus placed in the species of theft; if, on top of this, the aspect of place or time is considered, it is present as a circumstance. But because also the aspect of place or time (or such things) can be ordered, it can happen that the condition of place with respect to the object is accepted as contrary to the order of reason. For instance, reason orders that one not do offense to a holy place. So, taking the property of another from a holy place adds a special repugnance in relation to the order of reason. And thus place, which was first considered a circumstance, is now considered the principal condition of the object, repugnant to reason."

Moral Taxonomy and Moral Absolutes    241

bad because of a circumstance. It is good for humans to take nourishment, for example, but to do so during a religious ceremony is—or, at least, could be—sacrilegious. Or it is basically good to tell the truth, but to do so (rather than to remain silent) and thereby to betray one's comrades-in-arms in a just cause is wrong. But how can one allow an act to shift from an immoral species to a moral one without leaving the whole question of the morality of acts to the whims—or, worse, the ideologies—of those who would determine "what is reasonable"? When such winds blow, one feels drawn toward those whom Dewan accuses of blindness: that is, those who "doubt reason's ability to recognize good order for human life."

It is at this point that Aristotle becomes useful—in particular, the chapter in the *Nicomachean Ethics* most frequently associated with moral absolutes: chapter 6 of book 2.[8] Aristotle says there that virtue "is a state concerned with choice, lying in a mean relative to us, this being determined by reason and in the way in which the man of practical wisdom would determine it."[9] But then he adds the following:

But not every action nor every passion admits of a mean; for some as soon as they are named are bound up with badness, e.g., spite, shamelessness, envy, and in the case of actions adultery, theft, murder; for all of these and such like things—and not the excesses or deficiencies of them—are called what they are called because they themselves are bad. It is not possible, then, ever to be right with regard to them; one must always be wrong. (*EN* ii,6,1107a8–15)

Much ink has been spilt—and not just in recent years—in the attempt to show that Aristotle is not recognizing here moral absolutes.[10] As the argu-

---

8. There are (at least) two systems for dividing the chapters of the *Nicomachean Ethics* [*EN*], both of them in wide use and both represented in the standard edition of the Greek text (*Aristotelis Ethica Nicomachea*, ed. I. Bywater, Oxford Classical Texts [Oxford: Clarendon, 1894]): Bywater's primary system, which I follow whenever referring to *EN* (and according to which *EN* ii,6, for instance, begins at 1106a14) and a secondary system (according to which *EN* ii,6, begins at 1106b36). As it happens, the passage presently under consideration falls into *EN* ii,6 whatever the system of chapter division employed. The table of abbreviations for Aristotle's works (and also Plato's works) can be found in the front material of any edition of the Liddell-Scott-Jones *Greek-English Lexicon*.
9. *EN* ii,6,1106b37–1107a2. This translation, taken from the Revised Oxford Translation (*The Complete Works of Aristotle*, ed. Jonathan Barnes [Princeton: Princeton University Press, 1984]), presupposes ὡς ἄν in line 1107a1. In this essay I often make use of the Revised Oxford Translation, occasionally making adjustments.
10. See, for example, W. F. R. Hardie, *Aristotle's Ethical Theory* (Oxford: Clarendon Press, 1968), 137, but also "the Old Scholiast": Anonymous, *In Ethica Nicomachea II–V Commentaria*, ed. Gustavus Heylbut, vol. 20 of *Commentaria in Aristotelem Graeca* (Berlin: Reimer,

ment often goes, since Aristotle's position is that the various *names* imply badness, the badness is wholly bound up in the names: there are no particular passions or actions that, independently of the names eventually used of them, can be characterized as bad. The term 'envy,' for instance, refers to a type of sadness regarding the success of another; in effect, what it does is pick out this type among all the types of 'sadness regarding the success of another' and adds the connotation of badness so that envy becomes 'bad sadness regarding the success of another.' Similarly, when Aristotle says that it is not possible ever to be right with regard to certain actions, he would be referring to the bad instances of the relevant behavior. The members of such groups constitute groups only because they have been singled out as bad: bad killing (or murder), bad taking of goods not belonging to one (theft), and bad sleeping with the spouse of another (adultery).

As John Finnis points out, however, this account founders on this last case, the case of adultery, for Aristotle says just after the piece translated above, "Nor does goodness or badness with regard to such things depend on committing adultery with the right woman, at the right time, and in the right way, but simply to do any of them is to go wrong" (*EN* ii,6,1107a15–17).[11] Clearly, in the case of adultery, what we might call the 'bad-name' thesis does not go through: to say that adultery is 'bad sleeping with the spouse of another' implies that some sleeping with the spouse of another is acceptable, and Aristotle is explicitly excluding such a possibility or implication.[12] If one lies with the spouse of another, that is adultery—and that is bad: it is not possible ever to be right here; "one must always be wrong." But if the bad-name thesis founders on the adultery example, it cannot account for Aristotle's understanding of the other bad things, for he considers them all together. In the passage now under consideration, the expressions "such things" (περὶ τὰ τοιαῦτα—1107a16) and "any of them" (ὁτιοῦν τούτων—1107a17) refer to plural acts; they refer, therefore, to adultery *and* theft and murder. Aristotle's point cannot be that the badness of such acts comes in the assigning of names.

---

1892), 142.7–14. The latter is a comment on *EN* iii,1,1110a19–23; but reference is made to adultery (τὸ μιγῆναι ἀλλοτρίᾳ γυναικί—142.11) and this would seem to be a reference to *EN* ii,6,1107a11.

11. John Finnis, *Moral Absolutes: Tradition, Revision and Truth* (Washington, DC: The Catholic University of America Press, 1991), 32.

12. As we shall see shortly, Aristotle assumes here that the persons involved know that they are not sleeping with their spouse.

Moral Taxonomy and Moral Absolutes 243

## There Are Moral Absolutes—
## And Then There Are Moral Absolutes

But there is still a problem for those who would find moral absolutes in this passage. It is correct to say that for Aristotle the immorality of adultery is in the act itself: we apply that name because of what the act is; the act's being immoral—implied in the name—does not depend on the assigning of the name. But Aristotle himself recognizes that there are actions fitting what might be regarded as the basic description of theft, 'taking another's goods,' that are not theft; and he recognizes too that there are acts of killing human beings that are not murder. It may be that the immorality of acts such as adultery, theft and murder is in the acts themselves; but it is also clear that Aristotle holds that concepts such as 'adultery,' 'theft,' and 'murder' do not get all their content from the way things stand in the world, independently of the determinations of law and society.

There is a relevant passage in the first book of the *Rhetoric*:

Since it often happens that individuals agree that they have performed an action, but do not agree with its description in an accusation or that the fact in question corresponds to the description—for instance, they agree they have taken something but not that they have stolen it; that they have struck someone first but not that they have been wantonly violent [ὑβρίσαι]; that they have had intercourse but not that they have committed adultery; that they have stolen but not that they have committed sacrilege (since the object stolen was not sacred) [etc.]—for these reasons, it would seem obligatory to set out definitions regarding these things. What is theft? What is wanton violence [ὕβρις]? What is adultery? In this way, whether we wish to show that the fact is verified or that it is not, we should have something to present as just. All such disputes are about being unjust (or wicked) or not unjust, for the wickedness and the being unjust is in the choice, and such things—e.g., wanton violence and theft—include the choice in the signification of the names. For it is not the case that, if a man has struck another, he has always assaulted him wantonly, but only if he has done it for a particular reason: for instance, to disgrace him or for pleasure. Nor is it always the case that, if a man has taken something secretly, he has stolen it; but only if he has done so to the harm of another and to the advantage of himself. And as with these charges, so also with the others. (*Rhet.* i,13,1373b38–1374a17)

This passage helps us to understand what Aristotle is saying in *EN* ii,6, when he says that some actions "as soon as they are named are bound up with badness" (1107a9–10). This does not mean that the badness depends solely on the naming but that the badness of the act, which is "in" the choice—the choice being that which makes the act to be an act—is built also into the corresponding name. Says Aristotle, "such *things*" (τὰ δὲ τοιαῦτα—*Rhet.* i,13,1374a12) as assault and theft include the choice in the very meaning of their names (τῶν ὀνομάτων προσσημαίνει τὴν προαίρεσιν—1374a12–13). The direction is from the things (the acts) to the names.

But we also see in this passage that acts whose names imply badness presuppose some sort of political process determining which types of actions fall under such names—otherwise, it would not be possible to dispute such questions, as the passage clearly says can be done. In other words, even if the badness of adultery, theft, or murder is not *simply* a matter of using a negative name for a type of act picked out as not to be done—that is, even if such a meaning comes from the nature of the act itself and not from its naming—the naming does still involve a political process or (at least) situation that determines when such a nature is present and, therefore, that the name is being properly applied. Man does not find 'theft' in the world as he does, for instance, the natural kind gold. So, at least with some types of actions, the bad-name theory is not completely without sense: the name 'theft,' for instance, picks out, from a larger group of structurally similar acts, some that are immoral. It is not "always the case that, if a man has taken something secretly, he has stolen; but only if he has done so to the harm of another and to the advantage of himself" (*Rhet.* i,13,1374a15–16).

This is not to say, however, that there is no difference between adultery and the two other acts mentioned in *EN* ii,6, i.e., theft and violent treatment of another. It is significant that in the *Rhet.* i,13 passage quoted just above, Aristotle does not really discuss how an accusation of adultery might be disputed. Conceivably, he could have said that the basic structural characteristic is having sexual intercourse, the evil act being specified in accordance with how the law defines a spouse and therefore a non-spouse. But such a parallel would not be as neat as might at first appear. There is something already fixed about adultery, and this prevents such disputation. Adultery is *all* bad—and its opposite, conjugal intercourse, considered in itself, is all good. The excuses made when someone is accused of adultery are usually, therefore, not about what constitutes adultery but about whether one knowingly committed an act, the nature of which was acknowledged from the beginning.

Aristotle in effect acknowledges this in a parallel passage in the *Eudemian Ethics:*

Nor must we forget that some of the things mentioned cannot be taken to depend on the manner of action, if manner means excess of passion: e.g., the adulterer [μοιχὸς] is not so called from his excessive intercourse with married women—there is no such thing—but the act is already something wicked, for the passion is bound up with its character. Similarly with wanton violence [ὕβρις]. So men defend themselves saying that they did have intercourse but did not commit adultery (for they acted in ignorance or under compulsion) and that they struck but did not assault wantonly [πατάξαι μέν, ἀλλ' οὐχ ὑβρίσαι]; and [they defend themselves] similarly against all other such charges [*EE* ii,3,1221b18–26].

The resemblances between this passage and *EN* i,6 are apparent: one notes, for instance, the common use of the passive participle of συλλαμβάνειν (translated in the two passages as "bound up with").[13] And one recognizes from *Rhet.* i,13 the examples adultery and wanton violence, not to mention the forensic context ("So men defend themselves . . ."). It is also clear that in all three passages Aristotle's main concern is to show that the manner of performing an action has no bearing upon what it is to be that type of action. But Aristotle acknowledges here in *EE* ii,3 what we do not see in the other passages: that the way the person accused of adultery defends himself is different from the way the other accused defend themselves. The man accused of adultery in effect acknowledges that his act, had it been fully voluntary, that is, performed neither in ignorance nor under compulsion, would have been adultery; the man accused of wanton violence, on the other hand, puts forward arguments about what should count *as* wanton violence. Similarly, as we saw in *Rhet.* i,13, the man accused of theft typically disputes whether what he did voluntarily should count as theft.

## *Rhetoric* i,13: Universally Divined Ideals

One of our tasks in the rest of this essay will be to account for this difference between adultery, on the one hand, and theft and murder, on the other. Our basic question, though, is: How does such moral taxonomy work? And how, despite their being bound up with human political factors, can we say that acts such as adultery, theft, and murder (or wanton violence) are bad in themselves—that is, in the words of *EN* ii,6, that it is not possible ever to be right with regard to them; one must always be wrong?

We get at least the germ of an answer to these questions in the chapter of

13. *EN* i,6,1107a10: συνειλημμένα; *EE* ii,3,1221b22: συνειλημμένον.

the *Rhetoric* quoted just above, that is, in *Rhet.* i,13. The chapter begins with a remark about two kinds of law: "particular law" (νόμον τὸν μὲν ἴδιον) and "common law" (νόμον τὸν δὲ κοινόν).

Particular law is that which each community lays down and applies to its own members: this is partly written and partly unwritten. Common law is that which corresponds to nature [τὸν κατὰ φύσιν—1373b6]. For there exists something which everyone divines:[14] a common natural justice (and injustice) [φύσει κοινὸν δίκαιον καὶ ἄδικον—1373b7-8], even in the absence of a commonality or covenant among the parties to it. (*Rhet.* i,13,1373b4-9)

It is interesting, of course, that Aristotle speaks here of nature—practically using the modern expression 'natural law.' Elsewhere—to be specific, in *EN* v,7—he speaks just of natural justice. But truly extraordinary is what comes next, where he identifies some of the principles of natural or common law. He speaks first of Sophocles' Antigone's burial of her brother Polyneices, despite legal prohibitions. She held, says Aristotle, that this was "just by nature: 'Not of today or yesterday it is, but lives eternal: none can date its birth.'"[15] Then he refers to Empedocles, who bids us (says Aristotle) "to kill no living creature" [τὸ ἔμψυχον] and who says that this principle "is not for some people just, for others unjust, 'But the law for all, through the realms of the sky, unbroken it stretcheth, and over the earth's immensity'" (1373b14-17). The Ross edition of *Rhet.* adds a third principle: "And, as Alcidamas says in his Messeniac Oration, 'God sent forth all men free, nature has made no man slave.'"[16]

It is conceivable that Aristotle subscribes without qualification to the principle apparently expressed by Antigone, that is, that burying the body

---

14. The word is μαντεύονται (1373b7). In his commentary on the passage, Victorius says: "Quod cuncti mortales divino afflatu pronunciant, in quo omnes conveniunt tacito instinctu commoti μαντεύονται (ut opinor) valet" (Petrus Victorius [Piero Vettori], *Commentarii longe doctissimi in tres libros Aristotelis de Arte dicendi, nunc primum in Germania editi* [Basel: Ex officina Ioannis Oporini, 1549], 265). He cites *EN* i,5,1095b25-26 and Plato's *Chrm.* 169B4-5.

15. *Rhet.* i,13,1373b1013 (quoting *Antigone* 456-57).

16. *Rhet.* i,13,1373b17-18a: καὶ ὡς ἐν τῷ Μεσσηνιακῷ λέγει' Ἀλκιδάμας, "ἐλυευθέρους ἀφῆκε πάντας θεός, οὐδένα δοῦλον ἡ φύσις πεποίηκεν." The MSS do not contain the quotation, which is supplied by the scholiast. The "Messeniac Oration" does not survive. What appears in the MSS (καὶ ὡς ἐν τῷ Μεσσηνιακῷ λέγει' Ἀλκιδάμας ...) does call for a quotation of some sort. Grimaldi remarks: "Though the incorporation of the words in the text is a questionable procedure, and although they are better omitted, it should be obvious that the quotation ('God has sent all men forth free; nature has made no man slave') is quite apposite to the point at issue." William M. A. Grimaldi, *Aristotle*, Rhetoric I: A Commentary (New York: Fordham University Press, 1980), 290.

Moral Taxonomy and Moral Absolutes    247

of a relative is above any positive law possibly prohibiting it.[17] But what about the Empedoclean principle that one ought not to kill any living creature? Within a few lines of its introduction here, Aristotle also says that it is wrong for a man to refuse military service (*Rhet.* i,13,1373b24). Further along in the chapter, Aristotle discusses the problem of specifying in written law "the kinds and sizes of weapons that may be used to inflict wounds" (1374a32–33). And if we are to count the antislavery principle of Alcidamas as part of Aristotle's argument, this would appear to be contradicted by Aristotle's position in favor of "natural slaves" in the first book of the *Politics*, chapters 5 to 7.[18]

Let us consider the Empedoclean principle, the most interesting of the three since it appears to be so quickly and clearly contradicted. Ettore Bignone adduces this text in favor of his thesis that, in the lost early work *On Justice*, Aristotle was against the killing of animals. Bignone cites the Empedocles fragment and then remarks: "There is not any doubt, therefore, that on this point ... the *Rhetoric* has conserved for us an earlier phase of Aristotle's doctrine, appearing in works published by him and different from his ultimate doctrine, in which he prized so minimally the traits of common humanity even between the Greeks and the barbarians."[19] Bignone finds more evidence of this *On Justice* doctrine in a passage in Stobaeus that recounts ideas about ethics held by "Aristotle and the rest of the Peripatet-

---

17. See, however, Larry Arnhart, *Aristotle on Political Reasoning: A Commentary on the Rhetoric* (DeKalb: Northern Illinois University Press, 1981), 102: "Antigone's case is surely the strongest of the three; but while Aristotle might have thought the family to be natural in some sense, it seems unlikely that he would have thought it an absolute dictate of nature to bury one's brother irrespective of the circumstances."

18. For an analysis of Aristotle's position in this regard, see Nicholas D. Smith, "Aristotle's Theory of Natural Slavery," in *A Companion to Aristotle's Politics*, ed. David Keyt and Fred D. Miller (Oxford: Basil Blackwell, 1991), 142–55.

19. Ettore Bignone, *L'Aristotele perduto e la formazione filosofica di Epicuro*, Pensiero Filosofico (Firenze: La Nuova Italia, 1973), II, 276. In the corresponding note 1, Bignone cites *Pol.* i,8,1256b23–26 ("the art of war is a natural art of acquisition, for the art of acquisition includes hunting, an art which we ought to practise against wild beasts, and against men who, though intended by nature to be governed, will not submit; for war of such a kind is naturally just") and *Pol.* i,2,1252b7–9 ("That is why the poets say, 'It is meet that Hellenes should rule over barbarians,' as if they thought that the barbarian and the slave were by nature one"). He also cites *Aristotelis qui ferebantur librorum fragmenta*, ed. Valentinus Rose (Leipzig: Teubner, 1886), fr. 658: "He [sc. Alexander] did not do as Aristotle advised—act towards Greeks as their leader, towards foreigners as their master, treating the former as friends and kinsmen and the latter as animals or plants—and so fill his reign with many wars and banishments and festering factions."

ics." In the passage, notes Bignone, one finds a sort of progression of friendship (φιλία): from family, to fellow citizens, to race, and finally to humanity in general.[20]

The great Aristotelian scholar Paul Moraux dismisses the principles of Antigone and Empedocles as mere examples: "this habit of Aristotle's of taking refuge behind more ancient authorities does not imply that he wholly agrees with the opinions sustained by the witnesses he invokes."[21] And he asks, with reason, what the progression of friendship in Stobaeus, finishing as it does with humanity, has to do with the relationship between man and animals.[22] He might also have cited the place in the same chapter where Stobaeus asks, "Who would not rescue a man he sees overpowered by an animal, if he is able?"[23] This does not sound like friendship between man and animals.

Moraux also presents a more direct and positive argument to the effect that even the early Aristotle would have opposed extending a natural law-based respect for life to mere animals.[24] In Cicero's *De republica*, there appears a character, Philus, who in fact represents the skeptical philosopher Carneades (214–129 B.C.). Philus argues against the existence of any sort of natural law and, in particular, against the idea that natural law is understood by the good, who hold to the principle, "give that to each, which each is due."[25] Moraux argues convincingly that many of Philus's arguments are in fact directed against Aristotle's *On Justice*—and this would certainly be

20. Bignone speaks of a theory according to which "si passa, nel progresso della φιλία, dalla dalla famiglia ai concittadini, agli uomini della stessa raza, *all'umanità*, per concludere alla φιλία *verso tutti gli uomini*" (*L'Aristotele perduto*, 278, emphasis his). The passage in Stobaeus is Joannis Stobaeus, *Anthologium*, ed. Kurt Wachsmuth and Otto Hense (Berlin: Weidmann, 1884–1912), 2.7.13.

21. Paul Moraux, *A la recherche de l'Aristote perdu: le dialogue "Sur la justice"* (Louvain: Publications Universitaires de Louvain, 1957), 104. See also *Aristoteles: Rhetorik*, ed. and trans. Christoff Rapp, vol. 4.1-2 of *Aristoteles: Werke in deutscher Übersetzung* (Berlin: Akademie, 2002), 4.2.492.

22. Moraux, *A la recherche de l'Aristote perdu*, 105.

23. Stobaeus, 2.7.13.89–90: Τίνα γὰρ οὐκ ἂν ἐξελεῖσθαι θεασάμενον ἄνθρωπον ὑπὸ θηρίου καταδυναστευόμενον, εἰ δύναιτο.

24. Moraux, *A la recherche de l'Aristote perdu*, 107–8.

25. "An vero in legibus varietatem esse dicunt, natura autem viros bonos eam iustitiam sequi quae sit, non eam quae putetur? Esse enim hoc boni viri et iusti, tribuere id cuique quod sit quoque dignum" (M. Tullius Cicero, *De re publica librorum sex quae manserunt*, ed. Konrat Ziegler, Bibliotheca Scriptorum Graecorum et Romanorum Teubneriana [Leipzig: Teubner, 1955], 3.11.18). The idea that Philus opposes is found in both Plato and Aristotle: see Plato's *R.* i,331e2–3 and Aristotle's *EN* v,2,1130b30–1131a1.

Moral Taxonomy and Moral Absolutes   249

one of them. Philus argues in *ad hominem* fashion that, following the principle ("give that to each, which each is due") to its logical conclusion, one ends up with the position of the Pythagoreans and of Empedocles, who "affirm that there is one condition in law for all living beings and proclaim that there is waiting for those by whom an animal is done violence an inexpiable punishment."[26] This conclusion is clearly unacceptable—presumably also for Aristotle; therefore, Philus concludes, there is no natural law. Whatever we think of the argument, it is apparent that Cicero, who had access to early writings of Aristotle now lost to us, knew that these writings contradicted the Empedoclean principle that no living creature ought to be killed.

But, although Moraux stands on very solid ground with respect to Aristotle and the killing of animals, there are still some things he does not explain. Even granted that in *Rhet.* i,13 Aristotle is engaging in his standard practice of citing authorities (here Sophocles, Empedocles, and Alcidamas), why does he not give us one of his own principles—or even a suggestion of what one would be? And how can he so nonchalantly mention, within a few lines of the Empedoclean principle, the principle that it is wrong for a man to refuse military service?

The answer, I believe, is that Aristotle does in a way regard the principles stated in *Rhet.* i,13 as genuine principles of law, but his understanding of how such principles function in ethics is different from what we would expect. They are ideals that all people by nature—and/or by divine inspiration—find attractive and that might motivate noble and reasonable actions; but they are not principles to be employed in the resolution of all the related practical matters. We find such an ideal in the *Historia animalium* [*HA*], book 9, chapter 1, where Aristotle says that the members of the whole animal kingdom are at war against one another for the procurement of food. And then he says: "One might speculate, however, that, if there were abundance of food, then those animals that are now feared and are wild by nature would behave tamely towards man and in like manner towards one another."[27] As it is, there is lack of food and consequent strife—and that too is quite natural. Thus, Aristotle can say in another place that man rightly

---

26. "Non enim mediocres viri sed maxumi et docti, Pythagoras et Empedocles, unam omnium animantium condicionem iuris esse denuntiant, clamantque inexpiabilis poenas impendere iis a quibus violatum sit animal" (Cicero, *De re publica* 3.11.19).

27. *HA* ix,1,608b29-32. The phrase εἰ ἀφθονία τροφῆς εἴη might even be translated, "if there were freedom from envy for lack of food."

wages war against the animals and even against other men: "Now if nature makes nothing incomplete, and nothing in vain, the inference must be that she has made all animals for the sake of man. And so, from one point of view, the art of war is a natural art of acquisition, for the art of acquisition includes hunting, an art which we ought to practice against wild beasts, and against men who, though intended by nature to be governed, will not submit; for war of such a kind is naturally just" (*Pol.* i,8,1256b20–26).

But although an ideal such as that found in *HA* ix,1 clearly does not constitute for Aristotle a generally and concretely applicable principle, it does serve a function even in law broadly construed. Even given, for instance, the legitimacy of carnivorous behavior and war, if the conditions that legitimize such behavior were absent or if other factors were to suggest that otherwise legitimate measures ought not be employed, the ideal of peace is to be pursued. In cases where war is the issue, the area of decision beyond the conditions calling for war is not a sort of no man's land, where no principle has preference over any other; and the default principle is certainly not "Pursue war whenever possible." It must, therefore, be the ideal of peace among men. Or a more universal ideal would serve as well, as in the Prophet Isaiah: "The wolf shall dwell with the lamb, and the leopard shall lie down with the kid, and the calf and the lion and the fatling together, and a little child shall lead them" (11,6). Since law is ultimately about what is reasonable, it is proper that even such ideals be included in it. It is not reasonable for there to be an ethical no man's land.

This way of understanding the principles of common law gives us a more plausible understanding of the organization of *Rhet.* i,13 than we usually find in the commentators. As the chapter is typically understood, Aristotle first (1373b2–6) sets out in general terms the various divisions of law, then in a few lines (1373b6–18) gives us the principles of common law, then (i.e., at 1373b18) launches into an analysis of particular law, both written and unwritten, which takes him to the end of the chapter (at 1374b22), a full Bekker page later. On this view, contrary to what the introductory section leads one to expect, the chapter is basically about particular law.[28] This appearance of imbalance is increased by the apparently perfunctory manner in which Aristotle puts forward the principles of common law, neglecting to give us one

---

28. Grimaldi (*Rhetoric*, 287) contends that Aristotle does come back to common law for a few lines in the later section, i.e., in 1374a21–25, but there is no hint in the text that that is what Aristotle sees himself as doing.

Moral Taxonomy and Moral Absolutes    251

of his own. One is left with the impression that Aristotle has not fulfilled an implied promise to expound the relationship between common and particular law.

If, on the other hand, we understand the principles of common law along the lines suggested above, that is, as ideals, it is possible to see their influence even in the section dedicated to the exposition of particular law. Beginning at 1374a18 and going to the end of the chapter, that is, as part of the treatment of particular law, Aristotle discusses equity (τὸ ἐπιεικές). The latter can be understood as the application of the principles (or ideals) of Antigone, Empedocles, and Alcidamas, plus other factors that might go into the reasonable application of law, in order to fill deficiencies in the written law: deficiencies either not foreseen by the lawgiver or foreseen by him and left in the laws, with the expectation that others would apply them with equity.

Says Aristotle:

Equity bids us be merciful to the weakness of human nature; to think less about the laws than about the man who framed them, and less about what he said than about what he meant; not to consider the actions of the accused so much as his choice, nor this or that detail so much as the whole story; to ask not what a man is now but what he has always or for the most part been. It bids us remember benefits rather than injuries, and benefits received rather than benefits conferred; to be patient when we are wronged; to settle a dispute by negotiation and not by force; to prefer arbitration to litigation—for an arbitrator goes by the equity of a case, a judge by the law, and arbitration was invented with the express purpose of securing full power for equity. (*Rhet.* i,13,1374b10–22)

It is true: Aristotle does not explicitly say that he is applying here the ideals of common law; but it is not difficult to discern their influence in the application of equity. As we have seen, Aristotle holds that equity "makes up for the deficits of a community's written code" (1374a25–26). Certainly, Antigone's claim that burying Polyneices "was a just act in spite of the prohibition" (1373b10) is an appeal to equity. After the Empedocles remark, Aristotle does not again in *Rhet.* i,13 speak about friendship with animals, but he does speak a good deal about individuals who might be accused of one crime or another: assault, for instance, or adultery. If, because of extenuating circumstances or circumstances that put an act into a different—more favorable— light, a judge or "arbitrator" decides not to sentence a man to death, it is not implausible to argue that he is motivated by the universal benevolence that led Empedocles to say that no living being ought to be killed. If the realm of equity is still part of law (as Aristotle's calling it common *law* would suggest), it must be governed by principles: by reason. What more suitable principles than those that draw us toward universal benevolence and mercy?

## *Sent.* 4.36.1.1 ad 2: Nature's First and Second Intentions

Let us remind ourselves now of where the present argument is headed. We are looking for an account of moral absolutes such as explains the difference between the prohibition of adultery, on the one hand, and theft and murder, on the other. But we are also ultimately out to explain how Thomas Aquinas can claim in *ST* 1-2.18.10 that circumstances can take something that is basically bad and put it into the species of good acts. An appropriate question to ask at this point, therefore, is whether there is any evidence that Thomas employs the type of principles or ideals we have found in *Rhet.* i,13.

This question can be answered in the affirmative. In his commentary on Peter Lombard's *Sentences,* Thomas considers the question whether the condition of servitude (or slavery) can be an impediment to marriage. (The mention of servitude reminds us, of course, of the principle of Alcidamas that Ross finds in *Rhet.* i,13.) An objection argues that no: "[T]hat which is against nature cannot impede that which is according to nature. But servitude is against nature, for, as Gregory says, it is against nature for a man to will to dominate another man;[29] and this is also clear from that which is said about man in *Genesis* 1.26, 'Thus, he has dominion over the fish of the sea,' etc. He does not have dominion over man."

Thomas does not agree that the state of servitude can *never* be an impediment to marriage since he holds that it can be an impediment if the state is not known to the other spouse. So, he replies as follows:

[N]othing prohibits something's being contrary to the first intention of nature without its being contrary to its second intention, just as every corruption and defect and growing old is—as is said in *De caelo*[30]—contrary to nature since nature intends

---

29. Gregory the Great, *Moralium libri, Patrologia Latina* 75–76, gen. ed. J.-P. Migne (Paris, 1849), 21.15 (22), vol. 76, col. 203: "Omnes namque homines natura aequales sumus . . ."; see also Gregory the Great, *Regulae pastoralis liber, Patrologia Latina* 77, 2.6, col. 34.

30. *Cael.* ii,6,288b12–16: Ἀλλὰ μὴν οὐδὲ τὴν ὅλην ἐγχωρεῖ μεταβάλλειν· ἡ γὰρ ἄνεσις ἑκάστου γίνεται δι' ἀδυναμίαν, ἡ δ' ἀδυναμία παρὰ φύσιν· καὶ αἱ ἐν τοῖς ζῴοις ἀδυναμίαι πᾶσαι παρὰ φύσιν εἰσίν, οἷον γῆρας καὶ φθίσις. Besides here in the *Sentences* commentary, Thomas cites this passage at least three times: see *in Phys.* 5.10 (§739), *QD de veritate* 13.1 ad 2, *QD de potentia* 6.1 ad 1—not to mention, of course, in *Cael.* 5.9 (§375).

## Moral Taxonomy and Moral Absolutes    253

being and perfection, but is not contrary to nature according to the second intention of nature since, because nature cannot preserve being in one thing, it preserves it in another which is generated from the corruption of the first. And when nature cannot achieve a greater perfection it effects a lesser one, as when nature cannot make a male and it makes a female, which is a botched male, as is said in *De generatione animalium*.[31] Similarly, I say that servitude is contrary to the first intention of nature but not contrary to the second. For natural reason tends toward—and nature desires—everyone's being good, but in as much as someone sins nature also tends to bear punishment for sin; and thus servitude was introduced as punishment for sin.[32]

Aristotle and Thomas are often criticized, of course, for their way of conceiving the female, that is, as a botched male *(mas occasionatus)*; but if the first intention of nature is to be associated with the ideals mentioned in *Rhet.* i,13, their position might even be described as 'enlightened.' It is as if they were saying that, although women *are* subject to men and in that sense are unequal, more basic is their fundamental equality *qua* humans. When at all possible—that is, when reasonably constituted law does not prohibit it—women are to be regarded as equal to men. And, indeed, we find Aristotle at least inclined in this direction. He criticizes the "barbarians" because they do not distinguish between women and slaves (*Pol.* i,2,1252b5–6), for he considers at least some women "free" (*Pol.* i,13,1260b18–19). He says that the relationship between man and wife is aristocratic, "for the man rules in accordance with merit, and in those matters in which a man should rule, but the matters that befit a woman he hands over to her." If the man does not concede such rule to his wife, the relationship becomes oligarchical, "for he does this contrary to merit and not *qua* better" (*EN* viii,10,1160b32–1161a1). Aristotle also acknowledges that, in certain circumstances, a woman properly serves as head-of-household (*EN* viii,10,1161a1–3).

We find in Aristotle a similarly complex attitude regarding slavery. We

---

31. *GA* ii,3,737a27–28: τὸ γὰρ θῆλυ ὥσπερ ἄρρεν ἐστὶ πεπηρωμένον.
32. "Ad secundum dicendum, quod nihil prohibet esse aliquid contra naturam quantum ad primam intentionem ipsius, quod non est contra naturam quantum ad secundum ejus intentionem; sicut omnis corruptio et defectus et senium est contra naturam, ut dicitur in *De caelo*, quia natura intendit esse et perfectionem; non tamen est contra secundam intentionem naturae, quia ex quo natura non potest conservare esse in uno, conservat in altero, quod generatur corruptione alterius; et quando natura non potest perducere ad majorem perfectionem, inducit ad minorem; sicut quando non potest facere masculum, facit feminam, quae est mas occasionatus, ut dicitur in *De generatione animalium*. Similiter etiam dico, quod servitus est contra primam intentionem naturae, sed non contra secundam; quia naturalis ratio ad hoc inclinat, et hoc appetit natura ut quilibet sit bonus; sed ex quo aliquis peccat, natura etiam inclinat ut ex peccato poenam reportet; et sic servitus in poenam peccati introducta est" (*Sent.* 4.36.1.1 ad 2).

have already mentioned his position that some persons are naturally slaves (*Pol.* i,5–7). He holds too that a master stands toward his slave as an artificer toward a tool. In this sense, the master has nothing in common with his slave. "*Qua* slave, then," he says, "one cannot be friends with him. But *qua* man one can" (*EN* viii,11,1161b5–6). Aristotle also says that masters would not need slaves if they had machines that operated automatically (*Pol.* i,4,1253b32–1254a1). This is not unlike what he says in *HA* ix,1 about animals becoming tame if there were an abundance of food.

In the chapter of *De caelo* cited by Thomas (ii,6), Aristotle argues that any movement that falls short of perfect regularity—which is to say, any movement in the universe below the level of the fixed stars—to the extent that it is not perfectly regular, is against nature since any such irregularity or unevenness is a sort of corruption. Thus, everything in the world in which we live is bound up to an extent with the 'unnatural': that which is against nature. All things have good aspects, that is, the aspects that are consonant with their natural propensities: having life, for instance, or exercising the faculties of sense. But, to the extent that there is any 'falling away' from these good aspects, there is action that is against nature, even if the falling away is, in another sense, quite natural. Since the ethical life of man is certainly part of the sublunary world, it too is inescapably bound up with that which is contrary to nature (contrary, that is, to nature's first intention).

## Killing, Property, and Sex

This understanding of things gives us answers to the questions before us, that is, how to explain the difference between adultery, on the one hand, and theft and murder, on the other, and also how to understand Thomas's claim that circumstances can change the moral species of an act, either for good or for ill. We can answer these questions together. With respect to the second, as we have already seen, the problem is not so much in understanding how a good type of act (e.g., telling the truth) can find itself in the species of bad (telling the truth rather than remaining quiet when speaking would betray one's friends), but rather in understanding how a basically bad type of act can be considered good, when demanded by a "special order of reason." One worries that the moral character of acts might be changed from bad to good according to the whims of self-appointed arbiters of the reasonable. But such an eventuality is excluded by the Aristotelian theory of moral absolutes: intrinsically immoral acts such as adultery, theft, and murder are immoral because of what they are, not because of the arbitrary determination of any individual authority or group of authorities.

This is not to say, however, that even such moral absolutes are independent of the political. In *EN* v,7, Aristotle distinguishes legal justice from natural justice—the latter, obviously, being the same for all political entities. He mentions that some people object to this approach, arguing that the whole realm of human action is in constant and irregular motion: it has not the fixity we find in the natural world where, for instance, fire always goes up. Aristotle responds: "This, however, is not true in this unqualified way, but is true in a sense; or rather, with the gods it is perhaps not true at all, while with us there is something that is just even by nature, yet all of it is in motion; but still some is by nature, some not by nature."[33] To say that all justice, whether legal or natural, is in motion (κινητὸν) is just to say that it is political: it all belongs to the world of human action. But even *within* this moving realm, there are things that are according to nature.

Aristotle might also have pointed out to his interlocutors that fire's motion (as he argues in *De caelo* ii,6) is not as regular as they suppose—although this very irregularity gives it its natural constancy, that is, the characteristics it has as fire. It is true that one espies in the natural world regularities that, because they contrast with the irregularities of its proper lower-level movements, point to higher sources of regularity and intelligibility (the causality of "the gods"); and these higher regularities operating within the natural world can be described as the natural world's 'true' nature, just as man's true nature is located in his waking moments and not in his sleeping. But when we consider the natural world *itself*, that is, as a combination of act *and* potency, it has constant laws despite—or, better, because of—its natural motion. Although it is inclined toward perfect regularity, it is not going to change and suddenly shed its proper irregularity, which is as much a part of its nature as is man's sleeping a part of his.

Applying this approach, then, to moral matters, there is a sense in which, for instance, killing is in itself bad. That is the default position: life—any life—is better than death, just as knowledge is better than ignorance, act better than potency. But it is reasonable in this moral world, constantly in motion as it is, to say that some killing is good—and in a stable way, that is, as in

33. *EN* v,7,1134b27–30.

some sense, part of natural law or justice. Such killing would include killing in defense of one's nation, killing in defense of one's own person or kin, and perhaps some cases of capital punishment. Laws permitting certain types of killing have been part of the political realm from time immemorial: they are, we might even say, as constant as fire. But that same political realm includes a level that is above the natural necessities of war and self-protection and that considers all killing an evil. The principles of this realm, standing above the proper irregular movements of politics, are the principles that govern equity, which is not a 'free for all' but an application of reason.

So, there can be moral absolutes even in the mobile world of human morality and politics. How, finally, can we account for the different types of absolute prohibitions, that is, for the difference between adultery, on the one hand, and theft and murder, on the other? The difference depends on the fact that, in natural law—that is, at the level below the level of equity—the allowance of such things as killing is basically a derogation from a higher law. This has already been demonstrated sufficiently with respect to killing: the default position, that is, the rule to be followed when the conditions that allow killing are not in place, is not to kill. We find a similar position in both Aristotle and Thomas with respect to property. This issue is somewhat different from the allowance of killing, but it serves well as an illustration of what a derogation from a higher sense of moral law might be.

In *ST* 1-2.94.5 ad 3, Thomas responds to an objection according to which the natural law does change since, although St. Isidore says that "the common possession of all things, and a single liberty, is of natural right,"[34] this has been altered by human laws. Thomas argues that something can be said to be "of natural right" in two ways: either because nature *inclines* in that direction or because it does not tend toward the contrary. It is in this latter way, he says, that the principle "the common possession of all things, and a single liberty of all" is said to be of natural right: "because, that is, the possession of things and servitude have not been introduced by nature but by the reason of men for the utility of human life." But, if this is the case, when reason and utility no longer dictate the maintenance of individual property

---

34. "Ius naturale est commune omnium nationum, et quod ubique instinctu naturae, non constitutione aliqua habetur, ut: viri et feminae coniunctio, liberorum susceptio et educatio, communis omnium possessio, et omnium una libertas, acquisitio eorum quae caelo, terra marique capiuntur." Isidore Hispalensis (Archbishop of Seville), *Etymologiarum libri XX, Patrologia Latina* 82, 5.4, col. 199.

rights, the default disposition is for property to be held in common. This is, as Thomas says, "of natural right." Thomas does not deny Isidore's position; he just does not think that it contradicts the idea of personal property. His reason would be that an individual property right is just a granting to some person or to some entity the use of that which belongs essentially to all.[35]

In Aristotle we find similar ideas. He says in *Pol.* ii,5, for instance, "Property should in a certain sense be common, but, as a general rule, private; for, when everyone has a distinct interest, men will not complain of one another, and they will make more progress, because everyone will be attending to his own business" (*Pol.* ii,5,1263a26–27; see also *Pol.* ii,3,1261b33–38). This is basically the idea we have just seen in Thomas: that property is for the utility of man as established by reason. Aristotle goes on to conclude: "It is clearly better that property should be private but, when convenient, to become common; and the special business of the legislator is to create in men this benevolent disposition."[36]

So, the allowance of certain types of killing and the institution of private ownership are both derogations—permanent derogations—from a higher law. With sexual relations, we find no such situation. Recall, first of all, that in all three cases we are concerned with that which is reasonable. Self-defense and private property are lawful because they are reasonable; sexual relations too are lawful to the extent that they are reasonable—which is to say, to the extent that they take place within marriage and do not involve acts or attitudes that go against the goods of marriage. But the lawfulness of such sexual relations—at least, within the natural realm—is not a derogation from a higher law. Leaving aside the possibility of an afterlife where

---

35. See, for instance, *ST* 2-2.66.1c: "res exterior potest dupliciter considerari. Uno modo, quantum ad eius naturam, quae non subiacet humanae potestati, sed solum divinae, cui omnia ad nutum obediunt. Alio modo, quantum ad usum ipsius rei. Et sic habet homo naturale dominium exteriorum rerum, quia per rationem et voluntatem potest uti rebus exterioribus ad suam utilitatem." See also *ST* 2-2.66.2 ad 1: "communitas rerum attribuitur iuri naturali, non quia ius naturale dictet omnia esse possidenda communiter et nihil esse quasi proprium possidendum, sed quia secundum ius naturale non est distinctio possessionum, sed magis secundum humanum condictum, quod pertinet ad ius positivum."

36. *Pol.* ii,5,1263a37–40. I follow Thomas's interpretation of this remark: "Oportet enim possessiones simpliciter quidem esse proprias quantum ad proprietatem dominii, sed secundum aliquem modum communes.... Unde manifestum est quod multo melius est quod sint propriae possessiones secundum dominium, sed quod fiant communes aliquo modo quantum ad usum; quo modo autem usus rerum propriarum possit fieri communis, hoc pertinet ad providentiam boni legislatoris" (Thomas Aquinas, *Sententia libri Politicorum*, vol. 48 of *Opera Omnia* [Rome: Commissio Leonina, 1971], 2.4.112–14, 145–50).

there is no "marrying and giving in marriage"—which is a reasonable thing to leave aside since we are talking about what is *legal*, either strictly speaking or in equity—there is no playing of one level of morality against another: unlike killing in self-defense and property, the institution of marriage is no 'concession' made for the sake of safety or utility.[37]

The fundamental difference between licit sexual relations and, for example, licit killing is that, even when the latter *is* licit, it retains a non-moral aspect of badness. To kill is to put an end to the natural activity of an animal—and natural activities are good. Even when killing becomes lawful (in war, for instance, or self-defense), it still retains this aspect of badness. We discern this difference also in the animal kingdom, strictly considered. Obviously, both sexual relations and killing for food are natural in the animal kingdom—and, in that sense, legitimate. And yet, when we see one animal kill another—a wolf kill a lamb, for instance—we sense that there is something disordered here; not *wrong*, since it is perfectly natural, but not quite right: a natural activity has been cut short. We harbor a reasonably positive regard for Aristotle's ideal universe: "if there were abundance of food, then those animals that are now feared and are wild by nature would behave tamely towards man and in like manner towards one another." We do not have the same instinctive reaction to animals copulating: we are not pressed in any way to imagine a naturally chaste life for all.

The particular characteristics of legitimate killing are reflected in what Thomas says in *ST* 1–2.18.10 about circumstances that can take something that is basically bad and put into the species of good. The result (i.e., that type of act) is *all good*, and yet, given its natural origins, when the necessary conditions are absent the natural badness reasserts itself, and one is bound, in equity and reasonability, to prefer life. But there is no such interplay of default badness and legal goodness with respect to marital relations. Marital relations considered in themselves are good: the conjugal act is an *act*, that is, an activity natural to man. It is good in its own right. This is just to say that it is naturally good in the strictest sense.

Marriage is, of course, a political entity. Still, private property and legitimate killing are more dependent on the political than is marriage. With private property and legitimate killing, the details of the derogation from the law of equity are worked out in positive law. For this reason, as Aris-

---

37. See *EN* viii,12,1162a17–18, where Aristotle says that "man is by nature even more a coupling than a political animal." Many thanks to Michael Pakaluk for this point and reference.

totle says, legal defenses regarding taken property and violence very often seek to prove that the act committed should not *count* legally as stealing or as assault. On the other hand, when someone is accused of adultery, if he acknowledges the act but denies guilt, he will typically seek to prove either that he did not know what he was doing or that he was compelled to do what he did. To perform any of the acts mentioned by Aristotle in *EN* ii,6—adultery, theft, or murder—is wrong, therefore, independently of the circumstances: "It is not possible . . . ever to be right with regard to them; one must always be wrong." But adultery is more directly against the natural law. It is so because it is less bound up with—although not entirely independent of—the political.

Heather McAdam Erb

# Interior Peace

## Inchoatio vitae aeternae

IT WAS SAID OF THE DESERT ABBOT ANTHONY that he compared monks outside their cells to fish outside water, warning that as a fish must return to the sea, so must the monk to his cell, lest by tarrying without, he forget the watch within.[1] Saint Thomas's Dominican spirituality is as far from this version of interior peace as it is from the antiworldly passages of Cassian, which depicted the soul of a holy man as an anxious and vigilant watchman, shutting "both soul and body within the fence of its walls," or like a fisherman, intent and motionless as he judges the depths of his most quiet heart.[2] Thomas's comments on the nature of interior peace resemble more a cultivated garden or oasis watered by a secret source visited by a variety of pilgrims than an ascetic's watchful penetration of a vast solitude in the desert silence. This contrast of spiritualities illustrates the historical fact noted by von Balthasar, that side by side with the purely upward movement characteristic of Neoplatonism in the Fathers, there was now room found for the movement of descent, increasing as Christian insights came into play.[3]

---

1. As found in the *Vita B. Antoni*, in Rosweyde's *Vitae Patrum* (Antwerp, 1628), trans. Helen Waddell, *The Desert Fathers* (Ann Arbor: University of Michigan Press, 1957), 63.
2. Waddell, *The Desert Fathers*, 161.
3. Hans Urs von Balthasar, *Explorations in Theology*, vol. 1, *The Word Made Flesh*, trans. A. V. Littledale with Alexander Dru (San Francisco: Ignatius Press, 1989), 231. He notes that while contemplation is superior to action for Aquinas, as the two dispositions of the intellect reveal, there is nonetheless a complexity and paradox of the contemplative life that finds its explanation and source in Jesus' own contemplation: in the Son's earthly state "the *contemplata aliis tradere* was carried to the point of total renunciation, emptying, kenosis of contemplation in

Interior Peace 261

Here we will analyze three sources of Aquinas's spirituality, stressing, as he does, the roles of contemplation and action, love and knowledge, and metaphysical concepts involved in the mind's analysis of the achievement of interior or spiritual peace. First, we will analyze Augustine's influence on his theory of interior peace, in terms of the relation of the concept of peace to the concepts of immutability and rest. Augustine's main contribution to theories of interior peace, it will be seen, lay in his ability to reconcile the classical notion of "universal order" with Christian "spiritual peace," through his definition of peace as the "tranquility of order." Augustine's ideal of the Christianization of the world, framing as it did *The City of God*, reveals a notion of order as internal harmony and subordination within the self, and within society in relation to God. This association of peace with natural order in the soul and in the world influenced Aquinas's concept of spiritual peace far more than did the ascetic notion of peace as a spiritual "flight from the world" *(fuga mundi)*, a lived ideal reserved for elite ascetics, more popular in the early church and among monastics up until the twelfth century. In the second part of the paper, I will trace the biblical influences on Aquinas's notion of peace, as found in various passages taken from his biblical commentaries. We find this in his treatment of the beatitudes, in the Pauline "fruit of the Spirit" effected by charity, and in the all-enduring peace of Christ foreshadowed in Isaiah and in the Psalms. Augustinian themes such as the relation between earthly and heavenly peace, imperfect human contemplation as a foretaste of perfect happiness, peace as a "beginning of eternal life" *(inchoatio vitae aeternae)*, divine "rest," and others recur in Thomas's treatment of these texts. As well, the active and passive qualities of interior peace, and its coexistence with suffering, will be illumined. Third, the influence of Dionysius on Aquinas's theory of interior peace will be analyzed. In particular, Dionysius's concept of divine peace as the uniting force of all being, and his

---

action . . . when action ends by becoming passion"; "[C]ontemplation . . . is an act in which *actio* and *passio* are combined"; "Thomas was fully conscious of this paradox of the creature, namely that the more it is receptive to God, the more it participates in his activity" (ibid., 231–32). In von Balthasar's language, Aquinas's theory of spiritual contemplation combines the element of both ascent (speculative reason) and descent (practical reason), maintaining the primacy of contemplation from which action flows, to simple contemplation, as in the formula "contemplation *above* action." *Contemplata aliis tradere* means that only the action that is derived *ex plenitudine contemplationis* is to be preferred to "simple" contemplation. In Aquinas's words, "just as it is a greater thing to illuminate than merely to shine, so it is greater to communicate what is contemplated than merely to contemplate" (*ST* II-II 188.6). Thus his defense of the mixed apostolate of contemplative and active lives favored by the Dominicans.

concepts of *extasis* and *eros*, will be seen to be instrumental in Thomas's tempering of the ascetic motif of flight from the world and in his rehabilitation of the classical notion of peace as universal order.[4]

## The Influence of Augustine

The monastic theories of peace that began in the West with Gregory the Great focused on the achievement of spiritual repose in God during this life, through an ascetic detachment from the chaotic, sinful world. Augustine's theory, in contrast, reconciled many divergent senses of peace—the Stoic, classical notion of peace as cosmic order; the Christian understanding of peace as a fruit of the Holy Spirit, peace as a harmonic unity between soul and body; and the incomplete secular peace that he saw as a means to eternal, celestial peace.[5] His definition of peace as "tranquility of order" in Book 19 of *The City of God*[6] points to the celestial *ideal* of peace, never completely realized, but always dynamically influencing the submission of appetite to reason and human to divine will in this life. Various species of peace are listed, including the peace of the body, the irrational soul, the rational soul, the composite, among men, in a family, between the soul and God, and among the blessed in heaven,[7] all carrying the note of an ordered arrangement of parts disposed toward the good of the whole.

One sees the blending of several influences in Augustine's discussions of

---

4. We will reserve for another study a contrast between Thomas's theory and the Buddhist concepts of "indifference," "wisdom" or "insight," and "tranquility," in the context of these systems' content and goals. In light of Buddhism's popularity in the West, we hope to establish the key differences between Aquinas's theory and modern Buddhist thought on interior peace, and determine which theory possesses more explanatory power in terms of the human situation. Hans Urs von Balthasar's criticism of Buddhist meditation in light of its analysis of suffering, the call for worldly engagement, and the concept of "emptiness" *(sunyata)* could be examined against the background of Aquinas's theory of peace.

5. Thomas Renna, "The Idea of Peace in the Augustinian Tradition: 400–1200," *Augustinian Studies* 10 (1979), 106: "The world's peace was not a shadowy means to eternity; it was also a legitimate social arrangement with its own principles and techniques. Christians were supposed to Christianize the world, not flee from it."

6. *City of God*, 19.13.1: "pax omnium rerum tranquillitas ordinis." This definition is applied in the text to peace in its several instances: in the various types of bodies, souls, composites, within the community (domestic, political, and celestial), and in man's relation to God. "Order" is defined here as the arrangement of different types of things in their proper place.

7. Ibid. Cf. Étienne Gilson, *The Christian Philosophy of Saint Augustine*, trans. L. Lynch (New York: Random House, 1960), 173: "For a number of parts—and *a fortiori* a number of wills—to work together simultaneously in the pursuit of an end, each must be in its proper place, and perform its own function precisely as it should be performed. This is quite evident

peace: First, the classical notion of cosmic *concordia* prevails here as it does in Boethius, a sense of the universal order guided by divine providence, with the addition that spiritual peace is to be understood in eschatological terms—peace is never fully realized in this world.[8] Second, we see the patristic dichotomy of the true peace of Christ, versus the false peace of physical or emotional satiation and the temporary, negative sort of peace that is the result of war.[9] Third, there is peace as a result of Christian charity, seen through the progressive sanctification of history instead of flight from it, unlike ascetic models of peace. And fourth, we see the Neoplatonic theme of rest and immutability figuring into a Christian metaphysics of salvation, where created things are restored to their divinely assigned functions, the tug of appetites being finally stilled in contemplative *quies*.

The restless heart of Augustine's *Confessions* cleaves both to appetite and to a materialistic conception of reality, and is unable to find peace and enjoyment disconnected from its immaterial axis in the contemplation of divine love.[10] Knowing God as a spiritual and immutable substance that, as loved for its own sake, is also its own end, helps him direct his soul toward the eternal rest of heaven,[11] the peace without evening.[12] In *De doctrina Christiana*, Augustine discusses the types of love in terms of the soul's journey as a wanderer in exile, searching for rest in her true homeland. The wanderer is warned not to come to enjoy *(frui)* the means of traveling and traveling itself, but only to *use* these as a means to return home, the proper object of his enjoyment and rest.[13]

---

in the internal functioning of a physical organism like the human body, but it is no less true of the interior of the human soul and consequently, of the interior of a society."

8. *City of God*, 22.30. This deferment of beatitude is interesting in light of the fact that Thomas, while agreeing with Augustine that Moses and St. Paul experienced in this mortal life a "rapture" by which they were carried up even to the vision of the divine essence, nevertheless holds that their experience was transitory, like that of prophecy, and did not render them blessed simply speaking, since that would have demanded death and glorification. See the commentary on 2 Cor. 12; *De ver.*, 13; and *ST* II-II 175.

9. E.g., *City of God*, 15.4.

10. *Confessions* 1.1.1: "Inquietum est cor nostrum ..."

11. See, e.g., *Confessions*, 13.36.51. Cf. *City of God* 22.30: "Heaven, too, will be the fulfillment of that Sabbath rest foretold in the command, 'Be still and see that I am God.' ... And we ourselves will be a 'seventh day' when we shall be filled with His blessing and remade by His sanctification." Augustine also refers to this as the Sabbath of eternal life, which is the perpetual Sabbath or "eighth day" (*Confessions* 13.36.51). On this topic, see G. Lawless, "Interior Peace in the *Confessions* of St. Augustine," *Revue des etudes Augustiniennes* 26 (1980): 45–61.

12. *Confessions* 13.35.50.

13. *De doctrina Christiana*, 1.4.4. Cf. Oliver O'Donovan, "*Usus* and *Fruitio* in Augustine, *De Doctrina Christiana* I," *Journal of Theological Studies* [NS] 33 (1982): 361–97.

Aquinas's notion of spiritual peace adapts many tenets of Augustine's teaching, both within a system of infused virtues and gifts in his theological texts and within philosophical discussions of friendship as well as the passions. First, Thomas depends on Augustine's distinction between use and enjoyment in his understanding of charity as *frui*, noting that to enjoy is to love the good that is one's final good—that which is loved *for its own sake*. Citing Augustine as his authority for this principle, he says that "the ultimate and principal good of man is the enjoyment of God . . . and to this end man is ordered by charity."[14] Elsewhere, in a discussion on happiness, he calls this end our "peace."[15] Peace is antecedent to our final beatitude as the removal of all disturbances and obstacles; it is consequent to it as the rest of all desires and is identical with it as the perfect enjoyment of our sovereign good.[16] Thus, while "rest" *(quies)* applies first to physical movement, Aquinas takes it to apply to spiritual things in two ways: as the fulfillment of an act or operation, such as God's creating, and as the satisfaction of desire.[17] God is portrayed as resting "in himself" on the seventh day of creation, as the perfect fulfillment of his own desire for goodness, ironically resting in the act of giving rest to us, providing his own Self as the term of all desire.[18] This perfect state of rest is echoed by Thomas in citing Augustine on John chapter 14, where Christ leaves *his* peace with his apostles—a peace without anything left to overcome, the peace of the eternal Sabbath. Thomas also quotes Augustine's *Sermo* 59, where peace evokes the Augustinian nexus between rest, order, and interiority,[19] and is described as "serenity of mind, tranquility of soul, simplicity of heart, the bond of love, the company of charity and the inheritance of the Lord."[20] It is no wonder Thomas states

---

14. *ST* II-II 23.7. Cf. Augustine, *De doctrina Christiana*, 1.22.20.

15. *ST* I-II 3.4 ad 1: "Peace pertains to man's last end, not as though it were the very essence of happiness; but because it is antecedent and consequent thereto: antecedent, in so far as all those things are removed which disturb and hinder man in attaining the last end: consequent, inasmuch as, when man has attained his last end, he remains at peace, his desire being at rest."

16. *ST* II-II 29.2 ad 4.

17. *ST* I 73.2.

18. Ibid. and ad 3.

19. Cf. Lawless, "Interior Peace," 54: according to Augustine, "rest is inseparable from order, whereas unrest is always symptomatic of disorder [*Confessions* 13.9.10]. The nexus between rest, order and space, both inner and outer space, is, therefore, a patent Augustinian motif."

20. *Catena Aurea*, commentary on John 14:23–31, where Augustine's *Sermo* 97 ("What is peace?") is quoted in full. In his translation, M. F. Toal notes that the style is not that of Augustine, but rather that of St. Peter Chrysologus, to whom it has been ascribed: *The Sunday Sermons of the Great Fathers* (Chicago: Henry Regnery, 1959), 57n16.

that the special sanctification of the creature consists in its *resting* in God.[21]

Second, Aquinas adopts Augustine's interpretation of peace in relation to the passions and emotions. Repudiating the Stoic view of peace as the cessation of all passions in a state of *apatheia*, he substitutes the Christian view that while virtue directs emotions through the rule of reason, the supernatural gifts impart near complete tranquility to the arena of the passions, assisting the good will in their regulation.[22] Echoing Augustine, Aquinas reasons that it is not passions or emotions as such that harm the soul, but only inordinate ones, which are not controlled by reason.[23] In fact, the beatific vision is the coming to rest and fulfillment of every desire of nature,[24] for all being is present in the divine essence, and beatitude is the complete fulfillment of the entire person.[25] This rest or peace of the faculties applies even in the case of the intellect and will, which are in a qualified sense infinite. As open to the fullness of being, the intellect is infinite *extensively* but finite *intensively*. That is, by virtue of its immateriality, it is open to infinite fullness of being, but will never grasp, even in glory, the infinite plenitude of being with perfect *efficacy*.[26] The "rest" of contemplation thus underscores the fact that neither in this life nor in the next is peace a sort of static accident, but it is rather a dynamic ideal rooted in the inexhaustible enjoyment of God.

A third way in which Thomas's theory of peace is indebted to Augustine relates to the theme of cosmic harmony. Peace is the result of the divine law of providence, producing the ordered concord in which each person fulfills his function for the common good, and is ordered immediately to God.[27] Augustine's notion of *concordia* qualified the Stoic idea, however, with the

---

21. *ST* I 73.3.
22. See, e.g., *ST* I-II 69.3, on the beatitudes. Augustine repudiates Stoic *apatheia* in *City of God* 14.8–9.
23. E.g., *ST* I-II 24.2.
24. *ST* I-II 1.5; *SCG* I 100.
25. *ST* I-II 8.2: "It is impossible for any created good to constitute man's happiness. For happiness is the perfect good, which lulls the appetite altogether; else it would not be the last end, if something yet remained to be desired. Now the object of the will, i.e., of man's appetite, is the universal good; just as the object of the intellect is the universal true. Hence it is evident that nothing can lull [*quietare*] man's will, except the universal good. This is to be found, not in any creature, but in God alone, because every creature has goodness by participation. Wherefore God alone can satisfy the will of man. . . . Therefore God alone constitutes man's happiness."
26. *De ver.*, 2.9; 20.4 obj. 14; 2.1 ad 10. On this distinction between intensive and extensive infinity, see James Robb, *Man as Infinite Spirit* (Milwaukee: Marquette University Press, 1974), 44–47. Cf. *ST* I-II 30.4 and ad 2.
27. *SCG* III 128.

notion of original sin, in which the tug of passion detracts from perfect individual peace.[28] The complete fulfillment of this law is in *love*, its flower is *peace*, but its roots are in *justice*, guaranteed by a set of precepts and remedies such as are found in the Decalogue and civic law.[29] Ordered concord, or peace, is preserved among men when each is given his due, which is justice. Thus, he says, quoting Isaiah 32:17, the work of justice is peace.[30] The peace caused by justice and God's providence finds fulfillment, moreover, only in the order of the will, in the spontaneous and joyful response of love. In this way, the peace based on degrees of justice is also a sign of self-governance, where it is the liberality of charity that impels action rather than an extrinsic motivation hindering freedom, such as the fear of punishment.[31] The details of cosmic harmony in relation to the classical theory of order in the universe, however, must wait for Thomas's treatment of peace in his commentary on *The Divine Names* of Dionysius.

In sum, Aquinas adopts from Augustine the definition of peace as "tranquility of order" as well as its eschatological focus, and the application of the notion of ordered hierarchy, in the self, society, and the universe. The biblical distinction between true peace and false, worldly peace, and the conviction that true peace is not to be had by either the earthly city or even the natural virtues is also from Augustine. Finally, like Augustine, he links beatitude and peace in the rest that is contemplation.[32] Apprehension is to appetite as rest is to motion, he notes, in that cognition's completion is in assimilation, not in adaptation or "being borne towards" its object.[33] In a systematic fashion, he applies Augustine's insights within a Scholastic metaphysical anthropology. Nothing can be ordered to an end, he reasons, unless some proportion to the end, producing desire for the end, preexist *in it*—and thus in human nature there is some natural *inception* of the very good to which we are directed.[34] Just as faith is the beginning of eternal life,

28. Augustine, *Enarrationes in Psalmos* 85.7, Patrologia Latina 37 (Paris: J. P. Migne, 1844–64); *In Joannis Evangelium* 77, Patrologia Latina 35 (Paris: J. P. Migne, 1844–64). On this, see Renna, "The Idea of Peace," 108.
29. *SCG* III 128; III 146.
30. *SCG* III 128 [6].
31. *SCG* III 128 [8]–[9] on the connection between justice, peace, and charity as a sign of self-rule.
32. *ST* I 81.1 on the rest that is cognition.
33. Ibid.
34. He is treating the issue of faith here, but the same principle applies to peace, as our end: *De ver.*, 14.2.

so also is our imperfect possession of peace an *inchoatio vitae aeternae*,[35] as the fruit of contemplation. And having the character of an end, this peace involves joy, delight or pleasure in its possession. As a participation of eternal life, however, this peace will be partial compared with the limitless character of life that is God's eternity. Moreover, even our final peace will remain partial in comparison with God's perfect possession of peace,[36] since pleasure or delight requires cognition,[37] and creaturely knowledge of God is partial or noncomprehensive. Further, the peace that is achieved when being is subjected to order coincides with the good and the beautiful, for by tending to good, a thing at the same time tends to its proportion, to its specification, and to the removal of obstacles in attaining the good, which is an affirmation of its undividedness and uniqueness with respect to other beings.[38] The association of peace with rest in relation to appetite and cognition is expressed well by Umberto Eco in his treatment of Aquinas's theory of the relation of judgment and the aesthetic *visio:* "On the ontological level, peace is the perfection achieved when being is subjected to an order. It means things becoming stable in form.... On the epistemological level, peace means the total delight of a contemplative perception which, freed from desire and effort, experiences love of the harmony which the intellectual judgment has shown to it."[39]

Aquinas is less concerned with the psychological manifestations of peace than with its metaphysical nature. A sense of this is found in the questions he asks: "What is peace?" "Do all things desire it?" "Is peace the same thing as concord?" "Is peace the effect of charity?" "Is peace a virtue?" and so on.[40] Peace exceeds concord among several wills by harmonizing the appetites

---

35. On faith as *inchoatio vitae aeternae*, see *De ver.*, 14.2. On contemplation as the same, see *ST* II-II 180.4.

36. *SCG* III 61 [3]: "Again, acts are specified by their objects. But the object of the aforementioned vision is the divine substance in itself.... Now, the being of the divine substance is in eternity, or, rather, is eternity itself. Therefore, this vision also consists in a participation in eternity."

37. *Sent.*, d. 1 q. 4 a. 1, sol.

38. *De ver.*, 22.1 ad 12 (cf. *De ver.*, 1.1 on unity as undividedness).

39. Umberto Eco, *The Aesthetics of Thomas Aquinas* (Cambridge: Harvard University Press, 1988), 199–200. His own interpretation of Aquinas here departs from Maritain, who views aesthetic pleasure as a total, complete pleasure because it is experienced *prior* to the labor of abstraction. For Eco, the "joy and triumph" of aesthetic pleasure depends on the completion of the labor of cognition, on the *cessation,* not the *absence,* of such effort (200). For him, "intellectual travail is a necessary pathway to the knowledge of beauty" (201).

40. *ST* II-II 29.

*within* the soul.⁴¹ There is a connaturality of all appetites to peace, and all desires are mysteriously directed toward it; but only *true* peace can put order among the appetites, uniting desires by giving them rest in one object.⁴²

## Topics in the Biblical Commentaries

It is perhaps precisely because Aquinas was unacquainted with the language of the original texts, or with intricate modern problems of biblical criticism, that his biblical commentaries offer so rich a tapestry of theological insight. The concept of peace appears in many contexts here. We will deal with three: first, the Pauline doctrine that peace is one of the "fruits of the Holy Spirit," as a result of charity; second, the beatitude of the peacemakers and related texts; and third, those texts that affirm the possibility of peace in the midst of tribulation, which include the commentaries on Job and the Psalms.

Without attempting an exhaustive summary of the relevant Pauline texts, we turn to the fruits of the Spirit. In lecture 6 of his commentary on the fifth chapter of Galatians, Thomas explains the way in which the fruits of the Spirit (namely, charity, joy, peace, patience, goodness, kindness, longsuffering, gentleness, faith, modesty, continence, and chastity) relate to the beatitudes and infused virtues.⁴³ While a gift of the Spirit perfects our docility to the promptings of the Spirit, by giving our acts a supernatural mode, the fruit of the Spirit is an *inchoatio vitae aeternae*, an imperfect beginning of eternal life, a promise of future fulfillment. As Thomas says in the *Summa*, "It is one thing to hope that the tree will bear fruit when we see only the leaves [by which he means the 'disposition' for happiness]; another when we see the first fruits begin to appear."⁴⁴

In the commentary on Galatians,⁴⁵ the fruits of the Spirit are divided by way of their ability to perfect us *interiorly* (and here, "peace" signifies a sufficient and appropriate possession of a good), and *exteriorly*, as they signify the removal of obstacles toward obtaining the good (and here, peace is the

---

41. *ST* II-II 20.1.
42. *ST* II-II 29.2, and ad 1, ad 4.
43. As found by Thomas in the Vulgate, Gal. 5:22–23. The Septuagint only has nine of these. Cf. J. P. Torrell, *Saint Thomas Aquinas*, vol. 2, *Spiritual Master*, trans. Robert Royal (Washington, DC: The Catholic University of America Press, 2003), 216n49.
44. *ST* I-II 69.2.
45. Lectio 6.

perfection of love). The parallel text in the *Summa* divides the fruits by way of their proximity to man. As related to one's own self, peace signifies the full possession of one's mind or soul in good times and in bad. Peace is the perfection of joy, which is the rejoicing attending unity with the beloved; and the resting of desire in one object.

The architectonic of the *Summa*'s key article on the fruits reflects the theme of "setting an order" within the soul that the doctrine represents: all the fruits flow from charity, which both vivifies and contains them, with the first three fruits signifying a well-ordered self. The fruit of joy is present in being united to God through its root of charity, while peace is the perfection of joy in the sense of securing and focusing its possession on one object.[46] The next four fruits (goodness, kindness, meekness, and faith) describe the soul's relationship to things *near* to it (neighbors and God), while the final three (modesty, continence, and chastity) involve the soul's relation to things *below* it. "Perfect peace," he says elsewhere, "consists in the perfect enjoyment of the supreme good, by which all the appetites are at rest and united in *one* thing."[47] The tranquility of order that is peace requires unification—each thing functioning in the proper limits of its nature in cooperation with the rest, and with the unity of an end. A unified end is required since order is the arrangement of many things into some unity *according to some principle*,[48] and the perfection denoted by "end" coincides with the plenitude of being that is our goal. Only God, he says, suffices for all desires.[49] As infinite goodness, the highest end is an all-embracing unity: "The final end must so fulfill the total seeking of human persons that nothing remains to be sought outside it."[50] Thus, for Thomas, interior peace has its foundation in divine peace, which we will confirm in our analysis of Dionysius below.

The beatitudes are another context where the concept of peace is treated, in terms of the seventh, and second most noble, beatitude, that of the "peacemakers." The close connection between the beatitudes, the theological virtues, gifts, and the fruits of the Spirit is evident in Thomas's texts on the beatitudes, which are in essence those *acts* by which the Spirit leads be-

46. *ST* I-II 70.3.
47. *ST* II-II 29.2 ad 4.
48. The definition of order is found in *ST* I 42.3.
49. *Super II ad Thess.* 3, lect. 2 (Marietti #89).
50. *ST* I-II 1.5.

lievers along the way of Christ in daily life.[51] As Torrell puts it, "the beatitudes and fruits do not represent new categories of *habitus*, but quite simply the acts that come forth from them."[52] Each beatitude is analyzed in terms of its acts (blessed are they who do or suffer such and such) and rewards, and corresponds to an infused virtue; constituting together what Thomas regards as the complete program of the Christian life.[53] As found in Matthew, the first five beatitudes are said to be preparatory, and concern the active life, while the last three concern the contemplative life, culminating in the seventh, the beatitude of peacemakers; the eighth ("blessed are those who are persecuted for Christ's name") being a summary of all the rest.[54] This seventh beatitude, "blessed are the peacemakers, for they shall be called sons of God," is the act by which man attains the highest degree of conformity to God.[55] Those persons are called peacemakers, he says, "who bring about peace to a certain extent in themselves and in others. Both occur because those in whom peace is established can be reduced to right order.... In this manner, readiness for peace is adequately correlated with wisdom."[56]

Holy ones experience this peace as a foretaste of eternal life through the infused wisdom that views all things in relation to their first principle. As Torrell summarizes, "Thomas puts the whole of the spiritual life under the banner of hope of eschatological fulfillment."[57] As wayfarers, we can experience divine grace "in germ, as the seed of the tree contains within it the whole tree."[58] To be a peacemaker is literally to *make* peace, to be *active* in its production; but this human activity is a response to the call of grace, already present in our operations of knowing and loving. The peace that flows from wisdom is thus indirectly caused by justice and directly caused by charity. It is no accident that he places his treatment of peace in the very heart of the treatise on charity.[59] Citing Dionysius, he says that love is a unitive force, and peace is the union of the inclinations of the appetites.[60] Charity both orders and unifies desires within a person, by referring them to God and unit-

---

51. *ST* I-II 69.1: "Are the beatitudes acts or habits?" On the role of beatitudes as leading the believers in the way of Christ, cf. prologue to *ST* III.
52. Torrell, *Spiritual Master*, 216, quoting *ST* I-II 70.1.
53. *ST* I-II 108.3.     54. *ST* I-II 69.2–3.
55. Indeed, since the substance of God is identified with his action, the supreme resemblance of the person to God is realized in action: *ST* I-II 55.2.3.
56. *ST* II-II 45.6.     57. Torrell, *Spiritual Master*, 220.
58. *ST* I-II 114.3 ad 3.     59. *ST* II-II 29.3.
60. *ST* II-II 29.3 ad 3.

Interior Peace 271

ing our desires to those of neighbor, causing peace among men.[61] But since only the most perfect object has the power of unifying appetites, it is only through charity, which is from God, that peace is effected.[62]

The peacemaker *makes* peace, first, by avoiding obstacles to union with God; second, through supernatural wisdom, by viewing everything in relation to the whole, and third, by directing action through obedience to the Spirit's promptings. Thus peace is the work of love and the wisdom that springs forth from love.[63] An important corollary of this doctrine is that there can be no peace for the wicked, for the moral evil and the selfish end result in the dissension of desires and inner turmoil.[64]

A third context of the concept of peace in the biblical commentaries is the doctrine of inner peace amidst tribulation. There are three things to consider here: first, Aquinas's explanation of the distinction between interior and exterior forms of peace; second, his identification of Christ's sacrifice on the Cross as the instrument and channel of all peace; and third, his emphasis, especially in his commentary on Job, on the afterlife as the context for the experience of interior peace for the wayfarer. Taking the first point, Aquinas has, at times, been criticized for the lack of "interiority" in his writings, in comparison to the psychological approach of St. Augustine.[65] In a sense the distinction is justified, in that many of his texts that distinguish interior and exterior acts draw on Aristotle, not on Augustine.[66] But his de-

---

61. *ST* II-II 29.3.      62. *Super Heb.* 13:20 (Marietti #766).

63. Cf. *In Col.*, 3, lect. 3 (Marietti #164): "An immediate effect of the love of charity is peace, which is, as Augustine comments, that composure or calmness of order produced in a person by God."

64. Eleonore Stump explains Aquinas's view on this point, in opposition to thinkers such as Harry G. Frankfurt, in her book *Aquinas* (London: Routledge, 2003), 358–60. Summarizing Aquinas, she says, "The wise person is a peacemaker.... First, he is able to make peace for others by helping them sort out the rights and wrongs of their differences. Secondly, he is able to make peace within himself (*ST* II-II 45.6)." But Frankfurt (in his article "Freedom of the Will and the Concept of a Person," *Journal of Philosophy* 68 [1971]: 5–20) thinks that harmony in the will, or unified willing, is more important than the object of willing. In Aquinas's view, by contrast, "we need moral goodness and the wisdom that moral goodness accompanies" (Stump, *Aquinas*, 359). And this is why wisdom is an essential precondition of peace, and why his concept of peace signals an optimistic view of human nature, in that he supposes that moral evil will always fragment a person, no matter how unified their intentions toward what is objectively wrong: "peace is the natural reward for the wise" (ibid., 360).

65. See, e.g., Mark Jordan, *Ordering Wisdom: The Hierarchy of Philosophical Discourses in Aquinas* (Notre Dame: University of Notre Dame Press, 1986), 133: "the interior space in Aquinas is very small and very dark in comparison with that of Augustine."

66. See, e.g., where he ranks those activities flowing from contemplation as superior to

tailed description of the superiority of internal peace to external peace, and his rich portraits of the components of prayer in the biblical commentaries, belie simple categorization.

In his commentary on the Gospel of John, chapter 14, lecture 7, Thomas explains Jesus' words, "Peace I leave with you; my peace I give you. I do not give to you as the world gives" (John 14:27). In his commentary, Thomas outlines the relationship of the three ordered faculties of intellect, will, and sensitive appetite, and describes the threefold peace in man by reference to Augustine. The tranquility of order is present in the good will, as "simplicity of heart" (*simplicitas cordis*); in the self's relation to its neighbor, as "the bond of affection or love" (*amoris vinculum*); and in its relation to God, as "the community of charity" (*consortium caritatis*). Christ is said to leave peace through his example of life, and to leave *his* peace virtually, as a present participation in the eschatological possession of perfect peace. The "peace of the world" differs from Christ's peace present in the saints or holy men, in three ways. First, according to intention, since worldly peace is ordered to preserving temporal goods, not eternal ones. Second, worldly peace is called "false peace" to this extent, for it can coexist with an evil heart, whereas the peace of Christ reaches to the depths of the will. Third, they are contrasted according to perfection. In his commentary on Romans chapter 5, he describes this true peace as stemming from submission to God, through belief in Christ.[67] His commentary on Philippians offers the remedy for our external worries for our welfare, by outlining the four necessary elements of a prayer that will bring a peace that guards over our affections and mind: first, recognition of dependence through invoking divine help; second, recollection of God's goodness; third, a request for actual (not merely apparent) goods; and fourth, an earnest impetration.[68] One also recalls Thomas citing Augustine in the *Catena Aurea* regarding Jesus' stilling of the storm. The Gospel of Matthew tells us that when Christ was awakened in the boat, he commanded the sea, and there came a great calm. In a similar manner, Augustine notes, if our soul is endangered and we call Christ to keep watch over it, unruly passions, such as anger and fear, desist, and inner peace returns.[69]

---

those "consisting wholly in external matters, such as alms-giving, hospitality, etc.": *ST* II-II 188.6; 182.1–2.

67. *Super Rom.* ch. 5, lect. 1.
68. *Super Phil.* ch. 4, lect. 1.
69. *Catena Aurea* on Matt. 8:23–27. (Thomas uses Augustine's text "On Anger" here.)

Interior Peace 273

Taking the second point, the identification of Christ Himself as "our peace" in Ephesians 2:14, reverberates through many of Thomas's scriptural commentaries, including that on Ephesians itself, the commentary on Colossians, several psalms, the magisterial commentary on Romans, and the commentaries on John and on Isaiah. As the binding force reconciling creation to the Father, and drawing the body of Christ into one entity, Christ's peace flows from his role as mediator, specifically through the power of his Cross. In his commentary on Ephesians chapter 2, lecture 6, Thomas explains how in his crucifixion Christ established peace for us by killing all evil "in himself," referring to the hostility that existed between God and men through sin. The theme of peace as the gift of Christ the *reconciler* is recalled in the commentary on Colossians, where Christ's blood removed the evils in men's minds, affections, and actions.[70] Of course, for Christ's passion to be effective for an individual, that person must have both faith and charity,[71] which condition, he says, results in the peace of Christ. This peace, he notes, "consists in the love with which God loves us,"[72] and its presence depends on the continued presence of the divine effect of charity within us, which can be removed by sin. This peace thus comes to be in us voluntarily yet also remains *ad extra*, demanding a personal orientation to Christ.

We also see Aquinas asserting the coexistence of inner peace amidst tribulation both in his treatment of the emotions and in texts on Christ's passion. Thomas explains that Christ's suffering was the greatest that could possibly be endured, and while it carried the weight of physical as well as the totality of moral evil,[73] it coexisted alongside the most radiant peace, present in his higher faculties but not overflowing to his lower reason or sensitive powers.[74] Garrigou-Lagrange has given us the analogy of Christ's peace amid suffering as a high mountain peak whose summit is bathed in sunlight, while its lower reaches are in the grips of a terrible storm, com-

70. *Super Col.* ch. 1, lect. 5 (Marietti #51–#55).
71. *ST* III 49.1 ad 5: "The faith by which we are cleansed from sin is not lifeless faith, which can exist even with sin, but rather it is faith informed by charity.... And by this means, sins are remitted by the power of the passion of Christ."
72. *ST* I-II 113.2: "[T]his peace consists in the love with which God loves us. Now on the part of the act of God, the love of God is eternal and immutable. But with regard to the effect which it impresses on us, it is sometimes interrupted, insofar as we sometimes fall away from it and sometimes recover again. Now the effect of divine love on us, which is lost through sin, is grace, by which a human being is made worthy of eternal life."
73. *ST* III 46.6.
74. *ST* III 46.8.

paring it to Augustine's description of a penitent who rejoices the more he grieves.[75] In any case, the view can be defended metaphysically by the fact that nothing prevents contraries from being in the same subject, but not in the same way. Thus, Thomas reasons, Jesus' soul enjoyed God's essence by reason of his higher reason's proper act, while experiencing the grief of the Passion by virtue of its subject, by reason of the body and lower faculties.[76] The point he is making is that Christ's higher reason could not be deflected from its proper object involuntarily, and so his spiritual pain arose from the seat of the soul, or its subject. Perhaps a less obscure defense of the coexistence of peace and suffering is found in his treatise on the passions. Sorrow and pleasure, he says, cannot coexist with respect to the same object. But if their objects are disparate or are themselves contraries, then sorrow and pleasure *can* coexist. For example, sorrow at a friend's death *can* coexist with pleasure in contemplation; and to sorrow for evil and rejoice for good simultaneously *is* possible.[77] In this way, one could experience interior peace and both physical, external, and even some kind of spiritual tribulation at one and the same time. Indeed, this is what Aquinas asserts with respect to the eighth and supreme beatitude of the Gospels: in suffering for Jesus' name, there is a confirmation of all the preceding beatitudes, and an inchoate participation in their rewards.[78]

A third context where Aquinas asserts the coexistence of inner peace and tribulation is his emphasis on the afterlife as the focus for human happiness, in texts such as his commentary on Job, as well as in his commentaries on Hebrews and Isaiah. In her treatment of Aquinas's approach to Job, Eleonore Stump notes that Aquinas interprets the work as an attempt to come to grips with the nature of divine providence, *not* with the problem of evil, as contemporary thought presumes.[79] Although Stump does not state it plainly, Aquinas's starting point is closer to the author of Job and diverges from the modern starting point of agnosticism or even atheism, in that the theme of the work is to challenge conventional Judaism's theory of retributive justice and replace it with a version of intrinsic morality, where charity, not the fear of punishment or hope for reward, is the rule of action.[80]

---

75. R. Garrigou-Lagrange, *Our Savior and His Love for Us*, trans. A. Bouchard (Rockford, IL: TAN Books and Publishers, 1998), 276 [original French version: *Le Sauveur et son amour pour nous*, 1951].

76. *ST* III 46.8 ad 1.   77. *ST* I-II 35.4.
78. *ST* I-II 69.4 ad 2.   79. Stump, *Aquinas*, 460.
80. On the role of the book of Job in overcoming the theory of retributive justice, see, e.g.,

Connecting this distinction to the notion of internal peace, Aquinas sees that the purpose of Job is to displace a "this-worldly" concept of peace grounded in the acquisition of external goods such as wealth, honor, health, and the like, and to put in its stead a more advanced version of religious morality. The goal of happiness and peace with God centers on the afterlife, and by implication, on interiority, as Aquinas states: "If in this life human beings are rewarded by God for good deeds and punished for bad, as Eliphaz [one of Job's interlocutors] was endeavoring to establish, it apparently follows that the ultimate goal for human beings is in this life. But Job intends to rebut this opinion, and he wants to show that the present life of human beings does not contain [that] ultimate goal, but is related to it as motion is related to *rest* and the road to its *end.*"[81]

According to Thomas, in this life, God permits both physical and moral evils that can be turned into goods[82]—patience and humility are examples of virtues that result in part from antecedent evils. And as Stump indicates, Aquinas thinks that the author of Job is trying to instill in us the conviction that there is an afterlife, and that, consequently, our true happiness lies there, and that this is a truth we can imperfectly glimpse here only through the instrument of suffering.[83] This eschatological view of inner peace coincides with Aquinas's treatment of peace in his texts on the beatitudes, the Psalms, and the Gospel of John, in that he accords holy persons a measure of inner peace and a beginning of eternal life, even as pilgrims. It also echoes his conviction that only *rational* creatures can be peacemakers, since only they have an immediate order to God, and are capable of charity toward others.[84] Interior peace, according to this doctrine, is the work of the Holy Spirit, perfecting persons inwardly, giving them joy that subsists even in tribulation.[85]

---

Christian Hauer and William Young, *An Introduction to the Bible: A Journey into Three Worlds,* 5th ed. (Upper Saddle River, NJ: Prentice Hall, 2001), 187–88: "To assume that God's involvement with the universe revolves around the issue of retributive justice for humans is to place humankind at the center of the cosmic stage.... Job is chastised for making erroneous assumptions about God's ways based on too narrow a viewpoint.... [W]e are led back to the underlying question—Can there be disinterested piety? Will a person really maintain faith in God after realizing that there is no automatic reward for righteous behavior or punishment for evil deeds?"

81. *Super Job* 7.1–4, as cited in Stump, *Aquinas,* 461.
82. *Super Rom.* 8, lect. 6.   83. Stump, *Aquinas,* 469.
84. *ST* II-II 2.3.
85. *Super Gal.* 5, lect. 6. One could compare this with the literary account of inner peace

The general conclusion of Aquinas regarding inner peace and suffering is essentially that when one is not spiritually alienated from God through sin, it is possible to experience "rest in God" as a kind of consolation, which makes the sufferer capable of bearing the burden of suffering.[86] This sort of peace as reliance one finds also in his commentaries on Psalm 22 [23] and Psalm 4, for example. In his commentary on the latter,[87] the suffering just man is said to hold on to spiritual peace and possess the beginning of eternal life due to his having conquered moral obstacles and resting completely in the divine will. The commentary on Romans goes so far as to note that without suffering there can be no entry into heaven, since there can be no divine sonship, which is acquired partly by developing virtue and proving one's love of *eternal* goods.[88]

From a brief study of several texts in Aquinas's biblical commentaries, three conclusions have emerged. First, as a fruit of the Spirit, interior peace represents the interior working of the Holy Spirit, or as Thomas puts it, the spiritual sowing of grace setting the initial stages of the final end that persons will enjoy in eternal life.[89] The *unity* of this end was explained in terms of the necessity of unifying the appetites so as to achieve their rest. Second, the texts on the beatitudes reinforce the dimension of finality and add the interplay between the active and passive moments in attaining peace. Thomas's treatment of the seventh beatitude reveals the nexus he perceives between the notions of peace, supernatural wisdom, and sonship, by which our conformity to Christ is perfected. Here, Aquinas takes the position that a measure of interior peace is possible in this life, but as a world-transforming germ of that mysterious divine peace possible only in the next life, and as such, it is radically opposed to worldly, false peace. Our third conclusion deduced from the biblical commentaries concerns the coexis-

---

amidst tribulation as found in Herman Melville's *Moby Dick* (Ishmael speaks during a pause in a furious chase after Moby Dick): "And thus, though surrounded by circle upon circle of consternations and affrights, did these inscrutable creatures [viz., whales] at the centre freely and fearlessly indulge in all peaceful concernments; yea, serenely reveled in dalliance and delight. But even so, amid the tornadoed Atlantic of my being, do I myself still for ever centrally disport in mute calm; and while ponderous planets of unwaning woe revolve round me, deep down and deep inland there I still bathe me in eternal mildness of joy" (London: Panther, 1968), 27.

86. *Super 2 Cor.* 1, lect. 2 (see Stump, *Aquinas*, 476).
87. *Super Ps.* 4, #7.
88. *Super Rom.* 5, lect. 1.
89. *Super Gal.* 5:22–23, lect. 6 (Marietti #330).

tence of peace and suffering. In his commentaries on John, the Psalms, and Romans, for example, Aquinas juxtaposes true and false peace, comparing them as interior, eternal and exterior, temporal goods. Christ's role as mediator and reconciler in several commentaries made him the "bond of peace" and wellspring of interior order, emanating peace by uniting the faculties of the soul, the believers to God and to each other. The coexistence of interior peace and suffering is guaranteed by Christ's own Passion, and upon analysis, Aquinas does not find this pairing metaphysically contradictory. His emphasis on the eschatological nature of peace in the commentaries on Job and Isaiah also implies the view that the *hope* for complete peace in the afterlife increases the measure of the *reality* of peace experienced in *this* life, even in the midst of suffering.[90] A fuller picture of interior peace in Aquinas would thus also include a study of the role of many virtues, for example hope and faith, patience and courage.

## Divine Peace in the Commentary on *De divinibus nominibus*

In his commentary on chapter eleven of Dionysius's work *The Divine Names*, Thomas treats the theme of "divine peace" in terms of the power of

90. At this point it would be fruitful to compare the view of Aquinas with Nietzsche's rejection of Christianity on the basis of its deferment of beatitude to an afterlife, for the latter view is more prevalent in today's cultural milieu. Nietzsche's interpretation of Luther's position of *sola fide* was that it entailed the sacrifice of both "works" and "reason," leading to the paralysis of the practice of Christianity. Nietzsche's rejection of Christianity's deferment of beatitude lay in three points: first, he views the teaching of Jesus to be that the kingdom of God is in the hearts of men, not in another life; second, the conception of an afterlife has led to a deprecation of this life and human efforts to change this world; and third, the doctrine of the resurrection involved a new doctrine of retribution based on the arbitrary treatment or mistreatment of Christian believers. On the views of Nietzsche as found in *The Antichrist*, see W. Kaufmann, *Nietzsche: Philosopher, Psychologist, Antichrist*, 3rd ed. (New York: Random House, 1968), 345ff. Nietzsche's statements about peace in *Zarathustra*'s "On War and Warriors" align internal peace with a temporary rest on the way to winning the truth of argument—as a mere means, it is a state of necessary but imperfect complacency. In contrast to this state, the goal for humans is the strength of physical, mental, and spiritual independence ("I am *impassioned for independence;* I sacrifice all for it . . . and am tortured more by all the smallest strings than others are by chains." Letter to his sister, June 11, 1865: see Kaufmann, *Nietzsche*, 21). A contrast of Aquinas and Nietzsche reveals that their notions of peace depend on the concept of the afterlife, or on its absence. A detailed study of the relation between peace and eternity would draw on metaphysical and theological notions (and certainly the dialectic in Augustine between *operari (opera)* and *requiescere (requies)* in *Confessions* 13 affirms the balance between dynamic activity and rest in God—here, present time is contrasted with future time in terms of work and rest).

divine providence in the universe. That Dionysius's text provides him the most metaphysical account of peace there is no doubt; Dionysius is quoted as often as Augustine in the treatment of peace in the *Summa*. Whereas Augustine gave Aquinas the definition of peace, Dionysius left posterity a thorough metaphysical analysis of it, in terms of the various causalities present in divine peace itself, as it establishes universal order throughout the universe. In this chapter, the Areopagite treats the issue of peace in light of his earlier notion of divine *eros*, God's ecstatic being drawing back and uniting all things to himself.[91] As the "most unified" reality, God is Peace itself—having his will fully rest in its proper object, himself. That which is most unified serves, then, as the unifying cause within things, among things, and between God and creatures. As their *efficient* cause, God's peace creates things and institutes their operations and growth, causing a concord among natural appetites.[92] As their *formal* cause of peace and unity, divine peace permits creatures to participate by degrees in a similitude of itself. As their *final* cause, that peace directs these appetites toward their final end, a unity that is the fulfillment of their natures.[93] The tranquility of order that constitutes peace is said to involve three things: first, a distinction of beings; second, the establishment of each thing within the proper limits of its nature; and third, the conservation of each thing within the limits assigned to it as directed to a specific end.[94]

The metaphysical link between peace and unity is explored further in lecture 2, and supports the association of peace with a thing's natural perfection, reminding us of Dionysius's adoption of the classical doctrine of peace as universal order. Unlike the Stoic version of divinity that grounds cosmic peace, however, Dionysius's divine *eros* or uniting force of all being is a *personal "excessus"* of the divine nature, calling rational beings into a communion of knowledge and love. Divine transcendence is described as going outside itself in a loving and creative excess of goodness,[95] remaining within itself all the same, just as a seal that imprints its image on diverse

---

And Thomas's position that there cannot be perfect beatitude, and hence, perfect peace, in this life of succession and change, points to his insistence on the intrinsic connection between the ideas of peace and eternity.

91. *In De div. nom.*, 11, lect. 1 (Marietti #880).
92. Ibid., #885.
93. Ibid., #886.
94. Ibid., #891.
95. *On the Divine Names*, ch. 4 (712A15).

pieces of wax remains identical.[96] In an interesting twist, the love of concupiscence and friendship coincide in God, in that his ecstatic love both returns the loved object to the good of himself as final end, and yet also loves the good for the loved thing outside of anything that comes from it.[97]

Divine peace is this perfect self-possession calling creatures to imitate its own deep unity, through existing, living, and knowing.[98] Even the seeming restless motion of moving things is explained as a result of their "inward peace," which causes them to engage in the activity proper to themselves.[99] Even the disquiet of disturbed souls indicates a dim desire for peace, in their attempt to set various passions at rest, he notes.[100] The harmonic concord *(concors consonantia)* among things is possible through the "unshakeable bond" of one gathering cause,[101] uniting the universe by means of causal mediators (including angels) and joining things together in "natural friendship" with respect to their common end. Aquinas stresses the universal extension as well as the intensive power of divine peace, repeating Dionysius's claim that "nothing is so low as not to participate in the divine gift."[102]

Undergirding this entire treatment of universal peace is the person of Jesus, through whom God is said to "pour out" peace into the world[103] and by whom we are liberated from the sin that would disturb interior peace. Christ's providence and grace permits the harmonic integration of rational souls, allowing us to "work with the angels" to do "the things of God." Thus it is through Christ that "all things hold together" (*Col.* 1:17),[104] and from the Father's immutable center that the definitive grounding and operations of things derive.[105]

From this brief retrieval of sections of Aquinas's commentary on *The Divine Names*, it would seem that Dionysius's metaphysical approach sets the tone for Thomas's analysis of mystical experience in general. For neither

---

96. *In De div. nom.*, 11, lect. 2 (Marietti #896).
97. On the two types of love in this connection, see *In De div. nom.*, 4, lect. 10 (Marietti #430). On the topic of *extasis* in human and divine love, see Peter Kwasniewski, "St. Thomas, Extasis, and Union with the Beloved," *Thomist* 61 (1997): 587–603. The coincidence of loves is illumined by the following quote: "*Extasis* reaches its perfection with regard to both powers, apprehensive and appetitive, when the lover entirely rests in the good of the beloved as in his final end, the source wherein his own good preeminently subsists" (ibid., 595).
98. *In De div. nom.*, 11, lect. 2.  99. Ibid., lect. 3.
100. Ibid.  101. bid., lect. 2 (Marietti #908).
102. Ibid., #910.  103. Ibid., lect. 3 (Marietti #923).
104. Cf. *In De div. nom.*, 9, lect. 2 (Marietti #816).
105. This is one interpretation of the doctrine, based on chapter 11 and chapter 9.

man do the notions of "interior peace" and "ecstasy" refer to any private emotional or irrational experience, whereas both realities do involve the tug of grace. It could be said that while Dionysius recognizes the necessity of "going out of oneself" in the state of *xtasis,* Thomas *also* applied this condition of "radical dependence on Someone outside the self" for the achievement of interior peace.

## Conclusion

In general, both Augustine and Dionysius were largely responsible for the medieval focus on peace in terms of hierarchies, such as that between sense and spirit, souls, angels, and men, and souls and God. The eschatological emphasis of Augustine, combined with the metaphysical approach of Dionysius, Christianized the classical notion of peace as cosmic order, and ensured Aquinas's distance from the notion, common to many Church Fathers and ascetics, of peace as a dualistic flight from the world. Unlike Spanish and English mystics of the fourteenth to the sixteenth centuries, Aquinas's Dominican spirituality had not completely dissociated interior peace from its other forms, nor had the specialized study of the forms of interior peace yet emerged. Ironically, the latter study emerged only after the growing independence of mystical thought from its monastic setting.[106] Thus, unlike later devotional treatments of the topic, Aquinas's study of peace gathers together the metaphysical, psychological, and theological aspects in a unity reminiscent of Augustine's synthesis. Yet one can also discern in Aquinas the movement away from Augustine's attempt to Christianize the world, through the temporal application of *pax.* In contrast to Augustine, nowhere in Aquinas's treatment of interior peace do we see an emphasis on temporal peace as a necessary *means* to interior peace. Instead, both the *Summa* and the biblical commentaries illumine the necessity of temporal *trials* for the sake of attaining the soul's eternal rest in God. The attempt to *prescribe* Christian peace has given way to a *metaphysical analysis* of it, where the tranquility of order that flows from union with God through charity quiets conflicting desires and emanates from the love of God to love of neighbor. Still, Aquinas's analysis bears little resemblance to the devotional, monastic spirituality of a Saint Bernard, for example, who paralleled

---

106. Cf. Renna, "The Idea of Peace," 110–11.

various stages of interior peace with a developed system of the soul's stages of mystical ascent.

In conclusion, we have traced Thomas's thought on interior peace in terms of the influences of Scripture, St. Augustine, and Dionysius. More systematic than Augustine, Thomas searches the foundations of the saint's nexus of the notions of peace, beatitude, order toward finality, and the wisdom that is the fruit of love, as is evident in both the *Summa* and the biblical commentaries. In these commentaries, the pivots on which his notion of peace turn are first, a Christian concept of "happiness" centered on the afterlife, and second, the mediating role of Christ, setting us the example of self-gift, through which we get a glimpse of the peace of eternity here and now. Through meditation on Dionysius, Aquinas's thoughts on peace extend into the unfathomed depths of divine reality and then outward in an effusion of the divine presence in the universe of creatures. Through this metaphysical vision, Aquinas saw peace in terms of modes of causality, descending from the mysterious unity of the Father, and through Christ, into the human heart and down into creaturely vestiges. In this sense, Aquinas's treatment of the topic of spiritual peace reveals the full *theological* depth of the *rational* truth that although the universe is more perfect in extension, it is only the intellectual creature, by virtue of its intensity, concentration, and love, that has a capacity for the highest Good.[107] In the end, Aquinas discovered that it is only in Christian contemplation that the peaceful soul can marvel at the self-emptying of divine love.

107. See, e.g., *ST* I 93.2.

# Works Cited

## Primary Sources and Translations

Alexander of Hales. *Quaestiones Disputatae "antequam esset frater."* Quaracchi: Collegium S. Bonaventurae, 1960.

(Anonymous.) *In Ethica Nicomachea II–V Commentaria.* Ed. Gustavus Heylbut. Vol. 20 of *Commentaria in Aristotelem Graeca.* Berlin: Reimer, 1892.

Aristotle. *Aristotelis Ethica Nicomachea.* Ed. I. Bywater. Oxford Classical Texts. Oxford: Clarendon, 1894.

———. *Aristotelis qui ferebantur librorum fragmenta.* Ed. Valentinus Rose. Leipzig: Teubner, 1886.

———. *Aristoteles: Rhetorik.* Ed. and trans. Christoff Rapp. Vol. 4.1–2 of *Aristoteles: Werke in deutscher Übersetzung.* Berlin: Akademie, 2002.

———. *The Complete Works of Aristotle.* Revised Oxford translation, 2 vols. Ed. Jonathan Barnes. Princeton: Princeton University Press, 1984.

———. *Physics, or Natural Hearing.* Trans., with notes, by Glen Coughlin. South Bend, IN: St. Augustine's Press, 2005.

———. *Physics.* Ed. and trans., with notes, by David Ross. Oxford: Oxford University Press, 1936.

Augustine. *De diversis quaestionibus LXXXIII.* Ed. Almut Mutzenbecher. In *Aurelii Augustini opera.* Corpus Christianorum, Series Latina, vol. 50.1. Turnhout: Brepols, 1975.

———. *Enarrationes in Psalmos. Patrologia Latina* 37. Paris: J. P. Migne, 1844–64.

———. *In Joannis Evangelium. Patrologia Latina* 35. Paris: J. P. Migne, 1844–64.

Avicenna. *Liber de philosophia prima sive scientia divina.* Ed. S. Van Riet. Louvain-Leiden: Peeters, 1977–80.

Boethius. *De Trinitate.* In *The Theological Tractates with an English Translation: The Consolation of Philosophy.* New ed. Trans. H. F. Stewart, E. K. Rand, and S. J. Tester. Loeb Classical Library. Cambridge, MA: Harvard University Press, 1973.

Bonaventure. *Tria Opuscula Seraphici Doctoris S. Bonaventurae.* Quaracchi: Typographia Collegii S. Bonaventurae, 1911.

Cajetan, Thomas de Vio. *In De ente et essentia D. Thomae Aquinatis commentaria.* Ed. M.-H. Laurent. Turin: Marietti, 1934.

Cicero, M. Tullius. *De re publica librorum sex quae manserunt.* Ed. Konrat Ziegler. Bibliotheca Scriptorum Graecorum et Romanorum Teubneriana. Leipzig: Teubner, 1955.

Eriugena, John Scotus. *Periphyseon (De Diuisione Naturae).* Ed. I. P. Sheldon-

Williams. *Scriptores Latini Hiberniae*, vol. 7. Dublin: Dublin Institute for Advanced Studies, 1968.
———. *Periphyseon*. Trans. I. P. Sheldon-Williams (Montréal: Bellarmin, 1987).
Giles of Rome. *Theoremata de esse et essentia*. Ed. E. Hocedez. Louvain: Museum Lessianum, 1930.
Gregory the Great. *Moralium libri*. *Patrologia Latina* 75–76. Gen. ed. J.-P. Migne. Paris, 1849.
———. *Regulae pastoralis liber*. *Patrologia Latina* 77. Gen. ed. J.-P. Migne. Paris, 1849.
Henry of Ghent. *Opera omnia*. Leuven: De Wulf-Mansion Centre, 1979–.
Isidore Hispalensis (Archbishop of Seville). *Etymologiarum libri XX*. *Patrologia Latina* 82. Gen. ed. J.-P. Migne. Paris, 1850.
Newton, Isaac. *Newton's Philosophy of Nature: Selections from His Writings*. Ed. H. S. Thayer. New York: Haffner Press, 1953.
Pseudo-Dionysius the Areopagite. *De divinis nominibus*. In *Corpus Dionysiacum*. Ed. B. R. Suchla, vol. 1, 107–231. Patristische Texte und Studien, 33. Berlin: De Gruyter, 1990.
Siger of Brabant. *Quaestiones in Metaphysicam*. Edition revue de la reportation de Munich. Texte inédit de la reportation de Vienne. Ed. William Dunphy. Philosophes médiévaux, 24. Louvain-la-Neuve: Éditions de l'Institut Súperieur de Philosophie, 1981.
Stobaeus, Joannis. *Anthologium*. Ed. Kurt Wachsmuth and Otto Hense. Berlin: Weidmann, 1884–1912.
Suárez, Francisco. *Disputationes metaphysicae*. In *Opera omnia*, vol. 26. Paris: Vives, 1856–77.
Thomas Aquinas. *Glossa continua super Evangelia, seu Catena aurea in quatuor Evangelia*. 2 vols. Ed. Angelici Guarienti. Turin/Rome: Marietti, 1953.
———. *In Aristotelis libros De caelo et mundo, De generatione et corruptione, Meteorologicorum expositio*. Ed. R. Spiazzi. Turin/Rome: Marietti, 1952.
———. *In duodecim libros Metaphysicorum Aristotelis expositio*. Ed. M. R. Cathala and R. M. Spiazzi. Turin/Rome: Marietti, 1950.
———. *In librum beati Dionysii De divinis nominibus expositio*. Ed. Ceslai Pera. Turin/Rome: Marietti, 1950.
———. *In octo libros Physicorum Aristotelis expositio*. Ed. P. M. Maggiolo. Turin/Rome: Marietti, 1950.
———. *Lectura romana in primum Sententiarum Petri Lombardi*. Ed. Leonard E. Boyle, O.P., and John F. Boyle. Toronto: Pontifical Institute of Mediaeval Studies, 2006.
———. *Opera omnia: iussu impensaque. Leonis XIII. P.M. edita*. Rome: Commissio Leonina, 1882–.
———. *Opuscula philosophica*. Ed. R. M. Spiazzi. Turin/Rome: Marietti, 1954.
———. *Opuscula theologica*. 2 vols. Ed. R. A. Verardo and R. M. Spiazzi. Turin/Rome: Marietti, 1954.
———. *Quaestiones disputatae*. 2 vols. Ed. P. Bazzi et al. Turin/Rome: Marietti, 1953; 1965.

———. *Sancti Thomae Aquinatis doctoris angelici Opera omnia iussu Leonis XIII. O. M. edita*. Cura et studio Fratrum Praedicatorum. Rome: Commissio Leonina, 1882–. More recent volumes have been published by Éditions du Cerf, Paris.
———. *Scriptum super libros Sententiarum*. Vols. 1 and 2 (containing Books I and II), ed. P. Mandonnet. Paris: Lethielleux, 1929. Vols. 3 and 4 (containing Books III and IV, up to IV, dist. 22), ed. Maria Fabianus Moos. Paris: Lethielleux, 1933 and 1947. For Book IV, dd. 23–50: *Sancti Thomae Aquinatis Opera omnia*. Vol. 7/2, *Commentum in quartum librum Sententiarum magistri Petri Lombardi*, pp. 872–1259. Parma: Typis Petri Fiaccadori, 1858.
———. *Summa contra gentiles*. Ed. C. Pera et al. Turin-Rome: Marietti, 1961.
———. *Summa theologiae*, 5 vols. Ottawa: Commissio Piana, 1953.
———. *Super Epistolas sancti Pauli lectura*. 2 vols. Ed. P. Raphaelis Cai. Turin/Rome: Marietti, 1953.
———. *Super Librum de causis expositio*. 2nd ed. Ed. H. D. Saffrey. Paris: Vrin, 2002. [Original ed.: Fribourg/Louvain: Société Philosophique, 1954.]
Victorius, Petrus [Piero Vettori]. *Commentarii longe doctissimi in tres libros Aristotelis de Arte dicendi, nunc primum in Germania editi*. Basel: Ex officina Ioannis Oporini, 1549.

## Other Literature

Aertsen, Jan A. *Medieval Philosophy and the Transcendentals: The Case of Thomas Aquinas*. Leiden-New York: Brill, 1996.
Armour, Leslie. *Being and Idea: Developments of Some Themes in Spinoza and Hegel*. Hildesheim: Georg Olms, 1992.
———. *"Infini Rien": Pascal's Wager and the Human Paradox*. Carbondale, IL: Southern Illinois University Press for the *Journal of the History of Philosophy*, 1993.
———. "Knowledge, Idea, and Spinoza's Notion of Immortality." In *Spinoza, the Enduring Questions*, ed. Graeme Hunter, 48–63. Toronto: University of Toronto Press, 1994.
———. *Logic and Reality: An Investigation into the Idea of a Dialectical System*. Assen/New York: Royal Vangorcum and Humanities Press, 1971.
———. "Newman, Anselm and Proof of the Existence of God." *International Journal for Philosophy of Religion* 19 (1986): 87–93.
Arnhart, Larry. *Aristotle on Political Reasoning: A Commentary on the Rhetoric*. DeKalb: Northern Illinois University Press, 1981.
Bachelard, Gaston. *The Poetics of Space*. Trans. Maria Jolas. Foreword by Étienne Gilson. New York: Orion Press, 1964.
Balmaceda, Federico. "La doble causalidad ejemplar divina en Santo Tomás de Aquino." *Philosophica* 9–10 (1986–87): 155–66.
Bergson, Henri. *Duration and Simultaneity*. Trans. Leon Jacobson. Indianapolis: Bobbs-Merrill, 1965.
———. *The Two Sources of Morality and Religion*. Trans. R. Ashley Audra, Cloudesley Brereton, and W. Horsefall Carter. Garden City, NY: Doubleday, 1956.

Berkson, William. *Fields of Force: The Development of a World View from Faraday to Einstein*. London: Routledge, 1974.
Bignone, Ettore. *L'Aristotele perduto e la formazione filosofica di Epicuro*. Pensiero Filosofico. Firenze: La Nuova Italia, 1973.
Black, Deborah L. "Mental Existence in Thomas Aquinas." *Mediaeval Studies* 61 (1999): 45–79.
Bobik, Joseph. "Some Disputable Points Apropos of St. Thomas and Metaphysics." *New Scholasticism* 37 (1963): 411–30.
Boekraad, A. J., and Henry Tristram. *The Argument from Conscience to the Existence of God*. Louvain: Nauwelaerts, 1961.
Boland, Vivian. *Ideas in God according to Saint Thomas Aquinas*. New York: Brill, 1996.
Born, Irene, trans. *The Born-Einstein Letters*. New York: Walker, 1971.
Branick, Vincent P. "The Unity of the Divine Ideas." *New Scholasticism* 42 (1968): 171–201.
Brody, Baruch. "Why Settle for Anything Less than Good Old-Fashioned Aristotelian Essentialism?" *Nous* 7 (1973): 351–64.
Charles, David. *Aristotle on Meaning and Essence*. Oxford: Oxford University Press, 2000.
———. "Some Comments on Prof. Enrico Berti's 'Being and Essence in Contemporary Interpretations of Aristotle.'" In *Individuals, Essence and Identity: Themes of Analytic Metaphysics*, ed. A. Bottani et al., 109–26. Dordrecht: Reidel, 2002.
Charon, Jean E. *L'esprit, cet inconnu*. Paris: Albin Michel, 1977.
Chenu, M.-D. *Introduction à l'étude de saint Thomas d'Aquin*. Montreal: Université de Montréal, 1954.
Cole, K. C. "Annals of Science." *New Yorker*, June 2, 2003.
Colish, Marcia L. "Gilbert, the Early Porretans, and Peter Lombard: Semantics and Theology." In *Gilbert de Poitiers et ses contemporains: Aux origines de la "Logica Modernorum,"* ed. Jean Jolivet and Alain de Libera, 146–55. Napoli: Bibliopolis, 1987.
Coughlin, Glen. *Aristotle's Physics, or Natural Hearing*. Translation with introduction, notes, and essays. South Bend, IN: St. Augustine's Press, 2005.
Cousins, Ewert H. *Bonaventure and the Coincidence of Opposites*. Chicago: Franciscan Herald Press, 1978.
Craig, William L. "Is Presentness a Property?" *American Philosophical Quarterly* 34, no. 1 (1997): 27–40.
Cross, Richard. "Aquinas on Nature, Hypostasis and the Metaphysics of the Incarnation." *Thomist* 60 (1996): 171–202.
———. *Duns Scotus*. Great Mediaeval Thinkers. Oxford: Oxford University Press, 1999.
Cunningham, Francis, S.J. "Distinction according to Aquinas." *New Scholasticism* 36 (1962): 279–312.
———. *Essence and Existence in Thomism: A Mental vs. "the Real Distinction"?* Lanham, MD: University Press of America, 1988.
Dancy, Russell. "Aristotle and Existence." In *The Logic of Being: Historical Studies*, ed. Simo Knuuttila and Jaakko Hintikka, 49–80. Dordrecht: Reidel, 1986.

D'Andrea, Thomas. "Essence and Existence in Aristotle's Posterior Analytics." In *Saints and Scholars: Studies in Honor of Frederick D. Wilhelmsen*, ed. R. A. Herrera et al., 15–21. New York: Peter Lang, 1993.
Davies, Paul. *The Edge of Infinity*. London: Penguin, 1981.
———. *God and the New Physics*. New York: Simon and Schuster, 1983.
———. *The Mind of God*. New York: Simon and Schuster, 1992.
Davies, Paul, and John Gribbin. *The Matter Myth*. London: Penguin, 1992.
de Benedictis, Matthew M. *The Social Thought of Saint Bonaventure*. Washington, DC: The Catholic University of America Press, 1946; repr. Westport, CT: Greenwood, 1972.
Decaen, Christopher A. "Aristotle's Aether and Contemporary Science." *Thomist* 68 (2004): 375–429.
De Finance, Joseph. *Être et agir dans la philosophie de saint Thomas*. 2nd ed. Rome: Gregorian University Press, 1960.
De Koninck, Charles. *The Hollow Universe*. Quebec: Le Presses de l'Université Laval, 1964.
De Libera, Alain. "Albert le Grand et Thomas d'Aquin interprètes du Liber de causis." *Revue des sciences philosophiques et théologiques* 74 (1990): 347–78.
del Prado, Norbertus. *De veritate fundamentali philosophiae christianae*. Freiburg/CH: Ex Typis Consociationis Sancti Pauli, 1911.
Demoss, David, and Daniel Devereux. "Essence, Existence, and Nominal Definition in Aristotle's Posterior Analytics II 8–10." *Phronesis* 33 (1988): 133–54.
Dennehy, Ray. "Maritain's Reply to Gilson's Rejection of Critical Realism." In *A Thomistic Tapestry: Essays in Memory of Etienne Gilson*, ed. Peter A. Redpath, 57–80. Amsterdam: Rodopi, 2003.
Denzinger-Schoenmetzer. *Enchiridion Symbolorum Definitionum et Declarationum de rebus fidei et morum*. 36th ed. Rome: Herder, 1976.
Dewan, Lawrence. "Is Truth a Transcendental for St. Thomas Aquinas?" *Nova et Vetera* [Eng. ed.] 2 (2004): 1–20.
———. "A Note on Metaphysics and Truth." *Doctor Communis* N.S. 2 (2002): 143–53. (*The Contemporary Debate on Truth*, Proceedings of the II Plenary Session of the Pontifical Academy of St. Thomas Aquinas.)
———. "On Anthony Kenny's Aquinas on Being." *Nova et Vetera* [Eng. ed.] 3 (2005): 335–400.
———. "St. Thomas and Moral Taxonomy." *Maritain Studies/Études maritainiennes* 15 (1999): 134–56.
———. "St. Thomas and the Distinction between Form and Esse in Caused Things." *Gregorianum* 80 (1999): 353–70.
———. "St. Thomas, God's Goodness, and God's Morality." *Modern Schoolman* 70 (1992): 45–51.
———. "St. Thomas, James Ross, and Exemplarism: A Reply." *American Catholic Philosophical Quarterly* 65 (1991): 221–34.
———. "St. Thomas, Metaphysics, and Formal Causality." *Laval théologique et philosophique* 36 (1980): 285–316.
———. "St. Thomas's Successive Discussions of the Nature of Truth." In *Sanctus Thomas de Aquino: Doctor Hodiernae Humanitatis. Miscellanea offerta . . . al*

*Prof. Abelardo Lobato, O.P.*, ed. Daniel Ols, O.P., 153–68. Vatican City: Libreria Editrice Vaticana, 1995.

———. "Which Esse Gives the Answer to the Question: 'Is It?' for St. Thomas." *Doctor Communis* N.S. 3 (2002): 80–97.

Dillon, Thomas. "The Real Distinction between Being and Essence in the Thought of St. Thomas Aquinas." Ph.D. diss., University of Notre Dame, 1977.

Ebbesen, Stan. "Early Supposition Theory (12th–13th cent.)." *Histoire, Epistémologie, Langage* 3 (1981): 35–48.

Eco, Umberto. *The Aesthetics of Thomas Aquinas*. Cambridge, MA: Harvard University Press, 1988.

Edwards, Paul, ed. *Encyclopedia of Philosophy*. New York: MacMillan, 1967.

Einstein, Albert. "On the Ether." [Originally published in 1924.] Repr. in *The Philosophy of Vacuum*, ed. Simon Saunders and Harvey R. Brown, 13–23. Oxford: Oxford University Press, 1991.

———. *Relativity: The Special and General Theory*. Trans. Robert W. Lawson. New York: Bonanza, 1961.

———. *Sidelights on Relativity*. New York: Dover, 1983.

Einstein, Albert, with Boris Podolsky and Nathan Rosen. "Can Quantum-Mechanical Description of Physical Reality Be Considered Complete?" *Physical Review* 47 (1935): 777–80.

Evans, Gareth. *The Varieties of Reference*. Ed. J. McDowell. Oxford: Clarendon Press, 1982.

Fabro, Cornelio. "Elementi per una dottrina tomistica della partecipazione." *Divinitas* 11 (1967): 559–86. Repr. in *Esegesi tomistica*, 421–48.

———. *Esegesi tomistica*. Rome: Pontificia Università Lateranense, 1969.

———. "Il nuovo problema dell'essere e la fondazione della metafisica." In *St. Thomas Aquinas, 1274–1974: Commemorative Studies*, ed. A. Maurer et al., 2:423–57. Toronto: Pontifical Institute of Mediaeval Studies, 1974.

———. "The Intensive Hermeneutics of Thomistic Philosophy: The Notion of Participation." *Review of Metaphysics* 27 (1974): 449–91.

———. "Intorno al fondamento dell'essere." In *Graceful Reason: Essays in Ancient and Medieval Philosophy Presented to Joseph Owens, C.Ss.R.*, ed. Lloyd Gerson, 229–37. Toronto: Pontifical Institute for Mediaeval Studies, 1983.

———. *Introduzione a san Tommaso: La metafisica tomista e il pensiero moderno*. 2nd ed. Milan: Ares, 1997.

———. *La nozione metafisica di partecipazione secondo S. Tommaso d'Aquino*. 2nd ed. Turin: Società Editrice Internazionale, 1963.

———. "La problematica dell'"esse' tomistico." *Aquinas* 2, no. 2 (1959): 194–225. Repr. in Tomismo e pensiero moderno, 103–33.

———. "L'emergenza dello esse tomistico sull'atto aristotelico: Breve prologo." In *L'atto aristotelico e le sue ermeneutiche*, ed. M. Sánchez Sorondo, 149–77. Rome: Herder-Università Lateranense, 1990.

———. "Notes pour la fondation métaphysique de l'etre." *Revue thomiste* 2 (1966): 214–37. Repr. in Tomismo e pensiero moderno, 291–317.

———. *Participation et causalité selon S. Thomas d'Aquin*. Louvain: Publications Universitaires, 1961.

———. "Platonism, Neoplatonism and Thomism: Convergencies and Divergencies." *New Scholasticism* 44 (1970): 69–100. Trans. of "Platonismo, neoplatonismo, e tomismo," in *Tomismo e pensiero moderno*, 435–60.
———. "Sviluppo, significato e valore della 'IV via.'" *Doctor Communis* 7 (1954): 71–109. Repr. in *Esegesi tomistica*, 351–85.
———. *Tomismo e pensiero moderno*. Rome: Pontificia Università Lateranense, 1969.
———. "Un itinéraire de saint Thomas: L'Établissement de la distinction réelle entre essence et existence." *Revue de Philosophie* 39 (1939): 285–310. Repr. in *Esegesi tomistica*, 89–108.
Fafara, Richard J. "Gilson and Gouhier: Approaches to Malebranche." In *A Thomistic Tapestry: Essays in Memory of Etienne Gilson*, ed. Peter A. Redpath, 107–55. Amsterdam: Rodopi, 2003.
Farthing, John Lee. "The Problem of Divine Exemplarity in St. Thomas." *Thomist* 49 (1985): 183–222.
Finnis, John. *Moral Absolutes: Tradition, Revision and Truth*. Washington, DC: The Catholic University of America Press, 1991.
Frankfurt, Harry G. "Freedom of the Will and the Concept of a Person." *Journal of Philosophy* 68 (1971): 5–20.
Frege, Gottlob. *The Foundations of Arithmetic*. Trans. J. L. Austin. Oxford: Basil Blackwell, 1950.
———. *Translations from the Philosophical Writings of Gottlob Frege*. Trans. and ed. P. T. Geach and Max Black. Oxford: Basil Blackwell, 1980.
Frye, Northrop. "Spengler Revisited." In *Spiritus Mundi*, ed. Frye, 179–98. Markham, Ontario: Fitzhenry and Whiteside, 1991.
Garrigou-Lagrange, Reginald. *Our Savior and His Love for Us*. Trans. A. Bouchard. Rockford, IL: TAN Books and Publishers, 1998. [Original: Le Sauveur et son amour pour nous, 1951.]
Gauthier, René-Antoine. *Somme contre les gentils, Introduction*. Paris: Éditions Universitaires, 1993.
Geach, Peter. "Aquinas." In Peter Geach and G. E. M. Anscombe, *Three Philosophers*, 65–125. Ithaca: Cornell University Press, 1961.
———. *God and the Soul*. South Bend: St. Augustine's Press, n.d. [Repr. of the 1969 ed.]
———. *Providence and Evil*. Cambridge: Cambridge University Press, 1977.
Geenen, G. "En marge du Concile de Chalcédoine. Les textes du Quatrième Concile dans les oeuvres de Saint Thomas." *Angelicum* 29 (1952): 43–59.
Geiger, Louis B. "Les idées divines dans l'oeuvre de S. Thomas." In *St. Thomas Aquinas: Commemorative Studies*, ed. A. Maurer et al., 1:175–209. Toronto: Pontifical Institute of Mediaeval Studies, 1974.
———. "Les rédactions successives de Contra Gentiles, I, 53 d'après l'autographe." In *Saint Thomas d'Aquin aujourd'hui*, ed. R. Jolivet et al., 221–40. Recherches de Philosophie 6. Paris: Desclée de Brouwer, 1963.
George, Marie I. "Mind Forming and Manuductio in Aquinas." *Thomist* 57 (1993): 201–13.

Giacon, Carlo. "S. Tommaso e l'esistenza come atto: Maritain, Gilson, Fabro." In *Itinerario tomistico,* ed. Giacon, 137–65. Rome: La Goliardica, 1983.
Gilson, Étienne. "Art et Métaphysique." *Revue du métaphysique et de morale* 23 (1916): 243–67.
———. *Christian Philosophy: An Introduction.* Trans. Armand Maurer. Toronto: Pontifical Institute of Mediaeval Studies, 1993.
———. *The Christian Philosophy of Saint Augustine.* Trans. L. Lynch. New York: Random House, 1960.
———. *The Christian Philosophy of St. Thomas Aquinas.* Trans. Laurence K. Shook. New York: Random House, 1956; Notre Dame, IN: University of Notre Dame Press, 1994.
———. *Constantes métaphysiques de l'être.* Paris: J. Vrin, 1983.
———. *Elements of Christian Philosophy.* Garden City, NY: Doubleday, 1960.
———. "French and Italian Philosophy." In *Recent Philosophy: Hegel to the Present,* ed. Gilson, Thomas Langan, and Armand A. Maurer, 290–317. New York: Random House, 1962.
———. *From Aristotle to Darwin and Back Again: A Journey in Final Causality, Species, and Evolution.* Trans. John Lyon. Notre Dame: University of Notre Dame Press, 1984.
———. *History of Christian Philosophy in the Middle Ages.* New York: Random House, 1955.
———. *L'être et l'essence.* Paris: J. Vrin, 1948. English trans., *Being and Some Philosophers.* Toronto: Pontifical Institute of Mediaeval Studies, 1949.
———. "Lettres d'Etienne Gilson à Henri Gouhier." Ed. Géry Prouvost. *Revue Thomiste* 94 (1994): 460–78.
———. *The Philosopher and Theology.* Trans. Cécile Gilson. New York: Random House, 1962.
———. "Quasi definitio substantiae." In *St. Thomas Aquinas: 1274–1974, Commemorative Studies,* ed. Armand A. Maurer, C.S.B., et al., 111–29. Toronto: Pontifical Institute of Mediaeval Studies, 1974.
———. "Souvenir de Bergson." *Revue du métaphysique et de morale* 63 (1959): 129–40.
———. *The Unity of Philosophical Experience.* New York: Charles Scribner's Sons, 1937.
Goldin, Owen. *Explaining an Eclipse: Aristotle's Posterior Analytics 2.1–10.* Ann Arbor: University of Michigan Press, 1996.
Gomez Lobo, Alfonso. "The So-Called Question of Existence in Aristotle, *An. Post.* 2.1–2." *Review of Metaphysics* 34 (1980): 71–90.
Gouhier, Henri. *Bergson dans l'histoire de la pensée occidentale.* Paris: J. Vrin, 1989.
———. *Bergson et le Christ des Evangiles.* Paris: Fayard, 1961.
———. *Etudes d'histoire de la philosophie.* Hildesheim: Georg Olms Verlag, 1976.
———. "Introduction," in *Oeuvres de Bergson, edition du centenaire,* vii–xxx. Paris: Presses Universitaires de France, 1959.
———. *La philosophie et son histoire.* Paris: J. Vrin, 1948.
———. "Le bergsonisme dans l'histoire de la philosophie française." *Revue des*

*travaux de l'academie des sciences morales et politiques*, 4th series (1959): 184–93.
———. *Les grandes avenues de la pensée philosophique en France depuis Descartes*. Louvain: Publications Universitaires de Louvain, 1966.
———. *L'histoire et sa philosophie*. Paris: J. Vrin, 1952.
———. *Maine de Biran par lui-même*. Paris: Éditions du Seuil, 1990.
Graham, A. C. "'Being' in Linguistics and Philosophy: A Preliminary Inquiry." *Foundations of Language* 1 (1965): 223–31.
Greenstock, David L. "Exemplar Causality and the Supernatural Order." *Thomist* 16 (1953): 1–31.
Grillmeier, Aloys. *Christ in the Christian Tradition*. Vol. 2. Trans. James Bowden. Atlanta: John Knox Press, 1975.
Grimaldi, William M. A. *Aristotle, Rhetoric I: A Commentary*. New York: Fordham University Press, 1980.
Hardie, W. F. R. *Aristotle's Ethical Theory*. Oxford: Clarendon Press, 1968.
Hardy, Edward Rochie, ed. *Christology of the Later Fathers*. Philadelphia: Westminster Press, 1954.
Harré, Rom. *The Principles of Scientific Thinking*. Chicago: University of Chicago Press, 1970.
Hauer, Christian, and William Young. *An Introduction to the Bible: A Journey into Three Worlds*. 5th ed. Upper Saddle River, NJ: Prentice Hall, 2001.
Healy, Emma Thérèse. *Woman according to Bonaventure*. Erie, PA: Congregation of the Sisters of St. Joseph, 1956.
Hempel, Carl G. "Studies in the Logic of Confirmation." *Mind* 54 (1945): 1–26, 97–121. Repr. in *Aspects of Scientific Explanation*, ed. Hempel, 3–46. New York: Free Press, 1965.
Hempel, Carl G., and Paul Oppenheim. "Studies in the Logic of Explanation." *Philosophy of Science* 15 (1948): 135–75.
Hesse, Mary B. *Forces and Fields: The Concept of Action at a Distance in the History of Physics*. New York: Dover, 2005. [Originally published in 1962.]
Hintikka, Jaakko. "On Aristotle's Notion of Existence." *Review of Metaphysics* 52 (1999): 779–805.
Hintikka, Jaakko, and Ilpo Halonen. "Aristotelian Explanations." *Studies in History and Philosophy of Science* 31 (2000): 125–36.
Hittinger, Russell. *The First Grace: Rediscovering the Natural Law in a Post-Christian World*. Wilmington, DE: ISI Books, 2002.
Howison, G. H. "Steps in My Critique of Royce." Typescript C-B 1037 in Bancroft Library, University of California, Berkeley.
Hughes, Christopher. "Matter and Actuality in Aquinas." In *Thomas Aquinas: Contemporary Philosophical Perspectives*, ed. Brian Davies, 61–76. Oxford: Oxford University Press, 2002.
Irwin, Terence. *Aristotle's First Principles*. Oxford: Clarendon Press, 1988.
Jammer, Max. *The Philosophy of Quantum Mechanics: The Interpretations of Quantum Mechanics in Historical Perspective*. New York: Wiley-Interscience, 1974.
Janicaud, Dominique. *Le tournant théologique de la phénoménologie française*. Paris: Éditions de l'Éclat, 1991.

Johnson, W. E. *Logic*, Part 1. Cambridge: University Press, 1921.
Jordan, Mark D. "The Intelligibility of the World and the Divine Ideas in Aquinas." *Review of Metaphysics* 38 (1984): 17-32.
———. *Ordering Wisdom: The Hierarchy of Philosophical Discourses in Aquinas*. Notre Dame: University of Notre Dame Press, 1986.
Jubien, Michael. *Contemporary Metaphysics: An Introduction*. Cambridge, MA: Blackwell, 1997.
Kahn, Charles. "The Greek Verb 'to Be' and the Concept of Being." *Foundations of Language* 2 (1966): 245-65.
Kaufmann, Walter. *Nietzsche: Philosopher, Psychologist, Antichrist*. 3rd ed. New York: Random House, 1968.
Kenny, Anthony. *Aquinas on Being*. Oxford: Oxford University Press, 2002.
Ketchum, Richard. "Being and Existence in Greek Ontology." *Archiv für Geschichte der Philosophie* 80 (1998): 321-32.
Klima, Gyula. "The Changing Role of Entia Rationis in Medieval Philosophy: A Comparative Study with a Reconstruction." *Synthese* 96 (1993): 25-59.
———. "Contemporary 'Essentialism' vs. Aristotelian Essentialism." In *Mind, Metaphysics, and Value in the Thomistic and Analytic Traditions*, ed. John Haldane, 175-94. Notre Dame, IN: University of Notre Dame Press, 2002.
———. "On Kenny on Aquinas on Being: A Critical Review of Aquinas on Being by Anthony Kenny." *International Philosophical Quarterly* 44 (2004): 567-80.
———. "Ontological Alternatives vs. Alternative Semantics in Medieval Philosophy." *European Journal for Semiotic Studies* 3 (1991): 587-618.
———. "The Semantic Principles Underlying Saint Thomas Aquinas's Metaphysics of Being." *Medieval Philosophy and Theology* 5 (1996): 87-141.
Kneepkens, Corneille Henri. "'Suppositio' and 'Supponere' in 12th Century Grammar." In *Gilbert de Poitiers et ses contemporains: Aux origines de la "Logica Modernorum,"* ed. Jean Jolivet and Alain de Libera, 325-51. Napoli: Bibliopolis, 1987.
Kolakowski, Leszek. *Bergson*. Oxford: Oxford University Press, 1985.
Kostro, Ludwik. *Einstein and the Ether*. Montreal: Apeiron, 2000.
Kovach, Francis J. "Action at a Distance in Duns Scotus and Modern Science." In *Regnum hominis et regnum Dei: Acta Quarti Congressus Scotistici Internationalis*, ed. Camille Bérubé, tom. 1, 477-90. Rome: Societas Internationalis Scotistica, 1978.
———. "Action at a Distance in St. Thomas Aquinas." In *Thomistic Papers II*, ed. L. Kennedy and J. Marler, 85-132. Houston: Center for Thomistic Studies, 1986.
———. "The Enduring Question of Action at a Distance in Saint Albert the Great." In *Albert the Great: Commemorative Essays*, ed. Francis J. Kovach and Robert W. Shahan, 161-235. Tulsa, OK: University of Oklahoma Press, 1980.
———. *Scholastic Challenges to Some Mediaeval and Modern Ideas*. Stillwater, OK: Western, 1987.
Koyré, Alexander. *Newtonian Studies*. Chicago: University of Chicago Press, 1965.
Kwasniewski, Peter A. "St. Thomas, Extasis, and Union with the Beloved." *Thomist* 61 (1997): 587-603.
Laloë, F. "Do We Really Understand Quantum Mechanics? Strange Correlations, Paradoxes, and Theorems." *American Journal of Physics* 69 (2001): 655-701.

Lawless, G. "Interior Peace in the Confessions of St. Augustine." *Revue des Etudes Augustiniennes* 26 (1980): 45–61.
Langendoen, D. Terrence, and Paul M. Postal. *The Vastness of Natural Language*. Oxford: Blackwell, 1984.
Leonard, Henry. "The Logic of Existence." *Philosophical Studies* 7, no. 4 (1956): 49–64.
Levao, Ronald. *Renaissance Minds and Their Fictions*. Berkeley: University of California Press, 1985.
Lévinas, Emmanuel. *Autrement qu'être*. The Hague: Martinus Nijhoff, 1974.
———. *Totalité et infini*. 5th ed. Paris: Kluwer, 1992.
Lindley, David. *The End of Physics: The Myth of a Unified Theory*. New York: Basic Books, 1993.
Llano, Alejandro. "'Being as True' according to Aquinas." *Acta Philosophica* 4 (1995): 73–82.
———. "The Different Meanings of 'Being' according to Aristotle and Aquinas." *Acta Philosophica* 10 (2001): 29–44.
———. *Metafisica y lenguaje*. Pamplona: EUNSA, 1984.
Loux, Michael J. *Primary Ousia*. Ithaca: Cornell University Press, 1991.
MacDonald, Scott. "The Esse/Essentia Argument in Aquinas's De ente et essentia." *Journal of the History of Philosophy* 22 (1984): 157–72.
Mackie, John Leslie. *Cement of the Universe: A Study of Causation*. Oxford: Clarendon Press, 1974.
———. "The Riddle of Existence." *Proceedings of the Aristotelian Society*, suppl. vol. 50 (1976): 247–67.
Madaule, Madelaine Barthélemy. *Bergson adversaire de Kant*. Paris: Presses Universitaires de France, 1966.
Mansion, Suzanne. *Le jugement d'existence chez Aristote*. 2nd ed. Louvain: Éditions de l'Institut supérieur de Philosophie, 1976.
Margenau, Henry. *Open Vistas: Philosophical Perspectives of Modern Science*. Woodbridge, CT: Ox Bow Press, 1983.
Marion, Jean-Luc. *Dieu sans l'être*. Paris: Fayard, 1982.
———. *L'Idole et la distance*. Paris: Grasset, 1977.
Maritain, Jacques. *Bergsonian Philosophy and Thomism*. Trans. Mabelle L. Andison, with J. Gordon Andison. New York: Philosophical Library, 1955.
———. "The Bergsonian Philosophy of Morality and Religion." In *Ransoming the Time*, trans. Harry Lorin Binsse, 84–114. New York: Charles Scribner's Sons, 1941; New York: Gordian Press, 1972. [In England the book appeared under the title *Redeeming the Time*, with the same essay on pp. 74–100. London: Geoffrey Bles, 1943.]
———. *Court traité de l'existence et l'existant*. Paris: Paul Hartmann, 1947. [In English, *Existence and the Existent*. Trans. Lewis Galantiere and Gerald B. Phelan. Garden City, NY: Doubleday, 1956.]
———. *An Introduction to the Problems of Moral Philosophy*. Trans. Cornelia N. Borgerhoff. Albany: Magi Books, 1990.
———. "The Metaphysics of Bergson." In *Ransoming the Time*, trans. Harry Lorin Binsse, 52–83. New York: Charles Scribner's Sons, 1941. [In the British edition, *Redeeming the Time*, pp. 46–73.]

———. *Moral Philosophy: An Historical and Critical Survey of the Great Systems.* Ed. Joseph W. Evans. New York: Charles Scribner's Sons, 1964.
———. *Philosophy of Nature.* Trans. Imelda C. Byrne. New York: Philosophical Library, 1951.
———. *Science and Wisdom.* Trans. Bernard Wall. New York: Charles Scribner's Sons, 1940.
———. *Untrammeled Approaches.* Trans. Bernard Doering. Notre Dame, IN: University of Notre Dame Press, 1997.
Martin, Aaron. "Reckoning with Ross: Possibles, Divine Ideas, and Virtual Practical Knowledge." *Proceedings of the American Catholic Philosophical Association* 78 (2004): 193–208.
Martin, Christopher. "The Notion of Existence Used in Answering an Est?" In Martin, *Thomas Aquinas: God and Explanations,* 50–79. Edinburgh: Edinburgh University Press, 1997.
Martin du Gard, Roger. *Jean Barois.* Paris: Gallimard, 1913.
Maurer, Armand A. "Form and Essence in the Philosophy of St. Thomas." In *Being and Knowing: Studies in Thomas Aquinas and Late Medieval Philosophy,* ed. Maurer, 3–18. Toronto: Pontifical Institute of Mediaeval Studies, 1990.
———. "James Ross on the Divine Ideas: A Reply." *American Catholic Philosophical Quarterly* 65 (1991): 213–20.
McGovern, Thomas. "The Logic of the First Operation." *Laval théologique et philosophique* 12 (1956): 52–74.
McInerny, Ralph. *Being and Predication: Thomistic Interpretations.* Washington, DC: The Catholic University of America Press, 1986.
———. *Boethius and Aquinas.* Washington, DC: The Catholic University of America Press, 1990.
———. *Characters in Search of Their Author.* Gifford Lectures, Glasgow 1999–2000. Notre Dame: Notre Dame University Press, 2001.
———. *Praeambula Fidei.* Washington, DC: The Catholic University of America Press, 2006.
Melville, Herman. *Moby Dick.* London: Panther, 1968.
Merleau-Ponty, Jacques. *Cosmologie du $xx^e$ siècle: Etude épistemologique et historique des théories de la cosmologie contemporaine.* Paris: Gallimard, 1965.
Meyer, Hans. *Thomas von Aquin: Sein System und seine geistesgeschichtliche Stellung.* 2nd ed. Paderborn: Schöningh, 1961.
Michener, Norah Willis. *Maritain on the Nature of Man.* Hull: Éditions L'Éclair, 1955.
Mignucci, Mario. *La teoria aristotelica della scienza.* Firenze: Sansoni, 1965.
Miller, Barry. *The Fullness of Being: A New Paradigm for Existence.* Notre Dame, IN: University of Notre Dame Press, 2002.
Mondin, Battista. *Thomas Aquinas's Philosophy in the Commentary to the Sentences.* The Hague: Martinus Nijhoff, 1975.
Moraux, Paul. *A la recherche de l'Aristote perdu le dialogue "Sur la justice."* Louvain: Publications universitaires de Louvain, 1957.
Morris, Thomas V. "St. Thomas on the Identity and Unity of the Person of Christ: A

Problem of Reference in Christological Discourse." *Scottish Journal of Theology* 35 (1982): 419–30.

Munitz, Milton. *Existence and Logic*. New York: New York University Press, 1974.

Murdoch, Iris. *Metaphysics as a Guide to Morals*. London: Chatto and Windus, 1992.

Murphy, Francesca Aran. *Art and Intellect in the Philosophy of Etienne Gilson*. Columbia: University of Missouri Press, 2004.

Nagel, Ernest. *The Structure of Science*. New York: Harcourt, Brace, and World, 1961.

Newman, John Henry. *The Philosophical Notebook*. Ed. Edward J. Sillem, rev. A. J. Boekraad. Louvain: Nauwelaerts, 1970.

O'Donovan, Oliver. "Usus and Fruitio in Augustine, De Doctrina Christiana I." *Journal of Theological Studies* [NS] 33 (1982): 361–97.

Owen, G. E. L. "Aristotle on the Snares of Ontology." In *New Essays on Plato and Aristotle*, ed. R. Bambrough, 69–95. London: Routledge and Kegan Paul, 1965.

Owens, Joseph. "Aquinas on Being and Thing." In *Thomistic Papers*, vol. 3, ed. L. Kennedy, 3–24. Houston: Center for Thomistic Studies, 1987.

———. "Aquinas's Distinction at De ente et essentia 4.119–123." *Mediaeval Studies* 48 (1986): 264–87.

———. "Aquinas on Knowing Existence." *Review of Metaphysics* 29 (1976): 670–90.

———. "An Aristotelian Text Related to the Distinction of Being and Essence." *Proceedings of the American Catholic Philosophical Association* 21 (1946): 165–72.

———. *Cognition: An Epistemological Inquiry*. Houston: Center for Thomistic Studies, 1992.

———. "Common Nature: A Point of Comparison between Thomistic and Scotistic Metaphysics." *Mediaeval Studies* 19 (1957): 1–14.

———. *The Doctrine of Being in the Aristotelian Metaphysics: A Study in the Greek Background of Mediaeval Thought*. 3d ed. rev. Toronto: Pontifical Institute of Mediaeval Studies, 1978.

———. *An Elementary Christian Metaphysics*. Milwaukee, WI: Bruce, 1963; repr. Houston: Center for Thomistic Studies, 1985.

———. "Judgment and Truth in Aquinas." *Mediaeval Studies* 32 (1970): 138–58. Repr. in Owens, *St. Thomas Aquinas on the Existence of God*, 34–51.

———. "Quiddity and Real Distinction in St. Thomas Aquinas." *Mediaeval Studies* 27 (1965): 1–22.

———. *St. Thomas Aquinas on the Existence of God: Collected Papers of Joseph Owens, C.Ss.R.* Ed. John R. Catan. Albany: State University of New York Press, 1980.

———. "Stages and Distinction in De ente: A Rejoinder." *Thomist* 45 (1981): 99–123.

Pangallo, Mario. *L'essere come atto nel tomismo essenziale di Cornelio Fabro*. Rome: Libreria Editrice Vaticana, 1987.

Pascal, Blaise. *Pensées*. Critical ed., established and annotated by Zacharie Tourneur. Bibliothèque de Cluny, vol. 6. Paris: Éditions de Cluny, 1948.

Pegis, Anton. "St. Thomas and the Origin of Creation." In *Philosophy and the Modern Mind*, ed. F. X. Canfield, 49–65. Detroit: Sacred Heart Seminary, 1961.

Pini, G. "The Transcendentals of Logic: Thirteenth-Century Discussions on the Subject Matter of Aristotle's Categories." In *Die Logik des Transzendentalen. Fest-*

*schrift für Jan A. Aertsen zum 65. Geburtstag*, ed. M. Pickavé, 140–59. Berlin: de Gruyter, 2003.

Plantinga, Alvin. "On Taking Belief in God as Basic." In *Classical and Contemporary Readings in the Philosophy of Religion*, ed. John Hick, 484–99. Englewood Cliffs, NJ: Prentice Hall, 1990. Repr. from *Religious Experience and Religious Belief*, ed. Joseph Runzo and Craig Ihara. New York: University Press of America, 1986.

Renna, Thomas. "The Idea of Peace in the Augustinian Tradition: 400–1200." *Augustinian Studies* 10 (1979): 105–11.

Rescher, Nicholas. *Conceptual Idealism*. Oxford: Blackwell, 1973.

———. *A Theory of Possibility*. Pittsburgh: University of Pittsburgh Press, 1975.

Robb, James H. *Man as Infinite Spirit*. Milwaukee: Marquette University Press, 1974.

Roland-Gosselin, M.-D. Le *"De ente et essentia" de S. Thomas d'Aquin. Texte établi d'après les manuscrits parisiens. Introduction, notes et études historiques*. Bibliothèque thomiste 8. Kain, Belgium: Le Saulchoir/Paris: Vrin, 1926; repr. 1948.

Romera, Luis. *Pensar el ser: Análisis del conocimiento del "Actus Essendi" según C. Fabro*. Bern: Peter Lang, 1994.

Ross, David, ed. and trans., with commentary. *Aristotle's Physics*. Oxford: Oxford University Press, 1936.

Ross, James F. "Aquinas's Exemplarism; Aquinas's Voluntarism." *American Catholic Philosophical Quarterly* 64 (1990): 171–98.

———. "The Fate of the Analysts: Aristotle's Revenge." *Proceedings of the American Catholic Philosophical Association* 64 (1990): 51–74.

———. "Response to Maurer and Dewan." *American Catholic Philosophical Quarterly* 65 (1991): 213–20.

———. "Together with the Body That I Love." *Proceedings of the American Catholic Philosophical Association* 75 (2001): 1–20.

Ryle, Gilbert. *The Concept of Mind*. With introduction by Daniel C. Dennett. Chicago: University of Chicago Press, 2002.

Shook, Laurence K. *Etienne Gilson*. Toronto: Pontifical Institute of Mediaeval Studies, 1984.

Simon, Yves R. *The Great Dialogue of Nature and Space*. Ed. Gerard J. Dalcourt. Albany: Magi Books, 1970.

Smith, Nicholas D. "Aristotle's Theory of Natural Slavery." In *A Companion to Aristotle's Politics*, ed. David Keyt and Fred D. Miller, 142–55. Oxford: Blackwell, 1991.

Struever, Nancy M. *The Language of History in the Renaissance*. Princeton: Princeton University Press, 1970.

Stump, Eleonore. *Aquinas*. London: Routledge, 2003.

Sweeney, Leo. "Existence/Essence in Thomas Aquinas's Early Writings." *Proceedings of the American Catholic Philosophical Association* 37 (1963): 97–131.

Taylor, M. J. *Martin du Gard: Jean Barois*. London: Edward Arnold, 1974.

Taylor, Richard C. "Aquinas, the Plotiniana Arabica, and the Metaphysics of Being and Actuality." *Journal of the History of Ideas* 59 (1998): 217–39.

te Velde, Rudi. "Metaphysics, Dialectics and the Modus logicus according to Thomas Aquinas." *Recherches de théologie ancienne et médiévale* 63 (1996): 15–35.

Toal, M. F., ed. *The Sunday Sermons of the Great Fathers*. Chicago: Henry Regnery, 1959.

Torrell, Jean-Pierre. *Saint Thomas Aquinas. Vol. 1, The Person and His Works.* Trans. Robert Royal. Washington, DC: The Catholic University of America Press, 1996.
———. *Saint Thomas Aquinas. Vol. 2: Spiritual Master.* Trans. Robert Royal. Washington, DC: The Catholic University of America Press, 2003.
Toulmin, Stephen. *The Return to Cosmology.* Berkeley: University of California, 1982.
Utrecht, Daniel. "Esse Means Existence." In *Saints and Scholars: Studies in Honor of Frederick D. Wilhelmsen*, ed. R. A. Herrera et al., 87–94. New York: Peter Lang, 1993.
Van Bennekom, Riek. "Aristotle and the Copula." *Journal of the History of Philosophy* 24 (1986): 1–18.
Voegelin, Eric. *From Enlightenment to Revolution.* Durham, NC: Duke University Press, 1975.
von Balthasar, Hans Urs. *Explorations in Theology. Vol. 1, The Word Made Flesh.* Trans. A. V. Littledale with Alexander Dru. San Francisco: Ignatius Press, 1989.
Waddell, Helen, trans. *The Desert Fathers.* Ann Arbor: University of Michigan Press, 1957.
Wallace, William A. *Causality and Scientific Explanation.* 2 vols. Ann Arbor: University of Michigan Press, 1972–74.
———. *The Modeling of Nature.* Washington, DC: The Catholic University of America Press, 1996.
Watts, Pauline Moffitt. *Nicolaus Cusanus: A Fifteenth Century Vision of Man.* Leiden: E. J. Brill, 1982.
Wells, Norman. "Capreolus on Essence and Existence." *Modern Schoolman* 38 (1960): 1–24.
Whitehead, Alfred North. *Process and Reality.* New York: Harper and Row, 1960.
Winandy, Jacques, O.S.B. "Le Quodlibet II, art. 4 de Saint Thomas et la notion de suppôt." *Ephemerides theologicae Lovanienses* 2 (1934): 5–29.
Wippel, John F. *Metaphysical Themes in Thomas Aquinas.* Washington, DC: The Catholic University of America Press, 1984.
———. *The Metaphysical Thought of Thomas Aquinas: From Finite to Infinite Being.* Washington, DC: The Catholic University of America Press, 2000.
———. *Thomas Aquinas on the Divine Ideas.* Etienne Gilson Series, no. 16. Toronto: Pontifical Institute of Mediaeval Studies, 1993.
———. "Truth in Thomas Aquinas." *Review of Metaphysics* 43 (1989–90): 295–326, 543–67.

# Contributors

*Jan A. Aertsen* is emeritus professor of medieval philosophy and emeritus director of the Thomas Institute at the University of Cologne. Also a member of the Pontifical Academy of St. Thomas Aquinas, Aertsen has published more than 100 studies in the field of medieval philosophy, centered on the thought of Thomas Aquinas and on the doctrine of the transcendental notions. These interests came together in his book *Medieval Philosophy and the Transcendentals: The Case of Thomas Aquinas*. It was in 1984, as a research fellow of the Pontifical Institute for Medieval Studies, that Aertsen met Fr. Dewan.

*Leslie Armour* is research professor of philosophy at the Dominican University College of Ottawa, where he is a colleague of Fr. Dewan. Armour works in the areas of metaphysics and epistemology, the history of philosophy in the seventeenth and nineteenth centuries, and moral, social, and economic philosophy and their relations to culture and religion. A member of the editorial boards of *Laval philosophique et théologique* and *The International Journal of Social Economics* and a fellow of the Royal Society of Canada, Armour has published several books, including *"Infini Rien": Pascal's Wager and the Human Paradox*.

*Stephen L. Brock* is a priest of the Prelature of Opus Dei. Fr. Dewan was second reader for his doctoral dissertation on natural law at the University of Toronto in 1988. Since 1990 he has taught medieval philosophy at the Pontifical University of the Holy Cross in Rome. He is author of *Action and Conduct: Thomas Aquinas and the Theory of Action* (Edinburgh: T and T Clark, 1998). Other publications include studies on St. Thomas's Eucharistic doctrine, the physical status of the spiritual soul, natural inclination and the intelligibility of the good, and Aquinas's "Platonism."

*Christopher A. Decaen* took courses on metaphysics from Fr. Dewan while working on his M.A. and Ph.D. in philosophy at the Catholic University of America. Since 1999 Dr. Decaen has been teaching natural philosophy and physics at Thomas Aquinas College in Santa Paula, California. His published work, most of which concerns the relation between modern science and Aristotelian natural philosophy, has appeared in *The Thomist, The Review of Metaphysics*, and *The Aquinas Review*.

*Gregory T. Doolan* received his Ph.D. in philosophy in 2003 from the Catholic University of America, where he had the good fortune of taking courses with Fr. Dewan. Doolan is now an assistant professor in the School of Philosophy at the same university. A book, *Aquinas on the Divine Ideas as Exemplar Causes*, is forthcoming from the Catholic University of America Press.

Jude P. Dougherty is dean emeritus and professor emeritus of the School of Philosophy of the Catholic University of America. He is editor of the *Review of Metaphysics* and general editor of the series Studies in Philosophy and the History of Philosophy, published by the Catholic University of America Press. His books include *Western Creed, Western Identity: Essays in Legal and Social Philosophy* (2000); *The Logic of Religion* (2002); and *Jacques Maritain: An Intellectual Profile* (2003).

Heather McAdam Erb teaches philosophy for the Catholic Distance University. She has served as assistant professor of philosophy at Fordham University, senior lecturer in religious studies at Pennsylvania State University, and visiting professor of philosophy at Saint Francis University in Loretto, Pennsylvania. While a graduate student in Toronto she was a frequent student of Fr. Dewan, who also sat as external examiner for her doctoral dissertation. Her publications focus on the intersection of metaphysics and mysticism in the thought of Aquinas.

Kevin L. Flannery entered the Society of Jesus in 1977. In 1992 he began teaching at the Pontifical Gregorian University in Rome, serving as dean of the Philosophy Faculty from 1999 until September 2005; he continues now as professor of the history of ancient philosophy. In 2002 John Paul II appointed him a consultor of the Congregation for the Doctrine of the Faith; in 2005 he was appointed ordinary member of the Pontifical Academy of St. Thomas Aquinas. Publications include *Acts amid Precepts: The Aristotelian Logical Structure of Thomas Aquinas's Moral Theory* (The Catholic University of America Press/T and T Clark, 2001).

Peter A. Kwasniewski is associate professor of philosophy and theology at Wyoming Catholic College in Lander, Wyoming, and visiting professor at the International Theological Institute for Studies on Marriage and the Family, in Austria. During his doctoral studies at the Catholic University of America, he missed no opportunity for taking Fr. Dewan's courses. Kwasniewski's articles on Thomistic themes have appeared in such journals as *Angelicum, Communio, Mediaeval Studies, Nova et Vetera,* and *The Thomist*. He has prepared, with Br. Thomas Bolin, O.S.B., and Joseph Bolin, a translation of texts on love and charity from Aquinas's *Sentences* commentary (forthcoming from the Catholic University of America Press).

Ralph McInerny is the Michael P. Grace Professor of Medieval Studies at the University of Notre Dame, where he has been teaching philosophy since 1955. A student of Charles De Koninck of the University of Laval, he is thereby in the same genetic line as Fr. Dewan. McInerny is a fellow of the Pontifical Academy of St. Thomas Aquinas and a member of President Bush's Committee on Arts and Humanities.

Ralph Nelson taught in the philosophy and political science departments at the University of Windsor from 1961 to 2000 and is now professor emeritus. His research and publications have been in the areas of political philosophy and contemporary

Thomism, in particular on Jacques Maritain and Yves R. Simon. He supervised and coedited the latter's *Foresight and Knowledge* (1995) and contributed an article on Simon's philosophy of science to *Acquaintance with the Absolute* (1998). He met Fr. Dewan in 1982 at one of the earliest meetings of the Canadian Maritain Association at the University of Ottawa and has often enjoyed his company since.

*David B. Twetten* is associate professor of philosophy at Marquette University, where he has taught since 1991. He holds a Ph.D. from the University of Toronto and an M.S.L. from the Pontifical Institute of Mediaeval Studies. He has published extensively in the area of classical and medieval metaphysics.

*J. L. A. West* is assistant professor of philosophy at Newman Theological College. West earned his Ph.D. at the University of Waterloo in Ontario, Canada, in 2003. He is currently vice president of the Canadian Society of Christian Philosophers and serves as a consultant to the Catholic Archdiocese of Edmonton, Alberta. His research focuses on Aquinas's use of philosophy in revealed theology and topics in contemporary political theory. His articles have appeared in *The Thomist, Philosophical Forum, The Modern Schoolman, Nova et Vetera*, and other journals and books.

# Index of Names

Adler, Mortimer, 215, 223
Albert the Great, 76n109
Alcidamas, 246, 247, 249, 251, 252
Alexander of Hales, 90n15
Anaxagoras, 176
Anselm of Canterbury, 43–47
Anthony of the Desert, 260
Antigone, 246–48, 251
Arnold, Matthew, 151
Augustine, viii, x, 9, 46, 122–23, 154–55, 157, 162, 169, 261–68, 271–72, 274, 277n90, 278, 280–81
Averroes, 66, 96n32
Avicebron, 190–92
Avicenna, 23, 46, 55n42, 57, 59n59, 63n73, 69n88, 71, 78n114, 81, 89, 90n14, 95, 96, 99n39, 190, 195n60
Ayer, A. J., 110, 114

Bacon, Francis, 228
Bergson, Henri, 214–33
Berkeley, George, 92
Bernard of Clairvaux, 280
Bignone, Ettore, 247–48
Boethius, viii, 59n59, 60, 71, 86, 92, 99n39, 104, 166, 168, 187, 196, 263
Bonaventure, 90n15, 122–25, 137, 138n35, 141, 146–47, 151

Cajetan, Tommaso de Vio Gaetani, viii, 61n64
Calvin, John, 128–30, 139
Capreolus, Johannes, viii, ix, xiii, 62n71
Carneades, 248
Cassian, John, 260
Chenu, M.-D., 163–64
Cicero, 248–49
Copernicus, Nicolaus, 202

Darwin, Charles, 201, 216, 226, 228, 229
Davies, Paul, 124
de Biran, Maine, 223, 231–32
De Koninck, Charles, 189n45
Democritus, 176, 191, 223
Descartes, René, 110, 140, 150–51, 176, 219, 222, 225, 228–29, 231–32
Dewan, Lawrence, vii–ix, xiii–xxii, 3–5, 11, 13–14, 19, 20n30, 39, 44n8, 56n49, 76n111, 138n35, 140n41, 144n52, 154, 164, 168n52, 214n1, 238, 240–41, 287–88
Dewey, John, 202
Dillon, Thomas, 62n71, 77n111
Dionysius, viii, 70, 168n52, 237, 261, 266, 269–70, 277–81
Durkheim, Emile, 220

Eco, Umberto, 267
Einstein, Albert, 173–79, 181n22, 199–200, 201, 214n1, 226
Eliot, T. S., 109
Empedocles, 246–51
Eriugena. *See* John Scotus Eriugena
Euclid, 121

Fabro, Cornelio, 42n3, 47, 48n17, 50n21, 53n37, 59, 62n67, 63n73, 67–70, 77n111, 78n114, 82, 84, 167
Faraday, Michael, 177n10, 210
Fermi, Enrico, 203
Finnis, John, 242
Frege, Gottlob, 14–21, 25, 35, 37n84

Galileo Galilei, 201, 202
Garrigou-Lagrange, Reginald, 273–74
Geach, Peter, 14–16, 20–22, 26, 35, 37–38, 42n4, 110, 143
Geiger, Louis B., 155n9, 156n10, 163n32, 164n37, 169

## Index

Gilbert of Poitiers, 91n19
Giles of Rome, 42n3, 61n64, 64n76, 69n88, 77n111, 80, 93
Gilson, Étienne, viii, xiii, 68–70, 82–84, 89n12, 93n26, 116, 153–69, 214–17, 222–33, 262n7
Gödel, Kurt, 148–49
Gouhier, Henri, 230–33
Greene, Graham, 112, 114
Gregory the Great, 252, 262

Harré, Rom, 209, 212
Hegel, G. W. F., 130n13, 151, 213, 222
Heidegger, Martin, 69n88, 222, 223
Heisenberg, Werner, 201
Hempel, Carl, 203
Henry of Ghent, 69n88, 80
Hittinger, Russell, 119n8
Hobbes, Thomas, 176
Howison, George Holmes, 128
Hume, David, 202–4, 212–13

Isidore of Seville, 256–57

John Duns Scotus, 93, 122, 125, 134n22, 136–38, 140n40, 176n9, 179n16
John Paul II, ix, 109–11, 115, 121
John Scotus Eriugena (John the Scot), 137, 141, 146n56
Jordan, Mark D., 161n23, 271n65

Kant, Immanuel, 121, 176n9, 202–3, 213
Kenny, Anthony, 14n5
Kepler, Johannes, 202
Kierkegaard, Søren, 114, 151
Klima, Gyula, 14n5, 25n46, 34n76, 35n77, 36n82, 40n1
Kolakowski, Leszek, 217
Kovach, Francis J., 173n1, 175n4, 176n9, 179n16, 179n18, 189n45, 193n54
Koyré, Alexander, 173n1, 174n2

Leibniz, Gottfried, 131n17, 176, 219
Lévinas, Emmanuel, 123n1, 150–51
Linnaeus, Carl, 229
Llano, Alejandro, 14n4, 29n59
Locke, John, 91, 92n22, 127n6, 151, 174n2, 202–4, 206, 212–13
Luther, Martin, 128n10, 277n90

Mach, Ernst, 176
MacIntyre, Alasdair, 109, 111
Mackie, J. L., 42n4, 209
Malebranche, Nicolas, 225, 231
Marcel, Gabriel, xiii
Marion, Jean-Luc, 123n1, 150
Maritain, Jacques, xiii, 118, 214–33, 267n39
Martin, Christopher, 14, 20–26, 35n80, 38n89
Maurer, Armand, xiii, 47n15, 153–54
McInerny, Ralph, 215n4
McLuhan, Marshall, xiii
McTaggart, J. M. E., 131n17
Merleau-Ponty, Jacques, 232
Meyer, Hans, 46n11, 76n109
Milton, John, 128
Molina, Luis, 139
Monod, Jacques, 228
Moore, G. E., 110
Moraux, Paul, 248–49
Murdoch, Iris, 127

Nagel, Ernest, 203
Newman, John Henry, 118, 149–51
Newton, Isaac, 173–79, 181n22, 199–200
Nicholas of Cusa, 138n35, 139, 140n40, 147–48, 151
Nietzsche, Friedrich, 151, 277n90

Ockham. *See* William of Ockham
Owens, Joseph, xiii, 42n3, 45n10, 47, 53, 55n46, 71n92, 72n95, 95n30

Parmenides, 81
Pascal, Blaise, 148, 151, 152, 231
Pauli, Wolfgang, 203
Pegis, Anton, 46n14
Peter Chrysologus, 264n20
Peter Helias, 86
Plantinga, Alvin, 130n15
Plato and platonism, viii, 40, 68–70, 76, 81, 99–100, 122, 127, 144, 155, 162, 190–92, 202, 224, 246n14, 248n25
Plotinus, 176n9, 217
Popper, Karl, 202
Priscian, 86n3, 89n12
Pseudo-Dionysius. *See* Dionysius

Rescher, Nicholas, 206
Richard, Jules, 148–49
Robb, James, 137, 265n26

Ross, James, 42n5, 77n111, 153–58, 164–69
Royce, Josiah, 128n9
Russell, Bertrand, 114, 130n15
Ryle, Gilbert, 205

Santayana, George, 212
Sartre, Jean-Paul, 111
Scotus. *See* John Duns Scotus
Siger of Brabant, 75n105
Simon, Yves, 220n26
Sophocles, 246, 249. *See also* Antigone
Spencer, Herbert, 229, 231
Spinoza, Baruch, 143n48, 217
Stobaeus, 247–48
Stump, Eleonore, 271n64, 274–75
Suárez, Francisco, 80, 93n25, 139
Sweeney, Leo, 47, 50n21, 56, 57n52, 62n71

Torrell, Jean-Pierre, 156n11, 268n43, 270
Toynbee, Arnold, 110

Voegelin, Eric, 124
von Balthasar, Hans Urs, 260, 261n3, 262n4

Wallace, William A., 207n6
Whitehead, Alfred North, 144n48, 206
William of Conches, 89n12
William of Ockham, 176n9, 204
Wippel, John, 6n9, 47, 49–50, 52–53, 58, 61, 65n80, 89n10, 89n12, 90n17, 93n25, 98n37, 99n38, 153, 157n12, 159n19, 161n23, 162n27, 163
Wolff, Christian, 232

Zeno, 232

Addendum

# *In Memoriam* Lawrence Dewan, O.P. (1932-2015)

## Peter A. Kwasniewski

John Lawrence Dewan was born in North Bay, Ontario, in 1932, and took the B.A. and M.A. at the University of Toronto in 1953 and 1955. He did his doctoral work in two stints, 1954–57 and again 1966–67, leading to his dissertation "The Doctrine of Being of John Capreolus: A Contribution to the History of the Notion of *Esse*" (1967), defended before a committee that included Owens, Pegis, and Edward Synan. In these years he also studied under Etienne Gilson and Marshall McLuhan.

His first published article, "Leslie Dewart and Spiritual Hedonism," appeared in *Laval théologique et philosophique* 27 in 1971. Although to my knowledge no one has prepared a complete bibliography of Dewan's voluminous writings, he published well over 100 major articles, a Marquette lecture, and two collections of the work he considered his best: *Form and Being* with CUA Press in 2006, and *Wisdom, Law, and Virtue* with Fordham University Press in 2008. Among his major concerns throughout his career were the doctrine of *esse* and how it relates to form and substance; the doctrine of analogy in its various theoretical constructions; the interpretation of the Five Ways of proving God's existence; the relationship of natural philosophy to metaphysics, and the relationship of both to modern science; and the foundations of ethics and political philosophy. He sparred often with fellow Thomists such as Joseph Owens and the River Forest School. While it would be an exaggeration to speak of a "school" of Fr. Dewan, there is no doubt he shaped every facet of Thomism in the past fifty years.

# Addendum

How does one worthily honor the memory of a teacher who made an enormous difference in one's own life and in the lives of so many friends and acquaintances? There is always something far greater, more abundant and varied in the person and his legacy than any homage can do justice to. For me, Fr. Dewan was three things to the fullest: a teacher who dearly loved *his* teacher, St. Thomas, as well as his students, all potential Thomists waiting to be actualized; an intellectual who never stopped studying, researching, and writing, constantly advancing the science of metaphysics and probing the rich relationship between modern-day subjects and the perennial insights of Aquinas; and a priest who lived his life not merely as a scholar or professor, but as a genuine disciple of Jesus Christ, walking along the particular path of the Order of Preachers founded by St. Dominic.

I was blessed with many experiences of all three sides of Fr. Dewan. I enjoyed several semesters of metaphysics with him at The Catholic University of America from 1994–1998. Can anyone who attended his classes forget the owl-like eyes that gazed through coke-bottle glasses, the face that lit up with excitement as he engaged the intricacies of being and essence, form and matter, act and potency? I still consult the detailed lectures and collections of texts he handed out at the start of each class, with my own annotations in the margins, based on his improvised commentary. I remember the course on the Five Ways in which he assigned student presentations, and I had the fortune (or misfortune) to choose Gilson on the Third Way, not realizing yet that Fr. Dewan—an ardent admirer of Gilson's intellectual legacy—was a most severe critic of some of his interpretive moves. Needless to say, my presentation was subjected to the dialectical shredder and ended as a pile of slivers, but in the process I had grown in both knowledge and humility, the indispensable precursor of wisdom.

Towards the end of my time at CUA, I began to realize, in spite of the innate modesty and simplicity of this white-robed teacher, just what a formidable intellectual Fr. Dewan was. In class we always smiled when he looked up from his lecture notes, raised a forefinger, and said, brightening: "I have a *paper* on this topic!" (meaning a publication), but little did we greenhorns know at the time that he had published article after article on seemingly every question of importance in the field of classical metaphysics, natural theology, physics, cosmology, and philosophical psychology, with forays into logic, ethics, politics, aesthetics, cultural history, biography, and sacred theology (I'm sure the list could be extended). At a certain point I began to collect his work more systematically to deepen and diversify my own grasp of Aristotle, Plato, St. Thomas, and other scholastics devoted to the *philosophia perennis*. It wasn't an easy quarry to track, as he published in so many different (often obscure) journals, and, accordingly, it brought me pleasure, relief, and good hope for future scholars when Fr. Dewan decided to put together two collections of his best work.If I could urge an action to be taken, it would be to get and study both of these collections. They are pure gold.

Beyond these official publications, Fr. Dewan conducted a substantial correspondence with people who asked him philosophical and theological questions. I remember submitting to him some knotty difficulties that arose from a reading of St. Thomas's treatment of transubstantiation in the Tertia Pars of the *Summa theologiae*, and he replied with a mini-treatise of his own, making the distinctions I had failed to make. He often sent me papers of his own, either in response to my queries or just to share his recent work. He displayed no "proprietary" attitude over his writings and relished a vigorous debate, never giving the impression that he had heard or said the last word.

As for Fr. Dewan's religious life and priestly identity, he was a wonderful combination of total transparency and dignified reserve. You knew from the moment he entered the room in his white Dominican habit that he was a Catholic religious, and if you were in the right place at the right time you would see him involved in the celebration of Mass, but he discussed religious topics only when the subject of the class or a student question demanded it, and he neither pietistically mixed theology into everything nor arbitrarily excluded it from consideration—he was too much a son of St. Thomas Aquinas either to blur the lines of discourse or to compartmentalize and thus falsify reality. My warmest personal memories of him come from the semester he spent at the International Theological Institute in Gaming, Austria, where he co-taught a special seminar on Thomistic metaphysics and epistemology, and seemed to leave a gentle mark on the entire community's academic and spiritual life. My wife and I remember with special fondness the Masses he celebrated in the campus church and how he would bless our little children so lovingly, not in any rush, and with joy lighting up his countenance.

## Addendum

Fr. Dewan's dedicated students always wanted to show him how much they appreciated him, but it was not easy to find ways to do so with a man who was not exactly a social extrovert. I am glad to have spearheaded the publication with CUA Press of a Festschrift for Fr. Dewan's seventy-fifth birthday in 2007, under the title *Wisdom's Apprentice*, which brought together work by twelve authors, several of them students of his. When Fr. Dewan received his copy in the mail, the first thing he wrote to me—altogether typical of this dedicated intellectual—is that he found compelling so-and-so's argument about the real distinction and couldn't help but disagree with another fellow on a different point. He received the book simply as a philosopher in search of wisdom, not as a man looking for applause or resting on his laurels. It made me love him all the more.

One can say without hyperbole that Fr. Dewan's life was dedicated to pursuing truth and handing it on with unstinting generosity. May he now behold the beauty of that truth unveiled.

www.ingramcontent.com/pod-product-compliance
Lightning Source LLC
Chambersburg PA
CBHW020311010526
44107CB00001B/68